BHAGWAN
The God That Failed

BHAGWAN/
The God That Failed

Hugh Milne

St. Martin's Press
New York

Edited by Liz Hodgkinson

Library of Congress Cataloging in Publication Data

Milne, Hugh.
  Bhagwan: the god that failed.

  1. Rajneesh, Bhagwan Shree, 1931-   . 2. Milne,
Hugh. I. Title.
BP605.R343M55 1987   299′.93   86-24832
ISBN 0-312-00106-1 (pbk.)

First published in Great Britain by Caliban Books

First U.S. Edition

10 9 8 7 6 5 4 3 2 1

To Madam X

CONTENTS

ACKNOWLEDGEMENTS

A few of the characters mentioned in this book have requested that their names be changed to reduce the possibility of recrimination from Rajneesh Foundation International. I have complied with all such requests.

I would like to thank Tom Casey of the US immigration service for being unfailingly honest with me, and ultimately respecting my wishes for privacy while he conducted his investigation. Les Zietz, Jim Long and Scotta Callister of *The Oregonian* were instrumental in encouraging me to publish at a time when I feared to do so, and generously shared their time and research findings with me in a thoroughly professional way. My friend Jeannie added her encouragement to go public. Brett provided me with an IBM PC on which the original manuscript was brought up to date, and lent ceaseless support to the completion of the project. Dee Milne learnt the intricacies of the IBM and gave me invaluable assistance in transferring what was then three-year-old information onto floppy disks.

Cia Criss, Gerald Emmet and Kathy Schepps in the U.S.A. and Belinda Grant in London provided invaluable support and critical appraisal, and Tony Malmud in New Mexico helped me to authenticate historical data. Betty Balcombe of London and Hal Stone of Los Angeles, both of whom helped me in the darkest moments with selfless candour, intelligence and perception, have made their own contribution to the book—Betty with her quite remarkable clarity and Hal with his deeply human insight. Margaret Schwarzer of St. Martin's added her encouragement and selfless support to the updating of the book for the American edition. I am indebted to all of these people, and especially to a certain Madam X, without whom not a single word would have been put to paper.

DRAMATIS PERSONAE

Alpert, Richard   Wrote influential counter-culture books in the late 1960s and 1970s under the name Ram Dass.

Ambara   One of Bhagwan's disciples, a Canadian farmer's son, who was drowned in Oregon. Lack of concern over his disappearance precipitated author's departure from Rajneesh movement.

Arup, Prem   Dutch disciple, real name Maria Gemma Kortenhorst.

Barnett, Mike   Encounter group leader, early disciple who took the name 'Somendra'. He has now left the movement and set up his own centre in Zürich, Switzerland.

Bhagwan   Literally God. Also 'The Blessed One'; title

Byron, Helen   Former disciple who won a $1.7 million lawsuit against Rajneesh movement in May 1985.

Casey, Tom   Immigration investigator from Portland, Oregon, who handled Rajneesh immigration fraud case.

Champa   American disciple, photographer and *bon vivant* in Poona.

Chinmaya   Sheela's first husband, an American Jew, Marc Harris Silverman, who died of Hodgkins disease in Poona in 1980.

Chinmaya, Yoga   Bhagwan's first Indian disciple.

Cyriax, Dr James   British doctor flown to Poona to treat Bhagwan's back trouble.

Deeksha   Former disciple, an Italian who left the movement in 1982. Formerly in charge of catering, construction and maintenence in Poona.

Devageet   Bhagwan's dentist; real name Charles Harvey Newman, a British national.

Devaraj   Bhagwan's personal physician, a British doctor, real name Alexander Wynne-Aubrey

	Meredith. Now married to Prem Hasya.
Dhyandipo	Sheela'a third husband, a Swiss, whom she married after divorcing Jayananda in 1985.
Dhyan John	An American, John William Wally, formerly President of Rajneesh International Corporation.
Divya, Prem	An American, author's girlfriend from 1972-73 and again briefly in Poona.
Erhart, Werner	American founder of est movement who visited Bhagwan in Poona.
Frohnmayer, Dave	Oregon Attorney General, instrumental in investigating Rajneeshee activities.
Frye, Judge Helen	US District Court Judge who declared Rajneeshpuram illegal as an incorporated city.
Gayan	Beautiful German ex-ballet dancer and Bhagwan disciple; formerly author's wife, and still with the movement.
Gurdjieff, Georges	Russian philosopher much admired and emulated by Bhagwan.
Haridas	German electrician; the first German disciple and a particular friend of the author.
Haridas	Rajneesh's childhood friend, drowned in a swimming accident.
Harvey, Bob	Original ranch foreman in Oregon; hired by Sheela, never a disciple.
Hasya, Prem	Bhagwan's secretary since Sheela left the movement; American socialite, Paris-born Françoise Ruddy, formerly wife of film producer Al Ruddy. Married to Devaraj.
Isabel, Prem	Bhagwan's chief PR executive, of French-Chilean origin. Married to Niren, Bhagwan's attorney; author's girlfriend from 1979 to 1982.
Jayananda	Sheela's second husband, also American; real name James Shelfer.
Jeannie	American former disciple; left movement at same time as author.
Karuna, Prem	American disciple, also known as Wendy Cutler Wyatt, treasurer of commune in Oregon.
Kirti	Prince Wilf of Hanover, disciple who died of a

	stroke in Poona in 1980.
Kranti	Bhagwan's original Indian secretary; also his cousin.
KB (Krishna Barti)	American, boyfriend to Deeksha and photographer at Poona.
Krishna Deva	American disciple, former mayor of Rajneeshpuram, now a federal witness.
Krishnamurti	Indian sage and philosopher, very anti-Bhagwan, though admired by him, who died in 1986.
Laxmi	Laxmi Thakarski Kuruwa, Bhagwan's Indian secretary for ten years until replaced by Sheela.
Leela	Irish disciple, author's girlfriend for a short time in Bombay.
Levin, Bernard	Perceptive British writer who visited Poona in 1980 and wrote a glowing account in the London *Times*.
Maneesha	Australian disciple, still in the movement. Bhagwan's chief editor and early adversary of Sheela.
Mukta	Bhagwan's name for Mrs Catherine Venizelos, a Greek shipping heiress and one of the earliest Western disciples, who bought his house in Poona.
Nelson, Alan C.	American commissioner for immigration, who pursued Rajneeshees in Oregon.
Niren	American lawyer and disciple of Bhagwan; real name Philip J. Toelkes. Married to Isabel.
Pilot, The	South African disciple in charge at Kailash.
Poonam	Teertha's wife; organisational head of British centres.
Pratima	Early American female disciple; dropped out about 1975.
Price, Richard	Founder of Esalen Institute, died in 1985.
Puja, Anand	Diana Yvonne Onang, Filipino nurse who ran health clinic in Oregon, latterly known as 'Nurse Mengele'.
Richard	Sannyassi construction boss at Rancho Rajneesh, one of Vivek's boyfriends and an ex-real estate developer.

Rishi	British disciple, John du Cane, who was jailed in Bangkok for drug offences, but later freed on a Royal Pardon.
Ross, Diana	American singer who visited Poona ashram.
Ryan, Sharon	American disciple, daughter of American congressman Leo Ryan, who was shot and killed at Jonestown, formerly centre of Jim Jones' religious movement.
Sant	Indian disciple; Isabel's lover in Poona.
Sashi	Bhagwan's Indian girlfriend who died at the age of seventeen; supposedly reincarnated as his later consort, Vivek.
Satch	American martial arts expert, and chief karate teacher at Poona.
Sheela, Ma Anand	Sheela Ambalal Patel, Indian disciple who ran movement in Oregon before leaving in September 1985. Accused of conspiring to murder Devaraj.
Somendra	see under 'Barnett, Mike'
Stamp, Terence	British actor who stayed in Poona ashram for about four months. Renamed 'Veeten' by Bhagwan.
Sushila	American disciple, real name Susan Wallach. Bhagwan's chief fund-raiser in America.
Sushila	'The German Sushila', Eva-Marie Mann.
Teertha	Bhagwan's name for Paul Lowe, British former encounter group leader.
Turner, Charles	US attorney; whom Sheela plotted to kill.
Veena	South African disciple who founded first Rajneesh centre in London.
Veeten	Bhagwan's naame for Terence Stamp.
Vijayananda	Leading Indian film director who became a disciple.
Vivek	Real name Christine Woolf, Bhagwan's consort, by his side since 1972.
Whicker, Alan	British TV interviewer who visited Poona in 1978 to make a film about the ashram.

Krishna	One of the pantheon of Hindu Gods.
Krishna House	Main residential premises and offices of the Poona ashram.
Lao Tzu	Bhagwan's house both in Poona and in Oregon, named after his favourite Chinese sage.
Locket	Plastic bauble containing picture of Bhagwan, worn on the end of the mala.
Ma	'Mother' — Bhagwan's prefix for his female disciples.
Madras	Small town in Oregon, pronounced 'Maad-rus' to distinguish it from the Indian original.
Mala	The 108-beaded necklace, like a Catholic rosary, worn by all Bhagwan's disciples.
Mantra	Hindu or Sanskrit words repeated in a chant to enable stabilisation of the mind during meditation.
Martial arts	Oriental fighting techniques encompassing aikido, karate, kung fu and bushido, designed to train individuals to a high degree of competence in armed and unarmed combat, especially against multiple attackers.
Maya	A Sanskrit term referring to the illusory nature of the world.
Meditation	A means of quietening the mind to arrive at inner peace and harmony.
Mediums	Bhagwan's word for his special female followers, who would transmit his energies to the rest of the commune.
Namaste	Traditional hand clasp; literally 'I bow to you'.
Neo-Sannyas International	Name given to Rajneesh movement in about 1975, to signify a new kind of renunciate.
Orange People	Popular media name for Bhagwan's disciples.
Poona	Hill station, site of Bhagwan's ashram from 1974 to 1981.
Portland	Chief city in Oregon, and site of Rajneesh Hotel.
Prem	Bhagwan's prefix for certain disciples, signifying 'love'.
Rajneesh	New name for Antelope, the town sixteen miles from Big Muddy ranch.

Rajneesh Foundation International	Name given to the movement in America in 1981.
Rajneesh Friends International	Later name of the movement, given in 1985.
Rajneeshpuram	Name given to the city Rajneeshees attempted to build on Big Muddy ranch.
Rajneeshpuram Peace Force	The heavily-armed police force on Big Muddy ranch.
Rama	One of the Hindu Gods.
Rancho Rajneesh	New name for Big Muddy from 1981 to 1985.
Saffron	Orange colour traditionally worn by holy men in the East; colour adopted by Rajneeshees.
Sannyas	The act of renouncing worldly cares and responsibilities.
Sannyasi	One who has renounced the world. Name given collectively by Bhagwan to his disciples.
Satsang	A holy gathering, usually silent.
Shiva	One of the Hindu trilogy, literally 'The Great God'; the all-seeing one.
Shree	'Sir' — title of honour assumed by Bhagwan.
Surrender	State and practice of handing oneself over to God, or to a guru, and giving him total power over your life.
Swami	Holy man, prefix given by Bhagwan to his male disciples.
Tantra	Ancient system for using sexual energy to attain spiritual enlightenment.
The Dalles	Town in Oregon, county seat of Wasco County, where Rajneeshees allegedly sprinkled salmonella on a number of salad bars; seven hundred people suffered food poisoning.
Thousand Friends of Oregon	A land conservancy group which took up complaints against Rajneeshees on behalf of local people.
Transcendental	State of overcoming bodily desires to be at one with God.
Yoga	Literally 'to yoke' or 'to join'. Linking oneself with God. Also prefix given by Bhagwan to disciples.
Yogi	One who practises yoga.

INTRODUCTION

This book is the story of my attraction to, involvement with, and final separation from a particularly sensational Indian guru, Bhagwan Shree Rajneesh. It is not intended to be some kind of business manager's objective report: it is an insider's view—a view from the heart—of the intimate processes that act upon disciples in their love affair with their spiritual leader.

In 1970 an erstwhile University lecturer named Mohan Chandra Rajneesh changed his name to Bhagwan Shree Rajneesh—literally meaning Sir God—and with the help of some deeply devoted admirers set himself up as a guru in a small apartment in Bombay. His erudition, psychic perception, and intensely charismatic personality affected many of the people he came into contact with, and a nucleus of disciples formed around him. At first these people were all Indian, but by 1972 he had attracted his first Western disciples.

A few days after I arrived in Bombay in 1983, Rajneesh gave a celebratory evening at his apartment. Fifteen or twenty Western sannyasis were sitting in amongst about a hundred Indian followers and admirers. An Indian tabla and sitar duo provided the music. At one point a wealthy Indian industrialist disciple presented Rajneesh with an enormous diamond ring; it must have cost at least $10,000. Rajneesh slipped it on first one finger, then another, seeming to savour it gently and curiously. Then he returned his attention to the tabla drummer, who was lost in a fervent passion of drums. When the music stopped, he beckoned the drummer over, and presented him with the ring. Everyone in the audience was amazed. The industrialist, who had hoped to curry favour with his guru with such an expensive gift, was devastated, and stormed out. It seemed to me at the time a perfect example of Rajneesh's complete nonattachment to the world of money, power, and prestige. He cared only for his truth and his freedom. It was this quality of spiritual clarity that helped attract so many people to him.

By 1981 he had established a commune in Poona, India, that became known as 'The Esalen of the East', where he spoke daily to six thousand disciples, a large percentage of whom were professional people from Europe, North America, and Japan.

It was said of him at this time that he had so many German disciples that there was not a soul in West Germany who did not have one of his disciples either in their family or belonging to the family of someone they worked with. Even the most ascerbic and critical of Western commentators were impressed by what they saw in Poona. Bernard Levin of the London *Times* described how he felt everyone at the Rajneesh ashram had 'come home'. He described Rajneesh as 'a deeply disturbing influence' and said that his words 'had an effect that seemed to bathe the hearer in a refulgent glow of wisdom. His voice is low, smooth and exceptionally beautiful'.

By 1985 Rajneesh had some 20,000 Western disciples, a 120-square-mile commune in Oregon, and a personal fleet of 90 Rolls Royces. However, later that same year he was arrested and subsequently pleaded guilty to immigration fraud and to arranging the sham marriages of his disciples, was fined $400,000, sentenced to a suspended ten-year jail term, and was deported. Almost immediately his commune disbanded, and a year later Rajneesh—minus all but a handful of his flock—was back in Bombay, in what was one of the best publicised cult collapses of this century.

Rajneesh is not a simple man. The commune that arose around him reflected his complex and often macabre personality. He undoubtedly possessed remarkable gifts, but at the same time he was in the grip of a need for power and wealth that was nothing short of megalomaniacal. This struggle within himself found outward manifestation in the many contradictions and duplicities of his public lectures and his private life. It was a struggle that finally broke the enchanted harmony out of which he showered his gifts. It left him a disillusioned, embittered, and very angry guru. A man of quite exceptional consciousness, a man who in 1973 was literally giving away diamonds with both hands, became by 1985 a paranoid recluse who dismissed his personal secretary because she would not buy him a $1.2 million wristwatch. He was—and is—quite ruthless to an extent hardly known in the West. But he could also communicate a feeling of unconditional love that was, to everyone who experienced it, unquestionably the real thing.

It is not possible to tell an insider's story of living in his commune unless this fundamental paradox in Rajneesh's being is taken into account. Both the magic and the megalomania has to be encompassed. For me to claim that my experience was a typical one is obviously unjustified. It was part of Rajneesh's charisma that he affected so many different kinds of people, in so many different ways. But between 1973 and 1981 almost everyone who met him was so deeply affected by his presence that they gave up everything they had to move to India and be with him. Each one of these people could tell a different story. Some of those people claim that he was never a 'sex guru'—and for them, he never was. Others see him as some kind of master alchemist, one who irreversibly changed their lives for the better. Some embittered former disciples simply see him as evil incarnate, as an embodiment of the demonic. J. Krishnamurti called him simply 'a criminal'. The U.S. Immigration department collectively saw him as a criminal, too, but on a personal level were full of admiration for him, if only as the smoothest operator they had ever come across. But one thing that everyone agrees upon is that the man was quite extraordinary; he was not a simple man.

What happened around him did have aspects of both the demonic and the divine. It is a story full of paradox, of contradictions, a story of both deceit and beatitude. It is a story of a man and an organisation that changed so dramatically from its earlier origins as to be almost beyond recognition. No 'Dallas' or 'Dynasty' scriptwriter could possibly imagine a more astonishing and sensational plot. Murders, the poisonings of entire cities, machine guns, sex orgies, midnight flights from the law—all this existed side by side with 'surrender' and a continual influx of millions of dollars in donations, and six thousand 'beautiful people' sitting in absolute silence every day to listen to a man of God.

It is hard to recount the process of being duped without feeling even more of a lemon. The temptations to re-write history in one's favour are legion, but to do so removes that taste of authenticity that is so essential to understanding. Whilst it is obviously impossible to remember word for word conversations held thirteen years ago, I endeavour to stay faithful to their spirit. I have portrayed events as I saw them at the time, not as I might now interpret them. For instance, when he made me his bodyguard and envious friends asked me why I thought I had been chosen, all I could think of at the time were a few hesitant and superficial reasons. In retrospect the relationship was a good deal more two-sided than I dared believe at the time. If this simplistic thinking makes me appear naive then so be it. I was, and some 20,000 others would have given anything to be in my place. It is important to remember that a large part of Rajneesh's interpretation of the guru/disciple relationship was to emphasise such other-worldly things as total trust and surrender. And as the old Roman phrase has it, *Populus vulti decepi, ergo decepiatur*: The people wish to be deceived, therefore the people are deceived. . . .

It is difficult to describe the process of induction into what Jung called the most powerful single archetype, the guru disciple archetype, and be limited to the use of ordinary words in their ordinary contexts. The experience is both totally intimate, and quite universal—the quests throughout history and mythology for prophets, oracles, and seers bears witness to the importance we place at the feet of Teachers. The closest experience that most people have that can equate to the intensity of the guru/disciple relationship is that of marriage. But that institution lacks some of the peculiar twists and a good deal of the intensity of the guru game. To tell the story of a guru's effect on his people through a recounting of the salient historical facts means the story losing its real meaning, its archetypal impact. And to re-write history so that one appears wiser than one actually was makes the narrative misleading and dishonest.

While writing this book enormous amounts of information came my way which was more gossip than fact. I have excluded all such gossip except where I heard it first-hand at the time I write about. If it formed an important part of my life and decision-making process when I first heard it, then I include it.

Some six 'in-house' autobiographies, all written by loyal Rajneesh disciples, have already been published. Not one of them was written by a member of Rajneesh's exclusive *inner* circle, and not one has been written with anything approaching candour. The authors of these books were hand-picked by Rajneesh himself, and their work was vetted by him before it went to press. This is the only book written by a graduate of his 'mystery school', an ex-disciple whom he now calls 'Judas'. Rajneesh, however, needed no such betrayer—he did a perfectly good job on his own. The facts, as you shall read, speak quite eloquently enough about his personal responsibility to need no further defense on my behalf.

This is the story of my relationship with my guru over a ten-year period and of the ramifications consequent upon leaving his movement. For a great many Rajneesh disciples it is their story too, the story of what was both a quite magical and also a bewildering period of their lives.

Chapter One
THE ROUTE TO BOMBAY

I first met Bhagwan in his Bombay flat on March 31st, 1973. From the minute I made my initial nervous steps into his exquisitely clean, immaculately tidy, sparsely but beautifully furnished room, I had the overwhelming sensation that I had come home.

Here was my spiritual father, a man who understood everything, someone who would be able to convey sense and meaning into my life. It was a truly magical feeling. I was overawed, transported, and felt instantly that Bhagwan was inside my mind as nobody else had ever been able to be. From the moment his delicate brown hands with their perfectly manicured nails touched mine, I knew I was in another world. He radiated a palpable sense of unconditional love which was simply electrifying. I was swept off my feet, enchanted, afloat in a sea of compassion emanating from this wholly original, unique being.

During that meeting, called a 'darshan', time stopped. I was flying, and every care had disappeared. This was the man I had been seeking. Who needed to look anywhere else? This man, I knew, could teach me so much that was valuable. Indeed, who could have a better teacher? He was the goal I should aspire to, the perfect model for all attainment. If only I could partake of what he had to offer.

Bhagwan told me to wear orange robes from now on, and said that today was to be my new birthday, that the past was to be wiped out, and that henceforward I should have a new name.

And so plain Hugh Milne, an osteopath from London, became Swami Shivamurti — one who is like Shiva, the supreme Hindu God. Already I felt I had a lot to live up to.

After hearing about Bhagwan in London, and listening to his lectures on cassette, I knew I had to meet this man. I arrived in Bombay not knowing whether I was to stay there for one day, one week, or for the rest of my life. In the event I stayed there for six weeks, then Bhagwan suggested I return to the UK and come back five months later.

But after that first meeting I understood in my heart that I wanted nothing else but to be near him, to serve him, to listen to his lectures. I was to return to Bombay and spend a total of eight years in India, and then two more in America.

Why did this man and his teachings have such an enormous impact on me, and later upon thousands of other Westerners? I think we can find at least part of the answer in the sexual and social climate of the late 1960s and early 1970s. Bhagwan Shree Rajneesh, with his doctrine of free love, appeared on the scene when many young people were trying to throw off the constraints of a society they saw as repressive, self-seeking, empty, finished. Freedom of all kinds was in the air; everybody wanted freedom to express themselves, to live life in the way they saw fit, not in the way their parents and grandparents had laid down as correct. Those of us who were young wanted a chance to give free reign to our emotions, not bottle them in, to get out of the straitjacket of fear and anxiety. We wanted, in the language of the sixties, to let it all hang out.

Most of all, those of us who were young at the start of the seventies wanted sexual freedom. The pill, which came onto the mass market in the mid-sixties, had for the first time effectively separated sex from procreation. This meant that we could look ahead to a new golden age where we could make love freely, and where the shackles of puritanism and outdated morality would finally be removed.

At the same time there was a search to find a meaning, a purpose in life. And Bhagwan seemed to offer the complete package: permission to engage in transcendent sex, indulged in with the idea that it would lead to spirituality and enlightenment. For many young men like myself, a potent added attraction of the whole movement was that Bhagwan's initial female followers were a most attractive group of young women who dressed in a highly provocative way. Along with shedding mental, emotional and behavioural restraints, many of us also wanted to shed the heavy, restrictive clothing we had worn until then. In meditation sessions, Bhagwan's female disciples wore flowing robes which showed all too clearly their sensuality.

The fact that Bhagwan was Indian, and was preaching free love in a country well known for its prudish attitude towards sex and nakedness, was a definitely volatile ingredient. It was a heady mixture, difficult to resist. Here was somebody who was saying, with great authority: don't be ascetic, don't deny yourself. The path to true enlightenment is through indulgence and gratification of sensual pleasures, so long as it is done with conscious awareness. Through these pleasures you will eventually attain true spiritual transcendence.

Added to that there was the personality and charisma of Bhagwan himself. Few people remained impervious to his impact, his enormous fascination. When I first met him I felt that here was a remarkable being, an Enlightened Master, one I could follow. At first I had a few doubts, but these were gradually swept away. The cynicism and disillusionment that was to set in later can never take away the impact of that first audience, of those early years.

But as this is, above all, a personal account of my ten years with Bhagwan, I will relate the chain of events that led to my attending early morning meditation sessions at his newly-established centre in Chalk Farm, North London. I hope it may explain what to many, I realise, may seem inexplicable — how a Scottish lad from a dour middle-class background could become such an intimate of Bhagwan's, a key member of his charmed inner circle, and be utterly convinced that here was somebody who was showing people how they ought to live.

From my earliest years, I realise now, I had the strong sensation that something was back there, something almost out of sight, a vague beckoner, an intangible promise. Many children have this feeling, but most dismiss it in later life as daydreaming or fantasy. But for me, the feeling remained. It was as if somebody was saying to me: dance with me and I will give you gifts beyond your knowing, gifts that are already yours but you do not yet know of them.

The questions in my mind had always been: what were these gifts, and how could I harness them? I was born in Edinburgh in 1948, the eldest of four children. My parents were both students when I arrived, and were not really ready to bring up a family. Many years after my experience with Bhagwan, my father confided to me that he had never really wanted me, or at least not when I arrived. He found it hard to cope with having children, and my earliest memory of him was his lifting up the newspaper in front of his face every evening when he got home from work as a kind of barricade, so that his rowdy red-headed sons would not disturb his peace and quiet.

It hurt because we wanted more of him, more physical contact, more games, more laughter. He was always so serious! After he qualified my father worked in an alternative medical clinic that had been founded by my grandfather on my mother's side.

My brothers and I fought a lot, and when I was six my father gave me the task of setting a good example to them. Later in life I had a strong feeling of resentment, that this too-early assumption of responsibility had somehow cut short my childhood and made me grow up far too soon. Some of my very earliest memories are of being overwhelmed by identical twin brothers, eighteen months younger than me. Together, it appeared to me, they formed a solid front to frustrate me at every turn. I could not be victorious against them both as, like many twins, they had a secret language by which they communicated. The first ten years of my life were ones of continual warfare with my brothers.

My father's own survival tactic in all this was to opt out completely. He simply could not stand the noise, and banished the children from the adult meal table. I can vividly remember sitting on the dustbin lids outside the door to eat my dinner.

During the school holidays the noise and fighting became too much for either of my parents to stand, so they despatched me to a friend's farm in the idyllic Scottish lowlands. I came to love and cherish my contact with nature and livestock, wild animals, and above all the sky, the wind and the stars. Blue mountains in the far distance gave inspiration to my dreams. One peak was capped with a Viking burial mound, another flanked by a Roman fort.

As a small child I did not at first understand that these wars, when the Vikings and the Romans invaded Britain, were now over. It all seemed so real, so much in the here and now. I was named Hugh after one of my father's many friends who had been killed in the Second World War. During my childhood food rationing was still in force, and conscription was going on. I did not look forward to joining the army myself. Fortunately I never had to, as conscription was abolished many years before I became eighteen.

My father had lost so many of his own friends in the war that the experience of being a night bomber pilot remained with him for many years. It was such a tough, nerve-wracking experience that he wanted an easy life thereafter, and that was why he joined my grandfather's clinic rather than setting up one of his own. He became ultra-conservative, as he felt he had done enough dangerous things in his youth. He was rather a gloomy father in many ways, ever reluctant to open up his heart. In all these respects Bhagwan was so different when I first met him.

My father remained rather militaristic in his outlook, and I was always being given little jobs that reminded him of his days during the war. I would clean the car windows — "the better to spot Messer-schmitts" he said, and family journeys would always begin with the command "contact port outer" — a flight command — before inserting the ignition keys.

My mother, by contrast, was a staunch pacifist, and had remained so throughout the war. She was a very wholesome, intensely maternal and supportive sort of person. My parents sent me to a school run according to the teachings of the German mystic Rudolf Steiner. At the Steiner school we were taught by a rugged old character who had lost an arm during the First World War, in the trenches of Passchendaele. He had no time for what he considered to be softness, and treated complaints with contempt.

One day he overheard someone in class complain that his new shoes were too tight. "You laddies!" he yelled, trembling with unsurpressed rage. "When I was your age I had to walk twenty miles a day, do you hear me, and we were too poor to afford any shoes at all. Don't let me hear your milksops and bletherskites moan your wee spoilt mouths off that your nice new shoes are too tight, you schlecters you, blethering craters the lot of you . . . ". Though he would never use corporal punishment, he used a weapon that we found infinitely more intimidating: he would lose his temper and shout at us for minutes on end.

Our art teacher at the Steiner school was a softspoken South German man of about thirty. One day in a life drawing class he saw a doodle I had made at the margin of my page of a Spitfire shooting down a Focke-Wulf. I would have been about ten at the time. The German aircraft had a swastika drawn prominently on its tail. The art teacher came over to me and said softly, in man-to-man fashion, "We made a great mistake. Those days are over now, you know." Immediately I felt very ashamed and humbled. His sincerity and humanity were more of an education to me than all the drawing he ever taught.

As a child I had strange and unfathomable dreams of being a wise man in the hills, a philosopher, a sage. Perhaps it was a memory of some past life, as they would say in India. Maybe it was my highest yearning for myself in this life. When I was thirteen I wrote in a school essay that I wanted to be a philosopher when I grew up. At the time most of my classmates wanted to be engine drivers or janitors. The teacher read out my essay to the class, and showed it to his colleagues, who commented favourably on it. It all felt quite strange, I remember, as if some inner secret had come into the open at last. It was almost a shameful ambition, in spartan Scotland at least, to want to be a philosopher. As it turned out, I became a healer, but Rajneesh was to play a crucial part in my search for the truth.

But though I had publicly declared my ambition to be a philosopher, at the age of thirteen I was not doing very well academically. Docky, my class teacher (who always smelt musty, like old moth balls), put his arm round my shoulder one day and said: "You know, Hughie, it'll not be university for you. You're not the type. A gardener will be the thing for you, or a job like that. So I'll not be putting you in for the exams, the 'O' and 'A' levels."

The Harris tweed of his jacket burned my ear as he continued: "In two years' time you'll be free to go and enjoy a simple life. You will find fulfilment there."

I felt angry and humiliated. How dare this man presume to know what I was capable of? The last thing in the world I wanted to be was a gardener, with split fingernails and grubby hands, earning the minimum agricultural wage, which in Scotland in 1961 was a low sum indeed. I want to take exams, I shouted inside myself. I want to go to university. I want to be an airline pilot or an engineer. I want to be *something*! I went home and told my father what Docky had said.

It was all too clear why Docky had made that pronouncement. My performance in class was mediocre, to say the least. I was bottom in most subjects. But I was still enraged. Could not my teacher see deeper into my heart? Could he not see that I had not even started trying?

I decided for myself that the Rudolf Steiner school was no longer the place for me. I was by now too old to transfer to the Edinburgh fee-paying schools, so there was nothing for it but to go to the local secondary school, a hideous newly-built concrete and glass monstrosity whose chief claim to fame was the number of violent fights that went on in the playground. Knives were occasionally brought out. It was a very rough place, but I decided I had to go. I went down a year, and set to work.

Within three years I had the five 'O' levels I needed as a foundation, and a year later I had the 'A' levels necessary for university entrance. As it turned out I didn't go to university, but spent six months cramming at night to pass the science exams for getting into Osteopathic College in London.

True to his long-standing principles of self-sufficiency, my father never helped me financially during this time. I put myself through college, driving cars and thirty-ton trucks for Avis Rent-a-Car. By my fourth year at full-time college I had become Deputy Service Manager of Avis's truck rental in South London. I was making enough money to have my own car, and I drove to college during the week in my new Lotus Elan, the one with the racing engine and the wide wheels.

By the time I went to Osteopathic College in London, I had already worked as a concrete labourer, a heavy truck driver, a road survey official, a forestry hill worker and an agricultural labourer. I used the money I earned to build myself a high-performance motorcycle, a task that took a year. During college vacations I also worked as a junior masseur at various health clinics.

During my years at College I came into contact with the teachings of many spiritual teachers, including Krishnamurti and Gurdjieff. We were lucky at the College in that we were blessed with some inspired and quite extraordinary lecturers, who decided to broaden our limited horizons by introduucing a little metaphysics into the syllabus along with the usual anatomy and tissue pathology courses. An older classmate of mine had studied with Krishnamurti for ten years, so even at that time I was learning about new ways of thinking.

Osteopathy is a branch of alternative medicine which is concerned with joint, bone and back problems, and the relationship of the spine to general health. A good osteopath relies on more than a knowledge of bone and soft tissue structure, though. Intuition plays a large part in any successful healing process.

When I began studying, osteopathy was not recognised by the orthodox medical profession, and only now is it beginning to be incorporated into the British National Health Service. Though all osteopaths are still in private practice, any NHS doctor can now recommend a patient to see an osteopath.

We had many interesting students at Osteopathy College, and while I was there from 1967 to 1971 it was a venue for much experimentation with alternative lifestyles and modes of being. One of the three women in my class had a husband who had recently started a first-class vegetarian restaurant, one of the earliest in London. Another student was a Sufi. In our third year at College the drug LSD appeared, and almost the whole class tried it. While I was very interested in the concept of personal change, I never wanted to take mind-altering drugs, unlike many young people at the time. It seemed to me that there had to be another way to raise consciousness, to get at the inner core of being.

Nevertheless, all these goings-on aroused my interest, and made me feel there was more to life than I had previously imagined. Also, rebellion and unrest among students was going on all round me. The Art College at Hornsey was in the middle of its years-long sit-in to draw attention to students' rights. In 1968 there was the famous students' revolution in Paris, where bloody rioting took place in the streets.

It seemed to those of us who were students during those years that a new age was approaching, that the old order of educators was falling, and that a newer and better regime was emerging. My own college was not spared student unrest. Three of us were nearly refused graduation; I was one of them. Our senior tutor informed us that we had to toe the line, adding at the same time that he understood that the line was damn stupid at times. The three of us were eventually admitted to membership of our professional association six months after the rest of the class, as a mark of our tutors' displeasure.

Yet less than a year later I was welcomed back as a lecturer. It was after I graduated and began practising my profession that a series of strange experiences began to happen to me. In 1970 my mother died of cancer, and her illness and approaching death forced me to look again at the pattern of beliefs I had been born into, and to try and assess what was wrong with them.

Her illness brought us closer together than we had ever been during my childhood. While she was still able to, we would both go for long walks in the country, when she would try to convey to me what was going on in her, and why this disease should have invaded her body at the early age of forty-six. My mother's life had been devoted to healthy living, hard work, and the raising of four children. Ever stoic and uncomplaining, my mother refused the possibility of an operation, and instead tried to treat the condition by natural means. She was reluctant to take sleeping pills or pain killers until the very end, and her public face was always one of optimism and courage. It was hard to reassess my beliefs in the face of my mother's illness, especially as most of my beliefs had come from my mother herself.

When I had completed my training I began working at a health clinic near London. It soon became clear that I had a gift for healing. Patients would come in for their initial consultation, and in that instant I would know what to do, without knowing precisely *how* I knew, or what was wrong with them. Yet my training forced me to follow a set pattern of diagnosis and treatment.

I did all the orthodox side well enough, yet it was mainly because of my intuitive abilities that I became busy and successful beyond my wildest dreams. Eighteen months after graduation I was earning far more than I had expected to earn after five years. I had a Lotus sports car, a fast Honda motorcycle, a house in Oxfordshire and an office in Kensington, West London.

But through and above all this that inner voice came in and said: so what? It continued: Do you want to do this for the rest of your life? And that part of me which was brutally honest knew that there was another way to practise, to heal and to communicate. But what it was, and where to learn about it, I did not know. How did one find that inner space, that peace, that transcendence that so many of my friends seemed to be experiencing through LSD and other drugs? It seemed that all around me people were meditating, doing the whirling dervish ceremony, joining these new Californian groups the popular press was referring to as 'group gropes'. I decided that I had to get to the root of it all, and for the next eighteen months I participated in the available spectrum of humanistic psychology groups, encounter groups, and so on.

Since many of these groups flourished in the late sixties and are no more, or have lost the power they once had, I shall explain briefly what they were and how they operated.

Humanistic psychology encompasses a set of beliefs developed by the American therapist Abraham Maslow. He believes that everybody has free will, and that this will should be freely expressed. During the early seventies, 'growth' centres sprang up in Britain and America where ordinary people could go and explore themselves, come to terms with deep-seated hostilities and the anxieties which prevented them from achieving their true potential. The idea is that you should be able to strip off old defences in order to lead a new, freer life where it is possible to do your own thing.

Encounter groups, an offshoot of the above, flourished during the 'me-decade', as it was dubbed by the American journalist Tom Wolfe. In these groups, everybody tries to understand exactly who they are. Started by Carl Rogers, the idea is that you should strip off the layers of social conformity on a voyage to self-discovery. You could do this for yourself, and dispense with 'experts' who knew you, after all, far less well than you knew yourself. Encounter group sessions, at their most demanding, consist of 48-hour long marathons, where people can eventually relax and open up. You say and do just what you like. Many people find these groups frightening and forbidding as they are confronted with their own and other people's hostility.

est — Erhart Seminar Training, always referred to in the lower case — is another 'open up' type of therapy, again developed in America. est was devised by businessman Werner Erhart, who in the mid-seventies visited Bhagwan in Poona. These sessions aim to show people how, in the main, they live according to preconceived expectations and beliefs. In other words, they are not really living or being themselves at all. The 'training' involves sixty hours over two weekends, where trainees have to sit and listen to all sorts of truths about themselves, which might well be unpalatable. est became known as the 'no-piss' training, as toilet and lunch breaks were not allowed during the sessions.

I also became involved in Reichian bodywork. Wilhelm Reich was a disciple of Freud, and believed that the repression of sexual needs and the lack of abandonment to orgasm led to rigidity in individuals, and authoritarian regimes in society. He thought that energy which fails to be released through sexual orgasm becomes dammed up in the body in muscular tension, aches and pains. This pent-up energy leads to poor posture, bad circulation and shallow breathing. Reichian therapy sessions are designed to unblock this energy and allow it free passage through the body. They involve actual manipulation of the body, consisting of strenuous exercise or direct massage. Very often these sessions are carried out with the patient fully or virtually naked, with the idea of better releasing orgiastic potency.

Working on myself in the therapy groups, I sensed the desperate need for a personal quantum leap. The voice inside my heart told me: Get out of this rut, this money-spinning trap, and find out what this intuition is about. The voice of reason butted in with: But how will you earn a living; what will you do?

In the event the decision was made for me. In December 1972 I was informed that the residential health clinic where I worked was closing down in two months' time. The die, then, had been cast. I put myself into the hands of fate, and waited to see what would happen.

The day after the clinic closed, I went to my friend Bill Grossman, who ran the encounter group I had been attending, and made it clear that I wanted to embrace these new ideas. A former patient of mine offered me a room in one of the new encounter group houses. He was a shortish, wiry fellow about fifteen years my senior, with a bushy black beard and piercingly blue eyes. His name was Mike Barnett, founder of the therapy group People Not Psychiatry. After I had been with Bhagwan for about a year, Mike Barnett came out as well, and met with some of the most consistent wooing Bhagwan has ever given anybody. Mike became 'Somendra', and spent many years as a very prominent person within the Rajneesh organisation. He has now left too, and currently runs a religious and therapy centre of his own in Switzerland.

At about this time I read a book by a man called Richard Alpert, who had become a disciple of an Indian guru called Neemkeroli Baba, changed his name to Ram Dass, and advocated a way of life that made complete sense to me. The book, *Be Here Now*, told of a search to avoid the futility of war, waste and cruelty, and gain inner peace. It became a runaway bestseller in the early 1970s. I read the works of Jung, the writings of the pioneers of gestalt and psycho-drama, launched myself into encounter group sessions. I wanted to know finally, once and for all, what made my particular universe tick. I wanted to experience once again that space I had glimpsed up in the Scottish mountains as a child. All the experiences I was having as a therapist, of knowing instantly what was wrong with my patients, were leading me onwards in a search for knowledge, for the answers.

Then eventually my friend Bill asked if I would like to try some meditation. My wary and suspicious Scottish upbringing rebelled. I had previously included such activities under the same dubious heading as spiritualism, old ladies with crystal balls, Indian fakirs and other such nonsense, but Bill persisted. "There's this woman upstairs," he said. "She's about to start a dynamic meditation course. The first session is tomorrow morning. Let's go and meet her," he finished enthusiastically.

All right.

We went upstairs to see a vision that was indeed intriguing for London on a bleak, cold January morning. The lady was an apparition of gold and saffron. She wore an ankle-length religious robe with a wooden bead necklace, and emanated an aura of sandalwood, sensuality and camphor. Bill introduced us.

"Meet Veena," he said. "She's just off the 707 from Bombay, and has instructions to set up the world's first meditation centre for a man they call Bhagwan. That's him in the little picture hanging from Veena's neck. Look at him."

Veena continues as I look: "He's an Enlightened Being," she explains in her soft South African accent. "He lives in this small flat in Bombay, and has a few disciples he calls sannyasis. He gives them individual instruction, new names and a mala — that's this necklace. It's all great fun!"

I take a look at the photo. My first thoughts are that this man looks exactly like the Maharishi that the Beatles had followed for a time. He has, I think, a nice soft look, a Mona Lisa of a smile among the prolific beard. Yet I'm not sure that this is what I want to do first thing in the morning. Veena informs me that we have to get up at five-thirty in order to meditate properly. I demur. On the other hand, though, Veena is pretty, very pretty, and has very provocative hips beneath that thin robe . . .

"How much is it?" I hedge.

"Oh, it's free," she laughs, and dances away.

I listen while Veena explains what this meditation is all about. "There are four stages, and Bhagwan says we must wear loose clothing and a blindfold."

I decide to give it a go, thinking that at any rate I can have little to lose. At five-thirty the next morning I make my way to the upstairs room. Veena is already there, instructing everybody in what to do. There are about ten people in the room. "Here are the blindfolds," she says. "I hope they fit, as we only had them made last night, and there wasn't enough elastic to go round. Also I forgot the paraffin for the stove, so I'm sorry it's so cold in here.

"But you'll soon warm up with the breathing, and the final stage is terrific for bringing up the body temperature." The room was a freshly-painted loft in Chalk Farm, a long building beside the main London to Birmingham railway line. It was decorated and festooned with Indian artefacts. There were Indian print curtains, Indian incense holders, Indian fabric covering the cushions, and a signed black and white photograph of the Guru, Bhagwan, on a mini-altar along one wall. In every way Veena exemplified the exotic, by gesture, voice, fragrance, clothing, and her sun-bleached tresses.

The ten of us put on the blindfolds and began ten minutes of hyperventilation, the deep, fast breathing that worked us up to an intense pitch. Then came the stage they called 'catharsis' — letting go. There followed two more stages, one of dance, and the final one of complete stillness and silence. At the end of it all I was physically exhausted. The room had certainly warmed up considerably.

After the meditation session was over, we had mint tea, honey, biscuits and a talk, given by this man they called Bhagwan. It was on a very scratchy cassette player. He seemed to end each sentence with long trailing-off sibilances, making the lecture more like a seduction than a dissertation. There were long pauses between sentences, as if he was in no hurry at all, and not in the least concerned as to whether somebody would interrupt him. In the background was a litany of car horns, which took away from the impact somewhat. This lecture had been recorded in Bombay, not the quietest of cities. There was hardly a single space without several car horns going. At last, Veena lit incense, and its smoke curled in the air. Some people had to go off to work, and slipped out through the curtains, quietly excusing themselves.

It was all very magical.

As I continued with the early morning meditation sessions, I had the distinct feeling that everything was synchronising, coming together. As Bhagwan was talking on cassette about the ancient philosophy of tantra, so did the Hayward Gallery on London's South Bank mount a major exhibition of tantric art. As I went round the exhibition a large part of me felt that I had come home, that I belonged among people who could execute this kind of art. Then the Whirling Dervishes gave an exhibition at a major West End theatre. They were very inspiring, very elegant, and also seemed to say something important to me.

I met Neville, an enigmatic little fellow whose passion seemed to be smuggling antique carpets out of Tibet by mule train. "I'm not interested in what sort of day these city people had at the office," he told me. "If you have just crossed the Sahara underneath a camel, then I want to hear about it. Otherwise it's better to stay silent."

As we were excitingly rediscovering the mystic East, so did the sexual revolution get under way. *Time* magazine, in particular, charted the progress of this weekly revolution with zeal and verve. They wrote about wife-swapping, group gropes, all-weekend orgies, blind dates, one-night stands, blue movies, the emergence of marijuana, the establishment of upper class brothels. It seemed there had been nothing like this since the days of the Roman Bacchanalia.

At the time, too, sex-related diseases such as herpes, AIDS, candida, crabs and NSU were so far away they were not even small clouds to disturb the bliss of free love.

In the midst of all this, one can see how Bhagwan's appearance was perfectly timed. And he read *Time* magazine, too, as was evident from his speeches which we heard on cassette. It appeared that he took his clues from the media as much as the astral planes, and was bang up-to-date in everything he said.

Since I had enjoyed a sexually active adolescence, I was more than interested in what this man had to say on the subject. As he spoke it was as if the veil dropped from my eyes.

So *that's* what relationships are all about, I said to myself as I drank in his words. That is where I went wrong with this girl, that was my mistake with the other one. I had confused sex with love and possessiveness, and felt that Bhagwan was opening my eyes about the true nature of male/female relationships. He really understood, you could feel it. This man was not talking from dry memory, from scientific literature or some academic analysis.

He came over as a potent mixture of poet, artist, lover, sexual alchemist, sensual libertine, master magician, court jester, and without doubt one of the wisest men who had ever lived. He was somebody who seemed to promise the infinite, who hinted at worlds within worlds, knowledge beyond knowledge. It wasn't long before I made up my mind that I must meet this man, very soon.

Once I had decided to travel to Bombay at the earliest opportunity, I read up everything I could about Bhagwan and about tantra, the ancient doctrine which says that sex can be used to reach real inner peace and deep harmony with oneself and with nature. Tantra said don't deny yourself, but indulge, "that surfeiting, the appetite may sicken and so die," as Orsino has it in the opening lines of Shakespeare's *Twelfth Night*. The point about tantra, though, is that you harness sexual energies with the discipline of awareness.

One of the books I read about Bhagwan before going to Bombay was a slim booklet in the *Do Not Read* Series, Volume One, by V. Vora. It was published by Jeevan Jagruti Kendra, a firm run by one of Bhagwan's disciples. He was a close friend of Bhagwan's assistant Laxmi.

Entitled *Rajneesh — a glimpse*, the booklet is a twenty-four page panegyric to Bhagwan. Each paragraph begins with a new set of superlatives, a new indication of excellence or wonderment. A few examples will convey the flavour of the booklet. It starts off by saying: "Rajneesh is not a man of our times. He belongs to futurity. A modern Socrates he is, continually travelling the length and breadth of this country . . . His exposition of truths — or rather, The Truth — is universal, revolutionary and modern . . . Rajneesh's aim is to kindle religion in common man."

The booklet stated clearly that Rajneesh had no aims to be a leader, but went on to say that he imparts "a vision of prodigious proportions where definitions and limitations evaporate, which is beyond human thinking and imagination." Rajneesh, not yet called Bhagwan, at least not in this book published in 1970, was committed, according to the author, to abolishing poverty and demystifying religion. His intention, as spelled out in the booklet, was to make humans more like Gods themselves, and to show that religion and truth are not outside us, but within.

The point that interested me most in the booklet was Vora's assertion that Bhagwan guided "strictly by self-example". As I listened to those lectures explaining the tantric idea of sex, I realised that here must be a man who practised what he preached. There was no way he could speak so fluently and knowledgeably about sexual intimacy while being a celibate himself. He spoke more like a connoisseur of vintage wine than a dry academic. He trod very carefully, though, in the matter of his personal involvement. He did not actually say whether or not he was celibate, and referred only very obliquely to sexual experiences that might or might not have been of a personal nature. It was left to the listener to make up his or her own mind.

'Guiding strictly by self-example' is a cornerstone of tantra. Tantra is the alternative to yoga in Indian mystical teachings, and is in many ways its complete opposite. Yoga — the word means 'to yoke' or 'to join' — refers to the path of renunciation, whereas tantra encourages every kind of indulgence, so long as it is undertaken with awareness.

Though I had for several years tried to seek the truth, and I was becoming ever more interested in Eastern philosophy, I had never been in the least attracted to yoga, nor to those who practised it. I'm not talking here just about physical yoga, or exercises, but the mental attitude that goes with the bodily contortions.

I felt that people who went in for yoga were excessively sensitive, somewhat anaemic souls who were likely to be following a macrobiotic diet. I had never met any hale and hearty practitioners of yoga. They all seemed to be pale, hollow-cheeked, contemplative types whose only expression of vigour lay in defending their own ascetic practices.

The idea of sitting on the floor for an hour or more doing contortions seemed painful and unnecessary, and required an amount of patience I did not feel I possessed. And it was all so dry — no sex appeal, no earthiness, no panache. They were vegetarians who daren't eat meat in case it aroused the lower passions. I had been brought up as a vegetarian, so I knew how emotionally anaemic vegetarians could be. No, they were not my sort of people at all.

By contrast, here was Bhagwan introducing tantra. From what he said, this was an entirely different approach to enlightenment and self-transcendence. Someone who practises tantra will advocate the way to celibacy as being through wholehearted sexual indulgence. You can satisfy and satiate, but you should do it almost scientifically, so that you can be enabled to reach the end of your journey. To me tantra seemed a far more realistic way; do not suppress or repress, it said, but indulge as much as your fancy takes you. At the same time, you should not be carried away blindly by a passion, but enter into it with appropriate and adequate preparation.

Through tantra, passion and indulgence come to have a purpose. They are steps on a long journey of self-discovery. In one of his speeches Bhagwan pointed out that in an earlier epoch of Indian history tantra was a major religion, and had many full-time devotees. The temples of Kujaraho and Karnack, whose voluptuous solid stone carvings of intertwined couples combine sexuality in stone with a sensual lightness of touch, were carved during the flowering of the tantric religion.

Tantra teaches that nothing is intrinsically dirty, nothing good or bad, except as Shakespeare, who so understood these things, said: "Thinking makes it so". It is purely your own attitude which determines what you consider to be good or bad, moral or amoral. The sexual act, of itself, is neutral: we invest it with meaning, which can be positive or negative. But tantra is not simply concerned with taking you through and beyond sex; the main point is to free people from their previously hidebound conditioning. The ultimate goal of tantra is spiritual clarity, the disappearance of the personal and individual ego into a greater awareness, a disillusion of self into the whole, the eternal, the void, the blissful state of being. Five hundred years before Christ, Buddha called this space 'Samadhi', 'beyond the beyond, where nothing exists'. Jesus called this same state of mind the Kingdom of God.

Bhagwan referred to it as Enlightenment. He stated that he himself had attained it at the age of twenty-one, and that only eight or nine other beings on Earth at any one time could expect to reach the same peak. To make his own special case quite clear, he went on to declare that, whilst there were perhaps nine other Enlightened Beings, there was only one Enlightened Master in the world at any particular time, and that he was the one.

To attain in-depth, genuine spirituality, according to tantra, one has to harness all the vital and biological apparatus at one's disposal. We should not suppress it, indeed to do so is dangerous. It is possible to try and starve sex out through macrobiotic eating or fasting. It is possible to become an athlete and train so hard that there is little energy left for sex. It is possible to enter a monastery or nunnery where there is hardly an opportunity to express or indulge in sex. But whatever you attempt to do to drive it down, sex will still appear in one form or another. It will come out, if in no other way, through dreams and fantasies. Tantra says: let's be honest, let's face some facts about ourselves and admit that we are sexual beings.

The basic idea of tantra is that our dynamic energies can be awoken. The belief is that all energy is fundamentally sexual, and finds its origin at the base of the spine. When properly freed, it will travel up the spine to the brain, where it unites with the mind and the spiritual heart in an embrace of love and consciousness. In ancient images this is often portrayed sexually. Tantric followers firmly believe that it is through fulfilment and not through austerity that the supreme reality is found. All forms of self-mortification such as fasting or bodily contortions are seen as an insult.

Natural desires should be fulfilled intelligently and attentively, as repression of desire leads to endless trouble. Tantra says: enjoy the pleasures of the world, but at the same time discover in yourself the presence of God. The sexual act is never condemned, as the belief is that through conscious indulgence, practitioners of tantra will be brought into blissful union with the supreme consciousness. Through these practices an ordinary person can reach hitherto undreamed-of heights of awareness.

Tantric sex is not just about physical intercourse. It is essential to share a sense of love with one's partner. This does not mean one has to 'fall in love' — in fact such an emotion can make things more difficult and get in the way of enlightenment. The idea is that you learn to treat your partner as your guru, regarding their body as sacred, worshipping their form. You should become sexual without being in the least possessive, become sensual and delicate without ever surrendering your will to desire. If wild and passionate desire for a particular individual ever takes you over, then you have lost this meditative centre, your own core of being.

Bhagwan explained in his lectures the difference between 'peak' and 'valley' orgasms. In a 'valley' orgasm the sense of lingering union can be perpetuated for an hour or more, and you can retain your meditative core. If you lose your centre and become carried away by sexual excitement, then it is all a failure. The 'peak' orgasm is, Bhagwan told us, a poor thing in comparison with the art of prolonged lovemaking, which is the 'valley' orgasm.

In the later years, in Poona, many sexual experiments were tried. Bhagwan told one woman how to overcome her phobia of rats: she should indulge in oral sex. This took place in specific tantric sessions. In another tantric session at Poona, the male participants had to eat a ripe mango from between their female partners' legs. The mangoes were very popular with everyone. Interestingly, but perhaps not surprisingly, it was more often the men who withdrew first from these sessions, the men rather than the women who hid cowering in a corner as their most intimate fears confronted them.

Yes, tantra was the apotheosis of free indulgence, and goes a long way to explain why Bhagwan's teachings fell on such fruitful soil among young Westerners in the seventies. In later years, stories leaked out about how the tantric sessions led to broken bones, violence, and outbursts of wild hysteria. These reports were not exaggerated. "Falling up the steps on the way to the ashram" became a euphemism at the local hospital for those who had suffered injuries during tantric sessions. This was necesssary to avoid police involvement.

Now, looking back, it is easy to decry these sessions as licentious, sensational, and without merit. Yet nobody I know holds bitter memories of them. In the early days there was a very deep and genuine sense of family, of commitment to each other, and of love towards Bhagwan. Nobody, not even those who suffered broken ribs or worse, ever felt resentful about the sessions, or sued the Foundation. They were productive and positive, and a great deal of soul-searching went on. To us they seemed magical, alchemical, and we truly felt that we were working through our own problems, fears and inhibitions.

As we sat listening to Bhagwan in Veena's meditation sessions in the Chalk Farm loft, we were sure that whatever Bhagwan preached he must also practise. It was clear that Bhagwan's disciples were no ordinary people, but graduates of an uncommon and rewarding school. This was a master apprenticeship in the Tree of Life, and we could all partake of the fruits of wisdom and knowledge. Each of us was possessed of love, sexuality, sensuality, the capacity to give and to share, to receive, to teach, to protect. We could choose either to understand or to ignore. We could either acknowledge and wonder, or we could suppress and inhibit.

Tantra seemed to me to be a wondrous thing. Yet I doubt if I would ever have embraced this path had it not been for Bhagwan. While I listened to his speeches on cassette in the early hours of the day it seemed to me that his words were enchanted, that he was playing an irresistible pied piper's song as he said "Come, follow me".

The melody of his words captured my enthusiasm and imagination. He was asking me to dance with him, and he said it in words of love. It all made total and immediate sense. When I later asked others why they had been so attracted to Bhagwan, they all said the same thing: "He just seemed to be putting into words all the things I had been thinking about, but couldn't seem to express. Yes, he was *it*!"

The Western world had been made ready for Bhagwan by the Upjohn Corporation — the main developers of the contraceptive pill — the Beatles, the baby boom, the brief flourishing of the Western economy, the 'never had it so good' generation, and the demise of traditional religion. It was all the more fascinating for us that this tantric bacchanalia was being held in impossibly prudish India, a land whose high birth rates hid the most inhibited, sterile and unwanted sexuality. Bhagwan said that most Indian women had never had an orgasm, and my later experiences with Indian women made me realise how true this was.

For us, convening every morning in a little loft in Chalk Farm, London, Bhagwan seemed to be inviting us to the most magical and attractive of worlds. Before long I knew I was not going to be content with just having a toe in the water. I had to dive in with my whole being.

The way had been made ready for me. The health clinic where I had been working had closed, and there were no commitments to keep me in England a minute longer. I had saved up quite a lot of money, and I decided without further ado that I would go to Bombay to meet this wondrous being, and then see what happened.

Chapter Two
EARLY DAYS WITH BHAGWAN

From the moment I first met Bhagwan, I had the distinct feeling that I had finally met my real Father and Teacher, and that my search had now ended. I had reached my destination.

At the time, in 1973, Bhagwan lived in a small flat in Bombay with two full-time Indian female assistants, Kranti and Laxmi, and an English disciple who was also his lover, Christine Woolf. She came from prosaic Morden, in Surrey. Christine had been renamed Vivek, which means awareness, and was very beautiful in an ethereal, willowy way. She would have been about twenty-three at the time, and was one of the very first Westerners to seek out Bhagwan in India. She met him in 1971, and stayed with him as he travelled the world looking for sanctuary in 1985 and 1986. She has stayed steadfast throughout all the vicissitudes Bhagwan has endured or created.

There was in those days no established ashram, and the very few Westerners who gathered daily to hear Bhagwan's discourses—about two dozen people—lived in hotels in and around Bombay. Rajneesh Foundation International had not yet been set up, there were no overt signs of wealth, and few people in the West had ever heard of the man. However, Bhagwan had already become famous in India for his lecture tours, and until 1972 had been using the title 'Acharya' or professor.

After booking myself in at a Bombay hotel, I made an appointment to see Bhagwan. I can still vividly remember every aspect of that meeting, as it was to change my life for ever.

Laxmi, then aged about forty, was a tiny birdlike being with enormous eyes and the longest eyelashes I have ever seen. She was a former civil servant who had been instrumental in establishing Bhagwan as a leading spiritual teacher. In 1968 she had fallen in love with him, and had served him as a secretary ever since.

She sat outside his door, kept his appointment diary, and carefully vetted everybody who wanted to go in. It was already well known that Bhagwan was highly allergic to any kind of scent, whether this was a natural body odour or applied perfume. As early as 1966, when he first left his university post to become an itinerant lecturer, Rajneesh propagated the air of someone who was very special, and quite different from the rest of humanity.

As I approach his door, I am feeling very nervous, both at the prospect of actually meeting Bhagwan in the flesh, and also about my own possible reaction. What will happen? Will I conduct myself correctly? What will Bhagwan think of me? How will I take it all? I feel considerable awe as, even in those far-off days, Bhagwan was perceived by his disciples to be almost God incarnate, the saviour who would redeem humankind.

Anyway, I am told by Laxmi that it is 'good' to go in now. 'Good' was a word, I soon learned, that Bhagwan and his coterie used constantly and very loosely: it meant whatever they wanted it to mean at the time. Just now, Laxmi meant that the time was auspicious for me to have this meeting.

I open the door slowly and peer round. There doesn't seem to be anybody in the room. Why is it empty? I feel sudden panic and disorientation. Where is Bhagwan?

Suddenly there is a chuckle from the corner. There he is! My first impressions are how tiny, how exquisite he is. He is wearing immaculately-pressed robes and has a dainty little hand-embroidered towel over one wrist. He sits there so quietly, so peacefully, that I thought the room must be empty.

"Come here, come here," he directs gaily. He has deep brown eyes, arching poetic eyebrows, and an enormous overflowing moustache. Any Frenchman would be proud of such a mouser. The chair he sits in is a very businesslike, modern affair, brand new and upholstered in deep beige velour pile. "Come closer, come closer," he commands, making small rotatory gestures with his left hand, which is dangling over the side of the chair.

Can he mean me to sit quite so close, right under his wing, when we all know that the smell of the human body can easily upset him? Can he mean *that* close, rubbing my shoulder against the arm of the chair?

Awkwardly I sit down. The cold marble feels good against the soft outer soles of my bare feet. I pull in my ankles in what I hope is a passable imitation of the good disciple's cross-legged posture. A hand grasps mine. What a warm surprise! He is actually touching me, with rich, creamy, and yet at the same time dry and delicate brown hands.

There is a pause. Who should speak first? I glance in acute
embarrassment round the room. There is a double bed, on the floor,
and all is immaculately tidy. The floor tiles are highly polished, and
reflect the slatted blinds of the window shades. There is a tiny spot of
rusty water under the industrious air conditioner.

The room is painted in palest green pastel shades, and there are no
curtains, not one picture, not one ornament to disturb the stark
simple emptiness in this one small space that serves Bhagwan as
bedroom, lounge and dining room.

"So. You have come from London, hmmmm?"

He continues. "How is Veena? She is running the Centre well? She
has painted it? What colour has she painted it? Good. Green is good.
Veena is good. Much will be happening in London. Hmmmm."

I experience tremendous excitement and anticipation. These small-
talk questions somehow set the milieu, and are getting closer and
closer to me by discreet indirectness, the method of the East. It's as if
he is saying: through this orchestration of time and space let us take
bearings on this new child. Let us bounce simple and known
questions off him to establish the level of his understanding and
commitment. I sit there with a feeling of tremendous awareness that
something is going on, though I'm not at all sure what. There is no
doubt about it: I am definitely in the presence of something powerful.

He continues to ask simple questions, about the people in London,
Veena's lover, the location of the Centre. Any green grass around?
he asks. No chance. He also asks about bus routes, tube stations,
typical rents, the status of encounter groups in London. There is a
sensation that I am being warmed up. He asks my address and my
age, Mr Milne, with what seems like a slight sneer at the indelicacy of
having to pronounce my name at all. I feel like a target being cased,
as robbers case a bank, only it is all happening very gently. It's as if
reconnaissance aircraft are flying overhead, and I am still wary even
though I know they are friendly.

I experience excitement and at the same time a sense of fear. We
slide into more personal questions. How was my flight from London?
Did I have a hotel yet? Good, hmm. Hmm. Good. There are wafts of
pine forest and eucalyptus groves from the scent he uses. I find myself
irreverently wondering whether he puts it on his forehead or pads it
round the collar. At last the questions become directly personal.

"How is your meditation? Is there pain in the legs? That will go
away. Don't worry. Better to lie down. Hmmm. Go to meditation on

Chowpatty Beach in morning, then go to your room. That will be good, hmmm. Lie down and allow meditation to happen. "Stay all day, it will come to you. Don't worry, OK? Meditation will come." I think of the beggars outside, and contrast them with this palace of cool, aesthetic delight. The beggars and Bhagwan are of the same race, but impossibly far apart.

The sensation of time passing has gone. It's not that it stands still, it has simply disappeared and I am in a new dimension. I collect another waft of his cologne, the 'bugsy juice' that I've heard Laxmi mixes specially for him. It's wonderfully cool in here, and there are no flies. What an absolute contrast to those lepers just a few hundred yards away outside. Is this really the same land where I arrived at Bombay Airport, teeming, chaotic, dirty, and full of beggars and intinerants, only yesterday?

One hand still holds mine as the questions continue, as if he is practising the gentlest ever form of mind detection. It's an investigation by touch temperature. I am sure for a fleeting moment as he turns my hand over in his that I am having my palm read. It feels quite all right, and I'm not worried by it at all.

Whatever this marvellous being is doing, it is far more than the words that are passing between us. There is no invasion of privacy, no alarm, but it is as if his soul is slowly slipping inside mine, and in a split second transferring vital information.

Letting go of my hand, he moves his left arm up behind me. I sense a presence hovering over the crown of my head. He rests his hand there and stares off into the middle distance, sensing, checking, listening, all his being attuning itself to mine. Then the soft hand moves to my forehead, waits, listens, wafts to my throat and presses so gently on the cartilege there. Every chakra — the seven centres of energy in the body according to ancient Eastern tradition — is discreetly touched. The chakras recognise the arrival of a friend, and I feel deeply content.

The orientation now feels complete to me. The initial examination is over, and Bhagwan has drawn his parameters, established his primary goals, and evaluated this human being next to him. He shifts slightly in his chair, and his hand leaves mine. He gives me another curious, scrutinising glance, a quick one this time, before reaching for a nearby pen which rests on his neat bookshelf. One eyebrow arches quizzically above a deep, unfathomable brown eye.

"Are you ready for sannyas?" he asks.

'Sannyas' was traditionally the state of renunciation, and a 'sannyasi' one who had renounced all wordly goods, possessions and relationships to be at one with God. In Hinduism, a sannyasi is somebody who devotes the last years of their life to contemplation and meditation. This ancient Sanskrit word, as we shall see, meant something rather different for Bhagwan's followers. Nevertheless, he adopted the word 'sannyasis' to refer to those who had left their previous lives to follow him. It was to cause trouble in his native India, where purists accused him of debasing the word.

"Would you perhaps like to think about it first?" Bhagwan continues, pen in hand. But no, I had decided that I was ready, and indicated as much to Bhagwan.

"Good. You *are* ready. *Much* will be happening to you. You are ready. Hmmmm. Your name, what does it mean? Hmmmm. This is strange, nobody in the West seems to know what their names mean. In India, everybody knows. So, I will give you a new name. Hmmmm? Good."

He reaches for a sheet of his personal headed writing paper, and writes carefully, as if he is painting. The pen he uses isn't ancient at all, but a bright red Japanese magic marker. I had heard that Bhagwan was partial to these pens, and had a large collection.

I notice that everything is executed with exact precision, from the writing of the new name to the putting away of the pen. Suddenly I am acutely aware of my body, and how uncomfortable I am becoming in my Jaeger trousers. Bhagwan picks up a long string of beads which looks like a collection of brown nuts, and passes this garland over my head. This is the 'mala' — the 108-bead necklace which signifies renunciation. Then he hands me the piece of paper where he has written my new name.

Oh God, I think, let it be something reasonable! I look and read 'Swami Shivamurti'. Bhagwan explains what it means. "Swami means master or lord of yourself, your own destiny. Shiva is one of the Hindu Gods, and 'murti' means made in the image of Shiva. Do you know about Shiva?" he asks.

No.

"Well, in that case it will be good for you to go the library, read some books on Shiva, it will be meaningful to you. Shiva is known as the Great God; he has many aspects. Hmmm. You will miss your old name? Good. There is no need to hold on to the past. Now drop the ego and go into my work totally, without reservation. It will be good, hmmm."

He adds: "And wear orange from now on. Today will be your new birthday. Forget the old one. It will be good, OK?" As I hold the piece of paper with my new name, Bhagwan gives me more instructions. He says I have to make some orange robes, and not to wear underpants any more, as they stop the energy. Trousers are not good, he informs me. I am also instructed to meditate every day, and to go to the Camp, at Mount Abu in Rajasthan, which will be held soon. Bhagwan promises me that the camp, held at a hill station, will be far cooler than the hundred degree heat of Bombay in March.

Bhagwan indicates that the session is now over, and that I am to go out. As I get up to go, he tells me to ask Laxmi to introduce Haridas to me.

Haridas was a young German electrician who had gone to India in 1972, and had spent a year looking for a suitable teacher. Once he found Bhagwan, he had looked no further. Haridas was to become one of my main male friends during the eight years I stayed in India.

As I went out and closed the door behind me, I could see that Laxmi was smiling. Yes, indeed it was good. I felt as if I was walking on air, a euphoria stronger than anything I had experienced before, as if a wonderful large hand was enveloping me. I noticed that there were a few 'sannyasis' — average age about twenty-four — sitting on the platform by the french windows, cross-legged, with calm expressions on their faces.

I sat down by the window, looked out to a huge banyan tree, and gave thanks for the huge energy source I had just been uplifted by, been privileged to share. It was clear that this was the finest spiritual experience I had ever had. A little while later I went over to Laxmi and asked her what I needed to do to book a further 'darshan' with Bhagwan. 'Darshan' is the Indian name for audience, and the word has a spiritual connotation. Laxmi told me it had already been done, and that I could come and see him again at eight o'clock in the morning on Thursday, three days away.

Bhagwan's flat was at that time the rendezvous and spiritual heart of this small expatriate community. In the evenings we all packed into the large living room to be in Bhagwan's presence while he talked in Hindi. The fact that we didn't understand what he was saying didn't seem to matter. In the mornings we would sit in the delicious coolness as the sea breezes tumbled through the room from the french windows. And in the early mornings, at 5 a.m., we would all assemble on nearby Chowpatty beach for the dynamic meditation.

As I lived and stayed among these people, I gradually learned how it had all happened. Laxmi was fundamental in establishing the movement. She came from Gujurat, and was born into a good Shatria family (the warrior caste, immediately below the Brahmins) . She was well-educated, and her family had a large house in Bombay. She was, at most, four foot eleven, but in spite of, or perhaps because of, her physical smallness, she displayed the most extrovert and uninhibited behaviour at all times. She was a bundle of intense, humorous and mischievous energy. She was a borderline anorexic, and hardly ate at all. She had very beautiful jet black hair which she kept tightly hidden in a prim headscarf most of the time. When she let her hair down — literally — this cascade of raven tresses would escape. It was, it seemed, a secret sensuality, a hidden charm.

Laxmi's face would have been beautiful but for the scars of a childhood attack of smallpox. But if you ever noticed that it was only for an instant before her charm and effervescence carried you away. She had the skinny, wiry body of a little monkey, and would often challenge men twice her size to an arm wrestle. She was not averse to cheating, and as you made the big lunge was liable to kick you under the table to distract you.

We all believed that it was Laxmi who had made Bhagwan what he was, but it was apparently Kranti who managed his initial rise to public prominence. Kranti was a rather stiff, formal, strong-faced Indian woman who looked quite distinguished. She had high cheekbones and wore heavy dark-rimmed glasses. I saw her first when she brought Bhagwan some soda and medication during my second darshan. She had that aloofness and reserve that many high-born Indian women display when foreigners are present. Indeed, they may well have it all the time, for you never see them laughing or relaxing much. While Bhagwan's other disciples wore very simple orange robes, Kranti alwys wore an elegant sari.

There may initially have been a power struggle between Kranti and Laxmi, but whatever happened, Laxmi was to gain superstar status, while Kranti slipped into the background. I have never even seen a picture of her in one of Bhagwan's many books.

Between Laxmi's euphemisms and euphoric hyperbole, and Bhagwan's exuberant, persuasive rhetoric, it was difficult to get a clear picture of how it all began, but in time I managed to piece together most of what had happened.

Mohan Chandra Rajneesh showed early promise at school and his father, a cloth merchant of the Jaina religion, managed to put him through university. Bhagwan claims to have been a Professor at Mahakoshal Arts College, which is part of Jaipur University, but there is no record of his having held a professorial post there, though he was certainly a lecturer in the early sixties.

He began public speaking in 1964, and in 1966 left the University to become a travelling public speaker. He soon developed a reputation as an orator, and was in those days a fiery advocate of socialism. The Rajneesh Foundation International, which was established in 1975 after more Westerners started coming, claims in its official history that for the next four years, until 1970, Rajneesh travelled India by train and gave public discourses of a highly political nature. Enough Indians flocked to these lectures to keep Rajneesh solvent. When giving a talk to a group of Jainas in a small hall in Bombay, he met Laxmi Thakarsi Kuruwa, who was then working as a civil servant at a large public building in the city.

She fell in love with him at first sight, and became infatuated with this man she described as "a lion, a courageous warrior, a fierce and powerful speaker." Laxmi, who always referred to herself in the third person, said "Laxmi knew she had been waiting for such a man to serve." Laxmi soon became Bhagwan's groupie — his first — and an undemanding, unquestioning and devoted admirer during his years as a public speaker. Her eventual downfall and replacement by Sheela were very sad to see, but that was all still in the far-off future. In those days Laxmi reigned supreme, and anybody who wanted to see Bhagwan had first to get past Laxmi.

After Bhagwan decided to stop travelling round the country, a flat was arranged in Bombay for his permanent use. Laxmi helped to find the flat, and to decorate it according to his wishes. While still lecturing at the University, Rajneesh had gained a reputation as something of a Romeo, and his lectures on sex were what became the big draw for Westerners. One ex-sannyasi, John Ephlund, said in an interview with *The Oregonian* — the newspaper that conducted a twenty-part investigation into Rajneesh's activities — "He gives you the opportunity to sin like you've never sinned before." One of Bhagwan's most potent attractions was the way he taught a blend of Eastern spirituality mixed in with Western technology.

For many years the official picture was of a utopian community growing through the love and enlightenment of a spiritual leader. But almost from the start the reality was somewhat different.

Laxmi told me how Bhagwan had attracted his very first sannyasis, all Indian. "One day a few of us went down to the railway station. We felt it was right to wear saffron. When we saw that *he* was there, we joked to *him* about the saffron, the colour worn by religious renunciates and monks, and how this could mean us becoming *his* sannyasis, his followers.

"Just like that it came out of Laxmi's mouth: 'Make me your sannyasi.' He did not say anything, but a few days later at his flat we suggested it again. The saffron clothing felt so good that we wore it again, and after work hours we said the words to him again: 'Acharya, take us as your first sannyasis!'

"This time," Laxmi continued, "he looked at Laxmi for a longer time, and we thought that maybe he was considering it. Clearly, we told him, you are a man of Godly gifts. We would sit in his flat until two or three in the morning after he had given a lecture, and he would tell wonderful stories. It was *perfect*!

"In those days Bhagwan wore very soft homespun cotton, of the type favoured by Mahatma Ghandi, and a shawl round his shoulders. All his friends would laugh at his jokes, and before dawn we would leave him. Oh, it was such fun! Laxmi was flying!

"He told Laxmi to wear saffron, and buy a special mala, and so Laxmi became his number one sannyasi. Just like that."

Laxmi then told me how she had spoken to her publisher friend and arranged for the booklet *Rajneesh — a glimpse* to be published, and also ordered the very best paper for his letters. She told many people about her lion, and they became curious. More people wanted to hear the lectures, to become sannyasis, so Laxmi bought a whole stock of malas from Crawford Market in Bombay. Bhagwan's fame spread, so that in time politicians, actors, millionaires, poets and authors flocked to hear what he had to say. It soon became clear that better premises were needed, so Laxmi arranged for his present flat, for which the rent was paid by the A1 Biscuit Company in Bombay. The flat was A1 Woodlands in Peddar Road, a good address. Laxmi located a flat in the large tower which happened to be numbered A1, so she then approached the owner of the locally-famous A1 Biscuit Factory, who was a sannyasi. He was very flattered and happy to pay the rent. For him it was a wonderful omen!

Laxmi told me she foresaw the days when people from the West would also want to come and hear Bhagwan, and that he would need a full-time secretary and receptionist. Laxmi herself would fulfil this dual role. It was necessary to guard his door, she explained, as people wanted to see Bhagwan all the hours of the day and night, and he must have uninterrupted sleep. "So Laxmi gave in her notice at her important job, and we set up here," she said. She told me that in 1972 Bhagwan was ready to go to America if the right offer came. But it never did, and so they stayed in Bombay. It was about this time that Rajneesh changed his title from 'Acharya' to 'Bhagwan', The Blessed One. Originally, apparently, 'Maharishi' — which means 'great seer' — had been suggested, but that was already taken. An Indian scholar and pundit who also became a sannyasi, Yogi Chinmaya, suggested 'Bhagwan', and according to Laxmi this sounded exactly right.

This was Laxmi's version of events, but there were others which did not coincide exactly. There were stories about how Bhagwan had displayed hypnotic powers, even as a child, and that one reason for the heady atmosphere in his flat was the liberal use of 'Bhang Lassie' — a hashish-flavoured yogurt drink. Bhagwan would keep this concoction in his personal refrigerator, and hand it out after his discourses to his favoured guests. In the early seventies he was not in the least frail or spiritual-looking, but was very large and hirsute, with broad, powerful shoulders.

According to the brother of an Indian who used to run the London Centre, Bhagwan used to drive a small clapped-out Renault after he left his university post in 1966. He kept bundles of his published works in the trunk, and travelled from bookshop to bookshop hawking his wares, as well as giving his lectures. In time, of course, Bhagwan was to become the owner of more Rolls Royces than anybody else in the world. When asked on American television if ninety Rolls were not enough, he answered "Nine hundred and ninety-nine would not be enough."

It was hard for the Indians to accept Rajneesh as 'Bhagwan', as it seemed far too reverential a name for this self-promoting gourmet and lecturer who was gradually gathering round him a group of wealthy, unconventional foreigners. Many Indians take their gurus lightly, and regard them rather like a bunch of soccer fans see their team, as a mascot or talisman that one supports but does not take too seriously. Suddenly they were being asked to revere this man as nothing less than the true God.

It wasn't long before Bhagwan had moved his new sannyasin consort, Vivek, into one of the two spare bedrooms of the flat. Vivek reminded me of one of those little icons of female Greek saints with their radiant yet innocent faces, and she had about her a vibrant, self-absorbed sensuality. This liaison had happened a few months before I arrived, and Kranti — who was actually related to Bhagwan — was now occupying the other bedroom. If you look at the many photographs taken of Bhagwan and Vivek at this time, it is obvious that they were very much in love. Kranti made it very clear by her behaviour that she was having an extremely difficult transition being demoted from number one to number two in Bhagwan's affections. But within a very short space of time after Vivek moving in with Bhagwan, Kranti was paired up with a handsome Indian sannyasi, and the two of them were despatched to run a meditation centre somewhere far away. I never saw either of them again.

In 1973, the year I arrived, Bhagwan had already acquired a reputation as the 'sex guru'. This description seemed to refer both to his personal tastes and the content of many of his lectures. He became an arch advocate of the female orgasm, and devoted much time to explaining just how and why the majority of Indian women had never had one. He talked at great length about the clitoris, its function, and how it should be stimulated. In fact, the intimate anatomy of both female and male genitalia were described in enough detail for the talk to qualify as a lecture in gynaecology. These talks could have been embarrassing, but Bhagwan referred to it all in such spiritual terms, and explained carefully how tantric sex led to enlightenment, that nobody felt ill at ease.

Instead we felt that we could attain previously unimaginable bliss if only we listened to him before indulging in the next sexual encounter. However, Bhagwan made a point of never quoting the source of his knowledge or experience in this regard.

Most Westerners were fully aware of Bhagwan's proclivities before coming to India, and indeed it was to hear more and experience more on the sexual level that brought most of them out in the first place. Whatever Bhagwan did in his private life, that was all right too, as he was the most wonderful being anyway. Many of the female contingent fervently hoped that they would be chosen for a 'special darshan' — that is, for the purposes of making love with the guru himself.

This kind of sexual involvement was, however, deeply offensive to the Indians. During my initial stay in Bombay I was on many occasions, both on the street and in other public places, confronted on the issue of Bhagwan's unusual sexual morality. It occasioned much concern and gossip among the Indians, who considered it highly inappropriate to his new-found status as a guru. I was asked if Bhagwan instructed people to strip off in front of him. Yes, that did happen. He also had sannyasi couples making love in front of him, nominally to give them advice on how to do it properly, though there was certainly a degree of voyeuristic delight. While we were in Bombay, Bhagwan advocated all forms of gossip as an art form, and no attempt was made to deny or suppress stories about his private activities. But when we moved to Poona in 1974 a curtain was firmly drawn over these events, though that, of course, didn't stop them from going on.

Bhagwan's use of hypnosis was well known in 1973, especially among his very early group of followers. When I met some relatives of his in central India some time later, they all expressed their astonishment that 'Mohan' had any followers at all, especially female ones, as he practised hypnosis so much it was a wonder anyone could bear to be near him.

To foster his own reputation in those days, Bhagwan had an enormous number of carefully-lit studio photographs taken of himself. These were dramatically staged and lit to give an appearance of spirituality and religious awe. These pictures were, as Milton put it, "cast in a dim religious light", and most were taken while he was an adolescent and as a young man. In his autobiography, *The Sound of Running Water*, twelve photographs of Bhagwan are reproduced which were taken between the ages of thirteen and twenty-nine. One of them shows the young Mohan in a strikingly spiritual pose, and bears the caption 'Taken at 2 a.m.'. What, one wonders, motivated him to wake up a commercial photographer at that hour to pose a carefully-lit religious shot? It seems as though from a very early age indeed he had set his path, determined that he was going to be someone special, and was so certain of his future success that he set out to produce the documentary evidence to chronicle it for posterity.

When I first went to Bombay, the event that attracted most public interest was the morning meditation, held on Chowpatty Beach. Every morning at five o'clock about a dozen of us would assemble, all dressed in saffron robes. We all had malas, but wrapped them round our wrists as we began the dynamic sessions.

Our leader, almost always a woman, would appear and hand us our blindfolds, and take our valuables off us for the time being. We panted and cavorted and shadow boxed, and released all our inhibitions and pent-up anxieties through the cathartic movements. The natives of Bombay, fishermen and the few coolies out at this time, looked at us in complete astonishment. Here we were, a bunch of Westerners insulting Indian tradition by being so scantily dressed that the shapes of our bodies were all too clearly visible, wearing the holy saffron of the renunciate to take part in orgies. As we danced and moved, small knots of curious people gathered, along with the inevitable dogs.

It was not long before the dogs, excited by this unaccustomed energy flashing around at dawn, bit people's legs. This was serious in a country beset with endemic rabies, and those who were bitten had to have twenty-one daily anti-rabies shots. These are excruciatingly painful, as they have to be injected straight through the stomach wall. On another occasion a bystander walked among the foreign meditators — Indians attached to the Centre hardly ever attended these sessions — and punched a woman meditator hard in the face. He was insulted at our flouting of sacred traditions in full view of everybody on the beach.

Before the meditation sessions were finished the sun was up, and the sensation was as if somebody had moved a furnace close beside you. The meditators then stopped, rubbed the sand from their eyes, and either went back to their hotel rooms or ordered coffee from the beachfront stalls.

Whatever impression we may have created among the Indians, these morning meditations felt very good, and we all experienced a sensation of being cleaned out, refreshed, ready to start the day. I usually went back to my hotel to have breakfast in the restaurant, and would then lie down to meditate more. When I first tried the meditation that Bhagwan had given me, I found my mind constantly wandering to other concerns and worries. It was not at all easy. Every time I heard the air conditioner go on while I was meditating I thought of my bill going up. How much longer could I afford to stay here, I thought, and however would I support myself if I remained, as I wanted to, for ever? Then my mind would wander off again, to women, or the next meal, or private fantasies.

Two days after my darshan and initiation, I met a 'graduate' of our London meditation course who had also just come to Bombay for the first time. She had just had her own first darshan with Bhagwan and wanted to compare notes. I described my experience, starry-eyed and full of wonder.

She said slowly: "Well, mine wasn't quite like that. Frankly, I don't know what to make of it. As soon as I went into that room I felt very ill at ease indeed. Bhagwan gave me a name and all the intimate talk, just as he did with you, but I found myself not trusting the man. Throughout I kept saying to myself, he's a conjuror performing circus tricks. I just kept feeling that something wasn't right at all, and that there was some illusion going on.

"Anyway, he said to me suddenly: Take off all your clothes and lie on the bed."

"And did you?," I asked.

"Well, I thought, that's not so bad. So I did. He looked at me hard and then said turn over. I did that too. Then he made one of those long hmmms, as if it was a sign of approval or something, then told me to get dressed again. That was it."

She didn't know what to make of it, and neither did I. We were both used to naked and semi-naked encounter groups in London, and also to various kinds of Reichian bodywork, where the therapist sometimes needs you to be naked to work on you effectively. Perhaps Bhagwan was being a therapist, or perhaps, as she was a very attractive woman, he just wanted to see her figure. We discussed various theories and possibilities which gave Bhagwan the benefit of the doubt, but it did seem that the darshan was more like a harem interview.

The day after this somewhat disturbing incident, I was sitting in the Hanging Gardens, a large ornamental park between Bhagwan's flat and the ocean. A prim, well-dressed, and clearly educated Indian man approached me. He knew that I was a Bhagwan devotee because of my orange clothes and the mala around my neck. Without any preamble he came straight up and announced: "Your guru is not the right guru. He is sleeping with his female disciples!" He stormed off at a waddle, leaving me speechless. We sannyasis had become used to street tauntings, which took the form of locals chanting "Hare Krishna, Hare Rama". This came from a recent film in which a group of foreign thugs involved with drugs, sex and motorbikes had dressed in saffron robes and done forbidden things (off stage) with young Indian maidens, until the Indian hero arrived and vanquished the lot of them. We were supposed to be offended by having this song chanted at us, but we caught ourselves humming it. Eventually the song, which was repeated on every street corner, became irksome, and we learned to ignore it.

When I had my second darshan with Bhagwan, I knew more of what to expect. On his small bookshelf I noticed Tom Wolfe's book about the drug-taking hippy generation, *The Electric Kool-Aid Acid Test*. Veena had said that Bhagwan liked that book more than any other that had come out that year. He was a voracious reader, sometimes getting through ten or fifteen books a day, and liked to keep himself bang up to date with the world literary scene.

He took my hand again and said: "Hmmm. How are you Shiva, good? Yes, good? You are going well. Meditation is good, hmmm? OK, so then you drop the hotel, drop the meditation in the day. Now, it is too hot, hmmm, and camp is soon. That will be very good, keep your total energy for camp. You go swimming, visit my people in the day and do meditation on the beach also, hmmm? Beach is good for you, hmmm?"

I had the strong impression that part of him was already sharing my soul, and that he had completely accepted me and was one with me. He continued: "Hmmm, Shiva, and how is your love life?" I was stunned. This seemed too private, none of his business. We are British, after all! "All right," I mumbled. Kranti then brought him in ice-cold soda and Bhagwan popped a small pill into his mouth, then drank the soda.

He then made his shattering pronouncement: "Hmm. It will be good, hmm, move with a woman here, that will be good. Where are you staying now, Shalimar Hotel? That is good. OK. There is one sannyasin, Pratima, she is looking to take apartment. It will be good if you share with her. Meet her. Laxmi will introduce. Hmmm. You stay with Pratima."

Did that mean I had to go and *live* with her? I had never met this Pratima, never even seen her. I fervently hoped she would be attractive, and that we would be able to hit it off. Outside, Laxmi was smiling as ever, and obviously knew something of what had taken place during the darshan.

As I gazed across to the banyan tree, a largish, somewhat square-faced woman looked straight into my eyes, somewhat suspiciously. She wanted to know whether Bhagwan had said anything about her in the darshan. From her accent I could tell she was American.

"Oh, you must be Pratima," I replied. "Yes, he said something about living together," I mumbled, horribly embarrassed. I stared at my feet. She was about twenty years older than me.

"Did Bhagwan mean that we should share a flat, or that we should actually live together?" asked Pratima.

"That was my question too, but I gathered that what he meant was the more intimate variety."

"Oh," she intoned slowly. "Do you mind if I check, then?" Pratima seemed like an intelligent woman, pleasant and warm. This directive had clearly disturbed her as it disturbed me.

When she came back she was flushed and flustered, yet seemed determined to make the best of it. We had already learned to do exactly what Bhagwan said, however strange or distasteful it may seem. "Yes," Pratima told me, "he did mean live together. Believe me, this is very embarrassing. Perhaps we can meet for tea and get to know each other a bit first. Shall we try?" For both of us an arranged affair was a quite novel experience. I decided with a deep sigh that this would be a true test of my level of surrender, my ability to do whatever Bhagwan, in his infinite wisdom, demanded. So later Pratima and I had tea in the Shalimar Hotel, where she was also staying. Pratima was not an obvious lover for me. She was far more experienced at meditation. She had been practising meditation for ten years, and had gathered around her her own band of disciples. When she heard about Bhagwan, she felt that they all had to come out to India and meet him. About thirty of her disciples had travelled with her.

Pratima's disciples wore her photograph encapsulated in plastic around their necks. It was from this that Laxmi got the idea of making us all wear Bhagwan's picture in a plastic locket. When she met Bhagwan, Pratima knew at once that he was the man she had been looking for, and decided to stay. Some of her disciples stayed with her, and others went back to America. As we spoke, Pratima intimated that she had been 'brahmacharya' — celibate — for very many years.

This didn't make it any easier for me or for her. Taking a lover was something quite new and different for her, especially a raw young recruit such as myself. The whole meeting was painful, though we held hands and meditated together to try and make it easier.

We agreed to spend the night together first in the hotel, to see how it went. Truly, in my very first days in Bombay some strange things were happening.

Chapter Three
ABU AND AFTER

So Pratima and I attempted to establish a sexual relationship, to make love. It was a complete and utter disaster. It could hardly have been worse, and I was devastated by feelings of dejection and failure. What happened sounds amusing in retrospect, though it was far from funny at the time. When we got together to make love, Pratima used a mercury-based spermicidal contraceptive. I realised later that I must have been allergic to the mercury, because as soon as I came into contact with it I was in the most tremendous agony, and could not perform at all. At the time I couldn't work out what was wrong, but for days afterwards my penis was inflamed and sore, and very painful.

On the night in question there was no possible way in which I could have made love to Pratima. Added to this technical problem there was the fact that she had been celibate for ten years, that I was half her age, and that both of us found lovemaking to order very odd. As Westerners, we had both grown up with the idea that we should establish our own relationships, not be forced into them. In other circumstances it might have been possible for Pratima and I to have become sexually attracted, but as it was the relationship stood no chance whatsoever.

Oh dear, I had been here less than a week, and hard as I tried nothing was going right. I could not meditate lying on my back as Bhagwan had told me to, and there was no way I would ever be able to live with Pratima. I liked her, but sexually we could not have been less compatible. Would Bhagwan insist that we make another attempt, that we persevered? What a thought!

In my short time in Bombay I had already discovered both through my own experiences and through the gossip grapevine that Bhagwan could be a hard taskmaster indeed. I felt horribly wounded and discouraged by my uncompromising start. I had hardly got used to Bombay, and now here we were getting ready for the meditation camp at Mount Abu, twenty-four hours away by train. I dreaded that

Bhagwan would get to hear about our fiasco and would disapprove of me, perhaps send me away as he seemed to have done with others. What would he ask us to do now? Would he be furious?

The day after our sexual debacle Pratima knocked on my door. She didn't seem in the least concerned or upset; quite the reverse in fact. Sunshine flashed off her cheeks and she appeared to be supremely happy.

"Bhagwan says we can forget it," she announced. "He says drop it, let it go." She was so relieved, but I was confused by Bhagwan's response. It was so very unexpected.

Pratima then went on to inform me that she had told Vivek, Bhagwan's own beloved, all about what happened. A deep sense of shock ran through me at this news. How dare she disclose such deeply private affairs? At that time I hardly knew Vivek, and did not see why she should hear all about my sex life. But there was worse to come. "Vivek went in and told Bhagwan what happened, and he just laughed, then said we could forget the whole thing. Then he laughed again."

I shuddered. Whatever could Bhagwan think of me now? Not only was I a signal failure in the art of inner flying, but I was a failed stud as well. Whatever next?

At supper that night I was introduced to a Greek woman who was apparently a shipping tycoon and heiress to a Greek fortune. She seemed to be an extremely refined, cosmopolitan lady with an air of authority and contentment. She whispered to me that she had heard about my recent mishap and told me not to worry about it. So everybody knew! The Greek lady, I learned, was Mrs Catherine Venizelos, or Mukta, as Bhagwan had renamed her ('Mukta' means 'freedom' in Hindi). As I was introduced, a small bell rang in my head. I had first noticed this name in a small, exquisitely-produced booklet called *Turning In*. It was published in August 1971 by the same firm that had brought out the *Do Not Read* booklet on Bhagwan.

The dedication in the book was typically Indian: "A collection of thirty immortal letters written by Bhagwan Shree Rajneesh to H.H. Ma Yoga Mukta (Mrs Catherine Venizelos), President, Neo-Sannyas International, for North America, Seville Avenue, Rye, New York 10580, USA."

The 'immortal letters', a series of one-page missives, were a curious mixture of love letters, anecdotes, jokes and poignant messages. I had found the booklet very inspiring when I had read it in London before coming out to Bombay. As I read those letters for the first time, I had thought: fancy a man writing almost every day to a woman in such uncompromisingly loving yet such uncloying terms. Whoever wrote them must be quite somebody. And she must be quite a woman to have earned this degree of devotion from him.

Ever since reading those letters I had been intrigued by Mukta, and had long wanted to meet her. Now here I was sitting next to her in a Bombay restaurant. She was with a hearty group of young men, one of whom was her lover. She was about forty, and had three daughters. As she mentioned the incident with Pratima, I realised that she saw the whole Bhagwan thing in a completely different light from me. Whereas I was feeling depressed, she seemed very lighthearted about it all. For her it was all a joke, a cosmic dance, and not to be taken too seriously. As I got to know Mukta better, however, I realised that she could also get into a mood of reclusiveness, dark contemplation and loneliness, and remain out of sight for days. Her apparent lightness of mood at the restaurant belied a very profound person.

She was about five foot five, very striking, and always well-dressed. She never looked in the least dishevelled or unkempt, which was a rarity in those hippy days. She let her every emotion show on her face, and you knew immediately how she felt by looking at her. When she looked black, you understood that this was a time to avoid her. She did not allow her anger and frustration to build up, but let it all out at once.

When I first met Bhagwan he had jet-black hair, and there was a rumour that it was Mukta who dyed his hair and beard in secret sessions at his flat. Mukta's own hair was as black and shiny as his, and I conjured up to myself a scene of messy black puddles and blotchy towels, with Vivek looking on. I have no idea what really happened, but quite suddenly, in 1974, Bhagwan stopped dyeing his hair, and silver streaks started to appear almost overnight. Mukta immediately followed suit, and soon a fine train of silver threads appeared in her abundant head of hair. For Bhagwan, the new silvery hair made for the most dramatic change in his appearance, and I privately nicknamed him 'The Silver Guru'.

I knew that Haridas and some of the others would occasionally go to Mukta for money when they were running short, but also that she did not always give them the help they were expecting. Very often, instead, she gave them a lecture about their shortcomings.

Mukta had an unusual way of meditating. During meditation sessions she looked as though there was a secret whirlwind inside her, and at the same time she radiated a 'do not touch me' vibration. After the meditation it was the custom to embrace each other lovingly, sometimes even sexually, but Mukta always remained as still as a dead tree, locked into her own meditative space long after everyone else was on their second cup of tea. I would catch a glimpse of her and feel a complete fraud, as if she was experiencing the genuine article while my attempts were a complete sham. After morning meditation one might not see Mukta for the rest of the day, but then she would emerge from her room for supper sparkling and bright.

A few days after the incident with Pratima we all went to Mount Abu for the ten-day meditation camp. Bhagwan himself lived in a small ground-floor suite which looked on to the central courtyard of a large and distinguished country house which had been turned into a hotel. It was called the 'Abu Palace' or something equally impressive. Bhagwan's richer followers — there were two to three hundred at the camp — stayed with him at the hotel. The rest of us put up in the nearby village in hostels which were meant for short-staying sannyasis — the real ones — and sadhus, holy men. There were four of us in each small room. It made the flight paths shorter for the many mosquitoes.

The camp was physically very exhausting and demanding. There were five active and dynamic meditations every day, and part of Bhagwan's idea was to create the peace that comes with utter physical exhaustion. Most of the meditations were led by Bhagwan personally, except for those in the very early morning. After it was over we had a half-hour break for a steaming hot cup of tea — 'special chai' — and then filed in for the main lecture of the day.

Most of the meditations were being held on a pair of tennis courts, where a makeshift wooden dais had been set up at one end. The dais was covered with embroidered fabrics and covered with fat cushions, and had a parasol over the top. Two or three hundred people crowded into the tennis courts to hear the lecture.

I had not been at Abu very long when I got to hear of a major scandal the last time Bhagwan held a camp in the area. Apparently there had been nude meditations and the local people had objected strongly. The hotel had refused to let the camp return unless a solemn assurance was given that this completely un-Indian practice would not be repeated. In Bombay I had seen striking pictures of a black-bearded Bhagwan sitting in his low chair surrounded by two or three dozen naked people, eyes closed in bliss at the end of a meditation session. But this time there was to be none of this, and we all attended the sessions completely dressed, or at least according to our Western customs.

As soon as Bhagwan appeared at the tennis courts the audience became hushed. He never spoke immediately, but waited sometimes for several minutes before starting the discourse. Everything was silent, and the only interruptions were the pant-hoots of a nearby tribe of monkeys. For the first talk of the day Bhagwan was scheduled to talk in Hindi for an hour, and then in English for another hour. The previous year he had announced to Laxmi that he would never speak in English, but with Bhagwan what he said one minute could be completely contradicted the next.

As he takes his place on the platform we all sit there, covered as if in a soft silk drape by the peace that has settled over the audience, and we listen. Several people become painfully aware that the sun is getting up very fast, and soon it is so hot that even the multi-coloured rags and shawls that are on the ground start to heat up. Bhagwan begins in Hindi at eight in the morning and by nine he has finished, ready to start his English lecture. His body scarcely moves, and sitting cross-legged on his flat and stable perch he flings his shawl back over his shoulder, then arranges it in place. A spray of microphones surrounds him at mid-beard level, like a bouquet of inorganic flowers. Bhagwan is the only person sitting in complete shade.

He speaks, and all restlessness is at an end. "I have called you here, and you have heard my call," he starts. "And you have come." My Western scientific upbringing immediately objects to this. How could you possibly have called me from Oxford or Hampstead Heath? But if Bhagwan didn't call me, how do I come to be sitting here on this baking tennis court on a hill station in Rajasthan, surrounded by the motleyest crew of people ever assembled? Whatever happens in the end, this is certainly the strangest and most exciting of adventures.

As Bhagwan talks, the sheer persuasiveness of his oratory, the hypnotic sibilances of his lingering 's's', his habit of extending the last syllable of every sentence, conspire to lull, reassure, inspire and energise the audience. I can well understand how Bhagwan became the School Debating Champion. His words are like a love song sung specially for you and none other. His message seems targeted straight at every individual heart, and the fact that there are three hundred other people listening doesn't seem to matter. You feel that you are his only *real* disciple. Yet I know that every single person in the audience feels exactly the same, and as we compare notes afterwards we agree that we have all been similarly affected — 'ausgeblissed' the Germans call it, 'blissed out'.

Apart from the first meditation of the morning, all the meditations were led personally by Bhagwan. He would shout from the specially-constructed platform in the side garden where the afternoon meditations were held. "Be total," he yelled. "Put your whole energy into it. Hold nothing back!" These words were delivered so urgently that they added an immediacy, almost a desperate intensity, to the meditation sessions. I soon noticed that there were very few people who managed to complete every meditation every day. We all wore saffron robes the whole time, and between meditations trooped off to nearby tea and market stalls to buy drinks, food and cheap cigarettes.

Those on the camp ranged from Vietnam veterans to French ex-heroin junkies, English and American hippies and drop-outs to older, richer and more professional people. These were the harbingers of Bhagwan's message to the West, and were to be instrumental in spreading his word, so that by the end of the decade there was a Rajneesh centre in almost every major city in the Western world.

During the camp we all swapped stories about how we came to be here and why we were attending. The French junkies spent their time trading Kashmiri shawls for crumpled rupee notes; the British hippies on world tours retired to their messy Landrovers which were bedecked with jerry cans, shovels, and notices saying 'Private Property'. These were the days when Tibetan artefacts, beads and fringed garments were the height of fashion.

During our relaxation time we exchanged stories about lice and amoebas and dysentery disasters. We heard the story of one Bhagwan disciple who was on his way to camp from the Himalayas when he happened to put his hand on a scorpion. The first he knew about it was the searing sting from its tail. He realised he would die, said his surviving friend, so calm as you like he suggested they sat down there and then and smoked a joint, the best Nepali high valley stuff. The friend related: "Shit, man, I knew it must have hurt a lot, but he just spaced right on out and he was gone, man, peaceful as you like. What a way to go!"

Many of these people had gathered here after doing the hippy trail, or wandering round Tibet, Nepal and India hoping to find truth and the real guru. Many had already seen Sai Baba — the one who could apparently materialise watches and precious jewels, had seen the Dalai Lama, or read the Ram Dass book *Be Here Now*. Some had been to Benares; some had sat with Shankacharya, the Holy Man in Puri. Now they had all wended their way to Bhagwan Shree Rajneesh, the Acharya, 'the sex guru', and almost everyone who came to that camp was destined to stay with him for many years to come.

There were young English girls wearing tattered robes, who were homesick for the coolness of their home country and a pint of bitter. Nobody was in the least fat, and practically everybody had suffered at some time from amoebic dysentery. Travellers' tales and tips were passed back and forth. There were those who were expert on the cheapest place to stay in Calcutta, those who knew a sure way to get to the station at Abu Road without paying for a ticket on the bus. We were told how dangerous the local monkeys were, and given instructions as to how a woman could get a visa extension in Bombay without being pawed by policemen.

Many had embraced an Eastern lifestyle, and swore by local remedies rather than antibiotics to deal with infections. If you squashed out the jelly from cactus and applied it to a skin wound, keeping it covered, it would heal up in no time. As the camp continued, quite a few people went down with dysentery and fever.

Strange things happened. One of the sannyasis, an American, was sitting silently in meditation when he had the distinct feeling that he was being watched. He thought he must be imagining things, but when he opened his eyes at last he saw an entire family of monkeys not three yards away, all staring at him. There were fifteen of them. The sannyasi closed his eyes and silently asked them to go. They understood, and were gone.

When the last meditation of the day was over we all assembled at the chai-wallah's booth, the Indian equivalent of a coffee-bar. As we exchanged gossip and experiences, we all agreed that it was exhausting, but perfect. We gossiped about each other, and agreed that when it came to thieving and drug-taking the French were hard to beat. At night we could easily be kept awake by the noise of neighbouring sannyasis making love. Nobody minded: we all laughed, hugged and kissed each other, and felt a universal peace and kinship.

The girls dressed as alluringly as possible in the thinnest saffron robes, and the men wore 'lunghies', the wrap-around garments traditional in that area. On top they favoured tiny cotton waistcoats with many pockets, for matches and small change.

In the evenings there was a heady mixture of the perfumes of sandalwood, peppermint and camphor. Occasionally some sannyasi had a bottle of the treasured 'bugsy juice' that Bhagwan himself used. This was the most powerful and evocative fragrance for us all, as it reminded each one of us of the treasured few minutes we spent alone with Bhagwan in the individual darshan sessions.

At the camp, the Rajneesh movement was then referred to as the 'Life Awakening Movement'. The title 'Rajneesh Foundation International' was dreamed up a year or two later. When Bhagwan spoke, he had behind him a banner which proclaimed: "Surrender to me, and I will transform you. That is my promise — Rajneesh." The banner was about twenty feet long, and also bore the symbol of a cupped palm holding a small candle flame. What exactly did Bhagwan mean by 'surrender'? we asked ourselves and each other. He had already acquired a reputation for surprise, ingenuity and brilliance when he spoke to us in the darshan sessions. It was clear too that he was psychic and clairvoyant. We all wondered how he seemed to know so much about us, and theories abounded. One favourite was that Laxmi operated as a secret agent, and supplied him with personal details before he saw you, but even this could not explain it all away. Bhagwan maintained his air of mystery, and never revealed his sources of wisdom or said who his own masters and teachers were.

Indeed, he claimed to have been almost self-taught. He would say "In this life (like all Indians he believed in reincarnation as an absolute fact) I have never had a Master. In my many past lives I have studied with many masters from every tradition. Now I bring to you a higher form of teaching." We all agreed that he was definitely the genuine thing.

The elation experienced in his presence was unanimous, and nobody minded that he could be contrary, fierce, and a tough disciplinarian. It did seem that when he ordered two people to start a sexual relationship, some profound alchemy happened. Arranged affairs were common in Bombay, and were almost the only organised activity among us.

I heard one story of how it could be dangerous to flout Bhagwan's orders. An American woman, who had married the swami who was Bhagwan's chief male disciple at the time, told me how she had wanted to go to Calcutta with her new husband. Bhagwan agreed, and asked how long they intended to stay. She told him two weeks.

Bhagwan paused for a second or two, then after his usual hmmm, ordered her not to stay for longer than the fourteen days.

For the first fortnight in Calcutta everything went very well, so they decided to ignore Bhagwan's directive. But almost immediately their relationship, which had been so peaceful and supportive, soured and became difficult. By the time they eventually returned to Bombay, it was over. The thing about Bhagwan, this woman added, was that he would never say "I told you so," or dwell on their indiscretion for a moment. He would just dismiss it all with a hmmm, and leave you to work it out for yourself.

By the time we got back to Bombay after the Abu camp I was beginning to get the feel of India; how to move around, and what the public and private realities seemed to be. I began to feel at home in Bombay, to know my way round, to be able to change money on the black market, go to the best bazaars, and know where the best or cheapest restaurants were. It all seemed to be coming together after my earlier sense of being disoriented at every turn.

After returning from the camp at Abu, I moved into a 'dharmsala' — a kind of pilgrim's resting place — in Bombay, in an area with the distinctly odd name of Seepie Tank. My money was running out fast, and it was imperative for me to find cheaper ways of living in this very expensive city. In the dharmsala I shared a room with a new girlfriend, a black-haired Irish girl called Leela. Other sannyasis shared rooms on the same floor of the dharmsala, turning it into a miniature enclave of the Orange People, as we were becoming known. The dharmsala was not exactly a five-star establishment, and we shared our rooms with cockroaches, ants, mosquitoes, and green mould growing on the taps. The general squalour of the place was too much for some of the more sensitive Westerners, and some of the American girls would not go near the washing areas.

We were living in the 'real' India, and finding it very hard at times. But things were happening. Whatever the hardships and lack of money, we wanted to stay on, to be near Bhagwan, and also to move to a place where we could all be together. Soon after the Abu camp, Laxmi started her search for bigger and better premises for Bhagwan.

The numbers of new sannyasis was growing daily, and he had already outgrown the small Woodlands flat. Laxmi was looking at places within a hundred-mile radius, and told us that some Indian admirers had offered to buy him a house. It would be, she informed us, a considerable privilege to be able to buy Bhagwan a house.

At a lecture one day, Bhagwan made it clear that anybody who wanted to buy him a house was more than welcome to do so. There were, however, two things they had to realise. One was that he would be liable to leave at any time it took his fancy, and the other was that the purchaser should not be under the slightest illusion that the house would endear them to Bhagwan in any way, or enable them to come closer. At this the flood of offers dwindled.

On one of her house-hunting expeditions, Laxmi invited me to go along with her. She was going to Lonavala, a pleasant upper class hill station just outside Bombay. Laxmi had loved this place as a teenager, she told me, and used to borrow her father's car and drive round with her girlfriends at top speed. She was still something of a speed freak, and not the most careful of drivers.

We viewed the secluded villa, near the spot where Laxmi and her friends had once drunk their beers before racing back into Bombay, but it was not at all suitable. It was a slightly run-down two-storey house with faded pink woodwork. It smelt of damp, and apart from any other considerations would have been completely unsuitable for Bhagwan's rapidly growing library in this monsoon climate.

Back at the Woodlands flat I went for my third darshan with Bhagwan. I wondered what would happen this time. First of all he asked how the camp had been. "It was fine," I started.

"Fine? Good, Shiva. I have been watching you. You are doing well. Where are you living now? Hmmm. What are your plans? Hmmm. No immediate ones? And you have a girlfriend now, hmmm? She is having plans, hmmm?"

I told Bhagwan that Leela was planning to go to Lonavala to do his toughest course, twenty-one days of meditation and total silence.

"So, she is going to do the twenty-one days isolation meditation. It will be good, you go with her!" My face obviously showed my bewilderment at this possibility. The thought of twenty-one days spent in total silence — called 'mourna' — with no physical contact, no writing, no letters, very little food, and round-the-clock meditation, did not appeal in the slightest. I had found it an uphill struggle to meditate even for five minutes in the air-conditioned comfort of my hotel room.

The prospect of being holed up for twenty-four hours a day with my new girlfriend was not as attractive a thought as it might have been, as I hardly knew the girl. Bhagwan studied my face and attitude. "Good," he said. "It will be good."

As I departed limply I reflected upon what he meant by 'good'. Would I really be able to stand the prolonged torture?

At the Abu camp, Bhagwan had made many references about how he stayed in touch with all his disciples all the time by remote control. It was important to wear the mala and locket, he explained, as these were the vehicles by which contact was maintained. Once he had placed the mala round your neck, you could be sure of his presence all the time. As he put it on you he would say: "From now on I will be with you, wherever you go. Just hold the locket and think of me, and I will be there." He said that if at any time we were troubled, we should just go quiet, adopt a meditative attitude, clasp the locket against our heart, and then, through astral means, he would be there to support us.

As part of the gossip circuit, we naturally exchanged what had been said to us individually in the darshan sessions. Bhagwan would conduct as many as four or five in a morning, and we all passed on invaluable titbits of information. In particular we passed on details of Bhagwan's propensity for arranging sexual relationships, and even for giving highly detailed sexual instructions. Some couples told how Bhagwan had ordered them to make love in front of him. "Let the whole neighbourhood know when you are making love," he said, which made the Orange People extremely unpopular, to say the least, with our immediate non-sannyasi neighbours.

Bhagwan gradually began to acquire for us the characteristics of a supernatural being. If you only just managed to catch a train because a taxi was inexplicably standing in the right place at the right time, it was all 'through his grace'. It was mostly Laxmi who spread the idea that Bhagwan was a Godlike person who could influence events — the weather, financial matters, relationships, trouble with the police or with passports. She would say "He will take care. Don't worry." Bhagwan certainly did possess psychic gifts; of this I remain convinced. However much he enhanced a belief in himself through showmanship and Laxmi's adoration, there was still something beyond the usual range of abilities. He did have paranormal powers, though not perhaps in the measure he claimed or quite in the way it seemed in those enchanted early days when we felt he could do no wrong.

More than one person had the experience of starting to tell Bhagwan about a traumatic event, only to have him relate the end of it, complete in every detail. He had an almost uncanny accuracy for getting inside your head, knowing what you were thinking and what your wishes were long before you expressed them. The man was a genius in the art of communication.

How else could he have persuaded perfectly sensible and rational people to do what he told them, or make them believe that he was dispensing holy writ with every word he said? Most of us were not simple, gullible people; we were cynical educated Westerners who were used to questioning everything before deciding to believe it.

When I informed Leela that I had told Bhagwan about her proposed retreat, she was furious. "It was to be *my* meditation retreat, big mouth, and now you've spoiled it for me," she spat. She had been looking forward to this retreat for months, and saving up for it. "Jesus bejasus, just think of it — the two of us together in one small room for three weeks! *Why* did you have to tell *him*?"

But like me, Leela entertained no serious thought of defying Bhagwan. Whatever he said, it had to be. We hardly spoke to each other as we rode in the train up the flanks of the Western Ghats, through tinder-dry bleached forests, until we sighted the hill station. It was a relief after the hot dry journey to get out into the country and into this sleepy little village with its empty streets, a few goats, and brilliant blue and turquoise dragonflies flitting back and forth. Half a mile from the station there was a whitewashed enclosure, low set and clean. Our host met us, a slim, hollow-cheeked man of about fifty wearing homespun cotton clothes, and pointed out the hut we were to share. It lay on the far boundary, next to the railway track, and was no doubt extremely noisy.

Our host, the owner of the hut, explains the form. Our food, which his wife will cook, is to be brought to us twice a day, and we will also get tea three times a day. He points out the tap for washing, and asks how Acharya is doing. Is he well? Our host tells us that Acharya's fame has spread even out here, and they have heard him speak. We are to leave any messages on a blackboard near the tap, and that way silence will be maintained. We are told that the tap delivers water from six to eight in the evenings, and never on Mondays, OK?

The man 'namastes' — bows — to us, and leaves us. He is

extremely disconcerted by the presence of Leela and her exuberant sexuality. The Indians find it impossible to understand the Western girls, bra-less in thin saffron robes, and are confused at the way these girls look them fearlessly straight in the eye. They have never experienced women like this before, particularly not in these mountain villages. We all — men and women — wear the holy colours of India, and it offends and affronts the Indians. As someone remarked, it's as if an Indian came to London, put on a monk's brown habit, then walked down Piccadilly with his arms all over some half-dressed ravishing beauty. All our host could do in the face of this upsetting apparition was to revert to the safe and normal. "My wife will do all the cooking," he repeated, looking down at the ground and studiously avoiding Leela.

Leela and I go to inspect the hut. Inside there are two string-laced beds with very thin mattresses. The beds wobble and squeak. It is seven o'clock in the evening. We close the door behind us and immediately start the meditation marathon. Leela rearranges her sarong to expose her perfect breasts. No embarrassment on her part about this, but here goes nothing, I think. Great. No touching and no sex for twenty-one hot days and long nights.

The meditation marathon, for my part at least, was not a success. After eight days I had had more than enough. I soon took to walking in the hills, thus creating a distance between myself and my partner, who virtually never stopped meditating. She was blissed out in a moment, and remained so. Here I was, marching to someone else's orders, and it wasn't feeling comfortable at all. On one of my walks I met a small brown wild bear and envied the creature its freedom and exhilaration, unconstrained by someone else's commands. I made an immediate comparison between the freedom exemplified by the bear and my own incarceration in a nine-foot-square tin-roofed incinerator with a fiery Irishwoman who was blaming me for ruining her retreat and her chances of enlightenment.

I decided to return to Bombay forthwith, but before leaving I sat on a hill and looked down at the tiny village. It was time now to analyse and reflect on my relationship with the strange and wonderful being I called Bhagwan, the Blessed One. Yes, I had come to India to try and find someone who would teach me, point me in the right direction. Perhaps he was teaching me what my limitations were, showing me my impatience, my ego, my lack of perseverance. So far, it seemed, I had not been able to carry out successfully even one of the things he had asked me to do. I was a complete failure, I told myself again. Perhaps this surrender trip wasn't for me. Maybe I needed another path; maybe Bhagwan needs people who are more able to do what he says, more pliant clay. Enough was enough. I chalked up my farewells on the blackboard and caught the next train back to Bombay.

Back in Bombay again I found a new flat, then told the disciple I was sharing it with that I was going off to the mountains on my own for a couple of weeks to think things over. And no, I was not going to see Bhagwan first.

I packed my belongings in a rucksack and set off, arriving at another hill station that was far more spectacular than the one I had just left. I found a clifftop on which to sit, and mused at length on the peculiarities of this trip. I had to get to the bottom of it.

What was it about Bhagwan that attracted people so? He was undoubtedly very confident of himself and of what he was saying. He was intensely, almost overpoweringly, charismatic, a most persuasive orator and no mean magician. He had gathered round him a small group of intelligent, attractive and enlightened people. He himself *did* seem to be enlightened, but then, as I reminded myself, I had nothing whatsoever to compare him with.

There were others who had taken their spiritual search further and wider than I had, and they too avowed that they had never met anybody remotely like Bhagwan. But perhaps what was right for them was not so good for me. It was true that what Bhagwan said had the power to melt my heart, and he did seem to be able to speak directly to me, to look into my innermost being and know what I was feeling. He had the ability to read my mind, and say the things that I knew were true yet could not formulate or express myself.

In the darshan sessions I had no doubt that he was a healer, a mind-reader, a clairvoyant, a soothsayer, and the wisest man I had ever met. But was he right for me? I found it very difficult being ordered around all the time, being told what to wear, what to do, where to go, who to sleep with. Should I call it a day and go back to England?

Soon I had made my decision. I would go into the Himalayas to meet other gurus, then I would be in a better position to see Bhagwan in perspective. Maybe there were lots of wise men about, and I might meet someone who was far better for me than Bhagwan.

The Himalayas had beckoned to me since the first time I climbed a Scottish ben and was stunned by the view and the mental clarity one seems to gain on a mountain top. I needed to regain that clarity now. I would take the express train to Delhi, then venture into the fabled misty lands beyond where there were prayer flags and ancient bells, high mountain ridges where I could drink ice-cold water and smell the distant scent of pine forests.

I transformed my good pair of slacks into jagged-edged shorts with my scissors, and threw the bits away to float in the hot thermals eddying up the cliff-face. I ducked, startled, as a hawk drove past me in a shriek of tearing air, on its way to some already-spotted feast far below. India, with all its contradictions, its beauty, splendour, chaos and squalor, was a fantastic place. There was still so much forest, so many tiny villages and hamlets. From where I stood I could see the smoke rising from a thousand cooking fires, each marked by a tiny pirouette of smoke spiralling upwards. This land was impossibly far away in time and space from the urban civility of London and the Siberian fastnesses of Scotland. This was a land of beggars and shepherds, the very few rich and the many, many poor, a land of long, hot, dusty roads separating meagre villages.

Before dusk I went looking for a place to stay. The hotel was overcharging ridiculously, and when I made other enquiries some local lads tried to fleece me by renting me an empty run-down bungalow that was clearly not theirs. In an instant my desire to stay in this place evaporated, and instead I decided to go back to Bombay, pack up my remaining things, and head north. Now that I had made my decision I felt a renewed energy, and set off with a light heart to the railway station. It was as if a great burden, a malevolent yoke, had fallen off me, and I was now as free as the driving hawk.

I arrived at the railway station to discover that it was three hours before the next train arrived, but I didn't care. Intoxicated by my new-found energy, I walked all night in the direction of Bombay along the railway tracks. The huge harvest moon provided light. I broke off for an hour or two of sleep just before dawn, then set off again, passing through the plains of village India, through mango groves and rice paddies all dried up and dusty, coconut plantations and an endless network of dirt roads. They were peopled with ox-carts and shepherds, postmen on rickety bicycles, and gaggles of white-toothed children who came to stare at this Western oddity walking along in sawn-off shorts.

Some of the children had never seen a white man before, and they brought gifts of cucumber and tomatoes, and dubious glasses of drinking water. Though this water was visibly populated with green micro-organisms, I drank it nevertheless. It tasted sunburnt and good.

Chapter Four

BHAGWAN'S HOLD
GROWS STRONGER

Back in Bombay, my flatmate noted my rapid reappearance without surprise. "Of course, I knew you would be back today," he informed me.

"What do you mean, you *knew* I would be back? How come? I told you I wouldn't be back for two weeks."

He laughed and then explained. "Well, after you had left yesterday I went up to Woodlands and saw Laxmi. I told her that you had gone off into the mountains for two weeks without seeing Bhagwan first, and that your meditation with Leela had not worked out well. Laxmi went straight in to tell Bhagwan, who reflected on this piece of information.

"Then he laughed and predicted to Laxmi that you would be back tomorrow. He had called you back, he said. Then Laxmi came out and told me to expect you back today. So you see, there's no mystery. Besides, she passed on a message from Bhagwan that he wants to see you the minute you get back. So you'd better have a shower and change, and get straight over there."

I paused to digest all this. In the short time I had been with Bhagwan I had heard stories about how people had tried to leave him, but were inexorably drawn back. Vivek, for example, had tried to leave him the previous year. She declared she could not stand it any longer and had taken an evening train north out of Bombay, intending to go to Ahmedabad, Delhi, or even further, anywhere as long as it was very far away from *him*. But by the time she reached the northern suburbs of Bombay her intense desire to run away had simply evaporated; her whole attitude had changed and she knew that she wanted nothing more than to get back to him. So she got off at the next station, changed trains, and returned to Bhagwan's side. It was evident that our guru had far more of a hold over us than we were willing to acknowledge, or perhaps even to understand.

I felt suddenly excited: it was as if I had been given a secret insight into the inner workings of Bhagwan's mind. It was fascinating how he seemed to be influencing us all in subtle ways, and creating such an atmosphere of love, intimacy, peace and harmony within the group that was gathering so quickly around him. For the first time I felt the beginnings of a sense of purpose, the whispered intimation that this was going to grow into a worldwide movement. If he wanted to see me it was fine, though if I had not been summoned I would probably have caught a plane straight home to Britain after my Himalayan trip. As I prepared to see Bhagwan again, worried about having been disobedient and fearing a justified rebuke, I wondered what he might want now.

As I showered, I reflected on Bhagwan's apparent unworldliness. He seemed completely unattached to material possessions and personal relationships. He had the unmistakable appearance of one who did not want or desire anything, but was already complete and content. In common with most of the other sannyasis I had spoken to, I seemed to experience a definite sense of a higher reality in Bhagwan's presence. His eyes twinkled, and you felt at once that he was both wise and good, and completely at one with the universe. Then his eyes would suddenly go dark and blank, sending a shiver of awe through you.

Most of us had come to Bhagwan in search of this sensation of bliss, and some of us had already witnessed it. Once you have experienced this feeling, you long to have it again. It is a difficult thing to describe for those who have never had an inkling of it, but it's like the most wonderful and sustained orgasm, the light on the road to Damascus, or the high that can come from psychedelic drugs — only better. Many thousands of people experienced a tangible sense of upliftment and clarity in Bhagwan's presence. There were of course some who doubted his powers, and there were times when the whole thing seemed ridiculous, but having tasted honeydew, we kept wanting to go back for more.

I hastened up to Bhagwan's flat and spoke to Laxmi. She arranged a darshan for the next day. At seven thirty promptly I was ushered in to see him. He sat there, twinkling, impassive and peaceful as ever, and motioned me to come and sit nearer. Then he started to talk to me. "There are a few things you will have to understand, Shiva, hmmm. There are many people here who have real problems, but you are not one of them. You have no real problems at all. For you, it is all going to be easy.

"You have done so much already, and much, much more is going to happen. You will see. Do not be discouraged by these small things. Everything is going to be good, hmmmm? Now, what are your plans, hmmm?"

As I sat listening I was surprised. Suddenly the onus was on me. He was asking *me* what *I* wanted, rather than telling me to 'surrender' and obey his commands. He was such a chameleon, a magician of the first order. I had thought about what I would say when he asked me about the level of my surrender, and so was completely disarmed. There was no point preparing answers for Bhagwan. Now it seemed silly to go to the Himalayas: what would be the point? What would I have learned there?

Then Bhagwan told me what I had to do.

"The best thing will be for you to go back to London. Monsoon will not be good. You will avoid the worst of the heat still to come in India. Earn enough money to bring back so that you can stay here for a long, long time."

But of course. My future life was to be with Bhagwan. How could I ever have thought of doing anything else, of running away from him?

Now he became very specific as to what I had to do: "You come back in October, hmmm, October. October will be good." That word 'good' again! But this time it seemed to hold a special promise, and I felt I ignored these instructions at my own peril. I made a firm resolve to be back in October 1973.

A letter I wrote to my father in Edinburgh at this time underlines my first impressions of India, and of Bhagwan's world:

"Dearest Folks (I wrote),

Above is my new name, which means Swami — Lord — and Shivamurti — Shiva-like. Shiva is one of the three main Gods of India, who has over a thousand names and dances destruction, then rebuilds.

This is a very peculiar scene which doesn't suit me very well, to date. Living in Bombay on an equal standing to London costs more than in London. Living rough here is cheap, but very rough — hot, dirty and fundamentally pointless. I will stay in Bombay until June by which time I may move on if things don't metamorphise. It's almost impossible to make friends with Indians, as the religious and cultural gap is so deep, and none of the sannyasis has done, here. (Sannyasi means one who has renounced — meaning the ego trip.) Love, Shiva."

When I arrived back in London I continued to wear the orange robes, the mala, and the leather sandals I had grown accustomed to in Bombay. The garments attracted stares, but I didn't worry — I was back with a renewed sense of purpose, to spread Bhagwan's wonderful words, and to gather more people into his unique fold. The Rajneesh Centre had moved from its loft in Chalk Farm to better premises in Marylebone Road, and was attracting more people daily. There was such a bubbly sense of excitement, and none of us really knew what the next step would be. After India, London felt incredibly clean and well-organised, even *green*. There was so much water everywhere, and the cold wind that cut clean and fresh from the Atlantic was invigorating, very different from the enervating breezes from the Arabian Sea. This was civilisation, certainly, but not the way of the heart. Spiritually it felt like a desert, with little oases like the one we were providing to fill the deeply-sensed gaps.

Many growth and human potential groups were starting up all over Britain and Europe. People were becoming desperate for some sort of enlightenment, and were looking for new ways to raise their consciousness. They were looking for techniques to put them in touch with themselves, and help them to become aware of the harmony, sense and meaning of the universe. During the few months I was back in London these groups seemed to be mushrooming. More encounter groups were being started, together with psychodrama, guided fantasy, Rolfing — a kind of deep massage technique developed by Ida Rolf, and primal therapy, which took you back to experience and deal with the pain of traumatic experiences. There were also the spin-offs from est and the Esalen growth movement, which were both attracting large numbers of people to California.

Most of these movements started life in America, and were being enthusiastically taken up by young people who wanted more out of life than they seemed to be getting in ordinary ways. Television crews arrived to film encounter groups in action, and they became a controversial talking point. The 'Living Love' workshops came over from the States along with the 'Enlightenment Intensives', residential courses that were held in country mansions and charged what seemed to be very high prices for their experience of wisdom. Bhagwan was a topical subject of conversation among people who were busy exploring their 'inner space'. At that time there was a general movement away from hallucinogenic drugs, and towards an understanding that spiritual enlightenment could be attained without artificial means.

I noticed charts illustrating the chakras appearing on the walls of greengrocers' shops, mechanics' benches and other unlikely places. The days of student strikes and sit-ins were petering out, and guru Maharaj Ji, the overweight sixteen-year-old 'Perfect Master', talked at Westminster Hall to a capacity audience.

The Beatles had just separated from their own guru, Maharishi Mahesh Yogi, but their brush with Eastern spirituality had brought the whole subject out into the open. They sang "With our love we can change the world," and thanks to them everybody had now heard of gurus, pictures of the Maharishi appearing in just about every newspaper. The time was certainly ripe for Bhagwan to make his appearance. Those who sat listening to his lectures every morning in Marylebone Road were convinced of his authenticity, and fervently believed that he was the one who would lead us all from darkness to light.

While I was in London I fell in love with an American lady who practised primal therapy. Primal therapy, developed by an American psychotherapist called Arthur Janov, works on the belief that pain is basically rooted in the original trauma of birth. We try to suppress emotional pain, but like the archetypal pain of birth it remains locked in our bodies, where it is felt as tension and neurosis. Over time, this suppression blocks our ability to feel our feelings, both 'good' and 'bad', and it is then, according to Janov, that people become neurotic. Primal therapists take people back through all their suppressed traumatic experiences, and finally through the pain of their birth. While reliving the birth trauma people often scream in agony, and this is known as the 'primal scream'. There was a very strong link between primal therapy and Bhagwan's dynamic meditation sessions. Later, Bhagwan invited Janov to visit him, but he never came.

During therapy, people may whimper and wail, thrash their limbs around or drool like babies. According to Janov, the most common pain that is relived in therapy is rejection as a child. My father had not wanted me as a child, and I certainly experienced this sense of rejection. It was part of the reason why I was drawn to Bhagwan — he accepted me and became the father figure who emanated unconditional acceptance.

I fell head over heels in love with this primal therapist. It was love, lust and infatuation all rolled into one. I bought another fast Honda motorcycle and had a glorious summer relishing my new-found freedom. People I had known before I went to India told me that I now seemed very different. My encounter group friend Michael Barnett — who was to become Somendra and stay for eight years with Bhagwan — said that I had changed considerably. "You have your own light now," he told me. "Your eyes have changed. This Bhagwan may not be enlightened, but he certainly knows his business as a transformer of people." He was in India within the year.

Almost all the people I knew then in London were to go and see Bhagwan within the following three years. If you were in the growth movement at all, it seemed almost inevitable that you would end up with the 'orange people' and their charismatic leader.

I soon realised that my heart was no longer in my osteopathic work. I worked somewhat half-heartedly, did odd jobs, and toured Scotland on my motorbike. When October came I was ready to return to Bombay according to instructions. My new girlfriend said she was not ready to go to India just yet, and would prefer to go in December. I decided to wait and go with her. That was a mistake — Bhagwan's black magic working again? By December we were no longer so close, and the relationship had got into a distinct mess. I longed to see Bhagwan again, to be once again in that presence and make contact with the clear, unafraid, wise eyes that sometimes twinkled, and sometimes went black and blank. I longed to hear his voice, which seemed to come from somewhere beyond, and his words, which tapped a wisdom at the same time ancient and new. I longed for that incredible feeling of lingering euphoria.

So nine months after that first flight out to India I was back again in Bombay, but this time I did not go alone. I took with me ten potential new sannyasis, people who wanted to meet Bhagwan after doing Veena's early morning meditation sessions. As soon as I arrived in Bombay, Laxmi told me that she would arrange a group darshan for all of us. That didn't please me at all. What about my individual audiences? That was really what I had come back for. Now it was group darshans — what a disappointment!

We all filed in together. Bhagwan greeted me warmly. He raised an eyebrow in recognition, and said "Hello, Shivadas." *What?* I said to myself. Has he forgotten the name he himself gave me already? My pride was shattered. After all I had done for him in the nine months I had been away — helped develop his new centre, brought all these eager people to meet him, spread his word to all who would listen, meditated, worn orange robes all the while in London — all this, and he couldn't even remember the name he had given me!

"Hello, how are you, this will be your new name, hello, meditate, how are you . . ." he said to everybody in turn. So this was my reward for not coming back in October as he had ordered. It was all very different from the intimacy I had experienced before. Now I had to see him with hordes of other people, people who were new to all this, unlike me. Didn't he realise that I was special, that I was different, more committed?

Was this how it would be from now on? He turned to speak to me at last. "How long staying? Coming to next camp at Mount Abu? Good. See you there. Book a darshan at Abu. Next please . . ." It was like a production line. Our group was dismissed, like a class. Bhagwan turned to my girlfriend: "You stay behind," he told her.

In a flash I remembered what had happened to another woman who had stayed behind on her own: Bhagwan had ordered her to take all her clothes off in front of him. Would he do the same to my girlfriend? I remembered his fast-growing reputation as sex guru, 'The Guru of the Vagina', and the little Indian man in the park telling me that my guru was not the right one; that he slept with his female disciples.

The rest of us trooped out, and I waited outside for a long time for her to reappear. After twenty minutes she had still not come out, and I feared the worst. I wandered off to the apartment we were sharing, and waited. Eventually she turned up. Bhagwan had given her a new name: Prem Divya, or Divine Love. She said excitedly that she was going to see him again tomorrow morning, again alone. She was clearly in the seventh heaven of delight. He was explaining so many things to her, she said, clearing up so many mysteries. Another thing. She said she did not want to sleep in the same bed as me tonight. Just for tonight, she assured me, as she needed to be by herself. So I slept on the sofa, thinking how unfair it all was. I was jealous and envious that she was getting this special treatment while I had to see Bhagwan with a host of other people. It felt as if that special magic and precious intimacy had gone for ever.

It hurt even more when Divya continued to have private darshans every single day. On one day she had two, all to herself. Eventually I couldn't stand it any longer, and begged Laxmi to book me a darshan, but she turned me down with fierce finality and no explanations. It wasn't possible, I was told.

I was still infatuated with Divya, especially since I had been denied her. I knew I was being possessive about her, something Bhagwan had strongly warned us all against, but I went home to mope and sulk, and of course Divya then moved further and further away from me. The ultimate insult came one morning when Divya went off to one of those very special four-in-the-morning darshans, the darshans about which so much was rumoured, and which were euphemistically known as 'energy sharing'. Bhagwan would have one woman with him until midnight, then have four hours' sleep, after which another woman would come to him.

Four hours later I was found sulkily drinking a cup of tea in a chai shop near Bhagwan's Woodlands flat. The messenger was excited. "Laxmi says you are to come for darshan, now! Quickly, take a shower and put a clean robe on, come on."

As I waited outside Bhagwan's room I fantasised about his activities with my girlfriend. I had not seen Divya at all that morning. Why was Bhagwan calling me just four hours after he had seen Divya? Laxmi motioned me in in her usual effervescent and ebullient way, but I noticed that there was a curious caution in her eyes. It was as if she was warning me to tread carefully, for in going to see Bhagwan I was stepping on holy ground. Plus other territories, perhaps. Several years later, Laxmi told me that the caution I sometimes spotted in her eyes was because she was afraid of me: "We never knew what you would do, as you were such a tall man, so strong and big. Laxmi was always wary of you when you first came."

"How are you, Shiva?" said Bhagwan, pleasantly enough, and continued: "There are some things you have to understand. Listen, this is important. Divya cannot live with you now, as she needs space. Your relationship has become oppressive to her, to you both, so it is better you drop out of it just now. After the camp I want her to come back to Bombay. She can do her primal therapy here, and it will be very useful for my work. You will go to the farm at Kailash and help to build an ashram there. You can help build my commune."

Kailash. I had heard of Kailash. It was a farm situated in a remote, God-forsaken place about four hundred miles east of Bombay, the great bugger-all. It was owned by some distant relatives of Bhagwan's who had given him permission to send some of his disciples there to start an ashram. It was to be Bhagwan's new permanent home, or so we understood at the time. An advance team of about ten Western sannyasis had already been despatched there. Veetrag, a former pilot from South Africa, had been given enough money to lay the foundations and get the ashram started. Though Bhagwan's movement was not yet rich, several wealthy Indian industrialists and businessmen had already given him money to carry on his work.

Bhagwan went on: "I will be moving to Kailash later, once it is completed, and my people will all be there soon. It is a beautiful place, owned by one of my relatives. They are good people. Much will happen to you there, hmmm. Good, Shiva, don't worry. Everything will be good. See me again at the camp." It seemed unlikely to me that Bhagwan would ever really go to live at Kailash. In a 1984 semi-autobiographical account, Bhagwan describes Kailash as 'an experiment'; the most feasible explanation I have is that it was a device to test our mettle, to separate the wheat from the chaff, the real sannyasis from the hippies and hangers-on.

I felt doubly destroyed. First I had to accept separation from Divya, then be banished to Kailash, which had already been nicknamed Outer Siberia. The worst thing was that I knew Bhagwan was right in what he was saying. Divya and I had got ourselves into a terrible mess, and being city born and bred in New York she would be no use at all on a farm. But would I be any better? I had heard many stories about Kailash, about how it was infested with rats, vultures and wild dogs, and was little more than a jungle clearing halfway between Bombay and Calcutta. So far none of the ten survivors I had met had had a good word to say about the place.

But first there was another camp at Abu. About fifty of us boarded the train at Bombay, the same train as Bhagwan. A whisper went round that we were to protect him, as trouble was expected at Ahmedabad station. There had been rioting there, and the police had been tipped off that some right-wing extremists would attempt an attack on Acharya Rajneesh. He had upset these extremists with his comparisons between Hinduism and Islam, and though Hinduism preaches vegetarianism and pacifism, many of its adherents are capable of the ugliest rioting and violence. When aroused they spare nobody, and go for the nose, the jugular vein and the genitals. Meat cleavers and hatchets are their favourite weapons.

We were to change trains at Ahmedabad on the way to Abu Road, and as we pulled slowly into the crowded station, our old-fashioned steam locomotive belching and hissing, a few sannyasis tried to get off the train so as to position themselves in front of Bhagwan's first-class, air-conditioned coach. The station was packed to bursting with all kinds of people, but it did seem more densely packed than usual—when there are rumours of riot, many ordinary people head for the stations, believing them the safest places to be.

As we peered through the throng of porters in bright red tunics, chai wallahs bearing tiny cups of steaming hot brew, and panicking travellers, we momentarily caught sight of soldiers in riot gear in small, tight groups with fixed bayonets at the ready. It seemed that Laxmi had managed to call the police, as we glimpsed a small band of tough-looking sergeants with bamboo lathis standing beside a first-class carriage. In typically Indian fashion, however, it was the wrong carriage, and Laxmi started ordering them about. A few Western sannyasis crowded round, but they had been steeped too long in the gentle arts of surrender and meditation to be tough. Others, myself included, could make no headway at all, and we just saw the top of Bhagwan's shiny pate as he was escorted to a nearby train.

We heard some heckling, and then came the chant, clearly organised and orchestrated: "Rajneesh murdabad, Rajneesh murdabad"—death to Rajneesh. There was no further trouble, but the scare was enough for us all. It was to be the very last time that Bhagwan travelled by train, and also the final Abu camp.

It was good to be back at Abu. The freshness and mountain scenery of the hill station put a new sunrise in my heart. In this retreat where monkeys gathered to watch us, where gloriously-feathered birds twittered among the flowering trees, my infatuation with Divya, hopeless for so long, finally faded away and died. A tremendous release swept through me when I realised I was no longer attached to her. I was at last able to breathe without that sense of attachment and imprisonment, and my heart felt light.

At Abu this time I had the first inklings that I was in touch with a higher reality, a sense of inner calm, tranquillity and freedom. So this was what it was all about, *this* was what Bhagwan was trying to get me to see! It was *good!* This was the sense behind the senselessness. On the fifth day of the camp, after twelve hours of active dynamic meditations, I felt more full in my heart than ever before. The old yearnings, the sense of emptiness, had quite gone, and I was finally at home among a great spiritual brotherhood. I knew that I was privileged to partake in such a genuine teaching.

That night I woke from a deep sleep just before dawn. All the hairs on my head were standing on end. At the foot of the bed I saw what looked like a woman, preternaturally tall, standing with a water jug balanced on her head. She was looking at me with a mixture of love and serenity in her eyes. I was terrified. For just a split second I thought to myself how peaceful she looked, and then realised she must be a ghost of some kind. As soon as this interpretation crossed my mind the apparition was gone. Whatever was going on in this ancient place? I went outside to witness the dawn, shaken yet at the same time enriched. Was it going to go on like this? Would there be more such revelations?

At the camp I met some of the ten people who had already been to Kailash, and heard more about it. One of the women who had been there had a morbid terror of rats, in which the farm abounded. She had a private darshan with Bhagwan where she described her fear. At Kailash, she told him, the rats climbed all over the bed at night, and even — horror of horrors — darted under the bedsheets. They went pitter-patter all night, and in the morning there would be rat droppings in her sandals. Bhagwan explained that this horror was caused by a simple sexual hangup, and that there was a surefire remedy — unrestrained oral sex. She immediately had several offers to help her with her problem. Also, to add local colour, we heard that the foreman in charge of the farm, an Indian, every week beat his common law wife routinely — and severely — with that typically Indian weapon, his sandal.

I knew that I did not want to go to Kailash. It sounded like hell on Earth. So far Bhagwan had picked about thirty Western sannyasis to go there, and more were being chosen each day. It appeared to me that it was the Doubting Thomases, the rebellious and the riff-raff who were being chosen to go to Kailash. Those whom Bhagwan had earmarked as his special or wealthy disciples were let off the hook. All the Indians without exception, and my ex-girlfriend Divya, were excused Kailash duty. Could this be a continuation of Bhagwan's apparent revenge for disobeying his orders?

Eventually the day came for my darshan at Abu. A long queue had formed outside Bhagwan's room, and the darshans were being conducted on a production line basis. I was ushered in as the previous person was still kissing Bhagwan's feet — an affectation I found quite inappropriate.

Bhagwan asked: "How are you, Shiva, hmmm?" This time he had at least got my name right. I confessed to him that I was extremely reluctant to go to this dirt farm in the middle of the Indian jungle.

He looked at me, then looked away. He steepled his hands in contemplative fashion. "Oh well, then, if you do not *want* to go, then of course you do not *have* to! You can come back to Bombay with the rest of my people."

I got the point. I said "But I *do* have to go, don't I?" I knew somehow that I did have to go. Bhagwan turned slightly more towards me and caught my eyes. He nodded gently in confirmation. At this point tears came to my eyes and suddenly I knew that we were on the same psychic and intuitive wavelength, in direct contact. We were reading each other loud and clear. As soon as I acknowledged what Bhagwan was telepathically communicating with me and got the real message, my tears ceased. He looked down at me, smiled, and nodded slowly, twice.

"Yes, yes, Shiva," he confirmed. "Yes, you do have to go. Go. And . . . at the farm, hmmm, meditate, work, be loving. Be in silence for three months and do not read or write, OK? This will be very good. And I will send Divya to join you as soon as she is ready. OK? Good."

That night I saw the comet Kahoutek low on the horizon. The comet felt like a brother, a fellow seeker, a traveller. I felt I was getting nearer to the source, nearer to my innermost core of being. Immediately, something wonderful happened. Now that I had been lifted from my possessiveness of Divya, she came back, quite unannounced, into my life one humid night. We spent the last two days at Abu in a new and infinitely richer intimacy, on a basis of freedom and non-attachment. The lust and jealousy had gone.

Bhagwan had indeed been working his alchemy on us. Now I could look forward unreservedly to the time when she joined us at the farm. Bhagwan had promised she would come as soon as she was 'ready', whatever that meant. I knew enough about the vagueness of Bhagwan's promises to understand that he might not send her at all. The promises he made tended to be of the Indian variety — flexible, elastic, instantly forgettable, and made with an utter and complete disregard for chronological time.

On the final day of the camp everyone who had been detailed to go to the farm was summoned to a group darshan. We crowded into the little room and sat in a circle around our beloved Bhagwan. He was sitting there completely calm in the armchair which had been specially brought in the train from Bombay.

He said: "You are extremely fortunate to have been chosen to start this experiment, this Kailash ashram. More can happen to you at the beginning of any new development than at any other time. It is an enormously rich time — so much energy is being released. So you are all immensely privileged, you are lucky, hmmm. Go there. It is a beautiful place. I have been to that place many times in my childhood, and you will enjoy it tremendously. Do my work, build the ashram, prepare the site for the new experiment, my new commune. It will be of tremendous help to you all. Go with my blessings, enjoy, be blissful, and much will happen to all of you there!"

He was right: much would happen there.

Chapter Five

HEAT, HEAVEN AND HELL
AT KAILASH

Kailash was not an easy place to get to. It took more than a day by train from Abu to get to the nearest town, fifty miles from Kailash. Then we had to wait another two days until transport could be arranged to the farm itself.

As we waited for Bhagwan's relatives to come and pick us up, we wondered, not for the first time, what the hell we were doing. Were we completely mad? When the relatives did eventually arrive they were quite convinced that we were mad. They couldn't begin to fathom us out at all. We were Westerners, foreigners, used to comfort and luxury and here we were, setting off at the beginning of a hot season to go to a dirt farm in one of the hottest places in India. The relatives issued dire predictions to us as we journeyed there.

"But you will not last," they informed us matter-of-factly. "No one can. It is a bad place at this time." But we took little notice of them. We had a plentiful supply of money with us and were full of enthusiasm and boundless optimism. With our Bhagwan's blessing we could easily turn this God-forsaken place into an oasis and an ashram. I was curious to see whether the rats were really as bad as they were rumoured to be.

Within a week almost three dozen Westerners were camping out at Kailash. We were a strange mixture of people. There was a tall, slim, blonde Swedish ex-model and an American ex-grunt Vietnam veteran who kept complaining about everything. When his foot was pierced by a submerged branch in the river, causing a bad infection, he exclaimed: "Man, I got shot in the war, real bad, and it weren't nowhere near as painful as this." We also had with us a gay couple from Toronto, the former pilot from South Africa who was our leader, a vivacious Australian magazine editor, two very beautiful American girls — one tall and slim, the other petite and demure, and an English woman whom Bhagwan had instructed to masturbate three times a day. She took his instructions to heart and insisted that an area should be set aside for special tantric (sexual) meditations each day. So a part of the old two-storey farmhouse was curtained off and reserved for this purpose.

Haridas, the former German electrician who was one of my main buddies during the time I was with Bhagwan, came too, exuding gruff Teutonic charm. There was also an Austrian sannyasi, a tall blonde man, who had been given the 'stop' meditation to do. At odd times during the day he would stop in his tracks and stand completely still for about two minutes. This is an old Sufi practice designed to heighten awareness. He was quite a young chap, and every now and again we would glimpse him, a blonde and saffron scarecrow, transfixed in peculiar mid-frame postures. It was like musical statues, where you have to stand still the instant the music stops in whatever position you happen to be at the time.

As we worked and meditated, local people began to come by and stare at us unbelievingly. They could not make it out at all. As the weeks passed and the weather grew ever hotter we started to shed our clothes, and were soon walking around and meditating completely naked. It's not hard to imagine how the natives stared at us then. Indeed, we attracted a large crowd of sightseers on the far bank, some of whom, we heard, had walked twenty miles to see the 'naked foreigners'.

Everybody at Kailash had been at the Abu camp. Whatever our differences in background, upbringing or personality, we were united in our love for Bhagwan, and the words he had said to us in our individual darshans were our guiding lights, our protection.

We hung on to these when our work conditions seemed impossible to bear. It seemed that most people had been told to stay in this place for six months, which meant they would still be here when the monsoon came. Bhagwan had told me to stay at Kailash in silence for three months — thankfully he had never mentioned six. That would be too much. As the hot weeks passed a unity developed between us as we shared meals, sleeping spaces and meditations. We became a cohesive extended family, bound together by our love of Bhagwan and our devotion to 'his work'.

Veetrag, the South African pilot, had been given a large sum of money by Laxmi to pay for all the building materials the ashram would need. He gave out our daily work assignments and issued the rules and regulations. We did not know it at the time, but Laxmi and Bhagwan had told him to gradually increase the workload and the number of restrictive rules. He had been given instructions to remove privileges, reduce food, free time and days off, and to forbid excursions. He seemed to enjoy making our regime more and more repressive. He was a natural provocateur.

We had to pay a small housekeeping retainer to the pilot of fifty rupees (about £4), and surrender to him absolutely as our guru's representative at Kailash. The rules and regulations, combined with an acute lack of food and time off, caused some people to leave. The pilot had been forewarned about that too. When the rules became too much, he had been told to drop them without warning, then sit back and see what happened. But he didn't tell us about any of this, and all we poor toilers knew was that the stern rules caused great pain and suffering, both physical and mental.

Apart from the harsh rules, we had to contend with natural difficulties which included the heat, scorpions, the sheer isolation of the place, and being cut off from everything we had previously known as civilisation. Most of us were city people to whom any kind of farm life was alien.

When we arrived the pilot said that we did not need to take any precautions with the local drinking water, and there was certainly no need to boil it for twenty minutes as recommended in medical handbooks. The locals drank it, after all, and what was good enough for them would be good enough for us. After a few days it was clear that something was wrong, I had a word with Veetrag and politely mentioned that amoebic dysentery was already breaking out. The locals, I told him, were used to the water, and their systems could cope. Ours couldn't. I said that I was going to boil my own water, and he reluctantly agreed, complaining that it was a waste of firewood. I could do it after work hours, and scavenge my own wood in the nearby jungle.

Looking back, I cannot believe that Bhagwan had told him to go quite this far. Perhaps he adapted the rules, to make them harsher, for private reasons of his own. Perhaps he really did see no harm in his pronouncements. But the outcome was that within six weeks of his no-boil order, three-quarters of the community had gone down with amoebic dysentery. I had to drive one very weak pale-skinned English woman to the nearest hospital, in Chandrapur, forty miles away. She had been bedridden with dysentery for three days at Kailash, and was almost completely dehydrated. When we arrived at the hospital the doctor was aghast. "Whatever do you mean, you are not boiling the water?" he expostulated. "Are you mad? You surely know that you cannot live like a bunch of villagers. You are Westerners, and your bodies cannot cope with the local water. You go and tell your leader that he *has* to boil the water. This woman has nearly died. You go and tell him." When I repeated the consultant's warnings to the pilot, he simply told me to keep my 'negativity' to myself.

The regime altered completely the day the pilot himself became ill with dysentery. He immediately allowed all water to be boiled. A week later a scorpion stung him badly, but he sweated it out and lived.

As time went on more people left. By the fourth week the gay couple had gone. Haridas only lasted ten days. "Ze food is no good at all," he said. "I am hungry all ze time. Zis is not how Bhagwan wants it to be, zis is all wrong!" One Englishman nearly died from a scorpion bite. He coped with the pain by staying up all night beating a set of tom-tom drums to take his mind off the agony. No one slept.

Even so, there were some compensations. I came to love the wild Indian countryside and our expansive clearing in the jungle. I came to admire the ingenuity and contentment of the local people, who used cowdung to do everything from build their homes to wash the clothes, make fires and kill scorpions. To kill a scorpion you aimed a handful of fresh steaming cowdung at the scorpion, and when it was asphyxiated, nipped off the tail. Then you fried the scorpion in oil. It was considered a wonderful delicacy, but we, like Bhagwan, were vegetarian, and so did not indulge in this protein supplement.

I was sent with the Landrover for a five-day trip to a town about a hundred and fifty miles away, to pick up a calf which had supposedly been offered by some distant relatives of Bhagwan's. This calf was to be the start of our milking herd. Everything that could go wrong did. When I arrived at the town, Drug, I realised that the calf would be far too big to go into the Landrover. In the end that hardly mattered, since in typical Indian fashion the gift of the calf had been withdrawn by the time I arrived to pick it up.

The farm where the calf was was a miserable, fly-ridden dusty crumble of caked earth and green-slimed stagnant streams. Water buffalo stood around hopelessly, not even attempting to cope with all the flies that settled on their eyelids. As I wandered round the farm I glimpsed the calf, but nothing was said on either side. We went upstairs for supper, and the extended family gathered round to eat. Although the calf was no longer on offer, the relatives were still very hospitable.

At first they could not believe that seemingly sophisticated, sensible people like myself could think that 'Mohan' was the true guru, and that we had given up everything to follow him. They said with surprise: "You are following *him*, our Mohan? Is it true? Other foreign friends are also following him, not just yourself?" The family brought out pictures of Mohan and said, still wonderingly, "*This* Mohan, this is the one you are following? He is having lady disciples also, is that so? And is he still doing the hypnosis? He was experimenting terribly on all of us when we last met him."

There were about six children sitting cross-legged amongst their elders — grandfather, grandmother, two married daughters and their husbands. The men were all dressed in the simple cotton that Bhagwan had worn a few years previously but had now cast off in favour of more glorious and slim-fitting finery. We ate off highly-polished steel plates, sitting on the floor. It was absolutely delicious, and certainly nothing like the meagre amounts of poor-quality food we had been enduring at Kailash. I was given a few tips on eating Indian fashion, without the use of knives and forks. I ate prodigiously, and the family were delighted to see me enjoying my food so much, heaping more and more on my plate. We talked about the weather, the coming monsoon, local places of interest, and then they started probing with more personal questions. Was I married, or what? I told them no, but added that I had a girlfriend, and produced a picture of Divya. They were very surprised, and eventually the head of the family, the grandfather, passed the collective judgement: "Hm, your girlfriend, is she not a little *old*?" I said no, of course not, she was only my own age. Then it sank in. Of course, here in India the 'right' age for a wife was a third younger than the man, so they would have paired me off with a sixteen-year-old.

After a while the conversation drifted back to my guru. It became clear that 'Mohan' was considered the *enfant terrible* of this particular clan. They did not seem to be very fond of him, and frankly could not believe that he had now set himself up as a guru, an enlightened person. I felt too loyal to Bhagwan to admit of any reservations about him, but the way they went on about his hypnosis and how he had practised it on everybody for many, many years did worry me, causing a question mark to form in my mind. Later on, when it became clear how Bhagwan operated, I was to understand exactly what they meant by hypnosis, but for the time being I did not want to admit to any doubts.

Bhagwan's relatives were especially amazed that Mohan should be attracting lady disciples — to them this could only mean one thing, that there was more than just spiritual contact taking place.

As I listened I heard about Bhagwan's strange childhood, adolescence and early career. As his own parents had been very poor, he was brought up by his rich maternal grandparents. He was, apparently, a very beautiful baby, whose last birth was supposed to have occurred seven hundred years previously, when he established a mystic school in the mountains. Then he lived to be 106 years old.

Just before his death in this previous reincarnation, he entered a twenty-one-day fast in order to attain enlightenment. During this fast he was given the option of taking just one more birth, and decided to take advantage of the offer. He foresaw that there was a possibility of uniting East and West, and bringing about a synthesis between materialism and spirituality. According to this story, he was killed three days before his life should have ended. Rajneesh's mother, who later became one of his disciples, said that for three days after he was born he would not cry or take any milk, though his health remained excellent.

Another story I heard concerning his origins was that Rajneesh was the Christian Saint Bernard in a previous birth, and massacred a group of people, the Cathars, who were practising tantra, the sexual path to spiritual enlightenment.

Rajneesh became very attached to his maternal grandfather, who died when the child was seven years old. This left a permanent emotional scar. But even at this age, the young Rajneesh was displaying some highly peculiar tendencies.

He watched his grandfather die slowly for three days, after which he himself refused to eat or get up for three days. This morbid fascination with death and dying was to preoccupy Rajneeesh all his life, and this story provides an early glimpse into his rather voyeuristic personality. He loved the macabre and deathlike and, as an adult at least, appeared to remain unmoved by any event he witnessed.

An astrologer had predicted that Rajneesh would not live beyond his seventh year. When he did not die, another astrologer said that the child would face death every seven years. The numbers three, seven and twenty-one recur with mystical significance throughout Rajneesh's life.

After his grandfather had died, Rajneesh resolved never to become attached to a human being again. He said himself in his writings: "His death became for me the death of all attachments. Therefore I could not establish a bond of relationship with anyone. Whenever my relationship with anyone would begin to become intimate, that death stared at me . . . Since then, I have been alone."

Also at the age of seven, Rajneesh went to the Gunj School of Gadarwara, where his creative intelligence soon started to shine. He found it difficult to relate to his teachers, as he could find nobody who understood his needs.

He was anxious to discover what death was all about, and would follow people carrying dead bodies to the cremation grounds. Whenever he heard that anybody in his locality was dying, he would be there, watching and witnessing. His relatives confirmed what I had already heard, that he would go alone to cremation grounds and spend hours lying there at night.

Bhagwan described his attitude to death — and how closely that related to sex — in a writing of 1979: "If you listen to the phenomenon of sex that knocks at your door every day, year in, year out, and goes on knocking even while you are dying, you will be surprised to know that whenever prisoners are crucified, sentenced to death, the last thing that happens to a man is ejaculation. We cannot be so certain about the woman because she has no ejaculation. She must have an orgasm, but invisible. And this is my observation of many people I have watched dying: that has been one of my hobbies from my childhood.

"In my town I never allowed anybody to die without my being there. The moment I would hear that somebody was on his deathbed, I would be there . . . I would follow to the last pilgrimage, and I would go with every dying person, rich, poor, beggar — even a dying dog or cat — and I would sit and watch. And I was surprised again and again, the more perceptive I became; I have seen it happen again and again: that the last idea when a man dies is sexual, and so it is in the case with the dog and the cat."

He learned to swim in the time-honoured way, by being thrown in at the deep end. This was always Rajneesh's approach, and was exemplified at Kailash. He threw you in at the deep end, to sink or swim. As Rajneesh grew up he became a natural leader, and encour-aged the other boys to perform feats of great daring and foolhardiness, such as swimming when the river was dangerously high.

Two more deaths were to affect Rajneesh deeply. One was that of his childhood sweetheart, Sashi, when he was sixteen, and the other was the death of Ghandi, a year later in 1948. Rajneesh firmly believed that Sashi was reborn as Vivek, and that was why the relationship between the two of them could become so close. In 1983 he was to claim that Vivek was Mary Magdalene in another past life.

The astrologer's prediction that most concerned Rajneesh was the one that he might die at twenty-one. When this time approached he made a great effort to get through the year without dying, and as a result became 'enlightened' at twenty-one. Throughout his childhood and adolescence he was quite unafraid, either of natural phenomena or of people. In meditation he would let snakes crawl all over him. His relatives also told how he would climb up to a seventy-foot-high bridge and jump into a river in flood. He would dive into whirlpools, saying the experience was 'lovely'.

Rajneesh and his childhood friends were well-known locally for their hair-raising adventures, and would do whatever the fancy took them. Many of the pranks openly broke laws. It became clear as I listened that Rajneesh had always exhibited unusual powers, and had always been able to get people to do things. His pranks, entered into without fear of loss of life either to himself or others, often bordered on the psychopathic.

As a youngster Rajneesh was already fascinated by the occult, breath control, magic and hypnosis. Friends were often involved in experiments he would perform to see what happened when people were in life-threatening situations. Once he pushed a non-swimmer into the water, and on another occasion pushed the head of somebody who could not swim well under water — just so that he could ask what the experience felt like. Rajneesh was not averse to bribing people, and a favourite story was that he would bribe the policeman who stood on the bridge to prevent people from committing suicide to turn a blind eye to Rajneesh and his friends when they jumped off the bridge. Courage, he preached, was the very greatest human quality there was.

It seemed that Rajneesh had always hurt a lot of people, but whether this was intentional or not is unclear. He performed acts which were sadistic, but it is probable that his intention was not to hurt. He was simply coolly interested in the human response. He had little compassion or regard for the feelings of others. There were to be many deaths in the ashrams, both from suicide and from hepatitis and other diseases which could have been cured with proper medical attention. Rajneesh never gave enough money for food in the ashrams, and was not concerned when we worked too hard or slept too little.

I heard that Rajneesh became interested in communism while he was at school, because of his concern for the poor. This was interesting in view of his later wholehearted embracing of capitalism, and his reputation as the 'guru of the rich'.

As I listened it became apparent that Rajneesh was somebody who had put himself on a pedestal from a very early age. He had always regarded himself as different and special. He never made friends in the ordinary sense, or put himself in a position where he could be disappointed by others. It seems as though he may have tried to kill himself while at college, and finding himself inexplicably alive, had experienced a permanent change of consciousness — the 'enlightenment' that occurred when he was twenty-one. After that he became anorexic, refused to eat, and started to run sixteen miles a day, a practice he kept up for several years. It made him feel alive, he told people. He also suffered from mysterious diseases, headaches and nosebleeds.

He received his BA in philosophy in 1955, and his master's degree from Saugar University in 1957. These too were years of intense experimentation and rebellion, and he was eventually asked to resign from his lecturer's post at the University of Jabalpur. He began to criticise socialism at this stage, and also started to speak out against Ghandi. By 1968 he had begun to gather his own followers around him.

What emerged was a picture of a man who, above all, loved to experiment with people and cold-bloodedly observe their reactions. He wanted to see how far his own influence would extend, yet all the time he himself remained aloof, as if conducting a laboratory experiment. He showed no compassion at all for others, and loved to rebel against established authority.

He always read widely, and became a very isolated person. He loved to boast that he *was* an island, completely self-sufficient. In August 1968, two years after he had set himself up as a travelling lecturer, Rajneesh gave a series of public lectures on love, and startled his audience by proclaiming that sex was divine and natural, a first step on the way to heightened consciousness. The actual text of one of his lectures, as recorded in the official biography, *The*

Awakened One by Vasant Joshi, a prominent Western disciple, went: "If you want to know the elemental truth about love, the first requisite is to accept the sacredness of sex, to accept the divinity of sex in the same way as you accept God's existence — with an open heart." The lecture series, held in Bharatiya Vidya Bhavan, one of the most prominent public halls in Bombay, shocked and amazed the audience.

The lectures resulted in anger and abuse being directed at Rajneesh. Later he hit out at organised religion in the same forceful way. His belief was that religions nowadays are full of hypocrisy and deceit. In 1970 he introduced his technique of 'dynamic meditation', as he felt that the traditional relaxation type of meditation was not suited to modern people. Indian bystanders were horrified as participants screamed, shouted and took off their clothes. They had never seen anything like it before.

Rajneesh moved to Bombay on July 1st, 1970, and after this time he changed his title to Bhagwan, one of the Sanskrit words for God. At this time about fifty Indian people had gathered round him, and within the next year he began attracting people from the West as his power and influence spread beyond his native country.

He had never married. When he was at school his maternal grandmother kept asking his father to arrange a suitable marriage, but Rajneesh's father — usually called 'Dadda', and later also a disciple of his son's — was nervous about broaching the subject. As I heard the story, his mother did mention the subject of marriage once, but Rajneesh had already decided that he would never marry. Thus no marriage was ever arranged, a very unusual situation in Indian society, where everyone marries as a matter of course.

Later, I heard other stories about Rajneesh's childhood from other of his relatives. When he was young, for instance, he would go off on nightly expeditions along a perilous cliff path, hundreds of feet above a river gorge, where he acted as leader to the village lads. He had no fear of heights himself, and loved dark, moonless nights. I heard Bhagwan himself tell of a childhood friend called Haridas, whom he taught to swim. One day Rajneesh encouraged the boy to go swimming with him when the river was already dangerously swollen. Haridas was swept away and drowned. Bhagwan said that he had named the German electrician Haridas, who reminded him of his old friend, in memory of this drowned child.

Another story was told by an Indian follower who worked as an acupuncturist in London. As a young man, Mohan drove an ancient Renault, in which he carried stacks of his published works in cheap editions. Mohan had crashed the car in broad daylight, and as the other driver got out, Bhagwan suggested they cooperate in securing a better settlement from their insurers.

Bhagwan set a lot of store by the teachings of Gurdjieff, a Russian philosopher who flourished in the early part of the century. Gurdjieff advocated what he called 'Right action, right thinking and right greed'. Before coming to India I had read the works of Gurdjieff's main disciple, Ouspensky, so I was familiar with his ideas.

Gurdjieff was the main role model for Bhagwan who, needless to say, had read all Gurdjieff's works and the commentaries both in the original and in the version written by Ouspensky. In particular Bhagwan liked the way Gurdjieff had rebelled against authority and kept testing the strength of his disciples' faith. Once, Gurdjieff was supposed to be speaking at a meeting in Paris, and for three days he did not turn up. On the fourth day, when he did go to the lecture hall, he found that his audience had dwindled to just eight people. "You," he said, "are the people I've come to talk to."

Gurdjieff was sexually active with his disciples, just as Bhagwan was, and made much use of what he called 'confrontations and devices'—SAS-type character-building tests. The hardships of Kailash and later of Oregon were Bhagwan's versions of typical Gurdjieff devices. But there was a difference. There is no hint or record that Gurdjieff ever deliberately endangered a disciple's life: he never engineered dangerous devices. Bhagwan did.

Teertha, the oldest sannyasi at Kailash and a former encounter group leader, told two Gurdjieff stories that shed some light on our situation. In the first story Gurdjieff had an objectional pig of a man installed in his Priory, the place where his disciples lived near Paris. This peasant was paid by Gurdjieff to slobber through the genteel meals, and create bad feelings everywhere. Distress followed this chap wherever he went. He was the epitome of the anti-hero, and yet having him around taught the others valuable lessons about themselves. Gurdjieff paid the man to stay there. Everybody else had to pay Gurdjieff.

In another story, Gurdjieff had assigned a team to clear an irrigation canal. At a critical moment someone accidentally opened the sluice gate, and water surged into the canal, Gurdjieff also instituted the 'stop' meditation that was practised at Kailash. At intervals he would shout out "Stop!" and everyone froze on the spot. They had to stay there until allowed to resume their work by a second command. "Stop!" was shouted a few minutes before the tidal wave engulfed the canal crew. All except one scrambled out fast. The man who stayed put and was nearly drowned received all of Gurdjieff's praise. Gurdjieff pointed out that this man was the only one with the necessary will and dedication to succeed in his Work.

One of Gurdjieff's ideas was that you should pay attention to the task in hand without ever having your mind on the end result. You might build a house beautifully, only to see it knocked down the second you had finished. The point of these exercises was to instil into people the importance of concentration and dedication to what you were doing, and not to have your ego attached to what you might produce at the end.

If I had not been given this trip in the Landrover, with its blessed release from Kailash for a few days, I might have left at that point. I kept hearing stories about Bhagwan that contradicted the 'official' version put out by Laxmi. As I drove back to Kailash I found myself worrying about his family having asked if he was still 'experimenting'. It was true that Kailash did feel like a great big experiment, with us as the laboratory animals. Working away on this farm was not really what I had come to India for. I was searching for a higher teaching, for enlightenment. It seemed as if Bhagwan was making up the rules as he went along, and they were as strict as those in any monastic order. At least in a monastery there was less chance of contracting possibly fatal diseases.

I returned to Kailash minus the calf, but with our Indian foreman — the one who beat his wife — as navigator. He directed us back via the longest possible route so that he could show off the Landrover to everybody he knew on the way. I didn't mind, because it was a wonderful experience for me to meet so many happy and contented people, who had no possessions and no riches at all. They expressed admiration for the Landrover, but without any envy or greed. They said that water buffaloes were much more practical.

It had been good to break my three months of silence while meeting Bhagwan's relatives, but now I was back into non-verbal forms of communication.

Once I got back to Kailash, I decided to do something about our continuing starvation diet. I walked six miles to Saoli, the nearest village, and bought an enormous supply of sugar cane sweets. On returning, I was sold out within half an hour. Everyone was ravenously hungry. When the pilot found out, he was furious, and announced that in future day trips off the farm were prohibited. Three more people left at this news, so now we were down to twenty from an initial contingent of thirty-six. The pilot's reaction to this mutiny was to drive the Landrover to the nearest town, and return loaded with vegetables, fruit, biscuits, and the same sugar cane sweets. There may have been some logic and sense to the rules, but they were neither compassionate nor democratic.

As we later discovered, Bhagwan was continuously experimenting on us by first starving and then feasting us. Teertha explained how the hardships we were enduring were character building, and constituted trial by ordeal. Surrender to our master in all things was being tested, and the weakest would naturally not be able to stand it. When new and more stringent rules were applied, this was merely a sign that you had passed the first trial and were ready to undergo more. Ideally, you should take it all as a compliment. Meanwhile, more people left. Teertha easily rationalised this by saying it just proved that these people were not surrendered or committed enough to become the disciples Bhagwan needed for his great work.

But somehow there was a difference between the character-building exploits endured by the classical heroes and what was happening at Kailash, where we were largely creating our own problems. Not taking care of food and drink could mean a lifetime of liver trouble from hepatitis, or prolonged weakness resulting from amoebic dysentery. People could easily die, and many disciples were to die while with Bhagwan. Many of us who lived remained in very poor health for years afterwards. Bhagwan might be able to dismiss poor health as 'negativity', or even claim that he 'gave us' the illnesses we suffered. Tended by his own large staff of housekeepers, cooks, physicians and helpers, he was himself quite removed from our hardships.

By the end of the second month at Kailash almost everyone had dysentery of one kind or another. There were less than twenty sannyasis left, and most of us were very emaciated and unhealthy. Yet Kailash was beautiful, and I enjoyed and benefited from my silence. The shoe of meditation was at last beginning to fit.

I had a letter from Divya, now in England, telling me that Bhagwan had suggested she go back there. As I had suspected, she was not coming to Kailash. I had an affair with the slim — now *very* slim — Swedish model, in complete silence among the rushes by the river. After two months spent almost entirely without speaking, words had somehow become ridiculous as a means of communication. Other senses had developed to take their place, and I started to see auras around people. Clairvoyance opened up, so that I knew what others were about to do. I felt at one with the world, in harmony with nature, and at peace with myself. This prolonged silence had brought out many hidden abilities in me.

I kept thinking about Bhagwan and my relationship with him. It was no small thing to come to India and change your way of life completely. But did I need to be told what to do all the time to prove total surrender? Was it actually necessary to go down with hepatitis, dysentery and other tropical diseases to get to a higher spiritual plane of existence? I couldn't see that it was.

One day one of the American girls at the farm received a letter from the man she had shared a bed with at Mount Abu. He had developed gonorrhea. Free sex and sharing partners were very much integral to Bhagwan's methods. Free love was one thing, but sexually-transmitted diseases were quite another. Shaken, the girl left for Bombay the same day, and not many sweet words were heard as she hurriedly packed. I decided to leave at about the same time. I had had enough.

I decided to go off on that trip to the Himalayas. Before leaving, I meditated on whether this was the right thing to do. It was dusk when I began meditating, and an hour later, as I looked up at the emerging stars in the huge canopy of the Indian sky, a satellite streaked by, heading for the Himalayas. It was an elegant omen. I would bid farewell for ever to this dusty place, but first I would walk round it one last time.

Before I had walked a hundred yards into the darkness, I felt that something very large and very dangerous was out there. All the hair on the back of my head stood up in terror. I knew it couldn't be a villager out this late — they never went out after dark because of the man-eating tigers that roamed at night. Instinctively I clapped my hands and shouted once, very loudly. Immediately there was a piercing shriek and snarl from nearby. It *was* a tiger! A shudder ran through me. I was more terrified than I had ever been before in my entire life. Then there was a soft scuffling of gravel on sand, and I felt its presence disappear. Shit man, I said to myself, that was close. All the dogs on the farm began to bark furiously — they had heard the tiger too.

On the way back to the farm I hit my bare foot on a log and tore off a nail. I felt that these were strong portents that I should not leave the farm quite yet. Was Bhagwan trying to tell me something?

I did not leave for another week, but two weeks after the tiger incident I was trekking up the Nepali border towards Sandakphu, under the chest of Kanchenjunga, the world's third highest mountain. It was so good to feel clean and cold and clear and free again. I could see the curve of the Himalayan chain all the way to Everest and beyond. I felt full of pure awe at viewing this majestic sight. On the way down the mountain I passed through hundreds of square miles of brightly-flowering rhododendron bushes, and passed through tiny hamlets with tea shops full of wiry Sherpa porters. I was still wearing my mala and my orange clothes, since I had no others and was by now on a very tight budget.

I had firmly decided not to go back to see Bhagwan again. I had had enough of being ordered about, enough of succumbing to other people's questionable 'devices' to test me.

When I reached Bombay, it was three weeks since I had left Kailash. I discovered that the woman I had left in charge of my valuables, passport and remaining money had gone to be with Bhagwan. By now he was no longer in Bombay, but had moved to a plush new mansion in Poona. So I would have to go to Poona to recover my belongings before I could get my airline ticket and fly home.

When I got to Poona I had breakfast with the lady who had my money. Then she went off to have a darshan with Bhagwan. I would have to wait for my things until she got back.

When she returned from the darshan she proffered me an apple. "This is yours," she said, "a present from Bhagwan. When he heard that you were so hungry after Kailash he laughed and told Vivek to go and choose an apple for you. 'Shiva is always hungry,' he said. 'He will enjoy this. Oh, and tell him to come to darshan tomorrow!"

It was all so like my attempted escape a year previously! Just when I thought I had successfully distanced myself from Bhagwan, here he was, cajoling, enticing, challenging me to come back again. I was flattered and curious. What could he want of me, his errant and rebellious disciple? What would he say now? Yes, I would go and see him, give him one more chance. Perhaps there would be no more Kailashes to test me, no more dubious 'devices' or extreme experiments. Maybe something altogether more palatable would be in store. It could be that I had now passed the Herculean feats, so why not give it one more try? Anyway, individual darshans were so delicious.

That day I heard that Kailash had closed down permanently, less than two weeks after I had left. Perhaps the worst was over, and some good things were to follow.

Chapter Six
EARLY DAYS IN POONA

Though Bhagwan had started to attract many Westerners in Bombay, it was in Poona that he was to become world-famous — and notorious. He moved to Poona in March, 1974, taking up residence in a large and handsome house that had been designed by a Western architect with tropical needs in mind. The house had five bedrooms, and sat in two acres of dark brown soil. There was scarcely a tree or shrub growing in this soil, apart from a huge almond tree.

As soon as I had recovered my money and airline ticket, I went to this new house, where Bhagwan was due to give me my morning darshan out on the lawn. His brown velvet chair, an elaborate chaise longue, was out on the grass already. Laxmi was bustling about, giving orders as usual. "Bhagwan is due to come out," she said, "so we must hide inside until he has sat down. Then he will call you."

Five minutes later Vivek came in to fetch me, her eyes squinting from the bright early morning sun. "He wants to see you now," she said excitedly. "It's your turn." I went outside. Bhagwan sat languidly in the chair, dressed in one of his new pure white robes. I thought he seemed tired and world-weary. A small group of Indian and Western sannyasis sat around him. I sat down on the grass to one side of Bhagwan's chair. The dew on the grass dampened my clothes to a dark orange.

"So, Shiva," he said. "Still hungry?" There was a bowl of apples at his feet. "Take an apple!"

Then he turned to the other people assembled there and said: "Shiva likes food! Good, Shiva, you have lost weight, that's good, you look better. Hmmm, now you are planning to do what?"

This was a major change. Instead of Bhagwan telling me what to do, he was asking me about my plans. I hesitated and looked down at the grass. What *did* I really want to do?

"Well, I would like to go to Scotland and work with my father, and maybe open an ashram there." Questions followed, about my father, Scotland, the clinic, Kailash, my travels, together with a great many hmmms which held more meaning than anything he actually said. Teertha had mentioned to me that very morning that he had told Bhagwan how well I had managed at Kailash, and what an important role I had fulfilled there. Bhagwan had apparently pricked up his ears. Now he was double-checking the story from my perspective.

Bhagwan now turned to talk to another guest. I sat near his chair, and drifted off into that beautiful silent space I had found at Kailash. I felt that Bhagwan was in that space with me, that there was no separation in this enchanted time. When I had been in his presence before there had always been an urgent question, an anxiety. This was a new experience, and a sublime one.

After ten minutes Bhagwan looked at me again and asked a simple question about my health. He seemed to be assessing me with all his fine sensors; the question was merely a formality. He seemed satisfied, and moved on to speak to someone else. I knew that he sensed my quiet reality, and that I could feel him there. After a while, seemingly having considered the sum of his communication with me, he came back to me.

"Hmmm, Shiva. The climate in Poona does not suit my body. Next week I am returning to Bombay. I would like you to stay on here in Poona and run this house as an ashram with Teertha. Teertha tells me you managed very well at Kailash, that it was good there with you. Would you like to help run this place? Scotland needs an ashram, and Shiva will open it. But first, stay in Poona."

I was thrilled. What an opportunity! This would be far better than Scotland. I got on well with Teertha and he was a man I respected enormously.

Bhagwan continued. "Hmmm. You get along with Teertha? Yes, it will be good. He will be Kulpati (Chancellor) and you can be Ek-Kulpati (Vice-Chancellor) of my new ashram. OK?"

The following day I received a letter from my father, asking me if I would let him know for certain whether I was coming to help him run his successful alternative medicine clinic in Edinburgh. I wrote back immediately, saying that my plans to come home had changed yet again. Bhagwan's orders came first.

"Dearest Pa (I wrote),

Your letter hit me like a cyclone, having seen Bhagwan the day before, who said 'Stay in Poona'. A lot of impressions and feelings came up, and have continued to do so. My immediate feeling is to pack my rucksack and come straight away. Home is very tempting, with the good food, good climate, good worthwhile and rewarding work, a good car, and above all the learning experience it could be working with Pa and Leslie (my uncle). My allegiance lies I don't know where — I find myself saying things like, well, Pa doesn't need me that badly, and/or Bhagwan will send me back in two months anyway. Or will he? Also, I alternately intensely distrust Bhagwan, and then see him as part of God realised . . . But right now, my centre says, stay with Bhagwan. I've stuck with him through three months at the farm and things are just fitting into place . . ."

It was very hard, being with Bhagwan. We sannyasis were constantly changing our plans as a result of his contradictory orders, at the same time coping with our individual and irrational love affairs with the man. No one knew from one minute to the next what Bhagwan would do, what he would decide, where he would send you. In the event he did not return to Bombay after two weeks — he was to stay in Poona for seven years — so I asked to see him again.

"How is Scotland at this time of year?" he asked. "It will be good, hmmm, you go there now, open an ashram, continue the Work. When it is running well, you come back. OK?"

It was like a bombshell. I had just written to my father, and had geared myself up to staying in Poona for the foreseeable future. There was no doubt that he was playing one of his games, yet it was the most exciting game around. Where else would I find such a family, such girls, such magical, mysterious teachings, or be in the presence of somebody so extraordinary, so different?

So I went back to Scotland, and spent the next seven months working at my father's clinic, at the same time setting up an ashram devoted to Bhagwan's work. To give my father credit, he never once intimated that I was mad or being brainwashed as many parents do when their children go off to follow a strange cult. I later heard that he envied me my ability to go to India, to be free. It was something he would like to have done himself, but he was always too security-minded. In a sense, perhaps, I did it for him, led the sort of life that he would have liked to lead.

Though I worked hard at the clinic and at establishing the ashram, I became aware of an increasing homesickness for Bhagwan and India.

Wary of this illusion — I remembered those 120 degree days at

Kailash when I was homesick for Scotland — I resolved that if I did go back to India it would be for at least a year. I felt that I should make it a make or break effort, and cope as best as I could with dysentery, hepatitis and the rest of the legion of potentially lethal diseases. I had to see whether there was anything left for me in this connection with Bhagwan, and I could feel the balance tipping in the direction of returning to India as soon as possible.

Meanwhile, mysterious things continued to happen. I received a letter from a lady in Japan, who wrote in very neat handwriting and excellent English that Bhagwan was not the man he made himself out to be. Under the guise of advancing her spiritual knowledge he had actually raped her, and as a result she had become pregnant. She was sure that the resulting child would be deformed or even evil as a result of its traumatic conception. I did not know what to make of this at all, but only two days later I received a letter from Laxmi in Poona, saying that a Japanese woman was making libellous accusations about Bhagwan.

The truth of the matter, as Laxmi told it, was that this woman had been alone with Bhagwan in Bombay, but his energy had been too much for her. As a result she had become crazy and was now making wild accusations, and I was to pay no attention to her rantings. But my mind went straight back to that little Indian man in the Hanging Gardens who said "Your guru is not the right guru: he is sleeping with his lady disciples."

As autumn came, I wrote to Bhagwan from Edinburgh to ask when I could come back. I also asked what I should do about the 'running meditation' he had prescribed. Bhagwan had told me to run for one hour a day as my meditation, but I discovered that forty minutes was my absolute limit. Back came a letter from Laxmi. "Come whenever you are ready," it said. "Run for forty minutes, but come!"

I needed no further inducement. Within days of receiving that letter I was arranging air tickets and flights to Bombay. After arriving at Bombay, I took a night taxi ride to Poona through a two-hour meteor storm. During the time I had been away, many alterations had been made to Bhagwan's house and gardens in Poona. A huge lecture hall had been erected, which Bhagwan had named after the Chinese sage Chuang Tzu, and the wealthier sannyasis had been putting money into designing and planting a prolific new garden. A few hours before I arrived, however, this new lecture hall had collapsed in a thunderous roar of cracking concrete and severed steel.

The new beautifully-planned garden was enveloped by a thick layer of white dust. Thankfully, nobody was in the hall at the time. Bhagwan was furious, and in a message to Laxmi pointed out at great length that the auditorium had fallen as a result of the many dire predictions made about it by the Western disciples, particularly those, like Teertha, who had engineering backgrounds. It was all due to their 'negativity', he kept saying. In his message, Bhagwan made no mention at all of the patently deficient architectural design, nor that in the absence of adequate cement the hall had been built with a mixture of sand and cement that was not much stronger than a child's sandcastle.

Apart from this, it seemed as if Poona was suiting Bhagwan's 'body' after all. After much hunting, Laxmi had found this mansion, situated on the hill station the British made famous during their occupation of India. Laxmi had offered the owner eight hundred thousand rupees for the house before she knew the asking price, promising him a cash deal. Back in Bombay, she could not find the enormous stash of thousand-rupee notes she had buried in the front garden, but the rich disciples — mainly Mukta — donated the money, and the deal went through. It was only later that we learnt that the asking price had only been seven hundred thousand rupees. Though Laxmi thought she had made a bargain, she had in fact overpaid by at least a hundred thousand rupees. That was Laxmi for you!

When I returned to Poona it was December, and Bhagwan was having his birthday celebrations. Though his birthday was later officially fixed as December 11th, 1931, nobody at that stage, not even Bhagwan's mother, could remember exactly the day, or even the year, when he was born. Before I left Scotland I had received a huge shopping list from Teertha of things to bring back for himself and for Bhagwan. They were not exactly what you might think of as appropriate gifts for a guru, including the finest French brandy, chocolates, and a large piece of Chinese jade for Bhagwan's new cufflinks. This was the beginning of a new collecting phase. He had already been through pens and gold watches, was now on to cufflinks, and would end with Rolls Royces. Teertha also asked me to bring him a box of Roman Catholic altar charcoal to aid in the burning of incense, a set of pen refills for Bhagwan's Duponts, and a large packet of biological washing powder. I managed to get everything apart from the jade, which was not available in Scotland at a price that I was willing to pay.

After driving all night through the meteor storm, I arrived very early the next morning and made my way to Bhagwan's house, 33 Koregaon Park, only to be told by the Nepali servant that it was now permanently closed. It was clearly open. I was instructed instead to go to another house, number 17, which Laxmi had recently purchased for Bhagwan as an extension to the original property.

Teertha was there, waiting for me. He accepted the gifts from Scotland, but seemed unusually depressed. He told me that Bhagwan blamed him personally for the collapse of the Chuang Tzu auditorium. As Teertha was clearly in no mood for a friendly conversation, I went to have breakfast in Poona. When I returned later in the day I saw that the Poona ashram had doubled in size while I had been away. Laxmi had bought the house adjoining the original mansion, and Bhagwan had named it Krishna House. About ten disciples were already living semi-permanently in this new house, and all the rickshaw and taxi drivers now knew where 'Bhagwan's Ashram' was. Previously they had not heard of Koregaon Park, let alone of Rajneesh.

I soon discovered that many other changes had happened during my absence. Mukta, the wealthy Greek lady who had given Laxmi most of the money to buy the Poona house when Laxmi could not find her hidden fortune, was now personally in charge of giving darshan appointments to Westerners. These were being held in the evenings rather than in the early mornings, in the carport of Bhagwan's house, which was now called Lao Tzu. About ten people attended these each evening, when Bhagwan would ask those assembled if they had any questions. When my turn came, he asked me: "Shiva, this time are you staying long?"

So he knew I had come back for good. "Yes Bhagwan, long."

"Good, it will be long, stay now. Anything to say?"

"Well," I said, "I would like to be in my heart, to feel my heart more."

He knew what I meant. "How long is it since you have felt your heart?"

This question caught me by surprise. How long had it been? Since my mother had died three years previously, or before that? "I think it is a long time," I answered.

"Yes, I am also thinking it is a long time. Hmmmm. Do you know how to stand on your head?"

"Yes."

"Good. Stand on your head then."

I stared at him in disbelief. Did he mean *now*, in front of all these people? "Yes, now, stand on your head."

Horrors! True to Bhagwan's previous edict I was wearing nothing under my orange robe. I glanced at two elderly and distinguished-looking lady visitors sitting in the corner. How could I do a headstand without causing offence? How could I let Bhagwan know of my dilemma? I took the plunge. "Bhagwan, ahhh, I have no underpants on, and . . ."

"Don't worry," he said airily. "It will be OK, go ahead make sirsahsan (headstand)." I made a cautious headstand, and was grateful that my robe caught modestly at my knees. "Good, good," said Bhagwan. "Your energy is moving well, I can see that. Headstand will be good for you. Hmmm, do headstand for three minutes every night before sleep, OK? And one other thing, hmmm," he added, steepling his hands. "You have received much. Now the time has come to give, and start work. See Laxmi, she will give you work."

Bhagwan gave a quick nod to Laxmi, who was sitting primly beside his chair. She caught my eye conspiratorially.

And so it was that I came to spend the next eight years with Bhagwan, working for him, virtually never leaving his side, being part of the privileged inner circle of his ashram.

I had no doubt now that I had come home. Scotland, my father's clinic, my profession of osteopathy, all faded away, and I sensed in that instant that I would not leave Bhagwan for a very long time. It felt so good to be back with Bhagwan. He was such a Master. He knew everything; his perception was uncanny. When he had said "Now you stay long" it was as though he knew my innermost thoughts, and could open the door to my heart. In the following years many thousands of people were to seek him out, and it was his ability to perceive a person so accurately, to see what they really wanted, what they really thought, that was his single most admired quality. It did not matter how difficult or involved a situation might be, or how unfamiliar he was with a problem or a relationship. He would ponder on it for a few minutes and then come up with the brilliant, the perfect, solution.

A new direction was already apparent. In Bombay the emphasis had been on personal relationships, but now it was on Work with a capital 'W', the setting up of a new and large commune. I asked

Laxmi what work she had in store for me, and found it was to be tape copying. I was to make duplicate cassettes of Bhagwan's lectures. This work was carried out on a large balcony on the first floor of Lao Tzu House, where Bhagwan gave his discourses each morning. His intention was to move to the larger Chuang Tzu auditorium as soon as it was rebuilt.

Every morning, just before eight o'clock, about a hundred people, two-thirds Indian, would file into Bhagwan's house to hear him talk. A raised dais had been made by covering two coffee tables with an attractive Indian print cotton quilt. A small step had been put there to make Bhagwan's ascent easier. He had changed his style of dress from the lunghi and shawl, and was now wearing pure white robes that were very tight-fitting, and made it difficult for him to walk more than a short step at a time.

He himself looked very different from when I had seen him last. Mukta had discontinued her practice of dyeing his hair, and whereas before it had been jet black, it was now predominantly white. This white hair made Bhagwan look far older and more venerable than his forty-four years.

Not all was love and peace. About a week after I arrived, a young American woman started screaming and flailing about on the floor during Bhagwan's morning lecture. Teertha and I immediately got up to carry her out, not an easy task as she was heavy and kept thrashing about. Bhagwan stopped talking at once, and indicated that we should bring this woman to his feet. We laid her so that her shoulders and head were on the cloth-covered dais. Bhagwan gently reached down and placed a hand on the woman's head, saying a few soothing words as he did so. At the same time, he slipped a sandal off one of his feet, and placed the foot very gently on the woman's shoulder. The result was electrifying. The woman stopped sobbing, and became serenely quiet, though as soon as Bhagwan restarted his lecture she started to sob noisily again. Bhagwan looked across at me to ask me to take her out, and she screamed all the way to the rear of the house. The next day she was perfectly calm, and remained so. Her inner storm had blown itself out.

Then there was the occasion that Laxmi herself was viciously attacked. An Indian man to whom she had repeatedly refused darshan attacked her as she was going back to Lao Tzu after a long evening's work at nearby Krishna House. He had been lying in wait for her in some bushes, and as she passed he leapt out and fastened his teeth on her nose. This is a traditional Indian response to somebody who has offended your honour, and the time-honoured punishment for an unfaithful wife. Laxmi struggled and tried to scream out "Bhagwan! Bhagwan!" Luckily an Indian disciple heard her and went to her rescue. A doctor was called immediately she was inside Lao Tzu House. Her nose was badly penetrated, and she had to have an anti-tetanus injection and stay in bed for a few days.

But the next day her irrepressible high spirits had reasserted themselves. "What's a nose, child?" she said to me when I was summoned to her room. "It is *him* that is important, not Laxmi's body, only *him*. And now *he* has given Laxmi a new toy, a bodyguard. Shiva is to be Laxmi's bodyguard. Laxmi told *him* that she did not need a bodyguard, but *he* insisted, and who are we to argue? But it is *he*, not Laxmi, who needs a bodyguard. Laxmi is not so important. *He* is the important one. Without *him* nothing can happen. So, Shiva, Laxmi has been given a beautiful gift, such a strong good-looking man, but Laxmi does not need such a gift. It is for *him* that you will be bodyguard. You will start at darshan tonight, OK? Come to darshan to guard him!"

That was how I became Bhagwan's bodyguard. I was overjoyed at the news. No, that was an understatement — I was on top of the world. What greater gift could any sannyasi be given than to go to every darshan and every lecture? Could it really be true? Would such a dream really materialise, and if it did happen, would it last, or be merely a passing allocation?

That night I began my new job of bodyguard to Bhagwan. There seemed little possibility of trouble inside the carport, but I was aware of prying eyes on the outside, gazing through the latticework garden fence to peer at the strange sight within. As dusk fell every evening, the orange-clad sannyasis would fill the porch and listen to their white-robed guru. It made quite a sight. Whenever I detected a presence I would get up and wander over to the fence. I made a makeshift weapon — a short club — out of the shaft of a pickaxe, and kept it in a potted plant out of Bhagwan's sight, just in case somebody did come over the fence. It was the primitive start of a security system that ten years later culminated in hundreds of highly-trained guards carrying submachine guns.

In Bombay, Bhagwan had had a Gurkha bodyguard who had carried a formidable mountain man's knife. I felt that to do my job as effectively as possible, I should at least have something with which to

combat an attacker with a similar weapon. I was not sure what part
weapons played in Bhagwan's work at this time, since he preached
non-violence. Though I had tried to keep the club hidden, several
people got to know about it. One day Vivek asked me about the club.
Was I sure I really needed it? Bhagwan had said that I looked like a
samurai warrior sitting there. I said I thought I did need it. I wasn't
sure whether Bhagwan had asked Vivek to question me about the
club; you could never tell — she had a very close and delicate
relationship with him. Maybe Bhagwan did not want me to have the
club there, or maybe he did. I decided that since it was for his
protection, I would keep it.

A week later Vivek showed me a letter from an American disciple
who had complained about the club. This disciple had just come from
a political rally in the States where he had seen police brandishing
such weapons freely, and had been horrified to see one in Bhagwan's
ashram, the last place on Earth he would have expected it. "So no
club then?" I said to Vivek. She nodded happily and emphatically.
This was Bhagwan's way of telling me to do away with the potential
weapon. Then Vivek gave me a new order. "Shiva, from today,
whenever Laxmi gives you any task to do, or you hear any
information that might in any way affect Bhagwan adversely, I want
you to find me right away and tell me. Is that clear?" Yes, I said, it
was, thinking not for the first time what a very beautiful woman
Vivek was. She spoke in an upper-class English accent, and exuded
class.

Many other disciples envied my new job. Several people asked me
if I knew why I had been chosen, but I had no definite idea. I thought
it might have something to do with the way I had coped with the
screaming American girl when only Teertha and I had moved, or
perhaps the way I had stood on my head in darshan, but really I could
not fathom it out. Nobody knew the real source of any of Bhagwan's
inspirations.

In Bombay everybody had talked freely about their relationship
with Bhagwan, and gossip was condoned and encouraged. Now a new
phase of secrecy was starting, and it began with those women who
had been called to 'special darshans'. Laxmi called together all the
women who had been so honoured and told them they must never
talk to anybody else about it. It would create endless jealousy and
misunderstanding. The women were to realise that 'special darshans'
were a great honour, a blessing, and that not everybody would be

called to them. It had been the strangest experience for me in
Bombay to have almost every woman I slept with lean over at some
point and say "You'll never guess who *I* slept with last week!". At
first I had had no idea, but the experience was repeated so often that
I came to know exactly what the revelation would be. "I've no idea,"
I would say. "Beats me."

"Well, you mustn't tell anybody, but I slept with *him*"

Within a month of starting my new job I moved up to sit beside
Bhagwan himself. I had soon come to realise that not all the trouble
would come from without, and that there were quite a few disciples
who could easily flip and attack Bhagwan during darshan. One
evening, when Bhagwan came out from his room, I sat close to his
chair on the right-hand side. Bhagwan asked me what I was doing
there. I explained that there had been some pretty strange characters
coming to darshan recently, and I thought it would be better if I sat
closer.

Bhagwan looked at me wonderingly, almost accusingly. "Some
pretty strange characters," he repeated, mimicking my delivery. "So
you want to sit there to protect me, hmmm?"

"Yes, I thought it would be better." I wasn't at all sure at this stage
whether it was my duty to protect him seriously, or whether my
function was more ornamental. "OK," he said at last, "we will try.
Shiva, you can sit there for a few days. We will see, we will see."

The ashram was expanding all the time. There was still no real
wealth compared to that which was amassed later. The property had
been bought, and the running expenses were paid for almost entirely
out of donations. At the beginning of the Poona period there were no
therapy classes, and no objects for sale. Whenever new disciples
came, Laxmi would coolly assess them to find out how wealthy they
were and what their background was. She revealed this information
to Bhagwan immediately before the person concerned came for their
first darshan. Bhagwan certainly favoured the rich and influential.
Laxmi was constantly checking out new properties with a view to
further expansion, and Bhagwan would often turn to me and ask my
opinion about a proposed new property he knew I had looked at with
Laxmi.

After the morning lecture was over, I would spend my days sitting
with Laxmi in what she called her 'cabin', a smallish office in Krishna
House that was the nerve centre of the emerging commune. I
continued to meditate, and on several occasions reached that true

bliss and abundant joy which come from a deep meditative state. This meditative space was incomparably beautiful, and worth anything to experience. Those who dismiss 'evil cults' have no idea at all how rapturous this state can be, and how no other pleasure can begin to compare with it. Most people who have spent any time in a religious cult will have tasted this bliss, and it is what keeps them coming back for more. Whenever I touched a deeper sense of peace I knew I could have no greater happiness, and during this time at Poona it began to happen more and more often.

The early group darshans, held in the gathering dusk, were very intimate experiences. You shared your innermost thoughts, dreams and fantasies with other sannyasis, who immediately understood what you were trying to express. This sharing made the community cohesive, open and honest. We were all in this together, we loved one another, we shared our most intimate feelings. Most of the darshans were now taken as groups, but sometimes a specially favoured person would be allowed to ask a question in relative privacy. They would meet Bhagwan before the group arrived for darshan, when Bhagwan would be accompanied only by his intimate foursome — Mukta, Laxmi, Vivek and myself. Often the questions asked would be acutely personal or explicitly sexual.

As the ashram grew in size, many different groups sprang up, some from the burgeoning human potential movement, others from more Eastern traditions. One of the very first Eastern groups to be set up was the tantra group, where naked people would experiment sexually with each other, often making love with one another and changing partners in full view of everybody else. The group went on for at least five days. Looking at some of the pictures of these groups, they might seem pornographic, but this was not how they felt to us at the time. We were exploring a new dimension, the sexual one, in a way we never had done before, and it was a tremendous liberation.

Bhagwan explained carefully how he understood the ancient doctrine of tantra. The difference between valley orgasms and peak orgasms was particularly important, the former being infinitely more satisfying both physically and spiritually. For men, the art was to delay, or preferably avoid, ejaculation, but to stay very close to it, thus maintaining and extending the sexual experience. The whole point was to stay in that special zone just below the peak, so that both partners could attain a very deep sense of stillness and inner calm without hurry, worry or stress. It was thus the man's duty to bring the woman to orgasm several times while he restrained himself. Once this state was attained, Bhagwan said that it should be possible to make love for hours, and be in a state of profound meditation all the time. As soon as the man ejaculated, the meditative state came to an end and all was over. In 1974 and 1975 Bhagwan's lectures went on about this so much that he rapidly earned himself the sobriquet 'The Guru of the Vagina'.

Though Bhagwan placed so much emphasis on the physical side of sex, he was by all accounts hardly the world's greatest lover himself. Like so many who set themselves up as sexologists, his own sex life left much to be desired.

Many of the women Bhagwan slept with told me that far from practising what he preached and making sex last for an hour or more, it was often all over in a couple of minutes. He would, I was reliably informed, get on top of women in the traditional missionary position, enter her, then come almost immediately. Most of his sexual pleasure seemed to lie in foreplay and voyeurism rather than in active performance. Sometimes he would ask attractive women to strip off in front of him and lie naked while he peered at them intently. Then, after satisfying himself, he would ask them to get dressed again. He also had couples make love in front of him, a definite case of voyeurism.

Sheela, who first met Bhagwan in about 1972, boasted about her own sexual involvement with Bhagwan. It did not take the form of sexul intercourse, but she described how she would sit at his feet while he put his hands inside her dress and played with her breasts. That was apparently as far as it went.

As I had feared, my elevated position as Bhagwan's bodyguard did not remain unchallenged for long. One night in darshan an American disciple asked Bhagwan if he could also offer his services as a bodyguard. He pointed out that he was a martial arts expert, and thus well suited for the job. At the time I had no training in these skills, and suddenly felt acutely inadequate. Bhagwan looked at the sannyasi for a minute, then said "There will be no need for you to bother." I gave an inward sigh of relief.

Once, a Dutchman aged about thirty became very angry in darshan, having been instructed to go back to Holland to start an ashram and sort things out with his wife. The man continued to shout his bellicose invective at Bhagwan for four or five minutes, during which Bhagwan sat perfectly still and relaxed. I was ready to go into action at any second. Bhagwan calmly allowed the man to finish his diatribe, remaining completely unruffled. Then, as if nothing whatsoever had happened, Bhagwan quietly asked the man a few questions about his future plans. All the anger seemed to have gone out of the Dutchman, and he answered the questions meekly, factually and calmly. For the rest of the darshan Bhagwan showed no sign that he had just been given a prolonged verbal lashing. When the darshan was over, Bhagwan turned to the Dutchman. "You, swami, anything to say now? Is everything clear now?" I was astonished that he was prodding the hornet's nest again, but the anger had all evaporated, and the Dutchman nodded his agreement that everything was indeed now clear. Bhagwan floated out, a serene smile on his radiant face. He seemed to have no fear of anybody.

I knew, though, that people would come who would be bigger, stronger or faster than me. I started to train in karate so that I could protect my Master better, but above all I resolved that I would do everything I could to remain as alert as possible the whole time, then any attacker would have to get past me first. It seemed to work, since for many years there was no attack on Bhagwan himself. I seemed to have an intuitive sense of when there was danger in the air, and usually managed to pre-empt it. There were at least three attempts to attack Bhagwan when I was not there, and it was hardly surprising that he was at risk, considering that he was preaching such seditious ideas and dealing with such volatile people.

We were busy building and extending the ashram, starting more and more groups, feeding and looking after a fast-growing community. We were busy all the time, but what did Bhagwan do all day? After his morning lecture he would spend the rest of the day reading books in his room. He was such a fast reader that he could sometimes get through fifteen books in a day. He lived almost in isolation, like a hermit, which allowed him the time and space to replenish himself, like a powerful generator charging a huge psychic battery.

He seemed to be drawing out the power and wisdom of the many books he read, so that when he gave lectures or darshans, all the energy which had accumulated during his periods of isolation would shower forth in a firework display of wit, perception and clarity. It seemed, however, that there was a limit to his powers, especially in the evening, since after about ninety minutes he would seem to become exhausted, to wilt and become an ordinary mortal again.

When this happened he would summarily end the darshan, and impatiently brush off the poor souls who may have been waiting weeks to ask the Master their vitally important questions.

Bhagwan never travelled and never left the ashram, and probably as a result developed an ample waistline during this period. He sometimes used to stick his finger down his throat and vomit after eating. I thought he might be wanting to lose a bit of weight, but Laxmi explained the practice in terms of energy: "Energy is going *up*. Now with *him*, *his* energy is so fine that even digested food, which goes down, is affecting him. So vomiting happens in the body which makes food and energy go correct again — *up!*"

It was my job to set down Bhagwan's chair just before the evening darshan. It had to be placed in exactly the right position. A few inches to the right or left would not do. His official staff was increasing in numbers. After my first month in Poona, an Australian woman named Maneesha was given the task of resident observer, commentator, and editor of the darshan diaries. She was also assigned the job of keeping mosquitoes off the Master's chair. This she did far more delicately than Bhagwan, who until then had merely flicked his towel at them with devastating effect.

Other people started having permanent posts. Mukta became his gardener, and would go off in a rickshaw once or twice a week to a large garden centre, Pochas Seeds, in Poona, and spend a fortune buying exotic plants to enrich the brown and barren plot. Footpaths were planned, and Bhagwan himself took a great interest in the emergent garden. A disciple who had recently returned from Japan was given the job of building a 'Zen path'. This had to be constructed with special stones, which were sought in the nearby hills.

One of Mukta's three daughters would follow Bhagwan around with her camera as he made his tours of inspection, taking photographs all the time. Bhagwan still wanted as much publicity as possible. An Indian disciple took pictures of Bhagwan for Indian publications, and while I was acting as bodyguard I also took some photographs with my little Instamatic of Bhagwan as he wandered through the garden. It was typical of India that I got the photographs back from my uncle in Scotland faster than the professional photographers could have theirs processed in Bombay. When I showed Bhagwan my pictures he was impressed, and asked Mukta's daughter to provide me with a 'real camera' for my next session. Before long, I had the job of photographer added to my list of official positions, and soon had my work published in Bhagwan's books.

As soon as I started taking pictures of Bhagwan, I realised that his 'photographic' face was quite different from the one we usually saw. Mukta's daughter, who had up to that time been his 'official' photographer, told me that Bhagwan thought his nose was too long, and that he did not like his baldness. He was very emphatic that he wanted his body kept out of the photographs; he was only interested in carefully-posed portraits. As he explained to me later, it was really only his eyes that he wanted to have photographed, and his eyes were truly extraordinary: huge, hypnotic and lustrous. I discovered that a telephoto lens had the effect of foreshortening Bhagwan's nose. He thoroughly approved of the resulting portraits, and this revelation earned my promotion to being his personal photographer. I began to work in the darkroom when Laxmi did not need me.

Mukta's daughter wore a wide-brimmed straw hat to one of her photographic sessions, and this took Bhagwan's fancy. We took a few shots of him wearing it, and this started the hat craze. He ordered a variety of hats to be brought to the next session, and from that day on he was always photographed wearing a hat. This new addition pleased him immensely — he had finally discovered an effective way of hiding his bald pate. Later on a sannyasi was employed full-time to create these photogenic props.

Almost imperceptibly the rules started tightening up. One of the earliest changes was that Bhagwan no longer wanted more than three people photographing him in any one session. An American sannyasi who was also a photographer had recently returned to Poona. His name was Krishna Barti, always shortened to KB, and he was sharing an apartment with me about half a mile from Bhagwan's house. One day he turned up at the gate of Bhagwan's house and demanded admittance to a session. There were already three photographers there, and although I knew it would create problems, I told him about Bhagwan's ruling. He was not, however, prepared to take orders from me, so first he found Laxmi, who confirmed that he should listen to me, and then Vivek. Vivek had apparently not heard Bhagwan's ruling on the issue, and agreed with KB that it was probably a power game on my part. But it was now too late anyway — the session had begun.

When I next met KB he accused me of fabricating restrictions. An argument ensued, in the course of which he made it very clear that I was no longer welcome to stay at the flat I was sharing with him and his Italian girlfriend Deeksha, who was later to play such an important part in commune life. As of this moment, he informed me, I could get out. I went back, packed my bags, and left.

This meant I had nowhere to live. That evening, before people started coming for darshan, Bhagwan turned to me with a mischievous grin on his face. "So, Shiva, now you have no place to live, hmmm? I have heard what happened this morning." He chuckled and said: "What you did was good." He turned to Laxmi, ever attentive by his side, and asked her to find me a place to live inside the ashram. The next day, Laxmi moved me into a tent on the roof of Krishna House. I was delighted at this new turn of events, as it meant I was now accepted into the heart of the commune. Was this episode yet another example of how Bhagwan harnessed events, how he precipitated change through conflict?

We had our own monthly in-house magazine at Poona — the *Neo Sannyas*. Bhagwan was always very concerned about his public image, and when the Indian photographer used a picture of sannyasis meditating in the monsoon mud on the front cover, Bhagwan immediately summoned Laxmi. From now on, Bhagwan stipulated, only pictures of himself were to be used on the cover. Two months later the same Indian photographer was in trouble again for publishing a centrefold of the wedding of two of Bhagwan's most famous Indian disciples, the movie director Vijayanda and his beloved, the ravishingly beautiful actress Goldie. Laxmi called the photographer in, and told him that on no account was he to publish any photograph in any publication whatsoever unless Bhagwan had expressly approved it. The only full page photographs that were to appear were those of Bhagwan himself. No ordinary disciple could take up more than a third of a page. From then on Bhagwan maintained total control over editorial and artistic matters.

In spite of these events, the ashram was still a very relaxed place. The only people who could afford to stay in Poona for any length of time were those people who were either independently wealthy, or who had been given bed and board by Laxmi.

More professional people started arriving. A graphic artist and layout man came from England, and he was immediately given the task of producing the first English darshan diary, a book to be called *Hammer on the Rock*. This was intended to be an image for the difficulty Bhagwan had in getting his disciples to understand things without metaphorically banging them over the head.

Bhagwan asked me to choose two more photographers for the next session, an invitation I extended to the graphic artist. He was curiously reluctant to accept, and I found out why when we relaxed over a glass of cheap Indian wine later that day. The graphic artist, who had been named Yatri and was about ten years older than most of us, described how earlier that day he had meticulously scrubbed up with scentless soap and gone to see Bhagwan in a clean new robe. Bhagwan had outlined his ideas for new furniture, but then for the next thirty minutes kept changing his mind as to what he wanted. "Jesus," the artist said, "he couldn't even decide what height to make anything! After half an hour he kept turning to Vivek to ask her opinion, and as soon as she gave her views he'd change his mind again. I can't believe what a mess he's in when he's on his own."

The next morning we arrived for the session. Bhagwan came in and sat down in his chair, carrying an air of urgency with him. Yatri was summoned to his side, and Vivek was despatched to fetch a huge Salvador Dali publication, a book with an impressive solid gold cover. Yatri knelt down to hear Bhagwan describe exactly how he wanted the book. Bhagwan went on for a full forty minutes as Yatri began sweating profusely from the tropical heat and the concentration Bhagwan was demanding of him. Yatri looked more and more desperate as Bhagwan meticulously detailed his wishes for five new books, never wavering or changing his mind once.

Then, as Bhagwan finished and got up to leave, he turned to Yatri and said: "By the way, forget everything I have told you, OK? Do whatever you like!" As soon as Bhagwan was out of sight Yatri collapsed on the floor, exhausted.

All the time that Bhagwan had been speaking I had been taking pictures, and three weeks later I showed Yatri the photographs I had taken of him gnawing his fingernails in anguish. Yatri sent a framed set of them in to Bhagwan, who returned them, signed 'To Yatri with love'. This incident was typical of Bhagwan's methods.

The upstairs floor of Krishna House was occupied by the residential sannyasis, who passed the time playing cards, reading coffee table books, and sipping tall glasses of fresh iced lime juice. Few clothes were worn, and all the Westerners became very suntanned. Whenever the residents became bored, they would go to the Blue Diamond, the local four-star hotel, for a meal and a swim in the pool. By mid-1975, about fifteen people were working in the ashram six hours a day, six days a week, in return for their bed and board.

The resident staff needed feeding, so Laxmi hired a cook. He was not exactly a *cordon bleu* chef, and produced the blandest and most unappetising food imaginable. We had rice and lentils twice a day, every day, with vegetables thrown in very occasionally. After three months of this, Haridas, the ashram gourmet, went to Laxmi to complain about the food. She did not listen to him. She said the cook was well-paid, that he was given a generous budget, and that we were to blame, as foreigners, for being used to such gross eating habits in the West. We were in India now.

Laxmi was completely the wrong person to have been put in charge of the kitchens. She had no interest in food herself and was almost anorexic. But the food was so bad that it couldn't go on. Haridas mounted a petition which was passed round. We were to sign it and add our own comments about the food. I did not mince my words. 'They feed pigs better than this in Scotland,' I wrote. Teertha, even more diplomatic since the collapse of the auditorium, had become ever more obsequious and was the only sannyasi who refused to sign.

Two days later we were all summoned to Laxmi's cabin. "Bhagwan has told me to tell you that if anyone does not like the food, they are welcome to leave today," she announced. "He told me to tell you that he was enormously distressed at your ungrateful attitude. He has provided the best possible for you. *At all times* you are to remember how fortunate you are to have been given the honour of living in his ashram. Is that understood? He wants no more complaints of this sort, ever again. Is that clear?

Yet only a month later, Laxmi discovered for herself that the cook had been embezzling three quarters of the money she had been giving him to buy our food. A new cook was promptly installed—and a few weeks later turned bright yellow with infectious hepatitis. He went to tell Laxmi that he was going home to recover, but she would hear none of it. "Nonsense," she snapped. "You have to carry on with your work." In the West the cook would immediately have been put in solitary confinement.

Within the next few months, several disciples went down with hepatitis. The victims included Bhagwan's new editorial assistant, Maneesha. Bhagwan was quite unconcerned. A few years later Bhagwan was to say in his morning lecture: "There are two types of hepatitis—the one you catch, and the one I give you!"

While all this was going on, the various 'human potential' groups proliferated. Teertha, who had formerly led an Encounter Group Centre in London, was instructed by Bhagwan to start leading an encounter group here. He was reluctant, but of course acted on orders. One night he came up to my tent on Krishna House and said: "Shiva, do you think you could have a look at my arm? I think it's broken." It was. His new girlfriend had managed to fracture his forearm. It had happened in an encounter group when he was trying to protect his head while his girlfriend hit him in a fit of jealousy. Her blows had been so violent that, combined with our malnutrition, they had resulted in a broken bone.

It wasn't long before more bones were broken in encounter groups. New disciples were sent to these groups as part of their 'opening up' process, and though they were intensely feared, they were also enormously popular. There were more broken bones than the hospital had ever seen before, yet within the ashram community the trauma was accepted as ultimately 'good'. It seemed that there was some kind of release and relaxation when a bone was broken, triggering the letting go of deep-seated tensions. The local hospital, however, became extremely suspicious, and we had to invent stories to explain the casualties. To avert police interference, the hospital took to filling out police forms with such euphemisms as 'fell off bicycle on way to Shree Rajneesh Ashram' or 'fell off ladder at Shree Rajneesh Ashram'. These groups were the first step in Bhagwan's mission to deal with repressed anger, so that love and meditation could really flourish. The violence thus released often caused fights in encounter groups, yet it was all done in such an environment of trust and mutual understanding that not one lawsuit was filed in all those years.

On certain special days — Bhagwan's birthday, his Enlightenment Day, and the day known in India as 'Guru Poornima', the guru's full moon — Bhagwan would distribute gifts to the specially favoured. Vivek kept a selection of suitable presents in his room. The gifts might be a robe he had worn, a pillowcase, an embroidered towel, and very occasionally a gold watch or pen. Later, vast numbers of cufflink sets were ordered from Bombay and the West. I received a robe and later a set of imitation amber cufflinks. My next gift was a voluminous grey sweater which Bhagwan instructed me to dye orange. I noticed that the sweater was all wool, and made in Scotland. Six months later I was given a dark green towel which I

made into a little altar at the mouth of my tent. These gifts, known as
'prasads', were considered far too precious to use for their original
function.

Bhagwan did love his collecting manias and indulged in them
wholeheartedly. Before he began giving his cufflinks away he must
have collected at least three hundred pairs. Some were of pearls and
precious stones — diamonds, rubies and sapphires. They were all
very ornate. When he began wearing robes without cuff fasteners, he
gave all his cufflinks away. Vivek called Teertha and I and gave us a
matching set of lapis lazuli cufflinks surrounded with diamonds. She
told us that Bhagwan wanted us to have them made into rings, by
which we would always remember him.

Chapter Seven

POONA BECOMES
WORLD FAMOUS

As 1975 drew to a close, there was a tremendous sense of awakening in Poona. It was as if a sleeping giant had been aroused, stretched his long limbs, and was now about to extend himself and show the world what he was made of. More and more people were coming, intending to stay a week but remaining in or near the ashram for years. The English and Germans were the initial leaders, then French and Italians started coming in their hundreds.

Before long, countries outside Europe and America began to hear of Bhagwan. A contingent of Americans from the Arica movement arrived in 1976, and three years later the Japanese started to come in droves — the famous Japanese composer Kitaro was an early disciple. The German musician and composer Deuter, also known as Chaitanya Hari, came to stay.

A very high proportion of these new recruits were professional people — engineers, doctors, lawyers, psychiatrists, authors, architects, artists and craftspeople. Many from the so-called 'New Age' movement came and were intrigued, then sold up everything in the West to live with Bhagwan. Even by mid-1975 the Western contingent had begun to outnumber the Indians.

As the emphasis on work increased, and as therapy groups and workshops began to be set up, there was noticeably less meditation, and many Indians and less dedicated Westerners began to slip away. The card-playing, lime-sipping, lotus-eating days were over, and a new urgency spread through the ashram. Laxmi started instigating massive building projects, and employed dozens of Indian coolies to do the work. They were industrious but illiterate. Their primitive methods made the work horribly slow, and I wondered how long it would be before we sannyasis started doing their work instead. It was not to be very long.

Laxmi gave me my own room in Krishna House, saying "You have deserved it." This meant I did not have to live in a tent on the roof any more. My status was increasing, but my personal relationships were still stormy. One night a gorgeous Californian blonde who looked just like a young Candice Bergen arrived for darshan. Bhagwan called her 'Premda', meaning 'giver of love'. We soon became lovers, and she moved into my new room. It was good for a time, but I soon realised there was an enormous gulf between us, and I asked her to leave. Premda did not want to go. While she was my girlfriend she was entitled to many special privileges within the ashram, such as free entry to lectures and a free food pass — if we split up she would have to pay for everything, just like everyone else. She had very little money, but I was adamant, and she left.

At one o'clock the next morning she leapt through the window of my room and on to my bed. She tore off my new sixty-rupee mosquito net, then proceeded to bite, gouge and beat me for all she was worth. I was very glad I was sleeping alone.

The next day I came back from the morning lecture to find that my precious and newly-potted garden of cacti, morning glory and avocado trees had been flung through my window, smashing their flowerpots, and that graffiti had been written on my walls with a blunt crayon. I was so outraged by what she had done that I was afraid I might do her some damage, so I went to the library to cool off. I emerged two hours later, calmer but still simmering under the surface.

As I walked out of Lao Tzu gate I saw Premda on a barrow with Deeksha and a couple of other women, peeling vegetables. I kept going, but as I passed them I heard Deeksha hiss "Go on, get 'eem!" Premda ran up behind me, pounding her fists into the small of my back. I kept on walking, trying to ignore her. Then she yanked at my long hair. I turned round and pulled one of her arms up behind her back to stop her hurting me, and as I did so there was a gentle but quite definite snap, like a dry twig breaking. She fainted on the spot, her arm hairline fractured at the elbow.

I felt like the bully incarnate as I carried her in my arms to a rickshaw. Gradually she swam back into consciousness, and we embraced gingerly. At the hospital the nurse in emergency met us with a seen-it-all-before smile. "I suppose you fell down at the Shree Rajneesh Ashram?" We nodded. Her fracture soon healed, but our friendship took a long time to recover. Only a few hours after inciting Premda to attack me, Deeksha put a kitchen knife through her hand and severed the tendon to one of her fingers. Surgeons at the local hospital were unable to locate the tendon, and Deeksha's finger has remained crooked to this day. I felt that she had brought this misfortune on herself. It seemed like instant kharma.

By early 1976 the number of people on the ashram staff had more than doubled, and the number of visitors was three hundred per cent up on the previous year. Krishna House was fully occupied, and Laxmi was adding on extra rooms wherever possible. The ashram became like a gigantic rabbit warren. An entire new block was planned with rooms for eighteen more people. Therapy chambers were being excavated in the basement, and concrete dust floated everywhere. Some disciples started to build their own bamboo huts near wells and in the middle of sun-bleached deserted fields. A large palace, once belonging to a Maharajah and now a rooming house, was soon populated by two hundred and fifty sannyasis from all over the world. A self-service cafeteria opened, run by Deeksha, our 220 lb. Italian whirlwind.

The darkroom now had three full-time workers, and Haridas had become the head electrician. He was soon joined on the ashram staff by a full complement of handymen, plumbers, printers, editors and accountants, all united by a common goal—the pursuit of fun, fulfilment, happiness, meditation and enlightenment.

It was at about this time that the ashram's first suicide occurred. An American killed himself by jumping off the roof of a five-storey block of flats around the corner from the ashram. His death was attributed to a sense of deep unhappiness, though just before his suicide I had taken a picture of him at the end of a therapy group, and he had appeared to be one of the happiest people there.

A health centre was established, and as the doctors and medical staff were of many different nationalities, confusion reigned. It was initially staffed by two German physicians, who wrote all their medical notes in their own language. They were soon joined by a Paris trained Iranian doctor and a New Zealand nurse.

By this time I had several quite distinct jobs. My main task was Bhagwan's bodyguard, but I was also Laxmi's bodyguard when the need arose. I took charge of security arrangements inside the for major celebrations, but day-to-day security was now handled New Zealand disciple. I was also Laxmi's high-speed driver who made excursions to Bombay, and I worked in the darkroom and most of the ashram photographs. In addition I was respons Bhagwan's lab tests and medication. The tests involved thric rickshaw trips into the heart of Poona to get his specimens

Once this was done I had to go to the pharmacy with the doctor's prescription, but in order to avoid parading Bhagwan's dependence on medication I had to pretend the medicine was for me. As Bhagwan was a firm believer in orthodox Western medicine, these prescriptions were quite lengthy and they changed every week. The pharmacist obviously knew who all these medicines were really for, but as part of the discreet duplicity which is second nature to everybody in India, he never questioned me about it.

As soon as Bhagwan had made me his bodyguard, I had begun looking for ways to learn more about defending him. I practised rabbit punches and wrestling blows on the roof of Bhagwan's house to the amazement of his personal cleaner, who would stare at this wild redhead flinging fists at an old cushion under the noonday sun.

Then a very large black man from Chicago came to take sannyas, and I learned that he was a karate expert. I asked him to show me a few things, and practised the techniques he taught me. Two American brothers came to take sannyas on their way to study karate n Japan. They gave a demonstration for Bhagwan in the old car rch where he had been holding darshan, and Mukta decided that would make ideal bodyguards. I felt my position threatened.

time later an American kung fu fighter came and started the al martial arts class, with a lot of emphasis on blindfold and one-punch knockout techniques he called 'boom blows'.

r martial artist arrived called Molliko. He was, as they say , 'built like a brick shithouse', and was a tough, athletic ad been in the top Swedish commando unit, but had out, wherupon he went to Japan to pursue his love of d the toughest school in the whole of Japan, and had after acquiring his second dan black belt.

mastering the Oriental fighting arts myself, I s, starting at six in the morning on the roof of ore people arrived who were trained in the the CIA and the Israeli intelligence service — pidly-expanding security force. The Israeli- action, decisiveness and skill; the CIA

man arrived who was to play a crucial anisation. Her name was Sheela, and kitchen. I had met Sheela a year

she had come for a short visit with her American
Harris Silverman — renamed 'Chinmaya'. At the
mazed me with her fawning adulation, prostrating
ii's feet in traditional devotion — until then people
iis for Bhagwan himself. Now she had reappeared,
ay for good.

ni had assigned me to yet another job, that of co-
inning of the staff kitchen — perhaps she saw this as a
my complaints about canteen food and hygiene — so
ere immediately thrown together. Sheela seemed a
iimple person when I first worked with her, giving no
soever of the virago she was to turn into later. From
iings in the kitchen, Sheela began a quite
and meteoric rise through the ashram ranks, and
e had founded the ashram bank and become Laxmi's
sistant.

en born in Baroda, a town in a farming region about
iiles north of Bombay, and was the youngest of six
irents had been interested in Rajneesh, and for many
l host at their farm to an odd assortment of travelling
ople. By 1984 they had gained American citizenship,
ng attempt to keep Bhagwan in the USA, claimed to
i authorities that they had adopted Bhagwan as a
rself was already an American citizen by marriage,
t at the age of seventeen to study in New Jersey, and
, in 1969, married an American Jew, who soon
ajneesh himself. Sheela thus obtained the coveted
d was legally entitled to live and work in the USA.
hagwan when she was a child, and she would tell
e she was in America she had never forgotten him —
d her in thrall. From the time she returned to Poona,
iout twenty-six, Bhagwan gave her special attention.
in in the ashram grew stronger, power seemed to alter
Soon she was no longer content to kneel devotedly at
iut determinedly sought power and influence. The
arfulness vanished.

she barged her way into the darshan queue, where
ced that she had washed her hair with scented
efused her entry to darshan. Sheela hit the roof, and I
f for possible violence. She was furious at being told

what to do by a new disciple, a woman, and a foreigner to boot
went straight to Laxmi. Laxmi backed Maneesha up comple
giving Sheela a scarf to wear and telling her to go and wash her
Then she told Bhagwan what had happened.

It was a very hot night, and the crickets saturated the tired air
their vibrant rhythms. The darshan started, and Bhagwan went r
the semicircle of guests in his accustomed way. It was an hour b
he reached Sheela. He sighed deeply and his gaze became
"Sheela," he said, "I have heard what you did at my Lao Tzu ga
was *stupid*!"

"But Bhagwan," she began, flustered, "I . . . er . . ."

"Sheela, be silent and *listen* for once in your life! You ha
understand a few things. First, as the ashram grows many
departments are going to be formed, and each department will h
department head. Second, the person I choose to lead
department will have autonomy within their own depart
Thirdly, anyone entering that department should acknowledge
autonomy and observe whatever rules I have approved of. Man
I have put in charge of Lao Tzu gate, and you must surrender
when she is there. Is that clear?" Sheela's lips pursed as she tr
retain her self control and dignity. She was trembling with

"So now you apologise to Maneesha," Bhagwan went on. "Y
and touch her feet."

Sheela looked appalled. This was the ultimate humiliatio
someone of high caste to touch the feet of a foreigner. W
looking up, she crawled over to where Maneesha was sitting
atmosphere was electric, and Sheela's pain and degradation co
felt by every one of the twenty-five people present. As S
approached, Maneesha, who was crying, pulled her feet unde
but Sheela was determined to do it despite her obvious anguish
dutifully touched Maneesha's feet. Maneesha reached out to em
her, but Sheela could not return the affection, and slid back
place on all fours like a defeated animal.

Oh dear, I thought to myself, this is going to be very bad ne
Maneesha. Sheela had already earned herself a reputatio
keeping scores, never forgetting slights and insults. Her reven
Maneesha took a full three years to work itself out. When S
finally eclipsed Laxmi and began running the ashram, it wasn'
before Maneesha lost her darshan sniffing job, then her room
favoured Lao Tzu House. After that she was transferred

commune outside Poona, where she was assigned work as a toilet cleaner.

Given the atmosphere in the ashram in 1976, it wasn't long before Sheela and I were attracted to each other sexually. She made sure that I knew her husband had taken another lover, and that the coast was therefore clear for us. She told me how much I reminded her of an art teacher she had had at her New Jersey college, who was also Scottish and red-headed, and implied that she had had a mad but unconsummated crush on him. I had never had a sexual liaison with an Indian woman before, and it showed me just how great the cultural gap is in this respect between East and West. Though Westerners and Indians lived so closely together in the ashram, all engaged on what was supposed to be an identical search, we never managed to bridge that gap.

Time and again Bhagwan had informed us in lectures that most Indian women had never had an orgasm, and I was to discover during my affair with Sheela that this was all too true. Though I fell for Sheela's sweet and demure ways, and we did become lovers, it didn't really work out. There seemed to be a kind of deadness to her body, as if she did not really own it or live in it. It never really felt alive and vibrant. There were many people in the ashram who were highly body-conscious — athletes, gymnasts, actors, martial arts experts and students of the Alexander Technique — and they took great care with how they moved and used their bodies. Bhagwan himself had flawless carriage and posture, which were greatly admired. Sheela was quite different. She exuded a tomboyish, almost asexual, air, and treated her body with disdain. Instead of sitting crosslegged as most people did at darshan or lectures, she would slump over and fall asleep. She remained uninterested in and unmoved by sex; in conventional terms she would have been labelled as frigid.

There was, however, a complication to our affair. I was in the middle of a new relationship with my former girlfriend Divya, who soon got to hear of my liaison with Sheela. While I was guarding Bhagwan during a lecture one morning, Divya got into my tent and poured tomato ketchup and rubbish all over my bed. I was pretty angry to start with, but in the end, after I had cleared it up again, we were both able to laugh about it, and the incident brought us closer together again.

Sheela's husband was not happy about her relationship with me, and had written to Bhagwan about his concern. One evening, during that magic ten minutes as we sat with Bhagwan before the guests arrived for darshan, he asked Sheela to come to his feet. Without in any way acknowledging my presence or referring directly to my part in the affair, he turned to the kneeling Sheela and said, "Sheela, I have received a letter from Chinmaya, and he is distressed by this your other relationship. And this other relationship is shallow compared with the one with him, so it will not come to anything. So you do one thing, you drop it out."

Since I had no idea that Bhagwan knew about the affair, and had been convinced by Sheela that her husband was amenable to it, this came as a complete surprise to me. Now, by divine decree, it was over. I accepted the end of the relationship immediately and without question. Not so Sheela, who seemed to be hurt that I could drop her so easily. It was this incident that first earned me a place on her 'get even' list. Perhaps she remembered it when she denounced me so forcibly six years later in a public declaration that Bhagwan wrote, but she signed.

On the whole, though, Bhagwan encouraged our complete sexual freedom. He also, especially if things got difficult in one relationship, encouraged frequent changes of partner among ashram members. This, plus our own inclinations, engendered an atmosphere of frank promiscuity, a promiscuity for which the ashram was already becoming famous in the outside world, and it was about this time that frequent press reports began to appear about the sensational taboo-free environment at Poona.

Most of us had been brought up to suppress or control our sexual urges, yet here we were being told to forget all our inhibitions. The sexual freedom offered by Poona was quite phenomenal. Of the thousand or so sannyasis, at least six hundred were women, and nearly all were sexually active. All who came, female and male, had been attracted at least in part by a guru who advocated sexual experiment of the freest kind. It is no exaggeration to say that we had a feast of fucking, the likes of which had probably not been seen since the days of Roman bacchanalia. Never had people's carnal needs been so well catered for. Yet it was all done within an atmosphere of care, love and friendship that made it quite exceptional.

Most of the women were sexually voracious, and it was the men who found it difficult to keep up. An appreciable number of the men were almost or entirely celibate, and were astonished and terrified by the sexual aggression of the women. As the therapy groups became more firmly established, sexual liaisons often took the form of Gurdjieffian 'devices', to test our mettle, endurance or devotion. Other 'devices' involved getting very drunk, or eating ourselves silly. The only sensation that was expressly forbidden was that achieved through mind-altering drugs. These were not allowed inside the ashram gates, though they were widely indulged in outside them.

Because of my closeness to Bhagwan and my privileged position within the ashram, I had the good fortune to be propositioned by many highly desirable and sensual women. Poona undoubtedly attracted extremely beautiful women, and many of them sought me out. Laxmi, the perpetual virgin, did not know what to make of it all. In the midst of these energetic and uninhibited sexual scenes, she remained aloof and quite celibate. "Shiva," she would tell people, "has a new sari every day." It wasn't long before I became known as 'the ashram stud'.

For the men who were sexually active it was sometimes more than one sari a day: there were two, and even three on occasions. These were the heady days before herpes, AIDS and other sexually-communicable diseases had caught up with us, and a thousand of us gave expession to our long repressed and unfulfilled sexual urges.

On one occasion Laxmi gave permission to a visiting non-sannyasi London photographer to take pictures of the newly-formed tantra group. He couldn't believe his eyes as he captured amazing images of frank and free sexual exchanges among a mixed group of naked people. And it wasn't just free-for-all sex either — there was a conscious indulgence in wine, music, song, feasting and sensual massage. In the mango season, the men would eat ripe mangoes from between the women's legs.

Almost as soon as Laxmi had allowed the photographer into the session to record all this, one of her personal assistants rushed to query her authorisation, since it seemed impossible that she would have given permission.

"Child," she said, "what are you worried about? Let the photographer take the pictures. He is a good man, and his publicity will be helpful to our work."

The assistant pointed out that not only were they naked, but the sex was for real, not simulated.

Laxmi still appeared not to be concerned, and her assistant was becoming frantic. "Laxmi, they are using their *screwdrivers!*" she cried desperately, using a word that Laxmi understood.

"But Laxmi never knew the friends were taking off their clothes. Why did no one tell Laxmi? Get that man out of there immediately! Confiscate all his films!"

So the photographer's film was taken away, and Laxmi's innocence became enshrined in ashram folklore. On another occasion, Laxmi walked into one of her female assistant's rooms and thought she was having a fight with her boyfriend. She offered to help, and only then did she realise what they were actually doing.

Though we were enjoying such a feast of sex, we were not on the whole feasting in other ways. The ashram food was still barely sufficient for all the work we were doing, and many of us became extremely emaciated. Things got so bad for me that towards the middle of the year I broke a rib simply turning over in my sleep. It was done so easily that I resolved there and then to take some action — unilateral if necessary — to improve my diet. The major problem was that food needed money, and I was almost out of it. The last of my savings would run out in a month at the most, so I went to Laxmi and requested a small allowance. This was already given to certain highly-valued sannyasis, and though modest enough — fifty rupees or about four pounds a month — would cover basic essentials and enable me to buy a little food.

"We will have to ask *him*," said Laxmi piously. "Laxmi does not decide anything on her own," an assertion I knew only too well to be untrue.

I decided that I would wait until my money actually ran out before consulting Bhagwan, so that the answer I received would be of immediate importance. A week later I received a letter from my father in Scotland, telling me I had been left a thousand pounds in my grandmother's will, and that he would like me to come back to Scotland to collect it.

I went straight to Laxmi to find out what Bhagwan's answer had been. "Shiva has to find his own way," she said. I told her then about the inheritance, and asked her if she would like me to give her the money.

Laxmi said simply: "Child, keep it and *enjoy*!"

Like so many Indians, Laxmi often said what was expedient at the time. It was always difficult to believe any of her pronouncements, but she did almost always act in a spirit of love. While Laxmi's truth shifted and changed according to the situation, her heart remained constant. The same could not, unfortunately, be said for her protegé,

Sheela.

Now that I had a bit of money, I decided to set myself up as a freelance photographer in my spare time. I felt that I had now learned enough professional technique to be able to make money by selling pictures. I ordered a new camera outfit through one of our air hostess disciples, who bought the equipment in Tokyo. So began a successful career. I took sunrises, pictures of mountain scenery and vistas, which I sold for anything up to five hundred dollars each to an agency in New York. I was never again short of money.

The first priority was to supplement the meagre ashram diet with protein-rich food. There were to be no more midnight rib fractures from now on. I quickly learned how important a good diet is to good health, as I remained comparatively free from disease while many ashram members became seriously ill from not eating properly, and a few died.

There was little rationale in the way the ashram was run. The Indian photographer who had been at the receiving end of many of Laxmi's verbal lashings walked out at four o'clock one morning, never to return. For a whole year Laxmi kept his room empty, despite the severe overcrowding in the ashram, hoping that he would come back.

I soon lost my job as Bhagwan's personal driver — Laxmi divested me of that choice function after I had contradicted her in front of Bhagwan. She also dispensed with my services as a driver on her trips into Bombay, and started driving herself.

Laxmi already had a long and eventful career as a driver, including the demolition of a bullock cart in a high-speed crash in 1974 while she was driving Bhagwan from Bombay to Poona in his orange Chevrolet Impala.

When Laxmi went to Bombay to collect the new Mercedes 280SE later that year, she drove it back to Poona at night without lights. She couldn't work out how to turn the lights on, but knew she had an appointment to keep, so drove the hundred and twenty miles of poorly-surfaced, heavily-travelled, twisting road to Poona without them.

Following a further accident, Bhagwan forbade her from driving to Bombay, so my services were re-enlisted.

When we next went to Bombay, however, she dismissed me as soon as we arrived so that she could conduct her activities without my overseeing presence. When I innocently asked her when I should come back to drive her home, she laughed victoriously. "*He* never said Laxmi could not drive *back* from Bombay!" I was nonplussed, but Laxmi got her own way.

About a month after Bhagwan's no-driving directive, Laxmi was found in the middle of the night, wandering along the main Bombay-Poona road near Lonavala. Her robe was torn and she was covered with blood, disorientated and suffering from amnesia. She told her rescuer that she was looking for the god Krishna. She was sure he was nearby, but she could not find him. The new Mercedes, which had cost nearly as much as Bhagwan's house, was lying in a gulley, having rolled over several times. As usual, Bhagwan's ability to sense impending disaster had functioned faultlessly.

The next day I drove him in another car to visit Laxmi in hospital. She had been telling the nurses repeatedly that the Lord Krishna was about to come and visit her; they concluded that she had gone mad. As Bhagwan arrived, gliding into the room, immaculately dressed and with several elegant assistants following him, Laxmi's face lit up. "See, fools," she said to the surrounding nurses, "I *told* you Krishna was coming!" For Laxmi, Bhagwan was no less than God incarnate in human form.

She made a good recovery and was back at work within a fortnight. A permanent full-time driver was assigned to her, and she did not attempt to drive herself again.

It was during 1976 that the famous English actor Terence Stamp arrived. He was researching a film based on Gurdjieff's *Meetings with Remarkable Men*, and wanted to meet Bhagwan. He was the first really famous Westerner to visit Poona, and we were all very excited when he arrived. Several of the ashram women made themselves very conspicuous whenever Stamp appeared.

When he attended his first darshan, Bhagwan immediately motioned him to come and sit closer. Eventually Terence was sitting so close to Bhagwan that his legs were actually touching him. This was quite unheard of at a time when one of my main roles at darshan was to keep people from touching Bhagwan at all. I hesitated. Should I do anything, say anything? I moved closer to take the obligatory photographs, and watched while Bhagwan talked on and on, looking intently at Terence Stamp the while. I kept expecting the actor to keel over in the face of this verbal onslaught, but he hardly blinked. He just sat and listened, taking it all in. He did not give away just how much it was all affecting him, but Bhagwan made a very deep impression. Bhagwan gave him sannyas, and a new name, Veeten, which meant 'the transcendental one'.

As Terence Stamp sat in front of Bhagwan and was showered with all this attention and love, I was aware of a painful surge of jealousy. Why should this newcomer get so much consideration when it was the rest of us who had been working day and night to get the commune going? Was being famous and having money all that mattered now? Bhagwan had made it clear in his lectures that he did not care whether people were rich or famous, and that his ability to bestow love on all was quite unconditional. Now it did not seem to be true any more. The honeymoon was over, and it was to be a demanding marriage from now on.

Bhagwan picked up on my moodiness and negativity. The next day he sent Teertha to tell me that he was unhappy with my photography, my appearance, and some of my security work. I was invited to write Bhagwan an explanatory letter, so I did, outlining all my worries and dissatisfactions. I pointed out the vast range of jobs I was already doing — bodyguard, driver, photographer, darkroom technician, security overseer, pre-darshan sniffer, osteopath, laboratory runner and medication purchaser — and suggested that a reduction would be very welcome. I did not mention my freelance photography — by this time I was afraid that Laxmi would ask for a cut of my commission.

That same evening I was summoned to see Vivek for my answer. "Bhagwan said it was a good letter," she said in reply to my anxious questioning. "You are to give up the pre-darshan sniffing, and a woman will do it from now on. You are to concentrate on guarding in darshan, and Krishna Barti will take the darshan photographs. Bhagwan said that it would be good for you to find a woman to settle down with. He said I should tell Shiva that it will not be necessary to sleep with them all first!"

Terence Stamp continued to be given preferential treatment. He moved into his own room at Krishna House, and we exchanged friendly greetings as we passed each other in the corridor. He had not been given any work to do, and seemed to disappear during the day, no doubt to the Blue Diamond Hotel and its crystal-clear swimming pool. Within no time at all he was invited to live in Bhagwan's own house. I had by now accepted the inevitable rapid rise of this so-handsome and likeable man, and my jealousy had evaporated. A month or two later he left for London, and I gathered that his departure was accelerated by his feeling very lonely in the ashram.

He told me that all he had wanted was a friend he could go to the pub with in the evenings.

I heard many years later that Bhagwan had asked Veeten to investigate the Mevlevi order of Whirling Dervishes. They are Sufis who run a weekly whirling ceremony — one of the last genuinely traditional ones — in a large high-ceilinged room on the Cromwell Road in West London. The Sufis sensed that Bhagwan had asked Veeten to look in, and denied him admittance.

Also around this time John du Cane arrived at the ashram. He was then in his mid-twenties, and worked as an amateur film-maker — Bhagwan named him Rishi. About a year after taking sannyas he was accused of drug-running in India, and spent nine months in an Indian jail — where, he said, the food was a good deal better than in the ashram. Within eighteen months he was in jail again. He was accused of smuggling hard drugs in Thailand, and was confined in shackles in a primitive cell in Bangkok on a thirty-six year sentence. His father succeeded in petitioning for the release of his son and was able to secure a Royal Pardon. Rishi is one of many unfortunate sannyassis all over the world who have served time or are still in jail accused of drug-running offences. Rishi has received successful treatment for his addiction to drugs and is now pursuing a new career.

It was at about this time that the money-making at the ashram started in earnest. Admission charges were levied on all who came to the ashram. In his 1980 *Times* report, Bernard Levin called the admission charge 'trifling', but at eight rupees, it was twice what the average Indian labourer would earn in a day's very hard work. It was something approaching the daily wage of a minor clerk or small-time waiter, the equivalent in earning capacity of £10-15 sterling. The admission fee had risen four-fold since the move from Bombay.

Teertha was now in charge of the ashram encounter group. Formerly Paul Lowe, he had founded the first European growth centre, called Quaesitor, in London, after training at Esalen in California, the leading centre of the human potential movement. Teertha's encounter groups became famous for their explicit violence and polygamous sexuality. Bhagwan had told Teertha and his girlfriend to remain celibate, however. Teertha's interpretation of this edict was to restrict himself to prolific digital manipulation of his female group participants.

The most extreme test of detachment in Teertha's groups was for somebody to sit and watch while their beloved made love with someone else. Bhagwan had always said that true love differed from possessiveness, indeed that the presence of one ruled out the other. You could not truly love somebody if you wanted to possess their body. Thus the truly loving partner would be able to remain completely calm while their loved one had intercourse with another person, and would be happy to see them having a good time. Some people, it is true, were able to watch with equanimity, but not the majority. All too often the onlookers exploded in a fury of violence, often directed forcefully at Teertha himself, who was a provocateur *par excellence*.

Teertha's group was not for the fainthearted, or for the new arrivals. Before being allowed into this advanced group, you had to take part in several preparatory groups, to 'soften up', become familiar with the group processes, and gain awareness of your blocks and inhibitions. Teertha's natural propensity to push people beyond their limits of self-control led to many broken bones and other injuries. He sustained another broken arm himself. By 1980 it had become necessary to prohibit violence in the groups altogether.

As word of our activities spread, so curiosity grew among those who were interested in human growth and potential. We had a visit from Richard Price, one of the co-founders of the Esalen Institute, and I clearly remember his first darshan. When he got up from the marble floor he left a pool of blood behind, from a wound in his foot which had opened up while Bhagwan was talking to him. In this place of omens and portents, the pool of blood seemed very significant.

During his encounter group session, Teertha and Price had a bitter argument, at the end of which Price could take no more and left. About a year later *Time* magazine dubbed Poona 'The Esalen of the East'. Richard Price was not amused, and immediately sat down to compose a letter denouncing the Poona phenomenon, disclaiming all similarities with his own organisation. It was a well-written letter, and drew particular attention to the violence endemic in the Poona encounter groups, but if it was written with the intention of putting people off coming, it failed dismally. Droves of devotees continued to appear. Price's co-founder of Esalen, Bernie Gunther, came, stayed far longer than Price, and published some very successful photographic records of Poona. As a postscript to this Esalen link, I was sorry to hear in 1985 that Richard Price was killed by falling rocks while meditating in a canyon near Esalen.

Within a month of Bhagwan's commandment, I had found a

partner to 'settle down with'. Her sannyasin name was Gayan, which meant 'wisdom'. She was German, a ballet teacher and a single parent, and had her three-year-old daughter with her. The child's father, also a sannyasi, was living in a converted coach which he had driven overland from Bavaria, through Turkey and Afghanistan. Gayan started working in the canteen kitchens, and soon moved into my room. Laxmi explained to her that children were not encouraged in the ashram, and that her small daughter would have to stay with her father in the coach unless I wanted to share my room with her and her mother. I did not, and Gayan elected to leave her daughter behind.

Six months after we had established our relationship, we were accorded the ultimate privilege, and invited to move into Bhagwan's house. After nine months together, Gayan's visa was about to expire and she had to devise some means of staying on. There were two possibilities: either she could bribe the officials in Bombay to get the visa extended, or we could get married. In those days British citizens did not require visas — this only became necessary after the assassination of Mrs Ghandi in 1984. Without discussing it beforehand, I proposed to her one Sunday morning. Gayan's English was still very poor, and at first she did not understand what I was saying. When at last it dawned, and Gayan had agreed that it was a good solution, we decided to ask Vivek if it was acceptable. Vivek came back later and said that yes, it was, but added: "Bhagwan says it's okay for you to get married, as long as you understand that it's just for the visa." I felt secretly hurt by his message.

Bhagwan's own views on marriage were well known. He had never been married, and he violently disapproved of the institution. The official story is that when Bhagwan's mother asked him about getting married, he replied: "Mother, if you could have your life all over again, would you get married?" When his mother replied that she would not, that was the last word on the subject. He thought that marriage bound people to each other in such a way that eventually they could only end up hating each other, and very few married people, Bhagwan said, did not eventually come to do that. Bhagwan was also adamant on the subject of children, and did not want any couples having children while in the ashram. Thus in Bhagwan's eyes, any marriage within the ashram had to be regarded as being purely for convenience.

At the time, Gayan and I were deeply in love, and marriage

seemed to be the natural confirmation of our friendship. When I proposed to her it was out of love, and certainly not just a matter of convenience. Now Bhagwan was implying that it was to be a temporary arrangement, and not to let ourselves be under any illusion that the marriage was at all important. The only real relationship that Bhagwan acknowledged as important was that between him and his disciples. This was the only bond that actually counted.

One day Gayan confided in me that she had been having individual bodywork sessions with Teertha, and that she was worried about his interest in her. Several times he had told her to take all her clothes off and close her eyes while she performed some special exercises. Once, when she had opened her eyes briefly, he had been staring intently at her body in a way that was obviously not merely professional interest. I had my own encounter with Teertha after that, and it was a full six months before we became friends again.

Bhagwan continued to tell us that all our relationships other than the one with him were of secondary importance. The only reason we were at Poona was to further our relationship with him. He helped to foster this allegiance to himself by continuously re-arranging and breaking relationships, or ordering couples to seek different partners. If you loved Bhagwan totally, you should not become seriously involved in other affairs. As children interfered with the primary allegiance to Bhagwan, most women who became pregnant were instructed 'to finish with it' — in other words to have an abortion as quickly as possible. His alternative instruction was 'to finish with it absolutely' — to be sterilised at the same time as having the abortion, so there was no more risk of getting pregnant and interrupting 'the Work'. It was part of my job when addressing new people just before darshan to give them a list of 'forbidden activities' — this list included a directive not on any account to ask Bhagwan about becoming pregnant, having an abortion or being sterilised, since he had already made himself very clear on these points.

We could not become enlightened, Bhagwan kept telling us, until we had learned to become unattached to members of the opposite sex. His own enlightenment, he never tired of saying, came precisely *because* he had from an early age remained aloof from emotional entanglements. This had enabled him to think clearly, and pursue his own path unencumbered by the needs of another person. What about his relationship with Vivek, one might ask, the supposed reincarnation of his childhood sweetheart Sashi? This relationship remained inviolable until 1977, when Bhagwan separated from her of his own accord.

By 1976, four disciples had been given the task of writing autobiographies of their relationship with Bhagwan. All of these works had to be read by Bhagwan before going to press, and had to be officially sanctioned. They also had to be amended according to his instructions. Exaggerations were encouraged where they showed Bhagwan in a favourable light. In one of the autobiographies you can read about the excitement of twenty thousand people arriving for Celebration Day in 1977. I know for certain that the numbers did not exceed three thousand, since I managed the seating arrangements for the occasion. Exaggeration had always been one of Bhagwan's passions.

Chapter Eight
POONA GROWS APACE

Just over a year after the original Chuang Tzu auditorium collapsed, the new one was finished. It held six hundred people comfortably, and as I now felt rather nervous at being the sole bodyguard, Laxmi granted me an assistant. As ever more people came to sit in at the morning lecture, so did the rules and regulations begin to tighten up. The acoustics of the the place meant that coughing at the back of the hall could be heard quite distinctly, so the 'twenty second rule' was instigated. This was the time permitted for a brief spell of coughing. Anyone who continued for longer than that would be asked — or forced — to leave, by myself or my assistant.

Rows of ropes were laid down to separate the genuine disciples from the visitors — and the visitors got the worst seats, at the back. Anybody who had a 'catharsis' — flailed about, shouted or shrieked — had, according to Bhagwan's instructions, to be sat with for twenty seconds and calmed down. If they did not respond, they had to be carried out. This system worked fairly well, and soon I had an 'army' of five guards per lecture, which meant that we could carry people out and still have some guards in the hall. At this point, however, Laxmi still did not want me to train the guards in any way, as she felt that this would be inviting trouble. At that time Bhagwan's thinking was that if you allowed the concept of violence to take hold, this would inevitably attract it. Thus instead of discussing 'weapons', 'guns' or 'intruders', we talked of 'if something should happen' and 'if somebody points something at Bhagwan, then interpose your body'.

One of my more important jobs was to take photographs of Bhagwan, during lectures and at other times. Laxmi once said to a group of disciples when we were in her room discussing photographs: "Look, no one takes photos of *him* like our Shiva. Shiva drinks him into the lens. The photos are so beautiful — you can tell it." It was a rare compliment — most of the time Laxmi criticised rather than praised.

It was not easy to take good photographs in the new auditorium.

Bhagwan sat in front of one of Laxmi's bedroom windows, and the join in the windows intersected the crown of his head, making for a ruinous backdrop. I suggested to Vivek that a matt black curtain covering the area behind his chair would improve the photographs enormously. She said that a board would be better, as there would be less chance of allergies and dust affecting Bhagwan. Laxmi said she would fund the project, and the board arrived by handcart a week later. I painted it, and allowed a week to pass before inviting Vivek to come and give it the sniff test. "Far, far too strong!" she said. I waited another week and tried again. Still the same negative response.

After a third week I decided to treat the board as a write-off. Then one day, out of the blue, Vivek approached me and said that the board was fine now! I was astonished — but that was the way things tended to happen in the ashram.

Bhagwan was still very fussy about how he appeared in photographs. Only his head was important, he said, but it was not just a matter of leaving out his body. To be acceptable a picture had to minimise the length of his nose and not emphasise his bald head. His eyes were the thing. He would scrutinise all photographs very carefully, and only allowed certain pictures to be included in books and photographic records. This applied not only to photographs of himself, but to all official pictures of the ashram. I appear several times in *The Sound of Running Water*, the plush photographic record produced in Poona, but all traces of my presence were eliminated from the later book, *This Very Place, This Lotus Paradise*, which covered 1979-1984 and was produced in Oregon. By that time I had left the movement, and Bhagwan had forbidden the use of pictures or text references of people who had left the movement in any of the ranch publications. Ex-sannyasis were erased for ever.

Bhagwan could be infuriatingly difficult to please. I was very satisfied with my new backdrop, and I remember thinking as I sat taking pictures during the next morning lecture how I had always wanted a backdrop like this. It was perfect. Bhagwan's white robe and black and silver hair contrasted perfectly with the matt black, and was wonderful for black and white pictures. A few days after I had taken these pictures we had a private photo session in the garden. Halfway through Bhagwan turned to me and said: "Hmmm, Shiva, those photos with the board, they were not good. We will not use the board again, hmmm?" I felt utterly deflated, and could not fathom what he disliked about them.

But a month later he chose almost the entire series for a forthcoming book. You could never tell! He vacillated and changed his mind continuously, all the time maintaining an outward show of complete assurance and omniscience. In the end, though, he changed his mind yet again, and the board was replaced by a permanent white frame — better than the window frame, but definitely inferior to my black board. He even laid down the law about *when* photographs were to be taken during lectures. One day Vivek came to me and said: "Do wait at least fifteen minutes before starting to take any shots. That's how long it takes Bhagwan to hit his stride. After that you can do almost anything you like and it won't disturb him."

Strange things happened to me during the photographic sessions. Several times I sensed that Bhagwan was communicating with me through the lens on some kind of psychic level. I would look up from the camera to find him gazing intently at me, but was too astonished to get back to the viewfinder quickly enough to take the shot. Once, when I was about to snap the shutter, he gave me a broad schoolboy grin. The oddest thing was that nobody else seemed to notice it, nor were they aware that Bhagwan was looking straight at me when I was about to take pictures.

Some peculiar things happened to other people during Bhagwan's lectures, too. One woman had an epileptic fit, and three guards who thought she was having a catharsis found it impossible to carry her out. After that, diagnosis of epilepsy was part of the training I gave to my rapidly expanding force. On another occasion a young Japanese woman came to take sannyas. For a long time she sat demurely in front of Bhagwan, then suddenly sprang forward, put her head on his lap, and clasped her hands round his bottom. Laxmi leapt up and started clawing the offensive hands away. I had been too slow — the woman had caught me completely by surprise. Laxmi and I pulled the woman off Bhagwan, who had been grinning sheepishly throughout.

The incident did not go unnoticed by Vivek. "Shiva," she said afterwards, "you were too slow. You were sleeping. It had better not happen again." I felt an utter fool, and began to practise harder than ever, especially the art of responding without thinking — the ultimate goal of all the martial arts.

About a month later the same little Japanese lady came again for darshan. I sat beside Bhagwan, all ready to interrupt her should she make a move towards him. This time I was prepared, and focused my energy on the woman, so that I could pick up her intentions at the psychic level. She obviously sensed my hostility towards her, and so did Bhagwan. "Don't worry about him," he said to her dismissively. "Come close to me and let me feel your energy." Bhagwan touched her between the eyes, and I relaxed. Then he gave her a polished wooden box as a going away gift. She received it graciously, touching his feet and departing as daintily as she had come the first time. These boxes contained a strand of Bhagwan's hair or a nail clipping. He said these artefacts emanated his own enlightened energy, and helped his disciples to keep in touch with him.

Then there was the time that a woman started running towards Bhagwan at the end of the morning lecture. There was no doubt that this was going to be an attack. I gave the attack warning by urgent hand signal to the guard seated directly in the woman's path. He whirled round, then inexplicably froze. I waited a split second for him to intercept her, but he let the woman walk quickly past him. She was now very close to Bhagwan, so I took a few swift paces myself and intercepted her. "I've got to get to him, I've got to!" she hissed in my ear. As I held her, somebody opened the door for Bhagwan to leave. We escorted the woman away, then she received her telling off from Laxmi.

"Whatever got into you?" I asked the guard who had frozen. I had been training him for a year in how to respond quickly to an attack.

He looked confused and sheepish. "Well," he began, "that was my new girlfriend. We spent the night together last night, and I just couldn't stop her."

After that incident I coined a new phrase: Never Assume Anything. Teertha was full of praise for my prompt action. "I'm very glad you're taking care of Bhagwan," he said. "I feel totally safe when you are there."

There was some leg-pulling about the coughing rule. In one of his many humorous pre-lecture announcements, Teertha advised young women not to start coughing until they were surrounded by enough handsome guards to carry them out. In fact very few people did continue to cough after the rule had been established.

Around this time I was enjoying myself immensely. Here we all were, living in the commune of a truly incredible man, and there was the distinct feeling that you could have anything you liked. It seemed like an eternal Christmas Day, with Bhagwan as the generous Santa Claus. For me, the sensation of complete sexual freedom was an important dimension, but it was the sexual freedom, rather than actual sexual satisfaction, that was vital. If anything, the women seemed to get more out of this feeling of freedom than the men. But apart from this sexual freedom, there was a general awareness that two or three thousand like-minded souls were working together in this place to fulfil Bhagwan's dream. We felt as if we were new people, shaping the future, showing the world how people could and should live. When in 1977 Laxmi made the pronouncement that in ten years' time half of Red China would be sannyasis, it did not seem at all impossible. Nobody who had arrived in Poona wanted to leave. We were convinced that those who were sent back to the West were being given some kind of death sentence.

Once we had got over the first difficult year of malnutrition, disease and poverty, we found ways of keeping body and soul together, and the long-term sannyasis even had money left for little luxuries. Of the inner group of ashram workers, some of the men and a few of the women bought motorcycles for transport and enjoyment. With its hot weather and nine months of cloudless blue skies, India is a superb place to take to the open road.

One morning, sixteen of us on eight motorcycles took off for a lake about fifty miles away. Sheela was with us, together with her new boyfriend, the South African pilot from Kailash. She whooped it up on the pillion of the pilot's bike, and I took pictures of them both, legs out and orange clothes billowing in the wind. Sheela's perfect white teeth shone out beneath her goggles. She looked ecstatic.

When we arrived at the lake we were covered in dust and sweat, and we all went for a naked swim. Back at the ashram a few hours later, a very black-looking Laxmi greeted us. Bhagwan had noticed that we were all missing from the morning lecture, and Laxmi had found out where we had gone. Sheela, by this time Laxmi's deputy, was not expected to indulge in such childish pursuits, and she received a severe rebuke. It was the only time Sheela needed telling — she never rode on a Royal Enfield again. Laxmi, however, was more flexible. When Sheela opened a new commune at Saswat, not far from Poona, Laxmi was seen taking a guided tour round the place on Somendra's Enfield, and posed gleefully for photographs.

One day I surprised Bhagwan in his room and found him drawing up a highly complex plan on foolscap paper on a clipboard. As soon as he saw me he hastily moved the clipboard to the small bookshelf he always kept by his armchair, but I had already taken in the main elements of the diagram. He had arranged disciples' names in rows, using different coloured pens. It was clear that he was working out his weekly master plan, arranging the lives of those that lived there. I could imagine Bhagwan spending hours perfecting these blueprints, then quietly and authoritatively outlining them to Laxmi when she came in for their work sessions. Sometimes I would meet her coming out of Bhagwan's room, and she would accost me with "Wait, oh just wait, child, wait and see what the Lion has made happen today." She would then walk with me to her office, sit down in her dark green swivel chair, and order a special cup of tea while she issued a stream of new directives. Swami A was to move to department B; Ma C was to see Laxmi right away. This happened after every morning meeting with Bhagwan, and her directives would be delivered with great urgency. So and so was to be called *at once*, regardless of what they were doing. You might be gardening one morning when the feared directive would arrive, telling you to move to the kitchen, or to a building site, or — the dreaded one — to go back to the West and earn five thousand pounds before coming back.

Expansion was rapid throughout this period. By 1978 Laxmi had completed the building of an imposing gateway complete with a massive pair of brass-studded fake teak gates, which were to become famous in pictures which appeared all over the world. Above the gates was the sign: 'Bhagwan Shree Rajneesh Ashram'. Everything had to look as palatial and high-class as posssible. Laxmi had a weakness for ornate chandeliers, on which she spent tens of thousands of rupees, and these went up everywhere. New departments proliferated. There was now a bookshop, and a thriving public relations department. A large new apartment block became part of the ashram, and was named 'Jesus House'. Laxmi bought up more and more land round the ashram, and started building on it. Some of the land belonged to an Indian woman who, although nothing to do with the ashram, wanted to sell it. For complex family reasons this was proving difficult, but that didn't deter Laxmi, who started building on it anyway.

This was to be the site of the new 'Buddha Hall', an enormous auditorium with a seating capacity of six thousand, since the numbers of people had already outgrown the Chuang Tzu lecture hall. Alongside our splendid new buildings a workers' shanty town sprang up. It was a long line of tawdry hovels, reminding me of an endless string of black dead fish. There was constant activity as the coolies carried cement and bricks in iron baskets on their heads, inter-mingling with three thousand sannyasis. The place was alive from 5.30 in the morning, when the gates — named by Laxmi 'The Gateless Gates' — were opened for dynamic meditation, until 10.30 in the evening, when the music group finished.

Though some of us had managed to supplement our diet, the food, what there was of it, was still very bad. Haridas thought he had found the perfect answer by always choosing girlfriends who worked in Bhagwan's own kitchen. The food cooked for Bhagwan was incomparably better than any of the rest of us were given, and Haridas was able to eat there with the kitchen staff. But the day came when Vivek, who supervised Bhagwan's kitchen, banned everyone except her own cooks from the room, and Haridas was forced to eat with the rest of us in the canteen.

At lunch on his first day of plebeian meals he took one mouthful, spat it out, and cried "Zis food is 'orrible! Eet ees not made with luff!" For the next two days he refused to eat at all, and went to Laxmi in tears to appeal against his dreadful fate, but it was all to no avail. His girlfriend did manage to sneak him some titbits from Bhagwan's kitchen, but it was not enough, and eventually he had to join us in the canteen. "I don't know how you guys eat zis shit!" he would complain as he forced it down.

Deeksha, who had been put in charge of the catering arrange-ments,was busily empire-building. She now had full-time laundry staff, seamstresses and shoppers. She bought a van, two motorcycles and two large safes, for the ashram was beginning to make large sums of money. One safe was reserved for cash and gold bars. She kept her Swiss chocolate in the other.

Visitors were charged an entrance fee, charged to eat in the restaurant, and charged for therapy groups. Books were on sale, and we began making orange robes on a commercial scale. A soap and shampoo factory was set up to manufacture special scentless soap, and a little later a bakery was established by Deeksha, who also instigated an 'executive restaurant' for high-ranking sannyasi staff. This was a top-quality establishment, with white tablecloths, best bone china and real silver cutlery. Deeksha also installed her own accountants, to keep an eye on the finances accruing from her empire. The restaurants and culinary offshoots soon started to bring in more money than the therapy groups. By 1981, Deeksha was grossing 100,000 rupees a week just in canteen sales.

The health centre, originally staffed by the German doctors, became a thriving hospital in its own right, managed by a beautiful, slim Hawaiian lady called Jeannie. I promoted myself from darkroom assistant to health worker, and became part of the therapy team. As a qualified osteopath, I was soon in demand, and was also doing more healing work based on ancient Chinese methods. I was allocated a converted veranda to do my healing work, sharing this cramped space with a Japanese shiatsu therapist. By the time the hot season came round I was giving my treatments lying down beside my clients, where it was marginally cooler, a practice which gave rise to a malicious rumour that I made love to all my patients.

My own schedule began to alter. I was still getting up early every morning to teach karate to the guards, then some days I would motorcycle out of Poona to take photographs, both for the ashram books and for my New York agent. Healing now took up much of the rest of my time. Many highly knowledgeable people passed through the ashram, and I was able to learn useful new techniques, both in healing and in photography. At last I was beginning to make proper use of my healing powers, which had lain dormant for so many years.

I am naturally a high-energy person, and though I found it difficult to meditate for more than forty minutes at a time, I was always up and doing something creative. I still had too many jobs and was far too busy most of the time, but I loved it.

Not everything ran smoothly, though. After I had been in India for about four years, Laxmi took me into her office and gave me a summons from the Bombay CID. Why was I being summonsed? Laxmi wasn't worried at all. "Child, you can relax. Look at Laxmi, these things happen every day and she does not worry. Trust in *his* grace only, God will take care!"

She checked that I had enough money for the train fare, and sent me off the next morning with the address of a Bombay lawyer. I spent half an hour with a very young-looking lawyer before we went for my interrogation with the CID. His questions puzzled me to begin with: "So you are staying in India as a tourist? You are not fed by ashram? You are not given accommodation by ashram? OK?" But I soon realised what was happening. Though I had worked at Poona for four years, at the first hint of trouble Laxmi was protecting the ashram, and her loyalty to me came a very poor second. She was denying my intimate connection with the ashram, to protect Bhagwan and the ashram's tax-free status.

It turned out that a rich and influential young Indian disciple called Fali had reported me to the CID for suspected currency smuggling. He was jealous of my relationship with a woman he was infatuated with, and wanted me out of the country. Luckily for me, Fali let his secret slip at a party one night. Word got back to Laxmi, and Fali promptly withdrew his complaint.

The other major problem at this time was that my relationship with Gayan, my beautiful German wife, fell apart completely. After our registry office marriage, which we followed with a flamboyant Hindu ceremony, I had been faithful to her for eighteen months, refusing all other propositions — quite a feat in our intensely polygamous ashram. One night, however, I gave in. Afterwards I felt extremely guilty, and had no hesitation in turning down the next offer, but by then I was aware of how angry I was towards Gayan, because I did want to make love with other women, and had not because of her.

After a month of confusion over the situation I sought out Vivek, and asked her if she would consult Bhagwan about it. I would have written, but by this time I had been directed not to read or write, and only wrote about two letters a year to my father. When Vivek came back from Bhagwan she delivered the answer with great intensity. It was almost as if Bhagwan himself was standing in front of me. "Bhagwan says never feel guilty about *anything*! Be natural, and follow your feelings. That's a good message, isn't it?" She smiled. "Now you are free."

I walked down the corridor feeling enormously relieved. It was now more than two years since Bhagwan had told me to settle down with one woman, and the directive had eventually become very painful to both Gayan and to me. I felt trapped and inhibited. I had lost the sexual freedom that was supposed to be an integral part of the ashram's *raison d'être*.

Gayan and I talked it all over in adult fashion. Two weeks later she asked Bhagwan her own question, the answer to which was that we should split up that very day and move to separate rooms. In a celebration of pent-up longing, I spent the next week sleeping with all the women I had been attracted to in the last two years but had been denied.

It was not to be as blissful as I had anticipated. At the end of that licentious week my first liaison told me that she had gonorrhoea. I was horrified, and had to tell all my other contacts immediately. Later that day they were all sitting on the bench outside the health centre laboratory. As one of them later said to me, if I had walked by I would have been lynched for sure. Thankfully, nobody had been infected, but these ever-increasing incidents made us all stop and think. Modern times had caught up with the ashram. Not long after this scare, the first herpes attack occurred, and herpes spread very rapidly through the commune. One English swami developed a blister in his eyelid and nearly went blind. It was time to cool things off.

The Indian doctors who were approached for treatment had never seen herpes before. Because of the widespread ignorance about communicable diseases, sexual and otherwise, all the health staff were called together, and those who knew anything about such diseases were invited to pool their knowledge. Several sannyasis had already died of hepatitis, a Dutch sannyasi had died of a brain tumour, and tuberculosis and pneumonia were common — though I was not aware of it at the time, I was suffering from tuberculosis too. Pre-group medicals — especially for the tantra and encounter groups — were now instigated, and post-group pre-darshan examinations ordered for anybody who had become sick or infected. Given our sexual proclivities, it was not just sexually-related diseases that could spread rapidly, but lice and scabies too. It was a nightmare trying to keep track of contacts, since disciples were constantly flying in from all over the world as well as living all over Poona and participating in naked sex-therapy sessions, but it was essential if we were to avoid really serious infections. Before long a steady stream of doctors and lab technicians from the health centre could be seen furiously pedalling their bicycles up leafy lanes and to hotels, to tell yet another hapless soul that a sexual disease had possibly been transmitted to them. Long depressed queues formed outside the health centre.

It was difficult to earn money in India to stay in the ashram. There were few legal ways in which a Westerner could earn money, and before long many of the girls turned to prostitution. Sannyasin women would take a train to Bombay and make themselves available in the foyers of the most expensive hotels. The ashram grapevine had it that the Arab clientele was the richest, and should be approached first. This further complicated the problem of sexually-transmitted disease, but it appeared that the unfortunate Arab gentlemen got the worst of the transaction. It was not long before the grand and prestigious Taj Mahal Hotel banned all sannyasin women, because the prostitition had become so all-pervasive and distasteful.

The other main way of making money in those days was to mount a drug run. These were sometimes officially sanctioned, although very discreetly, and nobody who went on any of these highly illegal trips is willing to confess it even now. But everybody knew it went on, and the runners would even ask Bhagwan for oblique advice about the best day to go.

In order to raise the money to stay at Poona, many people got caught up in illegal and dangerous enterprises. Marijuana derivatives were easily available in Poona, and heroin and opium were obtainable cheaply in Bombay. Several sannyasis other than Rishi were caught running drugs. A German girl was caught in Canada and given a year's probation, and an English girl was caught on a run to New Zealand and given a two year sentence. Three English girls were caught in 1979, and their stories were given great prominence in the British press, where references were made to 'evil cults' and 'brainwashing'. Laxmi, who knew about these runs, had an informer at police headquarters who tipped her off when there was about to be a raid on the ashram. Drugs were, of course, not officially allowed in the ashram itself, but many disciples living elsewhere in Poona kept supplies, ready to deal in drugs or smuggle them out of the country.

Although Laxmi could give advance warning of possible police raids on the ashram, she could do nothing to protect people undertaking drug runs. One disciple received a three-year sentence in Bombay — an unpleasant prospect. And if Laxmi had informers at the police station, there was no doubt that the police also had spies within the ashram. One turned out to be Laxmi's personal typist, who Laxmi and I caught redhanded outside the local police commissioner's office one day.

Though the drug runs only had tenuous official support, they certainly helped the ashram to find its feet financially. Those who were successful gave huge donations, and sometimes bought themselves a permanent apartment within the ashram, which in 1977 cost about £5,000 each. Whenever a disciple was about to make a drug run, they would ask Bhagwan whether it was a good time to go to Thailand. "Wednesday would be good," he would say, or "Don't go until Friday," knowing exactly what they meant. Rumours abounded that both Bhagwan and Laxmi encouraged prostitution and drug runs, and though this was not directly true, Laxmi accepted very large donations without questioning too closely where they had come from, and Bhagwan certainly enjoyed the proceeds. By 1980 he had two white Rolls Royces in Poona, an unheard-of luxury in this land of poverty.

It was very clear that those who gave large sums of money earned themselves special advancement within the ashram, a covetous place to live or a prestigious position. One new disciple offered Laxmi more than half a million dollars, but Laxmi turned it down, saying "Keep your money, child. We only want it when you are holding on to it and it is a barrier for you." There were enough instances of both Bhagwan and Laxmi refusing money in this way to give the whole financial side a genuine sense of spiritual disinterest. Notwithstanding, less than a fortnight later the same sannyasi moved into Bhagwan's house, an honour not normally bestowed on anybody unless they had given two years of arduous service first. Only Terence Stamp had moved faster.

This man was assigned to my top security team, and proved to be very good at his job, but when two weeks later Sheela asked him for the money he had offered, he faltered and explained that he no longer had the money.

"Gone?" queried the astonished Sheela.

"Yes," he said, "it's gone. I lost it all in a business deal that fell through last week."

It wasn't long before Laxmi called me into her office and ordered me to fire him from the security force. I did so with a not very convincing lie that he saw straight through at once. Tears came to his eyes as he realised that I was lying in order not to have to tell him that these were simply orders from above. Though he lost a choice job, Vivek's intercession prevented him from being summarily evicted from Lao Tzu House.

As the building work progressed, it became necessary to raise capital through bank loans. Brett, a swami with the reputation of being a financial genius and gifted trouble-shooter, was detailed to try and raise an enormous loan from one Indian bank consortium. The consortium had already told Laxmi that such a loan was impossible, but within a fortnight Brett had succeeded in securing the loan. Thus Laxmi lost face, and she was not pleased. Despite my pleading on his behalf, she instructed me to fire him as a guard and aikido teacher, and within a month he had been sent back to England, permanently.

Meanwhile, Bhagwan's collecting manias persisted, and as his tastes changed a curious phenomenon emerged among the ashram staff who were close to him. As he collected pens, sheets or towels, so we would copy him, though we didn't notice it at first. His current mania was pens, though not fountain pens — he complained of the mess they made. If a particular brand of pen took his fancy, he would amass a collection of them, always ordering the most expensive diamond-encrusted ones from the top of the range.

Bhagwan was a real techno-freak, and loved every new piece of gadgetry he could lay his hands on. In this respect he was certainly following his own dictum that the way to transcendence lay through surfeit and overindulgence. It was one of Teertha's jobs to order new gadgets from the West as they caught Bhagwan's fancy, and with increasing abandon he sent away for things from Dunhill, Du Pont, Mont Blanc and Cartier. Once Teertha ordered a smart new IBM typewriter, explaining that he needed it to type up the notes for Bhagwan's daily lectures, and since it was for Bhagwan the type had to be clear and easy to read. It was far better than anything Laxmi had in her office, and she was furious. Teertha explained that Bhagwan had admired the professional quality of the notes prepared on the new typewriter, but Laxmi was not mollified. "Child!" she exploded, "Bhagwan does not either *need* or *like* anything! *He* does not care about these petty, petty things, fool. Bhagwan does not *like*, is that clear? *He* is. In is-ness there is no like or dislike. Bring that IBM here to Laxmi immediately, we have better uses for it. And *never* order such a thing for *him* again."

Teertha obliged, and the IBM was installed in her office, yet another example of Laxmi's ability to get what she wanted under the guise of total loyalty to Bhagwan. In this instance, however, Laxmi's wiliness failed her. Bhagwan complained to Teertha that his lecture notes were not as clearly typed as before. What had happened to that lovely clear typeface? Teertha had the IBM back the very next day.

One day Bhagwan suddenly announced in a morning lecture that he was going to stop carrying a clean towel with him wherever he went. This may seem a small thing, but it had become one of his trademarks — he had had a small embroidered towel over his arm the first time I had met him in his Woodlands flat. His announcement was greeted with loud hoots of disbelief and wonderment from the normally respectful audience. His towels were his most versatile affectation, and were used as fly swats, hand driers and comforters. They were also much-treasured gifts to sannyasis, the hand-embroidered ones being the most coveted. As Bhagwan's

photographer I was disappointed, since the towels were a valuable
prop. He went on to say that although the towels had been very
useful to him since his university days, he would now stop carrying
them as an outward sign of his unattachment to the material world,
and of his enlightenment. As a token gesture, he was going to throw
this, his last towel, into the audience. Nobody was to move, and
whoever it landed on could keep it. It landed at the feet of an Indian
disciple, who grasped it victoriously and turned to acknowledge the
many looks of admiration and envy from his fellow sannyasis.

At his lecture the next morning Bhagwan came without his towel,
and his discomfort was very apparent. The day after that the
customary towel reappeared, but nobody said a word. The day after
that he arrived twenty minutes late, but minus the towel. It was all
very strange.

A few days later I heard what had happened from Shanti,
Bhagwan's chief chambermaid. Vivek had become tired of keeping
Bhagwan in fresh, clean towels, and had given him an ultimatum: to
look after them himself, or to get rid of them all. He had a habit of
stuffing the dirty ones behind his bookcase after the lecture and
forgetting all about them. Vivek would find them days later.

So the first day he had come without a towel, but the next morning
he had found an old towel to bring with him, and took it without
Vivek's knowledge. When Vivek saw him with his towel again she
resolved to lock up all the towels. On the morning of the delayed
lecture he had told her that he would not lecture until she relented.
This lasted until Bhagwan gave in, and agreed to lecture without the
towel. "Every man is henpecked," he announced in a lecture some
time later, "and I mean *every man!*"

In the course of this year, Vivek's position within the ashram
changed drastically. At a photographic session in 1977 it became very
clear that something very unusual was happening. Bhagwan seemed
very ill at ease and uncharacteristically jumpy. Vivek appeared to
arrange his hair and hat, then sped off into the foliage. A minute or
two later we heard a most unearthly wailing, sobs of heart-rending
anguish. Vivek was in agony, sobbing her heart out. Bhagwan called
to her repeatedly to come back, but she refused. He did his best to
remain composed, but Vivek's sobs kept piercing the air. The session
ended, not very satisfactorily, and it was clear that Bhagwan had
other things on his mind.

Vivek had been his lover and constant companion for seven years, and now that relationship had changed. She still had her privileged position, but Bhagwan's attitude to her had altered. For so many years Vivek had remained aloof, unapproachable, doing only Bhagwan's bidding. It was difficult to make out what had happened. Was Bhagwan displeased with her, or was he looking for somebody else? Or was Vivek unhappy with him?

What was certain was that Vivek had taken a new lover, a German group leader called Prasad. When we found out we were speechless. In taking a sannyasi lover she had become ordinary, one of the populace like the rest of us. She continued to take care of Bhagwan as devotedly as before, supervised the preparation of his food, oversaw his laundry. But she also began to appear at our all-night parties, something she had never done before, dancing slowly and mysteriously with her new German lover.

Her new lover was not as faithful as he might have been. A few months after their affair started, Prasad met Vivek in the kitchen. She was pleased to see him, but where was his mala? He had to confess that it was on a bedside table in the Blue Diamond Hotel, in the room of a French woman.

Bhagwan's concerns about children and pregnancy began to have far-reaching repercussions on the health of Poona sannyasis. There was a boom in female sterilisations, an operation which was expensive, irreversible, and, in India, dangerous. In one week in 1979 two women nearly died while being sterilised. Laxmi and her assistants decided that it would be much better if the men had vasectomies, which were safer, faster and cheaper.

A month or so after Vivek's distressful scene I met Vivek's new boyfriend, a swami called Devaraj, otherwise Dr George Meredith. I had first met him when he was selling surgical instruments to our health centre from his small truck. He had driven overland from Arabia, where he had been in charge of a hospital, with his wife and young daughter. He seemed very laid back and relaxed, but he also had passionate and peculiar enthusiasms. One of his first projects in Poona was an anti-dysentery drive. Toilet paper had been considered an unnecessary luxury at the ashram, and Devaraj pointed out that the lack of hygienic alternatives was not helping his campaign. He was responsible for the installation of high-speed water jets that did the job of toilet paper, which were affectionately known as bum-wipers.

I was not as happy with Devaraj's next campaign. A few weeks later I bumped into Devaraj, and he told me his news: "I've just had my vasectomy. It was terrific, so easy! A real piece of cake, Shiva, and it only took a local anaesthetic" He indicated his genitals, covered by a cotton towel, and asked if I would like to look. I recoiled, wondering what this was all in aid of. Though I demurred, he insisted, and showed me the surgeon's handiwork. I got out of the room as quickly as possible.

A week later one of Laxmi's assistants approached me. "Have you considered the operation?" she asked.

"I've thought about it," I answered, "but it's not something I'd choose to do of my own accord."

She went on to tell me that it would set a good example to the rest of the commune if I did have a vasectomy. I promised to think about it.

By the end of the day I said I would have the operation. It was following Bhagwan's advice, I had no desire at that time to have children, and it seemed the right thing to do. It also fitted in with my feeling that the world was already overcrowded, and that every one of us must do our part to ensure its survival.

After I had had the operation I was asked to help promote the campaign in the commune, and in the next two or three months maybe a quarter of the sannyasi men had vasectomies. It was only possible to avoid the operation by being adamant that you weren't going to have it, and such refusal sometimes meant having to leave the ashram workforce. This kind of stance flew in the face of established ashram behaviour. Vasectomies became quite the vogue, yet another step on Bhagwan's road to total surrender.

Chapter Nine
PROTECTING BHAGWAN

During the late 1970s we were expanding so fast that overcrowding became a serious problem. About three thousand sannyasis, most of them now Westerners, lived either within the four-acre ashram or nearby in Poona. Many, many more people came to visit, and I became quite anxious about our security arrangments. For ten rupees a time anyone could come and visit, and it was not unusual for Bhagwan to be lecturing to three thousand people. By this time Laxmi had grudgingly alloted me twenty-five part-time guards to handle lecture security — it was barely sufficient to handle such a crowd. He spoke in Hindi for one month and then in English for the next, and though the most faithful went to every lecture, it was noticeable that the audience doubled on the English-speaking days. Those of us who went to the Hindi lectures would occasionally be rewarded with a few English words suddenly appearing in a sea of Hindi, such as "I am the one", but most of the Westerners stayed away.

Anybody at all could come to the early morning lecture at eight o'clock, as long as they paid their entrance fee. The darshans, which were held in the evening, were far more select affairs, and everybody who attended first had to be vetted by one of Laxmi's two senior assistants. A queue would start to form outside her office at about four o'clock, and one by one people would be ushered in to request a darshan. Darshans were divided into several categories — there were 'sannyas darshans' where new sannyasis were ordained, 'talking darshans', 'silent darshans', and 'group darshans', where you met Bhagwan as one of a therapy or activity group. On-going groups like the karate and music groups had a monthly darshan, where they would show off their skills to Bhagwan.

Potential darshan participants were more carefully vetted than ever before. It seemed that Bhagwan was becoming frailer, and the list of substances he was allergic to grew and grew. He could not now abide socks and woollen clothing. Two female sannyasins would stand at the entrance to Lao Tzu house before darshan and sniff behind the ears and under the armpits of every entrant, however famous or renowned they might be.

But the sniffing was not limited to scent or unclean bodies. As Bhagwan was now so famous and controversial, there was always the danger that a would-be attacker or assassin would try to get in. It was my job to spot potential troublemakers and forbid them entrance to darshan. Those who were violent or unstable, or who I felt were a possible threat, were conveniently found to have an unnacceptably strong 'fragrance' and turned away. Disagreements about this decision frequently came to blows, and here the French were the worst offenders. I had several bloody fights at the gate.

Once they were in the hall, those who were admitted were surrounded, unbeknown to them, by a small group of specially-trained guards. Security did not only apply to darshans. At the end of every therapy and activity group, leaders now had to fill in forms detailing anybody they felt was a possible security risk. These lists were passed to me through Laxmi's office, and whole lists of people who had been banned from entering the ashram were posted in the main guard's hut. It looked like a series of Wild West 'wanted' posters, as each name was accompanied by a brief description and a blurred Polaroid photograph. There were quite a few women in the banned category, with Germans and French always prominent among them.

Anyone who was sick had to produce doctor's notes saying they were fit enough to attend darshan, and another of my jobs was to distinguish between pre-darshan weeping, which was acceptable, and a cold, which was not. Bhagwan aroused strong emotions in people, and those who had been granted an audience with him were often overcome with uncontrollable tears.

The daily lectures were now held in the newly-completed Buddha Hall. I was in this hall teaching a class of karate students one day when I noticed a group of people who were on an enlightenment intensive. This class had to practise walking slowly and meditatively, with their eyes focused on the ground four feet in front of them, for half an hour several times a day. There were about thirty in this particular group, and as they walked round the perimeter of Buddha Hall I noticed among them a stunning raven-haired woman. She looked like a South Seas princess, a dusky maiden in her bright crimson batik-print sarong. As soon as I saw her my concentration for

Rajneesh during a photo session in his garden. Rajneesh gives one of his famous charismatic grins which tended to melt the hearts of his followers. Photo credit: Hugh Milne.

Rajneesh writing out initiates' new names during Darshan. Author Hugh Milne sits at his right. Photo credit: Carol Mersereau.

An "Energy Darshan." Rajneesh is about to touch the bearded sannyasi in front of him on his "Third Eye" and transmit "Enlightened" energy to him. The exclusively female entourage of mediums dance and sway around them. Photo credit: Carol Mersereau.

Rajneesh lecturing in Buddha Hall in 1980. The author is sitting facing the audience in the foreground. Photo credit: Carol Mersereau.

Sufi dancing in Chuang Tzu Auditorium, 1979. The group is lead by Aneeta, at center.
Photo credit: Hugh Milne.

This was how Rajneesh would look at you when he was in a decisive mood. "Look at me," he once said to a disciple. "I am absolutely certain about everything!" At other times he was not quite so certain. Circa 1977. Photo credit: Hugh Milne.

A Vipassana meditation retreat in Poona. The retreat leader is about to hit one of the meditators on the crown of the head with a tap from the stick. Photo credit: Carol Mersereau.

One of the group leaders venting her anger wholeheartedly: the so-called "Pillow Meditation." Circa 1977. Photo credit: Hugh Milne.

Rajneesh posing during a photo session in his garden in Poona, 1976. During this time he still wore a "Lunghai" under his robe and always had a brightly colored towel with him. The hats were worn solely during the photo sessions. Photo credit: Hugh Milne.

Rajneesh being served champagne by Sheela on board Pan Am Kit Carson, somewhere over the Arabian Sea. Note that the guru has already got both hands full. At this time the Foundation's press department described Rajneesh as a man with "a disintegrating spine" who needed medical intervention "as a matter of life and death." May 31, 1981. Photo credit: J. Lehman.

In a misty Montclair, New Jersey, Sheela shows her master the first of his ninety Rolls Royces. 1981. Photo credit: Hugh Milne.

Driven by an ecstatic Sheela, Rajneesh sweeps through the gates to Rajneeshpuram for the first time. Standing there, taking his picture, I wondered what he would think of the dustbowl he was about to see. August 1981. Photo credit: Hugh Milne.

A view of the central valley of Rancho Rajneesh, with the flashflood-prone creek in the foreground. One of the fifty plastic mobile homes is being towed in, followed by one of the Rajneesh's dusty Rolls Royces and his armed chase car. November 1981. Photo credit: Hugh Milne.

Rajneeshees looking wistfully after their guru as he leaves the ranch on one of his daily drives to Madras, in early spring, 1981. That spring, when many more female disciples had arrived, the male/female ratio began to return to Poona proportions. Photo credit: Hugh Milne.

"Nature does not care about us, so why should we care about nature!" Rajneesh's Heavy Equipment Department making their third attempt at a new road to their stranded guru's house. December 1981. Photo credit: Hugh Milne.

This poignant picture shows Sheela marrying Rajneesh's personal physician, Devaraj, to a rich and talented Los Angeles disciple, Hasya. Two years later, Sheela pleaded guilty to conspiring to attempt to murder Devaraj, and Hasya had succeeded Sheela as Rajneesh's personal secretary after Sheela and Rajneesh had a disagreement over the purchase of a $1.2 million wristwatch. 1984. Photo credit: S. Kaplan.

An "Energy Darshan" in 1980, with Rajneesh attending to the "Third Eye" of one of his entourage of hand-picked mediums. What the picture cannot convey is the intense tropical heat, the tangible sexuality, and the almost deafening jungle rhythm of the music group. 1980. Photo credit: S. Kaplan.

Disciples sitting during a lecture in Poona in 1977. Rajneesh's lush tropical garden forms the backdrop to the auditorium. Sheela rests her head down on the marble floor, as was her custom. The German musician, Deuter, sits behind her, at the far right of this picture. 1977. Photo credit: S. Kaplan.

Accompanied by a delighted Vivek Rajneesh alights from a chartered Lear jet at Redmond Airport in August 1981 Four years later, a similar aircraft delivered Rajneesh to a far less happy rendezvous, this time with the FBI Photo credit: Hugh Milne.

the karate class faltered. Whoever was she? I paired off the karate class to practise sparring while I went to have a closer look at this apparition. As I strode over in my bright red karate uniform my heart was pounding, but she kept her eyes obediently cast down and did not even look at me.

I knew that I had to get to know her better, and quickly. She came to take sannyas a few days later. Bhagwan called her 'Ma Prem Isabel' — Isabel being her previous name, and Bhagwan having given up the practice of issuing Indian names to Western disciples as a matter of course — and told her to go to the tantra and encounter groups, the really heavy ones. As I sat next to Bhagwan in that darshan, my heart did a flip-flop. Isabel was a bare eighteen inches away from me, and seemed even more beautiful and refined than before, a real princess.

Isabel was later to play a prominent part in Rajneesh Foundation International. A Chilean-born Frenchwoman, she had been working as a guide for the Tahiti Tourist Board — though I couldn't imagine anybody spending their time looking at the scenery with Isabel as a guide.

A week after I had first seen Isabel, I asked her for a date, but she turned me down. No, she said, she was too busy. I tried a different tack. Would she like to book a massage with me? Her eyes widened. "Yes," she said, "I will book one . . ." I told her I had a two-month waiting list, but if she wanted we could have a special session after the usual ones had finished. Isabel accepted. We met the next day and made love all afternoon. I was transported. What a beauty she was!

I was head over heels in love. I couldn't believe my fortune at finding such an incredible woman! Laxmi allowed her to come into Lao Tzu House, where I was now living in the room directly above Bhagwan's, and we slept together almost every night. I still preferred to sleep alone sometimes, as I needed privacy to meditate and reflect, and also to catch up on sleep, as my busy schedule sometimes left me exhausted. After a month of unguarded and trusted passion, and the most sublime tantric experiences I had ever had, I discovered to my horror that Isabel had also been sleeping with Sant, the senior Indian sannyasi guard.

I was angry and hurt, but when I questioned her about it, she said "But Shiva, what is wrong? Surely you can share me? What is the matter with that? Bhagwan says it is perfectly all right. If three people want to share like that, they can do it. Sant is beautiful, and I love being with him as well as with you. Can't we go on as we were?"

"I just can't do it," I said. "You mean too much to me. I couldn't stand being here on my own, knowing you were over there making love with Sant. You're much more to me than a good lay, you're the most fantastic woman I have ever met. I simply can't agree to a triangle. If you want to stay with Sant, then stay with him, but you can't have us both, or at least not as far as I'm concerned." I was sure she would stay with me. Surely she loved me best!

She chose to stay with Sant. I went through a month of heartbreak, disillusionment and despair, looking at women only to compare them with Isabel. Nobody else would do. I tried other relationships, but they didn't work.

After six months Isabel went to work as Laxmi's assistant and chaperone, so we could no longer avoid each other. Many of the other women in the ashram hierarchy regarded Isabel with suspicion, seeing her as something of an upstart. The only person Isabel looked comfortable with was Laxmi. Sheela was especially unfriendly, and darted looks of venom in Isabel's direction from time to time, but Isabel was just that bit too sophisticted and self-assured for Sheela to fathom.

As I was walking home from the health centre one day, I glimpsed Isabel walking past the end of the road. She saw me, and stopped and waited. I was still very guarded with her, but she had stopped to tell me that she had finished with Sant, who now had another girl. "She'll be good for him," she said. "Would you like to come for some tea at my hut?" Isabel lived in one of the thousand or so huts that had sprung up near the ashram during that time of rapid expansion.

"Yes," I said, trying not to sound too eager. "It would be nice to do that, to come and have a talk." At that point talk was all I could do, as I had just discovered a reinfestation of pubic lice, the bane of health professionals in India. As soon as the trouble had cleared up I was ready to try being lovers with Isabel again. And so was she.

We spent the whole of the next year together, locked in a fond, intimate and caring relationship. Isabel nursed me through dysentery and two bad attacks of dengue fever. We split up once or twice, but were always back together within a week. We agreed that if either of us slept with anyone else, we would tell the other straightaway. If one of us felt specially drawn to spend a night with someone else without actually making love, however, we didn't need to say anything.

One of the reasons why the Poona ashram became so famous was that Bhagwan loved publicity. He was addicted to it. Our public relations department put out press releases which were taken up by both the Indian and the foreign press. Media people soon realised that the ashram would make wonderful press copy and TV material, and a steady stream of journalists and reporters came to write and make programmes about our events. The well-known British TV journalist Alan Whicker arrived in 1978 with a six-man crew, and made a documentary about us which was mainly favourable. Two years later Bernard Levin came and wrote an extremely laudatory series of three articles about us in *The Times*. These were to have an important influence in making the name of Bhagwan respectable around the world.

Bhagwan did not divide publicity into 'good' and 'bad'. For him it was all good, and few restrictions were placed on press or TV reporters. Only tantra and encounter groups could not be photographed without express permission, but even so the German magazine *Stern* was allowed to take some carefully-posed naked shots of the tantra group without any censorship. The same magazine printed a picture of Vivek and Bhagwan getting out of a car, with me holding the door open. The caption read: 'Bhagwan with his two wives'. My hair was now waist-length, and in my orange robe I was easily mistaken for a woman. Bhagwan was highly amused, and referred to it during a morning lecture, saying "Shiva is so beautiful; what is wrong with it?" Talking about publicity in general, he went on to say: "I have now found the fulfilment of my life. Now it does not matter whether I am famous or notorious. I do not care whether people see me as Buddha or as Rasputin. Few people will think of me as Buddha, and the majority will probably regard me as Rasputin. That's beautiful. One thing I am certainly interested in is that everybody should think *something* about me."

By this time Bhagwan had his first Rolls Royce, a huge white specially-lengthened vehicle that Sheela had imported at vast expense from America. It came complete with gun ports, tear gas ejectors, a PA system, and one-inch thick windows. It weighed a ton more than the 'standard' model, and could withstand bullets, hand grenades and mines. Foreign cars are not allowed into India until an import tax of at least 120% has been paid, and everybody drives the 1950s-looking Ambassador or Fiat cars. Enough money will always secure a forbidden import. I used to drive Bhagwan the hundred yards to morning lecture in his Rolls. It was clear that he had already become the most successful and charismatic guru in India.

Bhagwan still had a special relationship with Vivek, but this was less close than it had once been. He used to boast that he made life hell for her, and this was certainly true. What he may not have realised is that Vivek took it out just as venomously on those who were near to her. If Bhagwan had made her furious for any reason, then she would get angry with her kitchen staff, the gardeners who brought in Bhagwan's special organically-grown vegetables, or me. For one six-week period it seemed that she turned on me viciously every time she saw me. Because of her privileged position one did not normally cross swords with Vivek, but eventually I had had enough. I was sure she was pursuing a personal vendetta. "I've had enough of this crap," I shouted. "Just stop picking on me. You've no right to treat me like this."

She went very pale, tightened her lips, and demanded to know what on earth I was talking about. I told her how I thought she had been behaving. "It's your imagination," was her reply. "You'd better watch out for your job, Shiva!" That did it. I started to cry openly, and this unmasculine and uncharacteristic behaviour pulled Vivek up short. It was as if she had seen me as a human being for the first time, somebody who could feel hurt. Her face relaxed and she embraced me. The storm had passed. "I'm sorry," she said, melting. "Don't take it so personally. Things get tough sometimes."

When I saw her the next day, she called me over and asked me how I was. Was she about to fire me? Had she spoken to Bhagwan about it? She looked me softly in the eyes and said again "How are you today?"

"I'm fine," I answered defensively.

"No, Shiva, that's not what I meant. How *are* you today?" Instantly I knew that all was forgiven, and went off to see Laxmi feeling wonderful.

After Alan Whicker, two very famous people arrived at the ashram from the States — singer Diana Ross and Werner Erhart, the founder of est, which had just opened its first centre in India. They were on a world tour. As soon as we knew that Diana Ross was coming, Bhagwan wanted to hear some of her music, and a wild search started in the ashram for one of her tapes. None could be found, and Bhagwan had to meet her without knowing anything of her craft. The darshan regulars always looked forward to Bhagwan's meetings with famous people, because it was then that he would rise to unprecedented heights of persuasiveness and salesmanship, and be quite a delight to watch.

As Diana Ross and Werner Erhart came in for their darshan, special front row spaces were reserved. Since Bhagwan was allergic to dust, feathers and wool, no mats or pillows were allowed to soften the cold marble, and everybody had to come with bare feet. For the first hour our celebrity guests squirmed in discomfort, trying to maintain as much dignity as possible, while Bhagwan sat in his large luxurious armchair, the image of Buddha-like stillness. He gave sannyas to a few new initiates, but was clearly pitching his messages in Diana Ross and Werner Erhart's direction. By the time he came to them, I expected them to be very open to what he had to say.

Erhart was very much the American businessman, prosperous, tanned, robust and forthright. He looked like an ex-marine, tough and healthy. At that time he was more famous than Bhagwan, though it was not to be long before Bhagwan's publicity surpassed anything that Erhart had ever received. "So, Werner, you have come!" Bhagwan said majestically. "What about you, hmmm. Anything to say?"

Werner made a renewed effort to ease the ache in his thighs, and clasped his hands round his knees for the umpteenth time. When he spoke he was loud and confident, in contrast with Bhagwan's dulcet tones. "I want you to know what an honour it is to sit in your presence, and that Diana and I have been looking forward to seeing you. We have heard so many good things about you."

"Hmm, yes, good, anything to say?" repeated Bhagwan.

"Yes, well, it really is good to be here . . ." said Werner, somewhat at a loss.

"And you are travelling on to somewhere, to Australia, hmmm? You cannot stay a few days, get accustomed to my people, feel the work that is going on here? If you did, that would be good. I have a feeling that you would see something here that is missing in your own work, an aspect of the Heart. If you can stay you will learn much . . ."

"Well, yes, thank you Bhagwan, that really is a most generous offer, but we have a tight schedule, and must be moving on."

Bhagwan's chat with Diana Ross was briefer and even more boring. Their darshan was very soon over, and nothing seemed to have happened. An hour or so later a few of us got together to share our impressions. Why had it been such an anti-climax? Why had Erhart not wanted to discuss anything with Bhagwan? The meeting had turned out to be quite inconsequential, and the distinguished visitors had not been in the least overwhelmed.

A month or two later a copy of the *est Newsletter* filtered into the ashram. Werner's World Tour was chronicled in detail, but there was not a single mention of Bhagwan or the visit to Poona. The slight did not go unnoticed, and Bhagwan lost no time in denouncing Erhart. He was a shallow man, Bhagwan said in his next lecture, a man who paid lip service to spirituality while really only being interested in people's money. A message also went to the sannyasin running the London centre that she should stop sending people to est trainings.

I had always thought that Laxmi had been too casual about Bhagwan's security. She had continually resisted the idea of my training guards or taking precautions against attacks. I was sure that sooner or later there would be a serious attack on Bhagwan, and I wanted to be ready, so I had prepared the best part-time team of guards I could to protect Bhagwan during lectures and darshans. There were some very peculiar and highly-charged people around, and you could never be too sure.

At eleven o'clock one hot pre-monsoon night, as I was asleep on the roof of Bhagwan's house, I was awoken by the sound of sannyasi guards' whistles. I grabbed a towel and ran downstairs into the hall outside Bhagwan's room. Vivek was already there, looking very flustered. An Indian man with a maniacal grin on his face had been rapping on Bhagwan's window. In the jungle of the garden I stumbled into a guard, who handed me a sodden slippery bundle. It was the man who had been banging on Bhagwan's window, and he seemed to be choking to death. In an instant I realised what had happened — he had stuffed his entire mala down his throat. We pulled it out, and then listened to his story. He had had an over-powering urge to see Bhagwan, and had had to answer the call. He was soon brought to his senses by Laxmi, who ordered him off the premises and banned him from the ashram.

These 'he's calling me' incidents were not uncommon. On another occasion an attractive lady had managed to slip past the guard at Lao Tzu gate by pretending to be accompanying a resident. The guard had then glimpsed her taking off all her clothes as she disappeared round the final corner before being in full view of Bhagwan's room. There was now only one guard between her and Bhagwan's window, and he was so deeply immersed in an exciting Louis L'Amour novel that he did not see her until her naked form flashed right past him.

The gate guard was now running after her, leaving the gate defenceless, and she was caught less than ten feet from Bhagwan's room in a desperate, slippery and embarrassed scuffle.

Regardless of these incidents, Laxmi remained indifferent to Bhagwan's security, thinking perhaps that he was magically protected from all attacks. We were not allowed weapons of any kind, which is why I felt that the karate training was so important. I only chose guards to assist me in lectures and darshans who did these voluntary classes enthusiastically. But the day-to-day guarding was far more lax. Unarmed combat was all that we could use. We were not encouraged by Laxmi to undertake any form of martial arts training, and she did her best to position the the young New Zealander's apathetic guarding crew in places where they could not see anything, and so would not be able to intercept an assassin until after he had reached Bhagwan.

Vivek, on the other hand, told me in no uncertain terms that she was disgusted by this lax approach to Bhagwan's security. Nobody seemed to care about his life or his privacy, she argued. The situation was getting more dangerous every day, and it was high time that something was done about it. I told Vivek about Laxmi's limitations on what I could do, but she would not be pacified, and repeated over and over again that something had to be done without delay.

After lecture I outlined my plans to Vivek. I proposed setting up a system of guards staffed entirely by trained martial arts experts and black belts, whose only responsibility would be to guard Bhagwan's quarters. I would stop doing my therapy work in order to train and co-ordinate them, and they would be quite separate from the ordinary system of guards in the rest of the ashram, the ones who until now had taken care of guarding Bhagwan's house. By speaking directly with Vivek the proposal would not have to go through Laxmi, who would be certain to block my plan if she knew about it in advance.

Bhagwan told Laxmi about the plan the next day. She later turned on me accusingly and told me that Bhagwan wanted only women black belts to sit in the most vital spot, just outside his room. There was only one female black belt in the whole commune to fulfil Laxmi's instructions — a slim and elegent American lady called Suresha. She was very fast, but far too slight for potentially deadly work. I relayed this to Vivek, who told me it was complete nonsense. I had half-believed Laxmi's story, as it was well-known that Bhagwan adhered to a belief in a 'female principle' whereby women found it easier to surrender to him than men, which is why only women held the highest positions in the commune.

I heard the real reason for Laxmi's 'female only' instruction later. For a long time Bhagwan had prophesied that he would be attacked in Poona by a sannyasi, who he said would be a male guard and a Westerner. Both Laxmi and Sheela were rather smug about this prophecy, as it meant that Bhagwan would not be attacked by one of their own, an Indian. Bhagwan had been threatened by a knife-wielding Indian in Bombay — he apparently said to his potential assassin "And after I am dead, then will you be happy?"; the man dropped his knife — but he would not believe that an assassination attempt might come from a fellow-countryman.

While there was only one woman karate expert in the ashram, my lecture hall security team already had eight men in it with black belts. One of Laxmi's assistants labelled my new platoon 'The Samurai Department', and within ten weeks fifty 'samurai' were working in the department. I was given the freedom to organise and train these men as I thought fit without Laxmi's interference. Vivek, freed from her bondage to Bhagwan, fell in love with one of the American samurais.

We had a makiwara — a straw-covered board — erected on the edge of Buddha Hall so that we could practise karate. I used to spend ten minutes each day delivering blows to this board with my hands, elbows and feet. Callouses the size of small cherries soon developed and hardened on my knuckles. A black belt called Satch taught a group of advanced warriors the art of bushido — traditional samurai training. We learned the use of the fearsome sai, a type of short and blunt practice sword. One thing that Satch taught us was humility, that however good you get, you can always be better, and there will always be somebody who is far better than you are. His school had only two grades of belt — black meant you *knew*, white meant you did not.

It was while we were organising and training the security force that we heard of the mass suicide of the followers of the Reverend Jim Jones in Guyana. I read that he too had a sophisticated system of guards, and was shocked that the name I had given to the guards under my command — angels — was the same as the name he had bestowed on his guards. Jim Jones' angels had administered the poison-laced Kool Aid to his disciples before taking their own lives.

Bhagwan made much of the event, answering questions about the Jonestown massacre and assuring us that such an event would be impossible with 'my people'.

Twenty minutes into the lecture on May 22nd I was handed a note with the terse words: 'Police inspector warns you attack expected today.' I flashed the 'extreme danger' sign to the twenty guards in the hall. Within seconds a robust-looking Indian man stood up about sixty feet from the stage, on Bhagwan's right. He shouted in Hindi "You are insulting our religions", then started to walk towards Bhagwan with a very determined look in his eyes. Five or six guards had already responded to my signal. A large Canadian sannyasi, Yogi, grabbed the man firmly, and three more guards quickly joined him. A second Indian then got up and grappled with the guards, apparently trying to free his co-conspirator. A brown arm briefly appeared at the top of this flailing of hands.

Two of my best-trained samurai were beside me. One of them pointed at the floor in front of us, where a rusty six-inch-long kitchen knife lay, having been thrown by the first Indian just as the guards had grabbed him. Meanwhile the other samurai leapt up behind me on the stage and started shouting directions. By now the hall was in uproar, with people in the audience screaming, sobbing and crying. Bhagwan, who had continued speaking until this point, now stopped talking and turned in the direction of the disturbance. "Be gentle with him, be gentle with him," he indicated as the Indian was carried out.

Bhagwan turned back to the audience. "Shanti, shanti," he said. Be peaceful, be peaceful. The sobbing subsided, and he continued with his lecture.

Before the lecture had ended a van-load of uniformed policemen arrived, armed with lathis. When the lecture had finished, guards surrounded the hall, and all the non-sannyasi Indian men in the audience were photographed by ashram photographers as they left. Potentially suspicious Indian men were taken aside by the CID for questioning.

Vivek, who had not been at the lecture that day, called me to her kitchen. She was furious. Why had I allowed a knife to be thrown at Bhagwan? Was I asleep? What had happened to my plan that if ever Bhagwan was attacked, he would immediately be surrounded by a huddle of samurai? I did not try to defend myself. I felt badly enough about the incident already. "I will have to talk to Laxmi about this," she concluded. "You will have to improve the guard. Bhagwan could have been killed!"

It transpired that five Indians had in fact planned a concerted attack, but all but one of them had stayed put when they saw how quickly the guards had reacted. In the subsequent court case the attackers were found not guilty, partly on the grounds that since Bhagwan had continued talking, it could not have been a serious murder attempt.

After the attack Laxmi withdrew her restrictions on training, and on the use of words like 'gun', 'knife', 'weapon', 'grenade' and 'attack'. She asked Bhagwan if I could wear a sai in lecture, the better to protect him. She described a sai to him as "very sharp-looking". He consented.

Until then all the guards in the audience had had to sit facing Bhagwan; now some could sit facing backwards so they could stop attackers without having to run after them first. Within a week the number of 'angels' in the lecture hall had doubled. A team of women sannyasins were brought in to frisk every lecture-goer, and metal detectors were ordered from the States, including several door-sized ones like those used in airport security.

Chapter Ten

DEATH OF A PRINCE AND LAST DAYS IN POONA

The samurai who had jumped up on the stage during the attack was called Kirti, otherwise Prince Wilf of Hanover, the cousin of Prince Charles, Prince of Wales. Although he did not speak much about his past, it had not been without adventure. He had arrived at the ashram with his wife and daughter several months before the attack, but this was not his first visit to the East. On a previous expedition he had stood off a band of dacoits—organised robbers—in Nepal.

Kirti was six foot four, willowy thin, with an aristocratic bearing and countenance. Part of his training as a prince had been in the martial art of tai kwon do, in which he had a black belt. He impressed me with his self-contained authority, discipline and composure, and when he let slip about his training in martial arts, I immediately applied for his transfer to the samurai, which Laxmi approved. Kirti, however, was not at all sure about it. He was enjoying a quiet life watering the ashram vegetable garden, and told me that after his gruelling years training at a dojo in Thailand he found karate distasteful: "Every time I hear a karate shout it turns my stomach."

At one point Kirti had unsuccessfully tried to renounce his royal title. He had succeeded in obtaining passports for himself and his wife without the customary and embarrassing 'Prince' and 'Princess' on them, but the German authorities rescinded the passports, saying that the titles could not be renounced.

Kirti had been educated with Charles at Gordonstoun, the spartan Scottish boarding school. Lord Louis Mountbatten of Burma had driven Prince Charles and Prince Wilf to school together on their first day, and they had become friends.

In 1980 Charles visited Bombay, and Kirti went to meet his cousin. As usual, Charles had an impossibly packed official schedule, and Kirti had been allowed only a five-minute audience with him. An usher announced his full title, and in went Kirti in his red sannyasi robes. It was the first time Charles had seen him dressed like this, and said that while he would have liked to visit the ashram himself, as the future royal head of the Church of England there was no way that he could visit such a controversial place.

In the five minutes that Charles and Kirti were together, Charles confided: "You know, since Uncle Louis was killed I have had nobody to turn to for real advice, no one. You are so lucky, Wilf, that you have your guru. I wish I had your freedom to go and see a man like that. It's the eyes of these men that are so fascinating, you can see it in their pictures." In the correspondence that had passed between them before Kirti met Charles in Bombay, Charles had asked Kirti if he could arrange for him to ask Bhagwan a question. Charles now wrote his question, and Kirti slipped it into his pocket. Charles walked his cousin to the door, and they parted company.

Only a month later, Kirti had a massive stroke while doing marine press-ups in the morning karate class.

The day before his stroke, Kirti had been standing guard outside Bhagwan's room with Bhagwan's Rolls Royce cleaner, Govind. They had been talking about how the constant shortage of food was making them ill, and Kirti had said "I feel so sick that if I was in Switzerland I would be taking a long rest in a sanatorium." Govind, who had just recovered from hepatitis, had agreed.

The next morning I had seen Kirti as he finished the midnight to dawn shift. He had looked deathly pale, and was about to go home and sleep until the 10.30 karate class. He had complained about having to get up again so soon, so I had said "Take the morning off then, and do an afternoon session later in the week."

"No," he had said softly. "I'll do this one and get it over with. By the way, could you tell Deeksha there was no soup again last night." I had tried to get Deeksha to provide soup for the guards on night shift, but for reasons best known to herself, there was plentiful soup some nights and then none at all for nights on end.

The karate teacher saw Kirti go down, but at first simply thought he was resting and didn't disturb him. When the rest of the class got up to do warm-ups, Kirti did not move. An aikido black belt went over to tell him to stop fooling about, but as soon as he saw Kirti's blue face he rolled him over and gave him mouth to mouth resuscitation and a thump over his heart to restart it. Kirti was at our health centre within minutes, and in intensive care at the local hospital within the hour. He was put straight on a life support machine, where he remained for several days.

After four days it became clear that he was not going to live. The stroke had been massive; Kirti was in a deep coma and was already brain-dead. Bhagwan arranged with the sannyasi doctors looking after him at the hospital that the life support machine should be switched off just before eight in the morning, so that news of Kirti's death would reach Bhagwan at the beginning of the lecture.

Bhagwan began lecturing that day as usual. Special arrangements had been made to seat Kirti's relatives prominently in the hall, as they had flown in from Germany on hearing about his stroke. The lecture began uneventfully, but after ten or fifteen minutes Bhagwan seemed to lose his way in a most uncharacteristic fashion, casting about to continue with his theme.

Forty minutes after he had begun, a note was passed to me to hand to Vivek. It was the news he had been waiting for. Vivek raised two fingers in an exaggerated V-sign, to let Bhagwan know that Kirti (his full name was Vimalkirti — hence the 'V') had died, but by now Bhagwan was in full flow and did not notice Vivek's signal for ten minutes or more, leaving those of us in the front row acutely embarrassed by his oversight.

When Bhagwan finally noticed Vivek's sign, he ended what he was talking about and announced to the three-thousand-strong audience that he had given Kirti permission to leave his body. Kirti had heard him, and accordingly was no longer 'in the body'. Outside the hall Deeksha had already arranged the firewood necessary for the cremation.

When two of the Indian consultants at the hospital heard what had happened, they were outraged at the way Bhagwan had played with someone else's life for his own self-aggrandisement, and made it appear that he was exercising supernatural powers. They found the deliberately stage-managed timing of the affair distasteful in the extreme. A dying man had been a pawn in Bhagwan's highly questionable spiritual game, and the doctors were not amused.

We later learned that although the life support machine had been turned off just before eight o'clock as instructed, Kirti had unexpectedly resumed normal heart and lung function on his own. Nearly an hour had passed before he had died of his own accord. In the light of this information, Bhagwan's lecture perfomance became more understandable.

Kirti's body was cremated on a traditional Hindu funeral pyre, with his parents and brother present. Their sorrow was compounded by the strangeness and primitive dignity of the occasion, and they seemed pained and ill at ease.

Kirti's young daughter remained in Poona with her mother, who was Teertha's assistant in the encounter group. The daughter was later invited to be a bridesmaid at Princes Charles' wedding to Lady Diana Spencer. While she was in England, the BBC screened a programme about Poona which showed her mother, the Princess of Hanover, in an encounter group, wearing only the flimsiest of garments, and violently slapping another participant.

Because of the Princess's highly questionable behaviour, Kirti's parents sought and gained custody of their granddaughter. In 1982 the Princess lost all right of access to her daughter, because when the visiting rights papers came she was too busy leading groups to look at them, and entrusted the job to a sannyasi office worker who did not attend to them in time. The Princess is still a disciple of Bhagwan's, and her estranged daughter lives with relatives in Europe.

By 1980, few people were granted a private darshan. The sniffing and vetting procedures before darshan sessions became ever more complex and ritualised after the attack in Buddha Hall, and it could be a full thirty minutes before people were admitted into darshan after they had been 'sniffed'.

One night in darshan, Bhagwan announced that he was going to experiment with a new kind of 'energy darshan'. He explained to his hushed audience that many of the female sannyasins were now ready to become vessels for his energy. He had been preparing them for this task for many years, he went on, and now he would begin a new phase of work with them. Ten or twelve chosen women would come to darshan every night — they would be known as 'mediums', and would be able to transfer his energy to the whole commune and eventually to the world outside.

Vivek had been chosen to lead these women, as he had now been working on her intensely for eleven years, and he and Vivek would instruct them. They were to wear special uniforms to stress the anonymity and ego-less nature of the divine capacity to channel energy. The choice of the first mediums would be announced shortly.

In recent months Bhagwan had been making much of how the enlightened master had no need of such lowly and fundamentally violent things as sex and physical contact with people, so his new plans came as something of a surprise. For years he had not allowed anyone except Vivek to touch him in any way. From 1974 to 1976 he did not touch anyone at all in darshan. Now it was all changing in the most remarkable way. Perhaps, like Ghandi, he needed to do it all just once more.

As a samurai co-ordinator I had to know who the new mediums were, as they were given unrestricted access to Lao Tzu House. It was a major headache keeping up with them. At the height of the speculation as to exactly what did go on in 'energy darshans' I bumped into Vivek, and asked her lightheartedly if Teertha and I were free to invite any of the mediums to stay the night. She said of course that she would have to ask Bhagwan. A day later, with a stern look clouding her face, she gave me my answer: "Bhagwan wants to know when you are going to grow up!" The boss was not amused.

As part of these experimental darshans, Bhagwan introduced music and flashing lights. Haridas made hand and foot switches which could be operated by Bhagwan. The darshans were transformed into a bacchanalia of light and sound, and whatever actually went on during those long minutes when Bhagwan turned off all the lights, it propagated an intensely sexual atmosphere. Strict instructions were issued that no photographs whatsoever were to be taken once the lights went out.

One of the mediums told me that they had specifically been forbidden to wear panties during these sessions. I relayed this juicy bit of gossip to my room-mate Teertha, who promptly told Vivek. Vivek sought me out at once to tell me never to talk about such things again, or I could go straight back to Edinburgh.

Bhagwan initially selected twelve mediums, and the knowledge that more would be chosen in time led to the most outrageous and sustained female behaviour wherever he went. Women who wanted to be chosen suddenly stared going to every Hindi lecture whether or not they could understand a single word. They bought low-cut robes in the finest silk, and wore them even in the early morning when it was bitterly cold. Exquisite batik sarongs jostled for visual supremacy with tie-dye shawls and flamboyant ear-rings. These scantily-dressed sirens tried to sit as close to the front row as possible at every lecture and darshan. It was the height of sannyasin inspiration to become a medium and have Bhagwan actually touch you. His touch could send you off into those ecstatic regions of pure bliss.

Answering questions in a lecture about the kind of women who could hope to become mediums, Bhagwan made it quite clear that only women with large breasts could hope for the honour. "I have been tortured by small-breasted women for many lives together," he

announced to a startled audience, "and I will not do it in this life!"
The slim boyish types slunk away disappointed, but only two weeks
later he chose three very slim women as his special mediums, and joy
spread through the small-breasted community.

I was thrilled when Isabel, my girlfriend, was also chosen to be a
medium. It was a special gift for us both to go to darshan every night.

During this period Bhagwan's illnesses seemed to multiply. He had
always been allergic to 'fragrances', and suffered from diabetes,
eczema and asthma, but these ailments were getting worse, especially
the allergies. Perfumes and toilet soap would make his eyes water and
his chest constrict and seize up. The slightest hint of smoke from a
distant wood fire made him choke. At darshans we would watch him
carefully, and if we noticed his eyes watering, we would search for the
source of the smell. If we were able to locate it, the offender would
have to leave immediately. Everyone who attended darshans was told
that this was necessary, since the slightest fragrance, even though
undetectable by most people, could upset Bhagwan.

Bhagwan now said in lectures that he was immensely glad that he
could touch us again. For many years, he said, he had been rendered
nauseous by coming into contact with our 'lower energies', and had
needed 'Shiva with the big nose' to prevent accidental touching, but
now we were ready for a new experiment. This was the creation of
the 'new man', who would change the nature of life on the planet,
render war and waste obselete, and create an ecologically-balanced
utopia. His people would be in the vanguard of twenty-first century
evolution, and his new freedom to transfer energy directly to us
would speed up the process of transformation enormously. "Many
things will be happening to you of which I cannot even tell you now,"
he said. His idealism was perfectly suited to the aspirations of the
average sannyasi, and brought the family even closer together.

In the energy darshans the noise and vibration would sometimes
approach the threshold of pain, and the flashing lights and tribal
rhythms could induce a trance-like state. These sessions had an
electrifying effect on me. When Bhagwan called me as the subject for
one of the first energy darshans, he sat me down opposite a medium
who was directly in front of his feet. Then, after the lights had gone
out and the music reached its tribal crescendo, he touched the point
on my forehead known as 'the third eye' I felt a new energy flowing
through me like molten honey. It rose in intensity until it felt as
though I was caught in a long dark tunnel with an express train

rushing towards me. Then it dissolved into peace, light, and the scary but exciting promise of the unknown. As that train of his energy passed into my being, some kind of internal fuse blew, and I floated blissfully in a sea of nectar, quite unaware of my surroundings. I heard Bhagwan calling, as if from a great distance: "Shiva, come back, you have to take the photos now."

I remember thinking: how could he be serious? How could I take pictures in this state? He repeated his directive, and as I stumbled to my feet Krishna Barti handed me the Nikon. If this was his energy, I wanted more of it.

Many people have asked me how a sensible, independent person could be mesmerised by someone like Bhagwan. The answer, as many sannyasis would agree, is that once you had been affected by his energy and experienced the sensation of being touched by it, you knew that there was nothing like it, no bliss to compare with it. Once you had experienced it, you had to go back for more, to try and regain that feeling of harmony and being at one with the universe. It is similar to a drug-induced high, except that here there is no artificial chemical at work. Bhagwan's touch could be just as addictive as the strongest drug.

As part of the general expansion programme throughout the ashram, a special dental room was being built in Bhagwan's house. The senior ashram dentist, a forty-five year old British man, was sent to London to buy the best dental equipment. No expense was to be spared. The dentist visited the leading supplier of dental equipment dressed in his flowing robes and mala, and asked for the very best reclining chair. He was told it would cost £12,000.

Without hesitation he said he would take it, and asked for it to be packed up immediately and flown to India. To the utter astonishment of the salesman he offered cash payment, and then asked for it to be "mucked up a bit", to make it look old and battered. The salesman was even more nonplussed until it was explained that this was to avoid the 120% tax levied on new goods brought into India. The packing boy was despatched to the corner shop for grey paint and red enamel to start mucking up the new chair.

Bhagwan's own parents eventually became his disciples, and were accorded special visiting rights at Poona. Bhagwan's mother, a tiny wrinkled old lady, was allowed to sit with him while he ate his midday meal from a circular silver tray.

One day as I stood in the driveway of Bhagwan's house I watched his parents bidding farewell to Vivek. His father, a dignified sixty-year-old, stood mutely by while his mother haltingly reached out her hand to Vivek. Although it was never done in her culture, this touch was their only common language. They looked at each other, the mother wanting to ensure that all was well with her son, the woman who was not even her son's wife reassuring her that it would be, and a tear trickled down his mother's wrinkled cheek. Bhagwan's mother suddenly embraced Vivek, and all traces of shyness between them evaporated. It was a touching moment.

The numbers of people coming to the ashram continued to increase, and overcrowding became an insoluble problem. The four-acre site could no longer contain all the people and activities associated with the ashram, and the city of Poona was bursting at the seams with disciples. Another larger site had to be found.

All the time we had been in Poona, Laxmi and her assistants had been looking for suitable premises, but nothing had been found.

Plans were now well advanced for a new commune at Saswat, twenty miles outside Poona. An ideal building had been found — a three-hundred-year-old castle, no less — which belonged to a Poona businessman, Amarssinh Jadhavrao. The old fortress had been inspected by Sheela, who undertook to organise the place into a commune. The building and surrounding lands were leased to her, and although a commune was established there, it never became anything more than an overspill site from the main ashram.

Violent things started happening at Saswat late in 1980. First the well was poisoned, then the generator was blown up, and finally the landlord was accused of attempting to rape a sannyasin woman. Sheela claimed that the violence to the property had been done by terrorist friends of the landlord, and stopped paying the rent. The owner brought a defamation suit against the Rajneesh Foundation, and the whole thing was further complicated by the fact that the man who attacked Bhagwan with the knife was distantly related to the landlord. There were rumours in Poona that the terrorist activities at Saswat had been undertaken by sannyasis themselves.

The incidents at Saswat, the drug runs, the prostitution and commune activities in general were turning the local population against us. One evening I was called to see Laxmi urgently. An English sannyasi had nearly been beaten to death in a block of flats nearby — he had apparently been attacked for making a pass at an Indian woman who lived there. Laxmi ordered me to rescue him, but when I reached the flats a group of twenty armed men barred my entry. A policeman had gone in, and they told me to wait until he came out again. A flick of a menacing-looking two-foot length of chain in one of the men's hands emphasised the point. A few minutes later the policeman appeared, followed by the sannyasi. His head was covered in blood and his clothes were in shreds. He was covered with welts and swellings, and in hospital he was found to have several broken ribs, a broken nose and severe lacerations.

This incident worsened community relations still further, and small groups of Indian scooter riders took to driving up behind walking sannyasis and hitting them as hard as they could on the head or neck with sticks or coshes. Sannyasin women were raped on the street, and one was shot in her thigh with an air rifle. Soon after this she was found dead one morning, having apparently shot herself with her Indian boyfriend's revolver. A month later her boyfriend, an Indian prince, killed himself by drinking an entire bottle of Scotch whilst recovering from a bout of hepatitis.

Sannyasis began to be admitted to the local psychiatric hospital by the ashram guards, and more drug-related arrests were now made by the police. One sannyasi murdered another in one of the hut villages about a mile from the ashram, and another was found dead with multiple stab wounds beneath the nearby Mulla-Matha bridge. A third sannyasi killed himself with a plastic bag after reading a passage in one of Bhagwan's books, where he said that if you held your breath with enough determination you wouldimmediately become enlightened. Another Western body was found with no clothes or papers, and was stored in the police morgue awaiting identification. A power failure put out the air conditioner in the morgue, so the body had to be disposed of at once. It was never identified. Another sannyasi went to meditate alone in the Lonavala caves, and his body was found, decomposed, a month later. Nobody knew what had happened.

By early 1981 there were about five thousand sannyasis living in and around Poona, and another two or three thousand appeared for Celebration Days. Every kind of local accommodation was bought, rented, or merely taken over. Several illegal straw-hut villages appeared along the river banks and by wells in hot dusty fields. A place called 'Laxmi Villas' — no connection with our Laxmi — became densely populated with orange-robed people, and apart from the communist countries, Rajneesh Centres started springing up in every corner of the world.

It was clear that we would have to move from Poona before long. The place was getting too hot to hold us, anti-Bhagwan feeling was growing, and the commune was far too small. At this point Bhagwan had never been out of his native country, but we needed a site where we could expand almost infinitely. Bhagwan sent Laxmi away to look for a property in her home state of Gujurat, while my friend Jeannie and an English nurse called Jaya went to Australasia to see if they could find an island paradise with its own sovereignty. They located a beautiful island, but then Bhagwan decided he did not want to go there after all.

Laxmi also found a place she considered perfect, at Kutch, near the Pakistani border, but when the plans were well advanced the project was apparently quashed by the Indian Prime Minister, Morarji Desai. Though nobody except Bhagwan really knew what was afoot, he decided about December 1980 that he wanted to go to America, and Sheela went several times to look for suitable sites. At the same time as Sheela was searching in America, Laxmi was told to continue looking in India, and given a deadline of April 1981. Bhagwan instructed her that she was not to come back to the commune until she had found the site for the new commune. If nowhere in India could be found by April of that year, Bhagwan and Sheela secretly planned to fly to America with a small entourage.

There were also other reasons why it became imperative for Bhagwan to move. The authorities were becoming increasingly uneasy about his activities, and through an effective informer network within the Indian CID and the local police, Sheela knew that at the very least Bhagwan would soon be put under house arrest for inciting religious unrest. He was publicly criticising Hinduism, a serious crime in India.

There was also a complex legal dispute which had arisen with the charity commissioners in Poona, who were questioning the charitable status of the ashram. The ashram had made vast sums of money — around $80 million — in the few years since it had been established, and an enquiry was launched into the Foundation's monetary and financial affairs. The ashram's eight accountants were accused of not keeping proper receipts for donations and subscriptions. Laxmi and Sheela fought the enquiry, which eventually went before the State charity commissioners in Bombay. It was taken through the Bombay courts, which ruled against the Foundation.

The local police started to pursue visa overstay cases with renewed vigour, and cases were brought against twenty-six ashram residents, including Prem Chinmaya, Sheela's American husband. As it happened, he died of Hodgkin's Disease at the age of thirty-three in 1980, before his case was heard. Most of the overstay cases were withdrawn after Foundation officials agreed that the sannyasis in question would leave the country. Many American and European sannyasis had got round the visa problem by marrying Britishers and applying for British passports.

Poona residents kept complaining about the drug smuggling, but the local police were hardly able to stem the flow at all. The Foundation's overworked public relations department—"far surpassing the efficiency of the Indian government" according to *The Times of India*—put out a news release denying any link with drug smuggling, yet only months after we had left for America, the Poona police told US consular authorities that narcotics dealing had lessened dramatically after our departure.

Bhagwan was not at all intimated by any of this, and took the offensive, pleading religious persecution. In its defence the Foundation listed several incidents of attempted assassination, arson, rape and assault.

Soon the ashram became embroiled in a dispute involving almost $4 million in unpaid taxes. The neighbours were becoming disgruntled, and complained of having their lives wrecked by the presence of the ashram.

Bhagwan did not leave India simply because of these contentious and often violent conflicts. Bhagwan left because he wanted to go to America. Though serious enough problems, the unpaid tax, the litigation and the impending trial and house arrest were not the main reasons for the move. The Indian government was certainly blocking any plans for a move within the country, but Bhagwan felt the time was ripe for a massive enlargement of his empire.

Having wrung India dry of attention, publicity and new disciples, it was time to move to fresh pastures. Bhagwan and Sheela kept their plans totally secret for several months. Everything was conducted in such secrecy mostly so that the vast sums of money which had been amassed could be retained. Bhagwan's first rule seemed to be that when you flee a country, you leave all your bills behind too. If he had made detailed announcements in advance, five thousand sannyasis would have wanted to go with him. By keeping the details of the move secret, he could rely on the resourcefulness of his followers without having to foot their travel bill.

In February 1981 Bhagwan hurt his back badly. Lectures were cancelled, and instead sannyasis were invited to attend silent 'satsangs', where they simply sat in the presence of their master's empty chair. Two ashram Rolfing experts were called in to see if they could rectify Bhagwan's problem, but they could not help. I was asked to treat him 'as a last resort', but Bhagwan had never been a believer in alternative medicine, and the manipulation I gave had little effect. Eventually, and at vast expense, a leading British orthopaedic surgeon, James Cyriax, was flown out from Harley Street to look at Bhagwan's back. Somendra, living in London at the time, paid his first class fare. He administered more manipulation and gave epidural injections which, Bhagwan later claimed, only gave temporary relief. "It was Valium that cured me" was his final verdict.

While he was confined to his room, Sheela, now his mouthpiece, announced to a meeting of group leaders, therapists and heads of department that Bhagwan had 'retired', and would not be speaking in public again. She explained that he had reached the final stage in his work, and did not need to speak any more because enough of his disciples could now hear and understand him without words. Sheela went on to tell us that darshans would now be run by Teertha, and that the mediums should decide whether they wanted to continue without Bhagwan being there. In an instant the whole organisation was turned on its head. Nobody had any idea what would happen next.

After a month of immobility, Bhagwan emerged from his room to resume his seat in the silent satsangs. He was very shaky, and was sitting now in a specially-made chair.

Teertha was busily appointing new mediums, as most of the old ones decided that they did not want to continue under the new arrangement. I stayed on as Teertha's bodyguard, a peculiar role, since we now shared a room and were mutual friends and confidantes. I was also told that I was to deputise for Teertha if he was ever ill. In one of the silent satsangs, Krishna Bharti was taking photographs when Bhagwan started nodding off to sleep. KB was immediately ordered to destroy the negatives. Bhagwan had always claimed that he never slept, merely changed his level of awareness to a lower one.

Out of the blue one day, one of Sheela's assistants asked me if my passport was in order. Nothing like that had ever been asked of me. Not a word had seeped out about where we were going, and as far as anyone knew, all that would be happening was that we would be going to a place that Laxmi had found in the north of India. I began to get very curious and excited. Then Vivek requested a list of my four very best samurai guards. It was all very mysterious. The department heads were then asked to prepare a list of their most dedicated and surrendered staff, in order of merit. The ashram gossip mill began to speculate wildly. Anxiety and fear grew.

Late one evening, about forty handymen, technicians, musicians and samurai were called to a meeting with Sheela and Deeksha in an upstairs laundry room. A guard was posted outside the door. Sheela announced that we were going to America with Bhagwan. We were all astonished, amazed and incredulous. Anybody who was not ready and willing to work twenty-four hours a day from now on should leave the meeting immediately, as they would be of no use in America, and so should anyone who felt they could not keep their mouth shut about the plans. Nobody outside the meeting was to know what was planned, not even our nearest and dearest. I thought of Isabel, at that very moment in distant Kashmir with Laxmi, looking for a suitable site. Finally, those who were not willing to surrender totally to Sheela and Deeksha could bid their farewells right now, Sheela added menacingly.

Everyone stayed put. Next the basic details of the plan were outlined. An advance party of handymen would get their hair cut and leave first to get everything ready for Bhagwan, and the rest would follow at a later date. We would be called individually to get instructions for going to Bombay for our American visas. Those of us who had money were asked to contribute a thousand dollars each towards our air fares. Sannyasis at the select meeting who had no money would have their fares paid. Meanwhile we were to tell nobody of these plans, and certainly not to rouse suspicion by selling or giving away our possessions. We all crept out after Sheela dismissed us, hardly able to believe our ears or our good fortune. Later that week I gave Sheela $1,000 from my photograph commission money.

By the beginning of April, a week or two after that first secret meeting, the ashram was abuzz with rumours. Most were inaccurate, but by this time everybody understood that we were going *somewhere*, and that the days of Poona were numbered. Sheela

held two large public meetings in Buddha Hall where she asked
people to guess the location of the new commune — those who
guessed correctly would eventually be given a small prize — but the
forty of us who were in on the secret kept silent.

Key people who would be important in our new life, like Haridas
and Shanti, began to disappear. Anyone from the core group who
gossiped found themselves transferred to Saswat, the unsuccessful
and unpopular protégé of Poona, which was regarded as a kind of
dusty Siberia.

Shortly after the violence in Saswat late in 1980, there was a series
of fire bombings in Poona. One of the ashram's main book
depositories was set alight — a peculiar event, as the English-
language books had already been removed, leaving only the now
unsaleable Hindi books to be consumed by the flames. Another
bomb exploded in the bicycle rank outside the sannyasi health centre,
injuring nobody, but resulting in a good deal of local publicity. An
insurance claim was filed for 700,000 rupees for the book depot fire.

The fortuitous nature of the fires and the bombings made me see
the 'steadily mounting anti-sannyasin violence' in a new light — it
became clear that it was all being engineered so that it would look as
though we were being persecuted. I felt relieved that there was no
new threat to Bhagwan's life, and if he saw fit to engineer events in
this way, then I in my admiration was quite happy to bow to his better
judgement.

I was loaned three thousand dollars to prove to the US embassy
that I had money, and given a thorough briefing by one of Sheela's
assistants. We went two at a time, to avoid arousing suspicion either
at the embassy or at the ashram.

Bhagwan obtained a temporary visitor's visa to the US after Sheela
had invited an American consular official to the ashram and given her
the red carpet treatment. One French sannyasin woman told me that
she was watching my hair — while it remained long, she knew that
Bhagwan was staying for at least one more day. People started to sell
off their goods — their handmade straw huts, motor bikes, bicycles
and apartments. Hysteria swept through the ashram population as
workers began to disappear and more people had their hair cut in
order to obtain visas easily. Sheela had been saying publicly that we
were going 'up north', and assured people that nobody would be left
behind when we moved. The Poona banks were suddenly deluged
with people changing money and asking for income tax clearance

forms, just in case Bhagwan was leaving the country.

At last Sheela told the forty of us exactly where we were going — it was to be New Jersey. It was cold there, so we should bring warm clothes with us. But where to obtain such things in tropical Poona? A few hastily-arranged marriages took place so that important people could get to America. A secret departure date was set only three days in advance.

The day we planned to leave, Isabel, who had come down from the north to see Bhagwan off, told me that an informer had tipped off the ashram that a warrant for Bhagwan's arrest was about to be issued on the grounds of inciting religious rioting. If Bhagwan was still in India to be arrested, it would mean certain confinement for two years at least. For this reason I was to be especially alert when we reached the airport. We left India on a Sunday, especially so that Bhagwan could not easily be served with a subpoena.

The day we left Bhagwan was driven in one of his two Rollses to what was to be his final appearance in Poona. Meanwhile, in the cloistered privacy of Lao Tzu House, I filled the other Rolls, the specially lengthened model which had been nicknamed 'The White Elephant', with petrol, oxygen bottles, ice coolers and towels. After the satsang a ramp was swung into place for Bhagwan to walk down into the White Elephant, and after closing the door for Bhagwan, Sheela got in too. The second Rolls had been stationed behind the first, and my four chosen samurai were in an anonymous brown van outside the gate to Bhagwan's house. I joined them in the van, and with two back-up cars the five-vehicle convoy set off.

The secrecy had been so effective that by the time the two white Rolls Royces swung into view and passed out of the Lao Tzu gate, nobody outside was remotely aware of what was happening. Even the gate guards had not been told. Some of the guards thought we were taking Bhagwan for another hospital visit, but the more experienced, like Sant, knew otherwise. Tears sprang to his eyes as he realised that he was being left behind.

We swept out through the deserted midday streets of Poona, the only Rolls Royces in the city, and sped off towards Bombay. Near Lonavala, about halfway to Bombay, Bhagwan's Rolls suddenly tunnelled off into the verge. As Bhagwan emerged to relieve himself, resplendent in his brilliant white robes, the traffic stopped. Everybody wanted to catch a glimpse of the famous Rajneesh. We had quite a job keeping people away, but finally got Bhagwan back into the car.

As we drove into Bombay, our samurai anxieties evaporated in a burst of ribald and enthusiastic singing. I looked at the beggars and the beautiful still lagoons by the roadside, and realised how much I would miss this country where I had spent almost all of the last eight years. What would the future bring, especially since Bhagwan had become almost a recluse, and Sheela, who was now in sole charge, seemed to have a personal vendetta against me?

We used an Indian sannyasi's house in the suburbs as a hideout until two the next morning, when everybody except Bhagwan, Sheela and Vivek was ferried to the airport. After passing through customs and passport control, I glimpsed Bhagwan's Rolls draw right up to the nose wheel of the 747. He had made it! A route had been engineered to get the car onto the airport apron and right under the aircraft, without any need to go through check-in, immigration, police or passport control. The baksheesh system had worked wonders. Apparently very large sums of money had changed hands.

I rushed on board the aircraft and met Bhagwan as he walked up the spiral staircase to the upper deck. Sheela had reserved the entire forty-seat first class section just for herself, Bhagwan and Vivek. A small team of sannyasi cleaners had been standing by to clean the upper deck, but the incoming flight from Australia had been delayed, and they had not been able to come aboard until after Bhagwan was already installed. White sheets were thrown over the seats, and the multicoloured cabin became a busy white workroom, a strangely surrealistic-looking morgue.

The captain came through from the flight deck and introduced himself to Bhagwan in a loud, confident voice. "I'm sure glad to meet you, sir," he said. "It is a privilege to have you aboard Pan Am 747 Kit Carson." He offered Bhagwan a meaty hand, but Bhagwan declined it by bowing to him, and said nothing.

Suddenly, on instinct, I felt the need to go downstairs. I found two policemen who wanted to know if one of Sheela's Indian assistants was upstairs. They tried to go up but I barred their way, telling them that their man was not there. Much to my relief they went away.

Twenty minutes later the gangways were swung away and the cabin lights flickered as the engines whined up to taxi power. At last we were on our way to America, without the subpoena. I felt an exhilarating sense of relief and excitement. We had made it! We had successfully smuggled our beloved Master out of India, and now we were ready to take the New World by storm. Bhagwan allowed himself a magnum of champagne, the finest French, and a tray of *petits-fours*. Sheela stood smiling behind Bhagwan's chair, and both she and Vivek broke into unsuppressable broad grins. We were off — bound for America, fame and freedom!

Chapter Eleven
THE START OF THE AMERICAN DREAM

Well before our meticulously planned flight to America it had been decided to disband the Poona commune as quickly as possible. The Rajneesh Foundation wanted no legally binding connection between the organisation that had left behind many debts and legal problems in India, and the new corporation, Rajneesh International, based in the USA. Apart from the $5 million or so owing in income tax, there were also large sums due to publishing houses, bookbinders, fabric manufacturers, and suppliers of raw materials to the ashram.

Another reason for our hasty departure was that the lady who owned the land on which we had built the enormous Buddha Hall was demanding it back, on top of which the entire Jesus House complex, one of the three main ashram houses, was in process of being handed back to its rightful owner in default of payment from us. When things began hotting up and the tide started to turn against Bhagwan, Laxmi's office became so efficient at compartmentalising information that we never learned the full extent of the financial, legal and immigration problems the commune was facing.

Within a week of Bhagwan's departure, the Poona commune began to be ripped apart. The vast Buddha Hall was demolished and the Jesus House buildings evacuated. Those left behind to close up the ashram conducted a giant yard sale of the remaining effects. The boutiques, therapy rooms, laundry, bakery, restaurants, clothing and other manufacturing businesses were shut down, and goods sold at bargain prices. Hundreds of sannyasi straw huts were sold, burnt down, or simply abandoned, and a glut of ex-sannyasi motorcycles flooded the second-hand market. So many Indians started coming to the ashram when the first rumours of the sale leaked out that the so-called Gateless Gates were in danger of being knocked down and trampled underfoot by the mob. Much to everyone's relief inside the ashram, riot police were called in to disperse the crowd, where the goods on sale resembled an Aladdin's cave of cameras, computers, air conditioners, metal detectors, dark room equipment, Rolls

Royces, gold-laden safes, electronic devices, and mountains of personal belongings. Many of these things were virtually unobtainable anywhere in India, and here they were, being sold off at knockdown prices.

By holding out the promise that those who helped clear up Poona would be the first to be invited to the new commune, Bhagwan hoped to ensure that the sale of the commune's property and the subsequent dispersal of sannyasis would be conducted in an orderly manner. When it came to leaving India, however, some of them had a very hard time. Many had no money at all, and had to be bailed out by parents, friends or embassies, or were forced to turn to the now traditional Rajneeshee ways of making a quick buck — drug running and prostitution. Some were assisted by the ashram to get home or to the States, but some had a very difficult time indeed. One Canadian who had worked as a gardener at Poona later said to me that he would never allow himself to be without escape money again.

Although Laxmi and Isabel had accompanied us from Poona to Bombay, they were not with us on the plane. It was very clear to us that Laxmi's days of supreme power were over. Sheela had superceded her, and was now making all the decisions that Laxmi would formerly have made. Married by now to her second American husband, a former New Jersey bank officer called John Joseph Shelfer, she was obviously far better equipped than Laxmi to take Bhagwan to the promised land.

During the flight we were all well-briefed on US immigration procedure. The samurai guards on board were told that State Department permission would be needed before any foreign national could have a bodyguard. This would entail explaining why such protection was necessary, a difficult step which might prejudice our entry. Therefore Sheela informed us that our status was to be that of ordinary tourists. The story of Bhagwan's back had gone ahead of us, so Deeksha and her crew of elite handymen, who were already in the USA, had arranged for Bhagwan to be met at JFK airport with an ambulance and stretcher. The official story was that his back condition was now so critical that there was nothing further that could be done in India, so he had come to the USA for major surgery.

Sheela arranged for Bhagwan to be cleared by customs and immigration while he was still on board, so everybody except Bhagwan left the plane, including Vivek. In the event Bhagwan refused to get on the stretcher, and seeing a limousine parked by the ambulance, he asked Deeksha whether the limousine was 'ours' as well as the ambulance. On hearing that it was, he chose to go in the limousine rather than the ambulance, against the advice of both Deeksha and Sheela. As he left the aircraft, he paused at the top of the stairs, looked around for a few minutes, and said expansively: "I am the Messiah America has been waiting for."

During much of the past year, Sheela had been flying backwards and forwards between India and the USA looking for a suitable new home for Bhagwan. Eventually she had purchased a ten-bedroom late nineteenth-century mansion in Montclair, New Jersey. It sat proudly atop a wooded ridge, and had an unobstructed view of Manhattan. Sheela nicknamed it her 'castle'. Though sannyasis had been working hard on the house to get it ready in time for Bhagwan's arrival, his precipitate departure from Poona meant that when he arrived it was not quite finished. When he arrived the small group of thirty-five handymen stormtrooper sannyasis was waiting on the lawn of the castle. He spent a few minutes sitting silently with them before walking up the stairs into the house. Deeksha had fitted an invalid's lift, but he took no notice of this at all. He was installed in a couple of tiny attic rooms on the top floor as work continued at a furious pace to get the large downstairs room ready for his use.

Deeksha gave the foreman $40,000 dollars for tools to speed up the work, and a number of local sannyasis, plus some non-sannyasi contractors, were brought in. Everybody was sworn to utter secrecy regarding Bhagwan's presence in New Jersey. At this stage Sheela wanted no press coverage in case thousands of unruly sannyasis started arriving — the place was too small to accommodate them.

The Montclair castle was soon unrecognisable. Deeksha was in charge of renovation, and had decided that for Bhagwan almost everything had to be painted white. She desecrated beautiful mahogany panelling with layers of brilliant white emulsion. Teak, walnut and cherrywood veneers were sledgehammered. One sannyasi craftsman called Samvid, horrified by the wanton destruction of beautiful craftsmanship, left. Almost priceless Tiffany stained glass windows which Deeksha regarded as junk were dumped into the skips which stood outside. Together with the other workers who had arrived on the plane, I was instructed to start work immediately. Sheela told me to pick my two best samurai, who were to be posted on twelve-hour shifts to guard the staircase to Bhagwan's rooms. Vivek immediately countermanded this, saying that neither she nor

Bhagwan wanted guards in future. "I'm sick of them," she said shortly. Instead we were set to work nineteen-hour building shifts, seven days a week.

It was not long before I realised that Sheela and Deeksha were out to break me. They had me in their power, and I was no longer Doctor Hot-shot. My relationship with Sheela had never been easy, and I knew that she still bore me a grudge. She had earned herself a reputation for getting even, and now she saw her chance.

I was assigned to the crack handyman crew, and we worked from seven-thirty in the morning to three or four the following morning, day after day. Within ten days of starting this punishing schedule, one of the former samurai developed severe kidney trouble. Three weeks later, another left. After six weeks of painting, decorating, sawing and renovating, I was barely able to keep my eyes open. One day I fell asleep with a paintbrush in my hand, lying supine on a scaffold. Soon some of the people who had been getting the New Jersey centre ready had left, and new sannyasis had to be flown in from Poona at short notice.

A couple of weeks after we arrived in New Jersey, Laxmi and Isabel joined us. Rumour had it that Laxmi had managed to get out of India disguised as a nun, a touchingly appropriate disguise. Laxmi had never been abroad before, and from the first was uneasy in America. Bhagwan initially gave her a great deal of attention, cossetting her through the extremely difficult transition, both from power and from her own country. He allowed her to have Isabel as a companion when everybody else was working like galley slaves, and granted her spending money, the use of a car, and frequent excursions to Manhattan.

Change was in the air. Those who had been powerful in Poona were suddenly reduced in status, and those who had been relatively insignificant suddenly became top dogs — or top bitches in many cases.

My own status had plummetted considerably. Three days before we were due to leave Poona, I had developed a mild toothache. I ha asked if I could get some treatment, and had been told in the heal centre that there was a long waiting list. Sheela had already told t favoured few in the secret meeting that we were not to do anyth that would attract attention, including asking for emergency me treatment. As I had been unable to get treatment in Poona, I wa to see what could be done in New Jersey. During the eighteen flight the toothache had become so painful that I couldn't sleep, and it had now become agonising. I asked Sheela what I should do, and she passed me on to Deeksha, who said "What's-a the matter with you? A leetle toothache only, so go to a dentist."

"But Deeksha, I have no money"

"Eyah, Shiva, you always have money, don't fool with me."

I told her I had no more than twenty dollars, and had heard that treatment in the States could cost as much as a hundred. Could she please therefore give me eighty dollars?

"Listen to you, whining away," she said. "'Oo de fuck you theenk you are now, mister the big samurai bodyguard? No, Shiva, now you are-a my handyman, an' you go round the people here and *you* getta the money. Don't-a come crying to me."

I thought angrily of the thousand dollars of my hard-earned commission money I had given to the office in compliance with their request that we should pay for our own flight if possible. I had also given Sheela a five-hundred dollar stereo set I had assembled myself, so that she could sell it to raise money. On the Indian black market, where it would have been very valuable indeed, she would probably have got at least twelve hundred dollars. What a fool I had been to be so trusting!

I asked a wealthy American woman who was staying at the castle if she could lend me eighty dollars, and she gave me two hundred. I knew that Sheela was going to see a sannyasi dentist in Woodstock in upstate New York, and her husband, renamed Jayananda, had offered to drive me there with Sheela. As soon as we got in the car, however, Sheela instructed Jayananda to drop me off at the nearest st's surgery, as my work at her castle was far too important for waste the whole day driving to Woodstock and back.

igh he had never before been outside his own country, adapted himself with supreme ease to his new living He changed his diet overnight and began eating eggs, ich, as a strict Jaina vegetarian, he had never done in were specially prepared for him by an Italian o tried meat-flavoured tofu, the remainder of which r work crew.

third day after Bhagwan arrived at the castle, a vce was delivered. It was a soft-top Corniche ertible. There were rumours that he had e it himself. It had been nine years since he

vek's
rors.
Rolls
gwan
. The
more
night
gwan
ar in
very
ke to
fear
n his

cket.
tted.
outs,
ith a
, and
pher
as he
into
d his
e he
, and
ssed,
ecret

e of
abel
and
ers.
no
asin
rself
e to
r. It
the
even
man

: wheel of a car, and it hardly seemed possible that
gile as Bhagwan could do anything as gross as to
e last time he had driven was in his battered Impala,
is acquaintances had judged him one of the fastest
s drivers on the streets of Bombay. He seemed to
narkably rapid recovery from the 'disintegrating
supposedly brought him to America; he never had
and once he had set foot in New Jersey never even
alist medical advice.
that our relationship with Bhagwan had to change.
'friend' — a word that he himself later used when
'followers' on television — and if we happened to
ing past, we had to wave to him as we would to any
t within a week this casual greeting had reverted, by
to the traditional namaste bow, and we were
and greet him *en masse* as he set out in the car. It
he only time we got off work in the whole day.
t week in America, the whereabouts of his hideout
lete secret. None of the sannyasis was allowed to go
le, except to the nearest medition centre. One
er, to the complete astonishment of his personal PR
an insisted on the roof of the Corniche being put
e wanted to drive in the open air. This would surely
finding out where he had got to. Vivek and her
l him on the back seat, and an older sannyasi, a
rsey, drove his sensational red and white entourage
wn Montclair and out onto the freeway.
three days of his newfound freedom, Bhagwan
nyasi drive. By the fourth day he was ready to try it
he first week of his driving he had amassed a very
passengers and a speeding ticket. Vivek's boyfriend
hey had shot through a 'Halt' sign and across a four-
n peak traffic, mercifully without hitting a thing.
riven through a set of red lights and made them all
fright. Then at the next set of lights he had drawn up
:o a police car that the two cars were nearly touching.
looked at this startling apparition, wearing a knitted
ous new robes, and had decided not to have anything

:et of traffic lights Bhagwan had driven very close to

another police car, almost touching its rear bumper. V
boyfriend could see the police scanning the Rolls in their mi
They too let it go — it did not pay to mess with Ay-rabs in
Royces. Doing top speed along the Garden State Parkway, Bha
glimpsed a patrol car ahead and slowed down as fast as he coulc
policeman gave him a warning. Driving back to the castle at a
solemn speed, the handyman suggested that a radar detector
be a good idea. His suggestion was met with silence. As Bha
parked the Rolls, he said he had had enough of travelling with i
the car. Anyone who did not want to travel with him wa
welcome to stop doing so; there were many others who would I
come. Electrical devices which derived their existence fron
increased the overall fear level, and he would not have any fear
cars. Was that perfectly clear?

On the next drive, Bhagwan collected another speeding
Without further comment, he ordered radar detectors to be

Soon the German magazine *Stern* got to know of his wherea
and one of our handymen caught their photographer up a tree
long telephoto lens. He was asked politely if he needed any hel
left rather shamefacedly. Two days later the same photog
drove through the castle grounds at high speeed, taking picture
went. A sannyasi who was cleaning the Rolls at the time jumpe
the car and headed him off. The *Stern* photographer abandon
car and ran into the adjoining building, a monastery, whe
requested religious sanctuary. Police cars and lawyers turned u
finally he was forced to hand his film to Sheela. As the days p
however, we spotted other photographers snatching shots. The
was out.

Our free and easy sex lives, which had been such a feat
Poona, were about to change for ever. Even after Laxmi and
arrived, there were still five men to every women at the castl
we learned from Deeksha that we would have to share pa
Sheela told us the day that Isabel arrived that there we
immediate plans to fly any more women in, so any female san
who did not have a regular boyfriend would have to make I
avaialble to the unattached men. She would now have to ag
sleep wih any man who asked her — this was the new surrend
was explained that this was a temporary measure until a site f
new commune was located, when more women would arrive tc
things up. The men were told that they could approach any w

they wanted, and be put on a waiting list. One of the cleaning ladies asked Deeksha, all twenty stone of her, whether she would be willing to take offers too. She said that she would when her boyfriend was too tired, and everyone laughed. Nobody dared bait Sheela about it though.

I was still theoretically with Isabel, but had to sleep in a crowded room with the three remaining ex-samurai. There was scarcely enough room for the mattressess, and as our room was next to the only bathroom on that floor, every night was disturbed by people walking past to use the adjoining toilet. In the new sharing arrangement I was of course the likely loser, since Isabel was easily the most attractive of the eight women living at the castle. Isabel and I resolved to spend each night together so that she wouldn't have to share herself, but as we had no privacy, and I was constantly exhausted from the nineteen-hour work shifts, our love life was hardly ecstatic. The edict to share the women soon came to a dramatic end, however, when herpes erupted in our small community just two weeks after the share-a-woman programme began.

Though Bhagwan was taking care to make Laxmi feel at ease, she was by no means reconciled to her new minor role, and suffered fits of black depression. In one of these moments she chopped off all her beautiful long black hair with a pair of blunt scissors, not even looking in the mirror as she hacked her way through the lovely raven tresses. A hairdresser was brought in later to tidy up the mess. Like me, Laxmi had always been a high-energy person, forever bustling about, constantly busy. Now she not only had nothing to do, but had lost all her power and was adrift in a foreign country. Sadly and desperately, she tried to win back some power and attention by buying Bhagwan a $20,000 platinum Rolex watch. It made no difference.

While we worked to make the castle resemble Deeksha's vision of white purity, Sheela was planning her search for a large permanent site for a proper international commune. From the start the plans for this American commune were ambitious, and when we had been in New Jersey about six weeks, she sent word to all the sannyasis in North America that the perfect place for His commune had to be located as soon as possible — Bhagwan had now acquired a capital 'H' when talking about Him and His commune.

A detailed list of requirements for the new location was given. It had to have pure, clean air, meadows, lush green forests, leafy glades, running brooks, wildlife, and good roads. Bhagwan also insisted on hot weather all the year round, with no storms and not too much rain. Nothing less than the very best of everything would do for Him.

Shunyo—Helen Byron—was detailed to check out southern Colorado, accompanied by Jayananda and Jaya, the English nurse. While in Colorado, Jayananda received an urgent telephone call from Sheela telling him to come and meet her in Arizona. From there they flew to Oregon, met an estate agent, and took his car to a desolate place known as the Big Muddy ranch—the barren site of several John Wayne westerns.

As they caught their first sight of Big Muddy, Sheela said on impulse "I'll buy it!" They had not even checked it out, and it seems that at the time she did not even know the asking price. Sheela promptly phoned sannyasis looking for property in various parts of America to tell them they could now call off the hunt, as she had found the perfect place. It was in eastern Oregon, which everybody assumed was all high desert country, but Sheela told her lieutenants that the place she had found was full of trees, had a small retirement town sixteen miles away, and was blessed with wonderful mid-seventies temperatures all the year round, with three hundred days of sunshine a year.

As soon as Sheela made her momentous decision, she celebrated on the spot with the ranch foreman, Bob Harvey, who with his wife Glenda and his two daughters, were the sole inhabitants of the place. Sheela became very drunk. She had already hired Bob as foreman at the princely salary of $50,000 a year. She started saying things he could not understand, but for the time being he did not question her or try to stop her flow of chatter.

A week or two later Bob established a firm friendship with Jeannie, one of the newly-arrived sannyasin women, a capable and astute department head from Poona. He started, gently, to try and sort out the mystery of Sheela's whisky talk: "Y'a know, Sheela an' all, well, she was a bittie drunk, and said things I could not git. One thing which was not too surprising was that she said she had been down here before. Lotta folk have. But then she started talking about some fellow called Chinmeyr, said he was going to come back here. Who is this Chinmeyr fellow—someone she was close to? And what does she mean 'come back'?"

When I heard this from Jeannie it made my blood run cold. Of all the typically Indian things to do — Sheela had gone and bought this desolate acreage because she thought it was the place where her late husband would be reincarnated! Jesus! So now we had to make an oasis of the place so that Chinmaya could return. What a farce. What about Bhagwan's dream, *his* requirements, *his* needs? Did she not care about him at all, or did she think she could get away with this madness? What on earth would Bhagwan think of it when he got here? Just the road from Antelope to the ranch would wreck a Rolls Royce very quickly. This area would be a poor place indeed after the luxuriant forests and paved highways of upstate New Jersey.

The ranch was bought in July 1981 for $5,750,000. It was situated across two counties, Wasco and Jefferson, and consisted of 64,229 acres. All the time that the search and negotiations were going on the Rajneesh Foundation had pleaded utter poverty. Sheela and Deeksha kept calling meetings to stress how poor the organisation now was, and how we had to work harder than ever, and pool whatever financial resources were at our disposal. Their language on these occasions was hardly spiritual; "Flying you bunch of misfits and bums over from Poona and buying this house for Bhagwan has emptied us of cash completely," said Sheela on one occasion. "We need money, and we need it now."

"We need your diamond rings and your gold watches," she continued. "We need the five dollars you've been keeping in your back pocket, even if that is all you have in the world." I felt all my old animosity towards Sheela rise up as I heard her speak. I had the solid gold Rolex which Bhagwan had given me, and was wearing the exquisite lapis lazuli ring. I decided that it was greed that was motivating her rather than need, and kept them.

As Sheela spoke, Deeksha went round the room requesting anybody who had any kind of wealth to relinquish it. People were told to phone their parents abroad and say they desperately needed $20,000 for an urgent kidney stone operation. I was publicly grilled about my family's wealth, and my father's clinic in Scotland. Deeksha asked me to phone him as soon as possible, reverse charges, to see whether he would send me the money. All the time she was looking at the watch on my wrist. There was no way I was going to deceive my father into believing that I was critically ill and needed a vast sum of money for an urgent operation.

Anyway, I was convinced that the commune did actually own large amounts of money, probably running into millions of dollars. Why didn't they sell the valuable Tiffany windows if they needed cash quickly?

Within a week of pleading for cash, Sheela bought herself a brand new bright red Mercedes, and Deeksha took delivery of a new Oldsmobile. A third Rolls Royce, this time a Camargue, arrived for Bhagwan.

After I had been in New Jersey about six weeks, I could tell that I was beginning to crack up. I would often collapse into bed at three in the morning utterly exhausted, yet so hyped up that I could not sleep. The three ex-Poona colleagues who remained had all been given easier shifts than me, and were in bed by midnight. I began to have serious doubts about my future with this outfit. If the future consisted of having every moment of my life controlled, and sharing Isabel with the other men, what was I doing here? I started to regret bitterly the vasectomy I had undergone in a moment of 'surrender', since it meant I could never be a father. How could I ever hope to lead a normal life if I left now?

As we workers toiled half the night without proper rest and sleep, Sheela and Deeksha began to live like royalty. They rose at nine or ten, then got into their cars and were driven to Manhattan on shopping sprees. We work crews were forbidden even the shortest excursions, and had been ordered not to leave the site even to post a letter. If we wanted to mail something we had to hand it in at the office, where, we later learned, it was opened and read 'for our own good'. If it displeased them it was destroyed.

No one was allowed to make telephone calls from outside the castle. On a trip to a local meditation centre, I darted into a nearby pub for a drink. I was happily surprised to see one of the sannyasi painters in the bar call box, talking animatedly, with a stack of unmailed letters in one hand. He started to move them out of my sight, then winked and laughed, and gave a shrug and a wave. I lifted my beer glass towards him in a toast to independence.

We were constantly being berated for our laziness, and Sheela kept saying that our days of luxury living were over. There was no time for meditation any more — work was our new meditation. Once, when installing an air conditioner in Bhagwan's own quarters, I caught a glimpse of him meditating. Thank goodness somebody still believes in it, I thought to myself. Sheela said that meditation was only for pansies.

Sheela had a heated argment with one of Bhagwan's ex-mediums.

She had found her playing a music cassette in Sheela's own Mercedes 280 while she was cleaning it. Sheela didn't want a cleaner messing with her equipment. Sheela bawled her out on the spot, and in the next day's work session angrily reported the woman's behaviour to Bhagwan. He heard Sheela out and asked a few pertinent questions, then told Sheela and Deeksha to come to see him early the next day, when he would explain a few things about the art of manipulating people.

The first thing Bhagwan said when they met the next morning was that Sheela had done it all wrong. He explained that when Sheela had seen the women playing the cassette, she should have gone straight to the office and sent an office worker to summon the woman. She should then have been kept waiting an hour or two, just to ensure that she was feeling as nervous as possible, whereupon Sheela should have got one of her assistants to lecture her on surrender, devotion and respect, along with a few meaningful threats about what might happen if this kind of thing ever happened again. "Never deal with such things yourself, Sheela," he said. "Delegate and isolate. Sheela, be more intelligent next time."

By now I was so tired that I was falling asleep at the coffee breaks. Even so, I resolved that they would not get the better of me. I would not quit, and if this was to be my ordeal by fire, then I was going to win. Deep inside, however, I knew that I was losing this particular contest. I had become so jumpy with lack of sleep that I started at the slightest unexpected noise. What had begun as the dawn of a new age, a glorious spiritual movement, already had the makings of a fascist nightmare. All my dreams of showing people how to live in love and harmony seemed to be vanishing. I was doing nothing more than working myself into a state of nervous exhaustion, decorating an old house so that Sheela could sell it at a massive profit. We were being used as slaves under the guise of spiritual surrender. While I was slumping over my coffee, Bhagwan would come out in his sumptuous new robes and knitted cap, get into his Rolls, and drive off like an exotic king. I was so tired I could not even raise my hand to wave as he went past.

This was the end. I wished somebody would give me a break. One day, as Bhagwan drove past, I sent a psychic message to him: Give me a break, Bhagwan; I can't take this any longer. Our eyes met, and he seemed to take his eyes off the road for a very long time. Was it compassion or disdain I saw in his gaze? The Rolls cruised off down the leafy avenue, and I went miserably back to work.

The very next day Deeksha announced that all the workmen were being granted a day off. Bhagwan had told her that we deserved it. Deeksha added that she did not agree, but orders were orders, so we were free for a blissful twenty-four hours, penniless but free. I slept solidly till four in the afternoon. When I woke up, I saw Deeksha laughing at the sleepers, a motley bunch with mattresses and blankets strewn everywhere. She told us that we had been given a second day off. I could hardly believe my ears. So Bhagwan had read the message in my eyes!

I met Deeksha outside the back porch later the same day. She looked at me quizzically. "Hey, Shiva," she said, "Why you not getting-a sick? I 'ear you work a-no bad for a cream puff guard, no-a bad. Hey, and don't-a worry, you are not-a going to be a 'andyman all your-a life. 'Oo knows, maybe someone make you a doctor again . . ."

After our miraculous two-day break the whole work schedule changed and became lighter. We even had a couple of parties. One night, Laxmi became bitterly drunk in a coach house party and I had to carry her home. Isabel was soon relieved of her duties as Laxmi's assistant, and Laxmi, without staff or status, descended further into disorientation and depression.

More people were flying in from Poona all the time, and sannyasis from various parts of the States arrived to see Bhagwan for a day or two. A few wealthy people came from Los Angeles, and one of the first, a woman who had come for a private darshan, walked straight into his new room and sat on his lap. She had not been checked for 'fragrance' and was wearing strong perfume, but Bhagwan said nothing. Later he sid that his body must be getting a lot stronger, because the perfume had not upset him at all.

Some of the heavy pressure now seemed to evaporate. Sheela informed us that Bhagwan was beginning to feel quite at home, happy and relaxed, and every bit as enlightened. In India, he had always said that his country was the highest spiritual location in the world and that there was nowhere to match it — yet another example of Bhagwan's ability to say whatever he felt like and not mind at all that he had contradicted himself completely.

My new work was in the nearby sannyasi canteen which fed the castle, as a driver and vegetable scrubber. My work as a driver involved going back and forth to JFK airport to collect incoming sannyasis, and involved some bizarre tasks. One day I had to collect an incoming sannyasi who was carrying the ashes of Kirti — Prince Wilf — and also those of Bhagwan's father, who had died recently. Bhagwan had asked for both to be brought over so that he could be near them — another example of his obsession with death. The ashes were later buried on the Oregon ranch, but the two lots of ashes had become mixed up, and nobody ever knew for certain which were the prince's and which were Bhagwan's father's.

I was much happier working in the kitchens of the meditation centre. It was a relaxed and light-hearted place, very different from the frenetic activity and dust of the building work going on in the castle. One day, however, the usually happy atmosphere in the kitchen changed abruptly. I came in to find the kitchen supervisor, a Brazilian woman who had been Teertha's girlfriend, in tears. "Sheela told me I'm negative," she sobbed. "I could hear Deeksha begging her not to do it, but after Deeksha had left, Sheela gave me eight hours to pack my bags and get out." The girl — who had been fondled intimately by Bhagwan in private darshan sessions in 1972 — left the following day. She had asked Sheela if she could have a ticket to join her mother in San Francisco, but Sheela had refused. A New York friend eventually drove the penniless woman across the country on his motorcycle.

This event turned out to be Deeksha's nemesis. She had contradicted Sheela in front of Bhagwan. Sheela had told him that the woman was negative, upsetting the staff and setting a bad example to others; she had been nothing but trouble ever since she had been flown over from Poona at ashram expense. "But Sheela," burst in Deeksha, "that's-a not-a true!" Sheela told Deeksha sharply to leave staff management to her, and outside Bhagwan's room warned her never again to contradict her in Bhagwan's presence. Deeksha had pleaded with Sheela to allow the girl to stay, but to no avail.

Sheela later summoned us all to say that the departure of the woman should be a lesson to us all. More people would soon be leaving if they did not look out. I knew that Sheela would like me to be one of them, and a sadness settled on my heart. Vivek's boyfriend observed that those who had taken sannyas before Sheela had in 1973 were not lasting long these days; the young Brazilian woman had come to Bhagwan in 1972. I looked down at my own mala — a pre-1973 model. Was I to be next in line?

Two months after we arrived in New Jersey a sense of desolation and depression descended on us workers. We felt that the love, light and laughter which were such an integral part of Bhagwan's work had gone. I allowed myself, however, to hope that once we moved into the new commune everything would come right once again. At present we were in limbo, not knowing what the next day might bring. I hoped that as soon as we were established in our new abode thousands of people would arrive, we would be able to recreate the love and vitality that were so prevalent in Poona, and establish our new utopia. Several hopeful and exciting rumours ran through the group at the mansion while Sheela was away looking for properties.

Sheela came back from the Big Muddy and held a meeting to tell us that we were all soon going 'to Madras'. She paused and watched us while we wondered why on earth she was talking about going back to India. Then she explained that this Madras was actually pronounced 'Maad-rus', and was a small town near the new site in Oregon. Apparently back at the turn of the century the local storekeeper had ordered fifty feet of Madras cotton from a Chicago warehouse; he had written the order out wrongly and five hundred feet of the material had arrived, whereupon he made his fortune convincing people that Madras cotton was exactly what they needed, and setting himself up as the only supplier in that corner of Oregon. Part of his entrepreneurial skill had been to rename the crossroads where his store was located 'Madras'.

Sheela also told us about Antelope, the nearest village to Big Muddy. It was a retirement village, she said, and launched into a description of how wonderful it was, with perfect warm weather, and leafy glades and forests. She made it sound very exciting. Then Richard, one of the crew bosses who had been an estate developer in New Mexico, asked Sheela solemnly how the area was zoned. In America, areas of land are zoned for particular purposes, and you cannot do anything you want with your land. Once an area has been zoned it is almost impossible to change the zoning, and Richard knew that Oregon had some of the strictest and most inflexible zoning regulations in the whole country.

"Well, Richard," said Sheela, "it's zoned as a farm, of course."

"Is any of it zoned commercial or residential?" he persisted.

"Richard, don't be *stupid*! Of course some parts of the ranch are zoned commercial, otherwise I wouldn't have bought it. And other parts are zoned residential."

"Sheela," Richard continued, "excuse me, but I've had quite a lot of experience with these regulations, and it strikes me as very odd that a farm would also be zoned commercial. And though parts of it *may* be residential, there would be restrictions on the number of people allowed there." Sheela and Bhagwan's plans had, of course, been to buy a site big enough to take up to two hundred thousand people, far more than the six thousand or so who had settled in Poona. The ranch, the second largest in Oregon, had been bought to house the biggest possible commune for America's new messiah.

At this confrontation, Sheela blanched visibly, and looked for assistance and support from one of her inner coterie of women. Her husband helped her to change the subject. At the time I had never come across zoning regulations, and did not understand the implications of what Richard was saying, but it was suddenly very clear to me that Sheela had just paid almost six million dollars for a piece of land without bothering to enquire about any restrictions that may be in force concerning its use. Having made his point, Richard very wisely backed off. It did not always do to be knowledgeable. I remembered the engineers who had foretold the collapse of the original Chuang Tzu auditorium, only to be accused of 'negativity' when it fell a week later. It was better to keep expert information to yourself, and let everybody else find out the hard way.

Soon after the handymen had completed Bhagwan's new middle floor luxury suite, he gave us a small satsang 'blessing' on the lawn. Bhagwan wanted to congratulate us on completing it in record time. Vivek's boyfriend had not fulfilled his earlier promise as a photographer, and Sheela and Bhagwan had decided to get a real professional in to take His pictures. Deeksha sidled up to me and intimated that just this once, before the proper photographer arrived, I would be allowed to take photographs at this session, just as long as I did not get too big-headed about it. I suspected that this was designed as yet another insult, but I was glad enough to comply, and I did enjoy taking the pictures. I was instructed that Bhagwan wanted lots of green in the pictures to emphasise the peace and tranquillity of his surroundings, and that I should use one of my own specialities — out-of-focus green foreground — to portray Bhagwan's lush new garden. "But don't-a let it go to your head," warned Deeksha. "You are-a still my 'andyman!"

Chapter Twelve
THE MOVE TO OREGON

In July 1981 the first batch of twenty handymen was sent to the new site in Oregon. Before they went they were allowed to look at a small photograph album compiled by Sheela, which showed herself and Deeksha standing under a large juniper tree by a stream. It certainly looked pretty. It was later that I learned that it was one of only two streams in the entire 120 square miles of the property, and that Sheela and Deeksha had walked miles to find this verdant spot. As she showed us the pictures, Sheela gave us a warning. "Some of you," she said sternly, "felt that you were special people in Poona. Some of you were given too many privileges, such as siestas and rooms of your own. I want you to understand that nobody will be special on *my* ranch."

After the first team of handymen went out, Sheela came back from a further visit to Oregon to let us know that this advance party had proved useless, and were a complete liability. "I will have no more cream puffs on *my* commune," she told us. I winced. Sheela's attitude was so different from Laxmi's — Laxmi had always deferred to Bhagwan, and had talked about 'we' rather than 'I', while Sheela seemed to be issuing orders and commands without any pretence of consulting Bhagwan first. The ranch was very clearly going to be Sheela's ranch. I was sure she had seen me wince, which meant that I was in deep trouble. Another ex-samurai was shipped off to the ranch the next day, promising before he left to write and tell us what it was really like. He did write, but we never received the letter.

Just two weeks after the confrontation with Sheela over the Brazilian woman, Deeksha was sent out to the ranch, while Sheela stayed on as the queen bee at the Montclair mansion. Sheela tried to control Deeksha at a distance, but failed completely. She had ordered Deeksha not to go outside the ranch, and not to use the ranch car, but Deeksha, undeterred, hired a car from fifty miles away and asked for it to be delivered as soon as possible. Sheela was furious. She told the workmen remaining at Montclair that Deeksha was now to be considered demoted, and treated as an ordinary person. She was no longer special, and no longer in charge of things in any way. We were instructed not to pay any attention to her when we got to the ranch, and not to listen to her.

Sheela went on to explain that thanks to Deeksha, who had wasted $200,000 on the building and renovation work, the Montclair castle was a financial disaster. In the event, the castle remained unsold for two years, and did in fact lose an enormous amount of money.

As I listened to Sheela running down Deeksha, I thought: "How are the mighty fallen." As she issued her instructions, Sheela looked defiantly round the room. Nobody said a word to defend Deeksha, and in the following weeks she, and she alone, was blamed for the totalitarian regime in the castle. She was blamed for putting her handymen's comforts before Bhagwan's, and of desecrating the house. This last accusation could not have been more true. The Montclair Historic Houses Association came round to view once the 'improvements' were finished, aand were horrified. It was obvious that trouble was to follow. The Mayor of Montclair had not been happy about our presence for some time, and after the visit by the Historic Houses Association, she wrote a carefully-worded but extremely forceful denunciation of our presence in her municipality. The neighbours, who had probably read something about our activities by now, started to complain about our evening music group. Though the music was amateurish, and we were doing no more than singing songs and playing a few instruments, they concluded that we were doing indescribable things, and termed our efforts 'goat sacrifice music'. We were highly amused, but Sheela did not want trouble while Bhagwan was still there and she was trying to sell the place, so she made us stop.

Isabel and Laxmi now flew out to the ranch, and moved into the first of many 'trailers'. These were prefabricated three- or four-bedroom houses made almost entirely of plastic, and had to be towed to the ranch in two long sections before being bolted together. They are the most instant form of housing ever invented, and form dwellings thirty feet wide and sixty feet long. One questionable attribute they possessed was being able to burn to the ground within five minutes of a fire starting.

Two weeks after Laxmi and Isabel were installed, it was my turn to go to the ranch. Vivek's boyfriend and an English plumber accompanied me. During our time at the castle we had been sleeping on large heavy futon mattresses, and Sheela told us to take these monsters with us to save her having to buy new ones in Oregon. The airport check-in clerk looked at them suspiciously, but did in the end let them through.

We arrived in Madras, and were driven from there through a minute hamlet with a sign saying 'Antelope: population 40'. Sheela had bought a trailer stationed on the outskirts of this tiny village. This trailer acted as the vetting office for the ranch itself, which was sixteen miles away down a very dusty rutted dirt track. As we drove, the rear windows became opaque with dust, and we coughed and covered our noses with handkerchiefs. "This is nothing, man," our Australian driver informed us cheerily. "Wait till you get to the ranch itself!"

We passed a neighbouring farm, and I was rather shocked to see five dead coyotes in various stages of decay strung up by the back feet from a barbed wire fence. It was a macabre sight, and did little to endear me to the place. The dead coyotes were supposed to scare off vermin, and were the present-day equivalent of a barbaric ritual — your enemies' bodies showed your power. So this is cowboy country, I thought, as we sped on.

We bounced over a hilltop, and the driver swept a calloused hand across the horizon. "So far as the eye can see," he said, "is ours." In front of us lay a succession of gently rolling hills, with valley after valley dotted with stunted juniper trees and tired sagebrush. I took off my sunglasses to get a better view of this land, which seemed to have a slightly bluish cast. Yes, it was blue, and the air was very clear. But it was hardly the lush paradise that Sheela had described. The land was tired out, and the tree growth looked like the survival of the fittest, the only things that could grow in this barren soil. There was not a bird in sight, nor a meadow, nor a brook. Dust swirled everywhere. We even had to stuff the fresh air vents in the van with paper and plastic bags to stop too much dust entering the vehicle. I wondered what on earth Bhagwan would make of this place. However would he be able to drive a Rolls Royce over thirteen miles of dirt track before reaching a proper road? I also wondered where Sheela had located the thirty-foot juniper tree and the brook for the photographs. Perhaps the valley bottoms would be more what I had envisaged.

Half an hour later we arrived at the ranch house, which was splendidly situated in a broad expanse of flat land on one of those valley bottoms I had been looking forward to. We stepped out, into three inches of dust.

A group of beautiful tall poplar trees shaded the farmhouse, which was surrounded by large barn, outhouses, machine shop, garages and stores. Sheela's office, a new wide double trailer, was already installed there, and overlooked a reedy brownish lake. There seemed to be dozens of sannyasis milling about. We got a great welcome, with bear hugs from the men and embraces from the women. Almost everybody was wearing a cowboy hat, cowboy boots and sunglasses. From what I could see of their faces they all looked bronzed and fit, not tired and played out.

Isabel was there, and we hugged rapturously. I noticed that she was not wearing a mala — nobody was — and I wondered why. Isabel explained that Sheela had thought it wiser for sannyasis not to wear them so as not to upset the local people. Trouble, she said, had already started. Only the previous day a government inspector had driven down to see how many people were really living on the site. As soon as the sannyasi supervisor heard he was coming, they had packed people off to River House, six miles away, so it would look as though there were only ten people living on the ranch. It turned out that the area was only zoned for ten people, no more. Isabel's eyes were shining. "Isn't this a wonderful place?" she enthused. I shook my head in disbelief, but Isabel, the PR expert, was adept at her job. As we walked off arm in arm, she told me that she had something important to tell me.

She said she was sure I wouldn't mind, but she had a new lover. "You don't mind, do you, Shiva?" She said she wanted to carry on seeing me too, but I felt suddenly overpowered by everything — the new country, the new commune, and Isabel with another man only two weeks after we had separated from a deep and precious intimacy in New Jersey. I said that I would need a bit of time to settle in and think about it. Perhaps we would be able to meet for supper?

I was assigned to the new heavy equipment department, and was given a choice of antiquated equipment to consider. I elected to try it all, to see what would prove the most challenging. The big caterpillar front-end loader seemed to demand the most handling skill, so I plumped for that.

The ranch turned out to be hotter than Poona — 110 degrees. One of our outside contractor friends guffawed at Sheela's description of the local weather. "Fella," he said disarmingly, "there's only two seasons in Ahreegan — July'n August, an' winter."

As I had promised, as soon as I had formulated an overall impression of the ranch I wrote to one of Bhagwan's three cooks back at the castle. "Surely," I wrote, "something in Sheela's unconscious must have fallen in love with how similar these barren hills are to the hills around Poona." Then I realised that that would not go down too well if Sheela read it, so, thinking of the girls in the castle office who seemed to be reading all the mail, I changed it to "something in Sheela's heart."

Vivek's boyfriend and I were assigned living quarters at the far-off River House, where we slept six to a room. Everybody else was near the farmhouse. I saw Isabel that night and told her I could not go through another triangular relationship with her. It had happened in Poona, and I did not feel that I could stand a repeat of that situation. We had adhered to our basic agreement to tell the other if either of us took another lover, and she had honoured it. Isabel then proposed that we should spend that night together, for old time's sake. My resistance dissolved in an instant.

For the next two weeks we went through various permutations of being together, apart, and enduring the triangular arrangement, and it was a very unhappy experience for me. At last we fell out even more seriously when I went off with another woman for a day.

I resigned myself to the life of a 'has-been' — or 'bin-has' as the locals put it. I had been important in Poona, and now, along with several other ex-samurai guards and ex-department heads, I was relegated to being an ordinary worker. Everything had changed, and it seemed clear that what had happened in Poona would never happen again. I kept telling myself that everything would work out when Bhagwan arrived.

After a week of trying to cope with the caterpillar, I was assigned dump truck work. It was safer but dustier. One day my ancient dump truck broke down while I was carrying turf for Bhagwan's new lawn, and a third of the turf died. It did not show, however, until weeks later, when the individual sections started to turn yellow in the completed lawn. I was very upset about this, but surprisingly Sheela was easier on me than usual, and told me not to worry about things I could not help. Sheela flew back to the castle two weeks after I arrived at the ranch, and we understood that Bhagwan was to join us any day. His own house, a triple-wide trailer, was hastily screwed together, levelled, carpeted, cleaned, plumbed, linoleumed and polished, until not a speck of dust or dirt was visible. By this time Vivek's boyfriend and I had moved into tents near the farmhouse, pitched where the government inspector could not see them.

The day before Bhagwan was due to arrive, to my utter surprise I was told that, along with Vivek's boyfriend, I was being moved into Bhagwan's own house. It seemed incredible, but when I returned to my tent after a hard day's work, I found that it was occupied by somebody else, and all my things had been moved into Bhagwan's house by the cleaning crew. So it was true! I could hardly believe my good fortune! So Bhagwan did hold the reins, after all.

The whole team, now numbering about seventy of us, was called upon to put the finishing touches to Bhagwan's house and the surrounding lawn. We worked until well past midnight, and I asked my new girlfriend to celebrate by spending the night with me. Isabel made a nuisance of herself by putting on her most seductive airs, letting me know she was available again. "Oh yes," I thought, "you didn't want me when I was living in a tent, but now I'm in Bhagwan's house you'd do anything to get in there as well. No thanks, ma'am.".

We were all very excited when we knew for sure that Bhagwan was coming. One of the sannyasi farmers rigged up a sprinkling device on the back of a tractor, and towed it up and down the dusty roads between the ranch house and Bhagwan's own house two miles way, in an effort to keep down the dust. Gardeners rushed around the house site planting shrubs and placing potted plants on verandas. The new name — Rajneeshpuram — had already been decided upon, and a rather imposing sign went up on a hill overlooking the ranch. All over the ranch, sannyasis were carrying special clean clothes to put on as soon as they heard that Bhagwan was near. There was no point in putting them on early — they would have been covered in dust in minutes. We had been briefed that we were to sit on the lawn to welcome Bhagwan with our smiles, our namastes, and our resident musicians. A large armchair was set out in front of us to welcome our Master. At ten in the morning Jayananda screeched up to my dump truck in a Rolls, and asked me where my camera was. Nobody had said anything to me. He explained that I had to take pictures of Bhagwan arriving at Madras. "Didn't anyone tell you?" he shouted, annoyed and flustered. "Bhagwan will be there in ninety minutes."

I followed Jayananda to Madras in a Saab, but by the time we got there we learned that the Lear jet that was flying Bhagwan cross-country had been diverted to Redmond, another twenty minutes away. We hoped against hope that the jet would be late, but when we arrived at Redmond there was no sign of the jet, and at the control tower we were told that it had disappeared from the radar screen thirty minutes ago. There had been no contact since. Was Bhagwan's propensity for breaking mechanical things at work again?

After ten minutes of anxious waiting we were relieved to hear that the Lear had reappeared on the screen and was now cleared for landing. I learned later that Sheela had instructed the pilot to fly low over the ranch, so that Bhagwan would not glimpse the magnificent forests of Mount Hood, a hundred miles away, and so be dissatisfied with what she had bought. I got some wonderful shots of Bhagwan coming across the windswept apron, as usual perfectly relaxed, bowing and smiling. Then we sped off back to the ranch so that I could get some good shots of Bhagwan's Rolls as it passed in front of the new Rajneeshpuram sign.

When Bhagwan arrived at his new house, he left the Rolls and walked over to sit with the assembled group of sannyasis for five minutes, the dust-clad flanks of the blue Rolls Royce behind him. Many of the sannyasis in the audience had not seen him since that final satsang in Poona. The original inhabitant of the ranch, Bob Harvey, sat at the back of the audience, a red shirt tucked into his Levis marking his concession to the occasion. Bhagwan got up to go into his new house. He namasted and looked around at the bluish view. Sheela and Vivek followed him slowly into the house, fussing over doors to let him in. We all sat on the marvellous lawn, amidst the dun browns and dusty blues, and rejoiced that *he* was here at last, and looking so well!

Within three minutes Sheela returned to the balcony outside Bhagwan's room. She smiled expansively, obviously tremendously relieved. "He likes it," she exploded. Everyone in the audience joined in her happiness, laughed and joked, hugged and cuddled, and wondered at our good fortune to have our beloved Teacher amongst us again.

Sheela complimented me on my photographs. How did I like these 'barren hills' now, she enquired. I told her I was getting to like them more and more, wondering to myself where I had heard that phrase before. Then I realised — so she did read my letter to the cook.

After Bhagwan was installed, Sheela called a public meeting and gave us all a pep talk. We were to remember, she said, that there was to be no negativity, no grumbling, so signs of dissatisfaction at all. We were going to have to be a hundred per cent positive to make it all work. She spoke directly to the men — the ranch was still eighty per cent male — and told us that we were to remember that we were specially privileged to be here with Bhagwan. We had to remember that things would be very different here. It would not be run like Poona, with outside villas and huts. Everything was going to be in the one enclosed and centrally-run commune. For the time being we were not to tell anyone where we were. The outside world was not to know that Bhagwan had arrived. If news leaked out that he had turned up, he was to be regarded as a visitor, and not as our leader. Bhagwan was still on a temporary tourist's visa.

As we were only zoned for ten people, the other sixty-five had to make themselves scarce when inspectors arrived. Discretion was to be observed at all times. This meant that nobody was to contact outsiders and tell them what was going on. We were to understand that there were only two Rolls Royces here, not six. The commune was to be a farming co-operative, and no more people would come in except for farm workers. If reporters came and asked us why there were so many people around, we were to say they were weekend visitors, or well-wishers come to lend a hand. They were not permanent residents.

Anyone who was feeling tired, negative, or in a complaining mood was not to go near the newsmen who would inevitably start arriving before long. Anyone who was interviewed had to be very careful what they said. This briefing, Sheela added, was to remind people how important it was not to put a foot wrong. We all had to trust Bhagwan that it would work out in the end, but before the utopia was finished there would be a lot of hard worked required from everybody. Anybody who was caught idling, complaining or causing trouble would be out in an instant. She glared round the room, then snapped her fingers. "Just to clear the air," she went on, "this is your last chance to bring up any complaints you have. Anyone with anything to say had better speak up now. Don't worry, nothing will happen to you if you do."

There was complete silence as sannyasis looked at each other. There was far too much experience from the Poona days to fall for this one. It would have to be low profiles from now on, especially among the has-beens. After a few seconds of painful silence, Vivek's boyfriend spoke up with a long list of complaints. He started with the beer, which was rationed to a pint a day. We all felt this was not enough in this intense heat. Then he complained about the half-hour queues for supper, and about the problems of making long-distance phone calls. There were only the two telephones — Sheela's and Bob Harvey's — and Bob soon had a lot of new friends. He finished his tirade by speaking out against the accommodation, which for most of us meant tents. He was voicing things that we all felt, and perhaps felt that his relationship with Vivek gave him the necessary status to speak out. Within eight weeks, however, he had been relieved of his job as Bhagwan's valet, had lost his room in Bhagwan's house, and his relationship with Vivek was over. He was put back to work as a concrete labourer, living in a distant house.

After he had finished, Sheela was noticably tight-lipped. "Anyone else?" she asked tersely. There was dead silence again. Sheela then added that Bhagwan had told her only yesterday that if this commune didn't work out, he would go off with just seven or eight specially-chosen disciples, and leave the rest to their own devices.

At another meeting Sheela launched into a tirade, saying that from now on the power games that had been practised in Poona would stop. Nobody was to give or receive gifts of either money or objects. Anyone who did receive such a gift should take it to Sheela's trailer, where it would be shown to Bhagwan. He and nobody else would decide what should happen to the gift. From now on we were not to indulge in all this lovey-dovey holding hands and kissing in public. "If you guys need to slobber over your girlfriends," she said, "you just do it in private from now on." Lastly, Sheela announced that there were to be no trips off the ranch and no outside phone calls without office permission.

"Oh dear," I thought, "whatever is coming next?" I remembered what Bhagwan had told us in Poona: "Never let *anyone* dictate your life to you. *Anyone!*" About the only thing which had so far been left unlegislated against was our sex lives. At least these were sacrosanct — as yet.

Almost as soon as we arrived at the Big Muddy, Sheela's public profile began to emerge and alter. Within six weeks of Bhagwan's arrival in Oregon, she began a round of public speaking appointments, where she assured local Rotary Clubs, women's social organisations and local county officials that they had nothing whatever to worry about. The Big Muddy, she said, was not going to be turned into some kind of international commune, and the absolute maximum number of people that the ranch would ever house would be 250. She assured them that she, like them, was a simple farmer, and that she and her friends were going to establish a beautiful, ecologically-rich and stable oasis. She declared that the overgrazed pastures would be turned back into rich farmland within two years.

She denied that Rajneesh was on the ranch, but agreed that it was likely that he might pop in for a short visit from time to time. Sheela was very careful to make sure that she was always accompanied on these trips by her husband, who always dressed in neat, dark suits. Bob Harvey, our non-sannyasi foreman, made glowing comments on local TV about how impressed he was with his new farmhands. He praised our industry, our farming knowhow, and our skill with sixty-ton bulldozers. Sheela hosted a buffet party in The Dalles, our local county seat, to which only the most presentable, clean-shaven sannyasis were invited. They made polite conversation with the ultra-conservative locals.

Sheela's PR campaign went well until one day about two months after it started, Sheela answered a question about the number of disciples that would eventually live on the ranch. Well, she said, there could eventually be as many as ten thousand. This admission brought astonished and outraged reactions, and Isabel, now head of PR, was brought in to reinterpret Sheela's 'misunderstanding'. But the damage had been done, and Sheela had unintentionally alerted the local people to Bhagwan's intentions.

Within two months of our arrival, two hundred sannyasis were actually living on the ranch, and complaints about us started. When one of the neighbouring farmers complained to the county authorities that we were infringing land use requirements with our sewage disposal arrangements, Sheela soon had her revenge. She sent me up in a twin-engined aircraft to take aerial shots of this farmer's ranch, and I was able to take pictures of infringements of the identical arrangements. These pictures were sent anonymously to county headquarters.

John Bannerman, one of the local farmers, came round one Sunday on a social call, mounted on a fine horse and wearing a splendidly weatherworn set of chaps, boots, jeans, and a cowboy hat. He was a coach to the American Olympic team, an erudite and companionable man with a handsome, distinguished face. We offered him a coffee at our canteen, and he told us how glad he was to see some ecologically sound ideas being implemented to resurrect this exhausted land. We could be sure of his support, he said, and if we ever needed his help, or the loan of any equipment, he would be very glad to oblige. We were all warmed by his welcome.

He soon turned against us, however, and before long both counties on which the ranch stood were determined to foil Bhagwan's plans. One county, Jefferson, had refused us all house building permission from the start. Wasco County, however, had given approval for fifty four-bedroomed houses, with an option on thirty more. Once Wasco heard of Bhagwan's intentions, they tried to rescind their approval, but it was too late. The conflict over zoning and housing eventually reached the point when in 1984 an attempt was made by some sannyasis to set fire to the Wasco County Court House, where all the zoning records were kept.

Bob Harvey, the ranch foreman, was certainly prepared to like us. In the first days after our Master's arrival, Bob had given Bhagwan a hat, a quaint and unconscious reversal of the normal gift procedure. "Seemed like a real cute fella," was Bob's initial opinion. At that time, Bob used to act as a bodguard, following Bhagwan's Rolls in a second car, carrying his .38 revolver.

Bhagwan soon added to his collection of speeding tickets, and in the next month drove one Rolls after another off the road. Two had to be sent back to the California dealers for major repairs. I wondered if Bhagwan's naiveté stretched to believing that because Rollses were the best car in the world, they could go round corners at any speed. Margaret Hill, then the Mayor of Antelope, stopped to offer assistance after one accident, but Bhagwan just ignored her and walked off. Vivek told me that this accident had terrified her, and she had been sure that both she and Bhagwan were going to be killed. After that Vivek took Bhagwan's car keys away, and in an attempt to stop him driving altogether Sheela promised to build him an indoor swimming pool, and to improve the airstrip so that he could go flying whenever he liked. She ordered a million dollar turbo-prop aircraft for his amusement, and work began at once on a swimming pool extension to Bhagwan's house, which was named, as at Poona, Lao Tzu House after Bhagwan's favourite Chinese sage.

In late 1981 Sheela began to be questioned more aggressively in her ongoing public meetings. One woman farmer asked her why it was that we needed ten people to feed our 150 hens. Her own grandmother could look after two hundred chickens all by herself. And how come we had a herd of beef cattle on a vegetarian commune? What was going on? The retired people in Antelope were already suspicious of our motives, and started worrying that the commune might be planning to take over their village. Sheela assured them that the commune would not be buying any more land than the one plot in Antelope where the office trailer now stood.

The organisation of the commune had not yet been formalised. Bhagwan had proposed to Sheela that there should be seven groups of people — seven was always a magic number for him — which would each have seven 'monitor members'. 'Monitors' had been senior disciples of Buddha's who ran his commune in India 2,500 years ago. All commune laws were to be discussed and passed by this august body. The monitors would have their own hall. The office — Sheela's office — would have an orange roof to denote its pre-eminence and special importance above that of the monitors' 'sangha' or parliament. All other buildings would have green roofs. Sheela apparently squashed the monitor idea.

It was very noticable that in all these arrangements Laxmi was given nothing to do at all. Bhagwan had told her to enjoy an uninterrupted retirement, something she could not possibly do. Leisure, in the sense that other people understood the word, was worse than death to Laxmi, and her health soon started to suffer as a result of her enforced idleness.

Before the winter really set in, Bhagwan went to take his Oregon driving test. He drove into the sleepy town of Madras to take the test. He occasioned astonished glances from the inhabitants as he glided by in an immaculate Rolls Royce. Much to the amazement of everybody on the ranch Bhagwan passed his test, and so was able to go on driving.

Between August and December the handymen set up a large number of building projects, and we worked night and day to turn the commune into something habitable. We started building on old avalanche sites and across dry creek beds which Bob Harvey warned us would become raging torrents at times of flash floods, and were ludicrous locations for homes. We took no notice and in our ignorance and chauvinism built on regardless. The road to Bhagwan's house crossed a bone-dry gulch. A couple of narrow culverts were laid down, and a road hastily and unprofessionally built over the top. None of us was trained as a builder or roadmaker, and few of us knew what kind of country we were building on. Six weeks after we had built our first culvert dam to Bhagwan's house, the whole thing was washed away. Two larger culverts were installed and a new road levelled on top of them. Four weeks and many thousands of dollars later, this too was washed away by another flash flood. A third culvert was installed, this time properly compacted and built with an over-flow spillway. Surely this would last, we thought, as we proudly sur-veyed the finished job. We were learning fast. It actually lasted until about Christmas, when the spillway eroded and widened until it was washed away under the onslaught of a forty-foot wide, twenty-mile-an-hour torrent.

After the second culvert disaster, Bhagwan was marooned inside his house for ten days, Vivek went onto the open wavelength of the CB radio and shouted: "Get me out of this hellhole!" Though we had all been told never to complain under any circumstances, she was rescued instantly.

We had a survey conducted of the ranch soil. The American soil grades go from 1, which is first-class agricultural land, to 10, which is almost solid rock, good only for minimal agricultural use in the order of one head of cattle per ten acres. Most of the ranch was graded 10. Although we had 120 square miles, there was little that could be done with it.

At the Antelope office, our PR front-line outpost, some sannyasis started redrafting the list of books and tapes which had been available in Poona. We had not yet realised that the Poona days of experiment were over, and became particularly excited about one of Bhagwan's tapes which very much reflected the free spirit of Poona. Called 'The Fuck Tape', it consisted of Bhagwan extolling and describing at length the forty different possible uses of the word 'fuck'. For the purposes of the Oregon public this tape was described as "a discourse in which Bhagwan makes jokes about human relationships." We still hankered after a new Poona here in Oregon, but it rapidly became abundantly clear that this was not in the minds of either Bhagwan or Sheela.

By degrees Sheela started cementing her absolute authority. First she ditched the monitor idea, then proceeded to demote most of those sannyasis trained and chosen by Laxmi who still had any status at all in the commune. Sannyasis who had been department heads in Poona were now given menial jobs far away from the nerve centre, and by December Sheela had picked a group of women to be her assistants who worshipped her and boosted her sense of power and authority. She soon had a retinue that surpassed even Bhagwan's, She had her own full-time hairdresser, a house boy, two personal house cleaners, and a doting — and largely redundant — husband. In addition she had half a dozen female assistants who were available to her at her beck and call, a driver, two pilots, two cooks, a personal nurse, PR people, communications staff and a valet.

While the rest of us worked long hours in perishing conditions, Sheela drove her new bright red Mercedes, wore Gucci shoes, carried Gucci handbags, and ordered Dior dresses and Dunhill sunglasses. Her hands glittered with gold, and she wore a man's solid gold Rolex watch on her wrist. Given her position of absolute authority, nobody dared challenge her excesses or attempted to check her in any way.

Meanwhile my relationship with Isabel had fallen apart completely. The triangular relationship had not worked, but after I had moved to Bhagwan's house, Isabel had tried to sidle back into my affections, and her change of attitude upset me even more. A month later we got back together again, and for six months our love affair had blossomed anew, but now it was clearly over.

As work progressed, Sheela invited a group of wealthy bankers to visit the ranch. They flew in from Portland, the biggest city in Oregon, from Seattle, and from San Francisco. An impressive tour of the ranch was laid on for their benefit, and we were all told to look as industrious as possible. Sheela was hoping to attract some large loans. As she drove them up to the fields ten miles from the ranch, Sheela told them how hard her people were working. None of them minded putting in a twelve-hour day, seven days a week. She assured them that we were going to produce an economic miracle, and make lush green vegetables grow where there had been only dry and infertile land before. When they finally arrived at the high fields, Sheela was embarrassed to discover her much-vaunted farmer fast asleep under a tree.

While Sheela assumed more and more power, Deeksha and Laxmi joined forces to try and oust her. Deeksha asked me at about this time what I would do if I left Bhagwan. I thought about it, and said I would probably go to California, a place I had always wanted to visit, but I was surprised by Deeksha's question. What I didn't know at the time, but Deeksha did, was that I was on Sheela's short list for expulsion.

Laxmi had requested her own telephone and car, and the freedom to go on shopping trips so she could send letters to India without Sheela's approval. All her requests were denied. She was told that she had to accept her retirement, and that we must be careful not to upset the locals by being seen in their towns. At this time even the grocery shopping had to be done in different towns each day so that nobody would know how many people were being fed at the Big Muddy — there were now 350 of us. In September Deeksha decided she could not stand it any more, and left quite suddenly with her boyfriend.

More and more people kept arriving to help with house construction, and by December we had built an enormous warehouse and licensed canteen which was large enough for the zoned 250 people, improved the airstrip, built a heavy equipment building complete with service bays and spares departments, and had nearly completed the fifty double-width trailers for which we had building permission.

Just before Christmas it became so cold that a pickaxe simply bounced off the ground, and building operations had to come to a halt. So much for Sheela's all-year-round warmth! We still did not really know what we were doing, but work proceeded at an immense pace. It was 'build and be damned', or at least build as much as possible before the authorities realised that what we were building was not a farm, but a city.

Chapter Thirteen
WINTER ON THE RANCH

Altogether, around $120 million was poured into the Big Muddy ranch during the four years of its existence as a Rajneesh commune. Though it did not make things any easier that we had to work in secret, from the start we worked frenetically to build Bhagwan the biggest and best commune ever known.

One of the major problems confronting many of us was how to stay on in America, as most of us only had tourist visas which would soon expire. From June 1981, hasty marriages began to be arranged so that those who were not American citizens could stay in the US and get American passports. These marriages seemed highly suspicious to the authorities, and it was not long before they began to be investigated. We began applying for visa extensions in different states of the USA, so that nobody in the immigration department should suspect that we were all Rajneeshees living at Big Muddy. We also had to learn passable American accents to make us indistinguishable from the real US citizens. Special classes were arranged in 'American', and I learned how to speak with a very passable American accent.

Where did all the money come from to fund the massive project we had undertaken? Large sums came from the sale of goods in Poona, and around $80 million had been amassed in India from donations, admission charges, and Deeksha's catering and therapy courses. But a lot of the cash raised specifically for Rajneeshpuram was due to the work of our chief fundraiser, Yoga Sushila, or Susan Wallach, from Chicago. She went on worldwide fund-raising trips, and spun such hard-luck stories that people stumped up wherever she went. One Lufthansa air hostess who was a sannyasin said later: "Sushila told me they did not even have enough money to feed Bhagwan the next week, so of course I gave her everything." Bhagwan at the time had just taken delivery of his eleventh Rolls Royce.

I was invited to take a portrait of Sushila as she worked, and sat through quite a devastating session. The middle-aged sannyasin woman who had given me money for my emergency dental work in

New Jersey, and to whom I owed a special debt of gratitude, was called in. A long and detailed examination of her financial status ensued.

Sushila told the woman: "Only yesterday Bhagwan told me how happy he was with your progress." A stiff brandy was brought in by one of Sheela's house waiters to celebrate, soon followed by another. "You'll need it, my dear, by the time you've finished with the lawyer," said Sushila. The lawyer came in with a stack of legal papers and a pen. He looked very smart and determined. Sushila went on: "And Bhagwan said to me that he could see you were ready for a great jump, but there was an impediment. Your money is a barrier to your surrender to him and the commune. The time has come to take the leap into the unknown and give everything! That is your message, isn't it wonderful? You must be so *close*! Look at me, huh, I haven't a cent in the world, and the commune takes care of me perfectly." Sushila sipped her coffee and picked out another *petit four*. "Look at me! Do you have any stocks? Shares? Antique furniture? Paintings, tapestry, jewellery? Believe me, dear, we need the lot, all of it! What about this apartment in Manhattan? How much is it worth? Can you sell it this week, right away? You have antiques in storage, you say? That's no problem· we'll send a sannyasi round with a truck tomorrow. I'll phone him right after you've left. My, you are going to feel so *good*, so *clean*, with all this shit off your hands! Now, what about foreign investments, futures, Krugerrands, property abroad; anything? Yes, that's fine, go right ahead, have another brandy. Why, it's hot on this porch today, isn't it?" The papers hovered meaningfully in the lawyer's hands. "Oh dear, how silly of me, I quite forgot. Bhagwan gave me this beautiful pen to give to you today. Here it is! Now, there's an idea! Why don't you use it to sign all these silly papers? You'll feel so *fine* afterwards!" I got a good wide-angle shot of Sushila proferring the pen to the woman over the spread of legally-binding documents.

I found myself rooting for the woman to hold out, and I was relieved when she demurely asked Sushila for three days to think about it. The lawyer's composure crumpled into a dissatisfied tightening of the lips. The woman slipped out, and Sushila immediately called in the next sannyasi. I excused myself as I heard her launch into: "You know, dear, Bhagwan was talking to me about you only last night . . ."

In October 1981 the immigration office in Portland sent their investigator, Tom Casey, on a 'friendly visit', the first visit of many. The Portland immigration office was used to dealing with impoverished Mexican farm workers, and at the beginning of their investigation they hard a hard time pinning anything on the wily Rajneeshees.

The insistence on 'not being negative' increased all the time. A few people had started to leave, so Bhagwan issued new guidelines which said that those who remained positive would be allowed to stay on the ranch, whereas those who tried to disrupt the smooth establishment of the commune would be told to leave at once. This made it sound as though he was sending away anyone who chose to leave, rather than them leaving of their own free will. Anyone who disagreed with the way the commune was being run could hand their mala in at once and leave immediately. This announcement was, I was certain, made in order to dispel the growing suspicion that Sheela was not running the commune in the way that Bhagwan wanted.

I began to settle into a routine. I drove dump trucks, took photographs, and did osteopathic first-aid treatments. I had the use of a powerful cross-country motorcycle to help me to take landscape photography, and I wondered what my eventual role would be.

Men still heavily outnumbered women at the ranch, and those women who did come in were hard-working, serious types rather than sexy, voluptuous females. Perhaps because of the dire shortage of available women, sexual jealousies became rampant at this time, and many of the men felt continually frustrated. One of the handymen later remarked that it was just as well we had no guns then, or there would have been a few gunfights at the corral. But after I settled into a routine of hard manual work with photography as a sideline, I became much happier, and there were moments in 1981 when I felt quite certain that the commune was going to work.

Mukta, one of the wealthier sannyasins, had invited me to give her weekly massages, for which she secretly paid me $50 a time, a fortune! I had readily agreed. As my dump truck work took me off the ranch from time to time, I had more freedom than many. Laxmi passed me letters to post to India for her in order to circumvent the sannyasi censors. I was happy to oblige.

Many of us had been applying for visa extensions through a sannyasi lawyer in Texas. One day he was arrested, and it transpired that the immigration service had known about the Texan ruse all along. An FBI agent posing as a local Oregon farmer came to the ranch to look for an Italian swami called Mario. He had reasoned that since Mario had given Bhagwan so much money while he was at Poona — over a million dollars — he would still be in the presence of his Master.

Things got no easier for Laxmi. A car was bought for her — an Eagle 4×4 as she had requested — but it was not the right model, and Laxmi refused to drive it. She complained about her trailer home, so a new one was built to her own specifications, small enough for her not to have to share it. But when she went to see it, she did not like the curtains and the lino, and was not at all happy with the way the rooms were arranged — the rooms were too small, she said, and there was nowhere to have a party. This of course was deliberate — Sheela wanted to ensure that Laxmi was not holding meetings in her trailer. Since Laxmi complained so much about the new house, it was given to Bhagwan's mother, Saraswati, who had recently arrived on a tourist visa from India.

Several more Indians arrived, including India's top male film star, Vinod Khanna, and they were set to work cooking and preparing food. All the outdoor work, however, did not by any means keep us healthy or free from disease. Within a few months of our move to Oregon, amoebic dysentery had broken out. The disease is carried systemically, and those who carried the amoebae, mostly Indians, were preparing food, so the disease spread rapidly through the commune. Gonorrhoea and herpes broke out again, leading to a clampdown on sexual liaisons, which became increasingly monitored and controlled. Another sannyasi came down with hepatitis. It seemed that all the old Poona diseases had followed us here.

Local feeling against us grew. Bhagwan had started to be harassed, and shots had been fired at the car escorting his Rolls Royce. It seemed to Bhagwan that sannyasis were being unfairly treated wherever they went, and that the commune had become involved in legal difficulties so quickly simply because of anti-sannyasi feeling. Why should this be? Bhagwan wanted quick answers, so Brett, an ex-trouble shooter for large multinational companies and one of my former martial arts trainers, was flown over to give some answers. His brief from Bhagwan was to answer three questions:

    — how could Bhagwan protect his visa, the most important asset on the ranch?

    — why were we being legally hassled?

— why was Bhagwan being attacked?

Brett was very specific and very sensible. "Bhagwan," he said, "your first mistake was to try and set up here as a non-profit company, when it is clear that you are making money. The first tax inspector to come along will see that. The three separate corporations that have been set up so far are obviously a false front. It's no good pretending that they are completely separate entities: the authorities will see through that in a second.

"The best thing you can do is come clean. Abolish them all and form one honest, profit-making company. If you pay tax in America, no one will bother you. The next mistake is that you have already bought eleven Rolls Royces. The Americans don't like that; they prefer you to buy American cars. Use modest cars until you get your immigration status approval, then go as big as you like. Get Lincoln Continentals — if they are good enough for the President of the United States, they're good enough for you. And one reason so many sannyasis get attacked and harassed is because of their unkempt appearance. Another is that they think they can do what they like, and are above the law. Then you don't pay your bills until you are threatened with litigation, and that doesn't make you popular either. Middle, America is a conservative and traditional place, and isn't likely to welcome with open arms the leader of a scruffy bunch of hippies who flout the laws of the land."

He pulled no punches, and Bhagwan appeared to listen attentively. He asked Brett how long it would take to change the tax structures, and how much it would all cost. Brett assured him that he could do it within a week, and that it would cost only a few thousand dollars, a trifling sum to the commune. Bhagwan then asked Brett if he would stay on the ranch for a while, and get the corporations and their finances sorted out. He suggested that Brett should go to Sheela and tell her that he was now in charge of finances. As he left, Bhagwan said: "Start the new company as soon as possible."

Brett accordingly started work the next morning in the accounts trailer. The very first receipt he found was for a large high-quality tent — and it was for twenty dollars. It was clear that this was an attempt to defraud, and he insisted that the tent be taken off the premises immediately. Sheela countermanded the order, saying the tent had valuable material in it and must stay where it was. She told Brett in no uncertain terms that she was in charge of running the commune, and that her word was final. Brett told her to go and jump in the lake, and made it clear that he would speak to her however he liked. Everybody gasped.

Brett worked all the next day in the accounts trailer, poring over the computer and making long distance calls. He made appointments with the right people to get the new corporation set up. By this time Sheela appeared to have cooled down, and invited him over to her trailer for a friendly chat. She and her bevy of female assistants picked his financial brains, and asked for the numbers of his important contacts in Washington DC. Then Sheela picked a beautiful sannyasin woman to give him a massage until he fell asleep. At midnight, Jayananda woke him up abruptly. "Could you step out into the living room for a minute?" he said.

Brett sleepily obliged, to find Sheela and about thirty handymen waiting for him. "Hand over your mala!" demanded Sheela. Brett looked stupefied. "Bhagwan says you are to be driven off the ranch immediately," she went on, "and you are to drop all your plans to set up a new corporation. Is that clear?" Brett remembered that the previous day he had called Sheela a two-cent barmaid. This was his reward.

As I was having a cup of coffee the next day, one of Sheela's assistants came and sat beside me. "I understand you are friendly with Swami Brett," she said. "Well, he is no longer a sannyasi. He has been driven off the ranch, and I am instructed to say that neither you nor any sannyasi is to have any further contact with him. You are not to try to write to him or phone him. Is that quite clear?" I said that it was perfectly clear, and resolved to make discreet inquiries to discover what had happened to my outspoken friend.

None of Brett's eminently sensible plans, which might have saved the day for the commune in the end, were ever implemented.

The local sheriff paid us a 'friendly visit' on October 30th. He told us that he would not visit again until the spring, as the roads would be impassable until then. That did not bother me at all — it gave me a wonderful cosy feeling that we would be holed up here together for several months. I soon discovered that the sheriff was not wrong. By early November the frosts became fierce and the first snow fell. The crop of sunflowers planted at Sheela's insistence was killed by the first frost. All the time, though, house construction went on at a furious pace. Everybody in the heavy construction department was issued with winter clothing, thick padded dark brown all-in-ones.

While more Rolls Royces arrived for Bhagwan, we workmen had

to eat outside, wearing our Arctic pack boots and parkas, the snow falling steadily into our rations. We evolved elaborate schemes to get ourselves a second and even a third pint of beer a day, and were each allocated twenty high-tar cigarettes every day — since I didn't smoke, I became very popular. A journalist from San Francisco who visited at this time reckoned that we must have the highest per capita consumption of cigarettes in the whole country. Isabel took photographs of us eating outside in the snow, and we had to admit that the pictures made us look very quaint and appealing.

I had always wondered why the ranch was called the Big Muddy, and now it became abundantly clear. The rains turned the roads into greasy ribbons. Sannyasis who had lived for years in tropical Poona now had to learn how to pull thirty-ton trucks out of ditches and fit tyre chains onto ten-wheel dump trucks at 25 degrees below freezing — without gloves. Huge bulldozers turned over and careered down embankments. The conditions we were working under led to the use of some very colourful language, but Sheela insisted that we must moderate our swearing. 'Shoot' had to replace 'shit', and 'golly' and 'gosh' ousted the more colourful expletives. At the same time, sewage disposal became a serious problem, since the thirty houses designed to house six people each were in fact accommodating fourteen sannyasis per house, not to mention the visitors and weekend guests.

As we worked in the snow in our brown canvas overalls, one of the carpenters pointed to a bunch of us. "Look!" he said. "Prisoners." It was true. That was what we did look like, and that was what we were. The description was so apt that we all burst out laughing.

As far as protection from the winter weather was concerned, however, the heavy equipment crew was much better off than the carpenters working on Bhagwan's swimming pool extension. They did not have our heavy overalls, and were issued with only one pair of woollen gloves every fortnight. People who could knit suddenly became very popular, and it became important to have friends who could buy leather gloves in Madras. We were allowed a half-day off every two weeks, and it was usually taken as an opportunity to catch up on sleep. On one of my days off, I snuck off to Madras in sub-zero temperatures on my cross-country bike to take my driving test.

By now the immigration investigation was growing apace, but no more people had been drafted in to help Tom Casey. The Rajneeshees were not an easy challenge. We complained that the agency was conducting an indiscriminate investigation when they had no evidence against us at all. We lodged counter suits and appeals, and used every possible legal device to stall them. The sheer size, dedication and financial power of Rajneesh Foundation International managed to swamp the tiny INS office. It did not dawn on them for a long time how badly out-numbered and out-manoeuvred they were.

The film *Ashram,* made at the height of Poona's sex-and-violence period, came to Madras and the local towns, and angered and opened the eyes of the natives considerably. On one of his daily drives Bhagwan found a large notice on a fence saying 'Sex Guru Go Home!', and on a shopping trip in Madras I was shouted at abusively from passing cars as I walked down the main street. On one occasion I had to take my dump truck in for repairs, and the mechanic, an Elvis Presley fan, was horrified at its condition. "He must be a powerful man, protectin' yo' all in a rollin' wreck like this. No way would you get me drivin' that thing, specially laden, hell no."

We were expanding fast, and not just on the ranch. A dark room was set up, and two American sannyasi doctors obtained state medical licenses to practice, one in Madras, the other, incredibly, as a psychiatrist in The Dalles. Very soon after saying publicly that she would not be buying any more property in Antelope, Sheela set out to do just that.

On one of his daily drives to Madras, Bhagwan stopped at Antelope and instructed Sheela to start buying up houses there. "Buy that one," he told her, "and that grey one over there."

"But Bhagwan, that's the Bell telephone exchange. It's not for sale."

"Good, so buy those two houses over there instead." Three years later Bhagwan claimed complete ignorance of what had happened to Antelope. "I was in silence and isolation the whole time."

At about this time, Laxmi had a private darshan with Bhagwan where she outlined a plan that had been forming in her head for some time. She knew of a ranch near San Francisco, she said, which had immediate zoning for five hundred people and was isolated in a beautiful redwood forest, yet had a good metalled road. She had already approached the Governor of California and met with an encouraging initial response. The asking price was six million dollars.

Bhagwan said there was no more money, since it had all been tied up in the Oregon venture, but Laxmi assured him that he had many friends who would be only too glad to contribute, but had been held back by not wanting to join Sheela's regime. Bhagwan seemed to assent to Laxmi's plans, and even gave her several official names for the new commune. She went away ecstatic, and told me all about it later that same evening.

The power struggle between Laxmi and Sheela had not abated, and no new house, new car, or other privilege could console Laxmi for the loss of her supreme position. The next morning Bhagwan called Sheela, Jayananda and Isabel in for a special work session, and told them that the commune in Oregon was not living up to his expectations. The weather was wrong, the location was wrong, and there were no trees, forests, meadows or birds. He went on to say that he was having great difficulty in staying in his body — always his ultimate threat — in this place, and that he could leave his body any day now. There were only three things that would enable him to stay in his body. One was to have a thousand more sannyasis at the ranch at the earliest opportunity — he felt more comfortable when he was surrounded by his own people, the second was to plant a forest, and the third was to get him more cars. "Every week I will be needing more," he told her.

A bare hour before Bhagwan called this meeting, Laxmi left for California, intent on initiating plans for the new commune there. That same day Sheela called an emergency general meeting, where she repeated to us what Bhagwan had said about leaving his body, and reiterated that more people, cars and trees were needed at once. We would have to work even harder. We were reminded of our supreme good fortune at being here at all with the Blessed One.

Two days later Laxmi was ordered to come back to the ranch at once. She managed to reach me by telephone from California and asked if we could talk. Did I know why she was being called back? What was happening?

The story soon came out. Sheela had discovered Laxmi's project and had presented Bhagwan with an "it's her or me" ultimatum. She had won. Laxmi was immediately ordered to cease all wordly activities and hand over financial affairs to Sheela. She was ordered to stay on the ranch from now on. Any more letters she wanted delivering would have to be handed to the sannyasi in charge of shopping. In another meeting Sheela told us that Laxmi was now an

'ordinary person', and should be treated just like anybody else.
Bhagwan had told her the time had come for her to focus on her
individual enlightenment, which was very close. So she had to be
allowed her privacy, and nobody was to visit her any more.

In contrast, I seemed to be back in official favour. I was called
regularly to Sheela's trailer to treat her stiff neck and several of her
assistants' bad backs. Sheela told me that Laxmi was still scheming
and trying to find ways of getting herself back into power. She told
me how happy she was with the way I had adapted to my new role,
unlike Laxmi. She would not give up.

In December we had a small birthday celebration for Bhagwan. A
few people were invited to attend from the West Coast centres, and
Deeksha, now in exile, was invited back for the day as long as she
kept a very low profile. I was asked to take pictures of this gathering.
Sheela proposed to Bhagwan at this time that he perhaps ought to
consider having just one guard stationed outside his door. Bhagwan's
reply was incredible, and when Vivek told me of the conversation
later in the day I wondered just who was in charge at Big Muddy.
"Sheela," he had said, "first the guard will be there to keep other
people out, but very soon he will be there to keep me in."

Meanwhile Vivek was having her own problems. It seemed to me
that she was bored with her life on the new commune. The
temperatures were sub-zero, and all she had to do each day was to
watch heavy equipment drivers go past. The canteen was crammed
full with a thousand hard-working sweaty people, still mainly men,
whose chief topics of conversation were mortice joints, masonry bits
and construction work. It was hardly a fitting milieu for a sensitive
soul like Vivek.

In early 1982 Vivek asked me to come and take some pictures of
Bhagwan in his dentists' chair. She mentioned something about daily
sessions, and said that he wanted pictures taken all through the
session. I was mystified. How could he need a dental session every
single day?

There was an absolute rule at Oregon that no drugs whatever were
to be allowed on the ranch. In Poona some sannyasis had smoked
marijuana and tried opium, but here in this high desert there was
nothing like that available. When I went to take the photographs, I
soon realised that Bhagwan had found his own way of circumventing
the stricture about drugs — he was taking nitrous oxide as a
consciousness-altering drug. I took shots of small clear tubes being

passed into his nostrils and being held in place by a specially-handmade clip. Bhagwan reclined. There were five people plus Bhagwan in the tiny dental room — the dentist, the dentist's female assistant, Vivek, Bhagwan's personal physician Swami Devaraj, and myself. The dentist twirled two knobs which were recessed in the wall, to balance the gasses. Bhagwan asked now for a little more oxygen, now for slightly more nitrogen. "Good. It feels right now." I clicked away, feeling uncomfortable, like a voyeur in a bridal suite. Bhagwan's physician knelt on the floor and the dentist and his assistant were perched on stools, sitting slightly higher than Bhagwan's head. I remembered the buying of the dental chair in London, and the orders to muck it up for export. So *this* is what it was really being used for.

As the gas began to affect him, Bhagwan started to talk. His speech became increasingly slurred and slow. His normally sibilant trailing 's's' became even more drawn out and exaggerated as the gas started to have its effect. I knew that nitrous oxide was also called 'the drug of the ego'. I had recently had a large dose of it myself for genuine dental work, and was aware of its ability to induce a euphoric, trance-like and almost out-of-the-body effect. Bhagwan himself had used the stuff regularly after he had noticed its effect in relieving his asthma during a dental session. He now incorporated nitrous oxide inhalation into daily one or two hour sessions. This had apparently been going on for about six months before I got to hear about it. Devious methods had been used to get enough nitrous oxide onto the ranch without arousing suspicion. The same system whereby shoppers had to go to different towns every day was also used for nitrous oxide. Thus each of the three or four sannyasi physicians and dentists now licensed to practice in Oregon would order the stuff from a different supplier every day.

Bhagwan spoke under the influence: "SSShhhheeeeeeeeellaaaaa," he said, "wants to buy me an aeroplane. But I don't need an aeroplane, I am flying already." I was glad that Bhagwan was flying again, but sad that this state had to be induced by a powerful chemical drug. The dentist's assistant wrote down everything that Bhagwan said in a little red book with a sharp pencil. Bhagwan went on to talk about the dentist. "You are such a stupid man," he informed him. The dentist just sat there impassively, not moving a muscle. "Your mind keeps on chattering," Bhagwan continued. "It goes on, so noisy. I am not a noisy man, I do not like noise, so shut up. Ssshhhhhhhiiiiiva is here, he is my bodyguard, he can make noise, he can make a karate shout! He understands me. I do not shout, but Shiva can shout, he is my bodyguard. He can shout at you to shut up . . ."

I noticed that everybody in the room apart from me seemed to be completely unaffected by what was going on. They were obviously all used to it. Suddenly I felt sorry for Bhagwan, trapped and manipulated by these powerful women, going out only on his monotonous daily drives round the ranch. So Bhagwan needs me, I thought, and in spite of Sheela's machinations to have me removed, he has refused to let her send me away. I felt myself silently saying to Bhagwan: "You want to get out of this huge mess that has taken you over, this enormous organisation that has swallowed you up." Bhagwan had asked me into this room to do this session not really to take pictures, but so that I could see and understand what was going on and how desperate he had become. At first I had been the willing and pliable disciple, then I became his bodyguard and protector, and now he needed me to help him. It seemed as if the tables had been turned, and I was the free spirit while he was the prisoner of his own creation.

Bhagwan went on: "I am so relieved that I do not have to pretend to be enlightened any more. Poor Krishnamurti" — who had denounced Bhagwan in no uncertain terms — "he still has to pretend." Are you serious, I thought to myself. If Bhagwan was not enlightened, then what was I doing in this hellhole, subject to a thousand petty restrictions, getting ill and working in sub-zero temperatures to build a commune that was angering and deliberately antagonising the local people more by the minute? Even by early 1982 I could not see any way that the commune could succeed. Bhagwan simply could not restrain himself from punching authority in the eye.

After the session was over, Vivek took the film from me. We discussed briefly where it would be possible to get this kind of film developed, and decided to send it to a professional sannyasi photographer in Boston. I wanted to ask Vivek what was really going on with Bhagwan. Had he suffered a stroke, or was he seriously ill? But I felt we were not close enough; there was not enough of a rapport. I knew that Bhagwan hated the place, but at the same time he needed adulation. That was why he needed thirty-five Rolls Royces — the number grew each week — and the biggest commune in the world. Though Bhagwan could no longer 'fly' on his own, he needed thousands of people round him to prove to himself that he was still important, that he still mattered. It gave him his identity. Without his extended entourage he would be a desperately lost soul.

One morning Bhagwan called Sheela to his room to tell her frankly what he thought of her choice of location for the commune. He told her very sarcastically that she obviously had exceptional vision, and that in ten years' time, with the full-time work of so many sannyasis, it could become a beautiful place. But, he added, he wanted somewhere that was beautiful right now. Vivek's new boyfriend, who had been present at this exchange, told me later that Bhagwan had told Sheela in no uncertain terms, but in his own polished language, that she must have had her head up her ass when she had bought the place.

While it was clear that he hated the Big Muddy, Bhagwan could not simply walk away from his trappings of wealth. He had sold his freedom for the rewards of the material world. It seemed a far cry from the man of peace and love in his little flat in Bombay nine years previously. I wished there was somebody I could talk to about what I had just experienced. It had hit me unbelievably hard to see Bhagwan like this. On one hand I wanted to try to help him escape, but I knew that he would never give up his power and wealth for his freedom, even if that power was fading fast. But there was nobody I could really trust enough to share my feelings with. I could not even trust Isabel since she was becoming ever more loyal to Sheela, and talking to Sheela herself was out of the question. I would just have to let it all settle and attempt to analyse it myself. In the meantime it was back to driving a sixty-ton bulldozer at 25 degrees below freezing point.

Chapter Fourteen
UNDERHAND DEALINGS

By early March the anti-sannyasi activity had hotted up. The government sent seventy-nine of us notices to leave the country, as they had denied visa extensions. These people had a fortnight to leave.

Isabel announced that she was going to marry a new sannyasi, an ambitious hard-nosed attorney called Niren, and a very important person to Sheela. The marriage had already been approved in Sheela's trailer. Isabel and Niren got married within the week, and on her return we remained close friends.

Laxmi's name was on the list, and I knew that I might soon receive my notice. I was told, however, that a professional person's visa application had been made for me and Gayan, who was still legally my wife, so we could both stay. We were assured by Sheela's office that there was nothing to worry about.

I immediately went to warn Laxmi. She was quite unperturbed. "Don't worry, child," she said. "They will tell Laxmi that she has been told to leave. They will do something. I trust in *him*." I admired her complete unflappability.

Soon after this I became ill myself, and lost touch with Laxmi. After a more than usually punishing month on the bulldozer I began to pass blood in my urine. One of the sannyasi doctors saw me and told me that I had to rest in the hospital ward, a specially-converted trailer. In a few days they would take X-rays. I shared a room with three other people, who were all as deeply exhausted as me. For the first week I seemed to sleep almost continuously, and hardly noticed what was going on around me. Isabel came to see me almost every day, and if she found me sleeping she would leave a flower to mark her visit. These flowers cheered me up a lot. The bleeding stopped as I rested, but it was only after ten days of complete rest that I began to feel even vaguely human again. The thought of enduring the noise of the bulldozer again, having to wrestle with it as it gouged its immense talons into hard rock, appalled me. I could not face it.

One of the English nurses, Jaya, also fell sick, and after a week she hardly looked any better than when she was admitted to hospital. She said she was feeling a bit better and was excited about going back to work, but as I took in her hollow eyes, her lank hair and sallow complexion, I could not help saying "And then what will you do?" She burst into tears.

Richard, Vivek's new boyfriend and our construction boss, arrived to see me one day. He suggested that as it was a fresh spring day we might go and sit on the veranda together. He implied that he had something important to say to me. Once we were alone and out of earshot, he confided that he was not at all happy with the profligate waste he saw going on all around him. It transpired that neither of us was happy with the way that Sheela was running the ranch. Bhagwan had made it clear many months ago that he did not like the place, and the so-called monitor system, which was supposed to give at least a semblance of democracy, was not being implemented at all. Sheela had become an absolute dictator, and ruled with complete power. We both realised that Bhagwan felt imprisoned, and knew how angry he had been when the culvert dam had been washed away the second time, leaving him stranded. It was as if his last link with freedom had been washed away with that bridge. Sheela now had such a grip on ranch activities that it was impossible to speak openly without being reported to her. Her spies seemed to be everywhere. It was almost impossible to have a conversation with a friend without fearing that our words would be relayed to Sheela at the earliest opportunity.

What could we do? asked Richard. We still wanted to stay with Bhagwan, and still believed that he had unusual, important powers. We felt we had both gained a great deal since throwing in our lot with him. An idea came to me. I told Richard about the island that Jeannie, the health centre co-ordinator from Poona, had found for Bhagwan in the South Pacific in 1978. The woman who had gone with her had been the English nurse who was now so ill in the hospital ward. I suggested to Richard that we should find out whether the island was still on the market, and perhaps send Jeannie back to make the necessary unsupervised enquiries. Richard decided that it was worth a try, and said he would mention it to Vivek. The next day Richard told me that he had seen Vivek, and she had relayed the suggestion to Bhagwan, who liked the idea. Then we could have our own commune without Sheela. It sounded marvellous. Nobody in the office was to know about our plan. I did what co-ordinating work I could manage from my sick bed, while Richard devised a way to send Jeannie to Portland.

It all went well. Jeannie came back from a week in Portland to report that the island could still be bought for $5 million. She showed Richard and I some photographs she had asked to be sent to her express, and the place looked like the perfect paradise. It had a barrier reef surrounding a fertile deep green island set in a turquoise and indigo sea. It looked about two miles long, and had a coconut or banana plantation on it. It appeared to be ideal.

Here on the Big Muddy we were still embroiled in litigation, as Sheela refused to pay the agent's commission for finding the ranch and the New Jersey castle, or even her own attorney's fees in New York. Neither she nor Bhagwan enjoyed paying bills. She had finally sent him half his fee both for the ranch and for the castle. I had even been sent down to Antelope one night in case one of the real estate men, who had threatened to come down with a gun, turned up. Jeannie knew the man who was dealing with the island; he was almost a friend by now, and she did not want the same trouble arising again. She told me to tell Vivek that she was unwilling to show Bhagwan the photographs of the island unless Bhagwan would personally guarantee the payment of the agent's commission, which would exceed $500,000. Until he did this Jeannie was not prepared either to send the photographs to Bhagwan, or to divulge any definite information about the island's name or whereabouts.

I relayed all this to Vivek, who said she would tell Bhagwan. When she came out there was a shadow over her face. She said that Bhagwan wanted to see the photographs *now*. Jeannie was adamant: no guarantee, no photographs. Vivek asked her to go back to work and await developments.

During this time Sheela was away in California, and an English girl, Sally Anne Croft, was deputising for her. Bhagwan told her that Shiva and Jeannie had made a secret approach to him about an island, and he informed the accountant that he wanted nothing to do with such plots. A week later, when I was discharged from hospital and back at Lao Tzu House, Sheela drifted in on her way to a work session with Bhagwan. "Oh hi, Shiva," she said briskly in an offhand way. "Enjoy playing politics while I was gone, did we?" I was glad that was all I heard about the abortive island project.

Meanwhile, the notices to seventy-nine sannyasis to quit the country became final. Sheela waited until the last possible moment before telling Laxmi that her name was on the list. Laxmi was issued with an ultimatum from Bhagwan: she either had to marry an American or leave America instantly. Laxmi's reply was that she would never get married, and anyway, who would believe that a marriage with a celibate like Laxmi was genuine? Nor would she fly straight back to jail in India. Sheela notified her on a Friday, and she had until Sunday to leave the country. By now she had no car, no unsupervised telephone, and could trust almost no one. How could she get to a good immigration lawyer in time? This was intended to be the *coup de grace*.

Laxmi sent a messenger to me in the ward, telling me what had happened. She had seen Bhagwan for a darshan and informed him that his time, too, was nearly up, and that he had better leave the country himself. She told him that he was a fool to trust Sheela, and should get out now while the going was good, as he could not trust Sheela to handle the situation. Bhagwan remained unfazed by all this, and professed to have complete trust in Sheela. After much argument, Laxmi got Bhagwan to agree for her to have ten thousand dollars for lawyer's fees so that she could stay in America. The next morning, however, Laxmi was only given five hundred dollars. She was told that was all the money that was available, and she could have no more. Laxmi rose to the occasion. "Then you had better keep it," she told the accountant, "you obviously need it more than I do." She left empty-handed, but proudly.

Laxmi had no choice but to leave the ranch. A month or two later we heard that she had apparently fallen into a deep fever as soon as she left, and obtained a doctor's letter to postpone her departure for India. She then filed a petition of some sort to extend her stay and possibly make it permanent. For the next three years she lived in the USA without proper papers under an assumed name, Ella, and changed her address often. While in Woodstock she sold chapatties in the street market, enthusiastically shouting out her wares. She must have been quite an incongruous sight, this tiny twig of a woman with no money and nowhere to live, yet wearing a solid gold Rolex watch on her wrist.

As soon as it was known that Laxmi was in Woodstock, one of the ranch co-ordinators was despatched there to tell all the sannyasis in the area to have nothing whatever to do with her. If she knocked on their doors they were not even to invite her in for tea. The door was to be closed in her face. While Laxmi was in Woodstock she received three letters, all apparently signed by Bhagwan, demanding that she send her mala back.

Laxmi did not turn a hair. She laughed and said: "Bhagwan is just testing me," and carried on as before. In July 1982 the immigration authorities in Portland called her and asked her to fly west for her 'green card' interview, the green card being the alien registration document enabling people to working legally in the USA. As soon as the plane touched down at Portland, she was whisked off the plane and taken to a hotel, where she was confronted by three government officials. The INS were willing to grant her a green card if she would give testimony that would prejudice Bhagwan's immigration status. Laxmi would not do it. She went into hiding again.

Two years later she was summoned to the New York immigration offices, where she had applied for a visa as a Zen Master — modesty was not her strong point — but was subsequently arrested and detained. She claimed that she was beaten up and held in jail for twenty-four hours. "They hit Laxmi's body because Laxmi laughed at them," she said later. The officer handling her case denied any knowledge of her having been beaten up, and said that he had merely handed her over to the detention officer in the lift. He thought it was unlikely that she had been physically mistreated in any way.

Sheela had announced when Deeksha had left that she had embezzled $200,000 of commune money, but we now heard that Laxmi had outdone her and appropriated $600,000 for herself. We old hands did not believe a word of it. Deeksha had money of her own, and we knew Laxmi of old. Laxmi was now over fifty, and two years after leaving the commune we heard that she had developed cancer. Many of the new sannyasis, however, who had known neither Deeksha nor Laxmi, believed the slanders.

We were informed that we were not on any account to have anything more to do with either Deeksha or Laxmi. They were, we were told on a small notice that appeared in the canteen, now 'negative'. The notice went on to describe how when people lose power they often become negative and try to form opposing camps. The notice also said that the ranch represented the teaching of our Master, and that those who followed the 'opposite camp' would forfeit their chance of becoming part of the real thing. A canteen supervisor took the notice straight down, suspecting it was some kind of joke. Laxmi and Deeksha were no opposing camp, just two disoriented ex-sannyasins clinging to each other for support and wondering what on earth had happened to them. They had gone from having complete power themselves to being denounced as criminals and traitors.

Alongside this notice was another, listing those sannyasis who were in sexual quarantine. A new list went up every day. Now that sexually-related diseases had become an everyday feature of commune life, those who were infected had to let everyone know about it. It was pretty horrible, but most of us agreed that it was a necessary public precaution. Many pints of beer were drunk in celebration when a sufferer came off the list.

My own recovery from kidney damage took a long time, and was marked down as 'negativity'. From now on anybody who became ill was diagnosed as 'negative'. If they had been of a more positive frame of mind, so Sheela's argument went, they would not have become ill in the first place. When Bhagwan's chief accountant came to see me in early April to ask how soon I would be able to take photographs of Him, she too implied that I had become 'negative'.

I could not take it, and exploded at her. "Do you know what it feels like to be two feet away from a hundred and thirty decibels for twelve or fourteen hours a day, when you can't even hear someone who's shouting in your ear? Do you know what it's like to work in a rock crusher, tottering above a thousand feet sheer drop, when you can't even see the edge for the dust? Why does nobody believe that working a ninety-hour week like this for eight months damages your health?" I added that it seemed that many of the things that Sheela said were coming from Bhagwan sounded as though they were coming directly from Sheela herself.

I knew that there would be repercussions from giving vent to such observations, but I was so angry I felt I could take no more, and continued to say all the things that had been annoying me for months. I said I felt oppressed by Sheela and her officers, and that the constantly multiplying rules and regulations, the paranoia and suspicion, and the lying we were having to do to official bodies, were all getting me down. I objected to the monitoring of telephone calls and the checking of mail, the lack of privacy, the ban on trips outside the ranch, the growing fascism of the regime. Was this really the new age, the paradise we were building to show the rest of the world how it was possible to live?

The accountant seemed to understand, and left to report my

grievances to Bhagwan, the Great One. Maybe he would understand as well. She came back an hour later. "Bhagwan says he understands why you feel oppressed. It is because you have been doing manual work, and you need creative work. If you want you can go away for six months and come back when things will be more comfortable for you. Right now pioneering work is the only kind possible here. He also says that you need three weeks away from the place immediately, so take a holiday. Bhagwan says that things will change soon, and you will be happy again. Oh, and he says that Sheela carries his messages perfectly . . ."

I waited for the familiar feeling of euphoria which had always come in the past when a message had successfully relayed to Bhagwan and his answer received. But nothing came, nothing at all. Instead of a feeling of bliss and wonder, there was only a sense of having been sold out. I felt no inspiration from Bhagwan's words, no deep truth. He had understood nothing of my plight. Where was the heart to heart communication he excelled at? I knew all about these 'holidays' — once you left, the chances of being allowed back were very slender. I already knew that I was no longer 'special', but it now seemed that I was being discarded altogether, told I was no longer useful, and that if I wanted I could go now, and nobody would care.

Everybody understood that no holidays were permitted in Bhagwan's work. When everything was going well we did not want holidays, we wanted to be with Bhagwan. We all knew that the outside world was a hostile and uncomfortable place — we had had ample evidence of that since we came here. Who wanted to be out there? There was no heart out there, we were constantly being told, no family, no love. It was not at all easy to go back into the world. Most of us had no money, and had long since lost contact with former colleagues. Parents tended to be unsympathetic or smother-ing. Having long hair and wearing beads and orange robes didn't help.

The next day I asked Vivek if she thought it would be a good idea for me to go on holiday, and she said yes. I made up my mind that I would take the risk and go, but I did stay long enough to experience the run-up to the Antelope elections.

This tiny town of forty inhabitants had decided that its only hope of economic and social survival as a community was to hold an election to disincorporate itself as a city. Bhagwan wanted to take over the city council so that the authority's ability to grant changes in zoning laws would be in his own hands. The people of Antelope knew this was his plan, and feared that if they did not disincorporate the council would be taken over by Rajneeshees. Their rates would go up, and many elderly people forced to move out. Disincorporation would mean that Bhagwan would be less interested in taking over the village.

I was given an assignment to photograph all the houses of the original Antelope residents, and try to show the residents themselves outside their homes or with their car licence plates. I was to liaise with a lawyer dealing with our affairs in Antelope. This exercise was to try and prove that many residents actually had their first homes in other parts of Oregon, and were therefore ineligible to vote as residents of Antelope. It also doubled as very effective harassment.

Sheela was buying up houses in Antelope as fast as they became available, and sannyasis were moving into them. Before long it became obvious to the local press that the Rajneeshees were trying to take over Antelope and force the long-term residents out by moving eighty sannyasis in the fortnight before the election. Under Oregon law, only two weeks' permanent residency was required to become eligible to vote in a local election. To encourage locals to sell up, all-night parties were held as noisily as possible near the homes of elderly people. In contradiction to the earlier edict, we were encouraged to kiss and hold hands in public. Soon Sheela had managed to buy enough properties in Antelope to instal eighty sannyasis there. Thus before we had been in the district a year, we outnumbered the old-timers two to one. This would ensure a landslide in the disincorporation election, and mean the city — with its zoning prize — would be ours.

All the time, sannyasis kept a twenty-four hour watch on Antelope, to see what the residents might try on, and radios were used so that we could keep in contact with each other in every part of the village. I was sent round other parts of the state, from Portland to Coos Bay, to photograph other homes supposedly owned by people living in Antelope. The feeling on the ranch was that these people were making trouble for us, so why shouldn't we go on the attack and make trouble for them? As I went round clicking my camera, I thought: "What on earth am I doing? These people came here to retire, live this way, and die peacefully, and we're forcing them to leave."

Before the election, one of the sannyasi lawyers kept a careful log of all the insults and threats purportedly received from Antelope residents. These came mostly in the form of telephone calls and letters. We received calls from vigilante groups, religious extremists and individuals who had a grudge against us. All harassment was also carefully logged.

An Antelope man saw me stalking his premises with my camera. "Come out and talk to me like a man," he called. He was angry beyond speech, and his impotent rage reached me, but there was little he could do, a harmless old man who had come to retire here and live peacefully. This was not saintly behaviour, not at all spiritual. It seemed that our sole aims were now money and greed, and the material expansion of the ranch. We were empire-building on a grand scale, and had little time or thought for those who stood in our way.

I watched another elderly Antelope man limp out of his house. We drew up alongside him at the bottom of his garden path. He turned to look at me, and defeat was clearly written on his face. He had come here to retire, and now these alien Reds were taking everything over. They wouldn't stop until they had driven everybody out.

One women who left Antelope at this time gave an interview to *The Dalles Weekly Reminder*. She was asked if she had left her house as a matter of 'free choice', as Rajneeshees had claimed all such sales had been made. "We had a nice little place in Antelope," she replied. "It probably wasn't much by most people's standards, but it was everything to us. We had put an awful lot of work into it, and we had fixed it up the way we wanted it. We had planned to stay but we just could not take it any longer. The constant picture taking and all the rest. I had lost twenty pounds and my husband had lost thirty. I'd go to the table to eat and my nerves were so bad I just could not get anything down. I'd just get up and walk away. And the tax we knew would be coming. It's going to be about thirty dollars" (per thousand dollars of assessed value, a rate comparable to a major city). "We are on social security and we just couldn't have made it. It was heartbreaking the day we left, just heartbreaking. When I go back to Antelope, I never look at the old house. It just hurts too much."

In a letter to *The Madras Pioneer* dated May 13th, 1982, Rajneeshpuram Mayor Swami Krishna Deva wrote in reply: "Nobody seems to take into account that each piece of property was sold purely as a matter of free choice by the owner, mostly through brokers, under no compulsion whatsoever."

On the day of the election, two of us were installed at the back of a smallish darkened room with a view onto the schoolhouse entrance, where all the voting would take place. We left a foot of space between closed curtains to get our line of sight. Our cameras were fitted with huge 'mirror' lenses which would enable us to get portrait shots of every non-sannyasi voter as they left the school. Then our lawyers would confront any voter who was actually ineligible with pictorial evidence, which would enable him or her to be disqualified.

On the day of the election, Antelope, normally a very quiet place, became a circus. Advance publicity had reached every major American TV network, who all sent crews to film the proceedings. There were also video teams, and journalists who had flown in from all over Oregon and California. The press men easily outnumbered the voters, even with the sannyasi contingent. It was billed as the old folk versus the Reds.

By nine o'clock nothing had happened and not a soul was about, and when the first voters only began to trickle in before midday we realised that something very peculiar was going on. Within a very short time more than two hundred unknown faces had come and gone, some several times, and we were nearly out of film. We radioed our lawyer to ask what was up. He radioed back fifteen minutes later to say that a canteen had been set up in the schoolhouse basement for the 'Save Antelope' fund, and a morning rally had been held, attended by all the Antelope residents and many of their supporters.

The sannyasi voters had all been briefed to be as polite as possible to the residents, especially with the press and TV taking everything in and looking for trouble. An Antelope radical was wearing an imitation mala, with spent .303 shells instead of beads, and the slogan 'Better Dead Than Red'. A local was interviewed for the nationwide *Sixty Minutes* TV programme. He was a fervent anti-cultist, an outspoken critic whose family had lived in Antelope for about eighty years. He had been a cowboy, and was now working as a County Road Department dump truck driver. I knew him quite well.

The interviewer asked him: "Do you see any hope of a peaceful and amicable settlement of the dispute here in Antelope, Eastern Oregon?"

"Nope. Only thing is to go down there with our guns and *waste 'em, waste 'em* proper."

"Does that mean you fear for your life, sir?"

"Bet yo' life I do. Sleeps with my .38 under the pilla and my rifle down there on the floor. They ain't gettin' me easy, no ways."

"I see, sir, and you intend to keep contesting the Rajneeshees' activities?"

"Well, hell, yes we do, git them people outa our town, I'll fight to the last drop of blood. I will, you'll see!"

"And how long have you and your family lived here?"

"Since time immemorial!" The last said with enormous and immediate conviction.

"So you intend to stay?"

"Bet yo' ass I do!"

"Then how come your house is for sale?"

An awful pause, and a long instant of betrayal and bewilderment. "You'll have to ask ma wife," he said with as much vehemence as had been offered with 'the last drop of blood'. "You'll have to ask ma wife." He turned on his heels and stormed off, defeated.

We won the election by eighty votes to thirty-nine, and the disincorporation was thus successfully blocked.

The tension arising from our pre-election activities led the Antelope residents to contact the US Community Relations Service for help. A report from this agency dated April 27th 1982 rated the situation at 'tension level four'. A riot rates as tension level five. Although the tension continued to rise, nothing was done, since 'overt violence was not anticipated'.

At another election later in 1982, a new sannyassi Mayor was elected. The great majority of her office bearers were also Rajneeshees. The rates were increased to the level of those of the metropolis of Portland, and in 1983 the name of Antelope was officially changed to 'Rajneesh'. It changed back in 1985, but in that time several maps noted the change.

Later that week, as I sat above the ranch taking photographs, I wondered whether I was right to take this projected holiday. I now had three jobs, and was living in Bhagwan's house. I could communicate with Bhagwan through Vivek, even though he was still officially 'not speaking'. I had my secret income of fifty dollars a week. I had the freedom to travel all over the ranch, and Sheela even seemed to have eased up on me of late. Twenty thousand Rajneeshees all over the world would give their eye teeth to be in my shoes. So should I take the risk and go on holiday, or stay at home? If I left and was not allowed back it would be very difficult to make my way in the real world again. The Rajneesh organisation had now been my whole world for nine years.

Chapter Fifteen
I LEAVE THE RANCH

I could not feel proud of the part I had played during the Antelope elections. What had for many years been a quiet and sleepy retirement village was gradually being turned into a commercial enclave of alternative lifestyle.

Though to the oldtimers we looked scruffy and unkempt, we were very astute when it came to making money and winning legal disputes. The old Antelope village store was turned into a Zorba-the-Buddha Rajneesh restaurant, while in the attached shop the prices of basic necessities rose appreciably, and groceries and hardware jostled with shelves of Bhagwan's books, tapes and merchandise. On the ranch itself money-making, collecting donations, house building and legal work became the chief activities. While we sannyasis worked fourteen-hour days with no pay, cash was being raised from all possible sources. We already had a highly complicated system of parent companies and subsidiaries to handle all the money-making schemes.

While still in Poona, Bhagwan had said that in the new commune we would grow money on trees, and that is just what we were setting out to do. He was not known as 'the guru of the rich' for nothing. We were busy setting up therapy centres, boutiques, restaurants and hotels, and charging high prices to visitors. At the Rajneesh Institute for Therapy, part of the Rajneesh International Meditation University, we were charging top prices for therapy, massage, and all kinds of bodywork. We also started preparing for the very first World Festival at about this time, which was to be held in July, and was seen as a large money-making enterprise.

In 1981, donations from the European centres — for some time our chief source of extra cash — amounted to over $280,000. A great deal of this was used to plant trees in Rajneeshpuram. Bhagwan had said he wanted trees, and though money may grow on them, they also needed money to buy and plant them. Once they were planted, however, nobody remembered to water them or protect them from the deer, and by the spring of 1982 90% of them had died. We spent around $2 million on the ranch in 1981, and in the following year $6.1 million was raised, mainly from donations and the sale of goods.

There were constant calls to centres in other parts of the world to finance our business enterprises, which now included nightclubs, casinos and publishing houses. Some of the more unusual money-making schemes never got off the ground, such as the one to establish a sperm bank from unsterilised Rajneeshees, and sell the 'superior' sperm for artificial insemination babies.

Bhagwan himself was quite open about the fact that the primary object of the ranch was to make money, and said that if ever money-making became a problem, he would abandon his vow of silence. Though he was officially in silence, Bhagwan still wanted publicity, and was not averse to having his photograph taken. One spring day a professional sannyasi photographer from Boston came with me to take some photographs of Bhagwan. As he was worried about the way the organisation was changing, he also wanted to ask Bhagwan some personal questions, but I warned him that this should not be done during the session, which by long-standing protocol was exclusively for taking photographs.

Bhagwan seemed to be unusually self-conscious and without his usual self-assurance. When, despite my warnings, the Boston photographer asked a personal question, Bhagwan agreed to answer it. "Bhagwan," he said, "this place is so different from Poona. Seeing it, I am at a loss to know how to run my commune in Boston. How should I do it?" I was interested to hear what he had to say, as I had not heard his views since his previous utterances while he had been under the influence of the nitrous oxide. Would he still have his orator's tongue, the gift that had moved Bernard Levin to write: "What he says is couched in language of great power and fluency: he is one of the most remarkable orators I have ever heard, though there is no hint of demagogy in his style"? As I bustled round setting up the shots I hoped to hear something that would settle the storm raging in my heart. There had been too many doubts in the last year for my liking.

Bhagwan spoke to the photographer: "You have to understand a few things, hmmm," he started in his time-honoured way. "First, this is a very different place from Poona. This place is huge, one hundred and twenty square miles, and I want every square mile to be full of *my* people." He drew out the 'hundred and twenty', and I was struck by an image of 120 tightly-packed versions of the Poona ashram, all crowded in on each other. So his master plan was to have a hundred thousand sannyasis here, in spite of the damage it would do to this fragile ecology. I wanted no part of that.

Why this emphasis on numbers? Sheela was now quoting the eventual goal of Rajneeshpuram as being a city of a million sannyasis, and I was remembering Bhagwan's own oft-quoted vision of the final stage of his work, where he would "go into silence and retreat to the mountains. I will take only five hundred people at the most with me," he had said. "At any one time on Earth there are only eight or nine enlightened beings. Only with a small group of totally dedicated and surrendered sannyasis can the ultimate jump happen — the leap into enlightenment. Only the real sannyasis will still be with me then. Until then I will be weeding you out. I am very good at weeding . . ."

He continued speaking to the Boston photographer: "The whole of America will eagerly be watching my commune, my people. We will set an example to the whole world of how to live creatively, productively, peacefully, meditatively. And it will not be like Poona, because there were many things wrong in Poona. Here we are isolated. Here we can control our environment. And in Poona the wrong people were in charge. They were cunning and deceitful people."

This statement hit me in the stomach. What did he mean, the wrong people? Bhagwan did after all choose those people, monitored and guided them. If they were cunning and deceitful, then it was Bhagwan himself who had encouraged them to be that way. Laxmi, for instance, never wanted anything for herself once she had her Rolex and her Mercedes, and now she was roaming round in exile, living on charity, desperately trying to find ways of staying in this foreign country. Already the past was being buried and rewritten to suit the present situation. It was to happen again when Sheela left the organisation, and yet again when Bhagwan finally left America. As soon as important people left or a commune was disbanded, the truth became twisted and altered. Historical revisionism was becoming quite a sannyasi art form, perhaps to replace the now-forbidden one of gossip.

Bhagwan went on: "The commune and the ashrams throughout the world will become more and more important. First, people will have to be prepared there before they come here. Only then will they fit here, float with my people. You in your communes have to prepare these people. The other communes will become oases where my work can continue, and people can be sent here to help build the city. You understand, hmmm? There will be one large commune in every country of the world. Then they will send their best people here as space becomes available. Now," he said to the photographer, "you train a successor in Boston, someone who can take over the work, so that you can come here, forget everything, and be absorbed in the commune, in my work. You are ready for it. If you have no one suitable, I will send someone to your commune. Then you can forget the world and cut all your ties with it. It will be good."

As I listened, my distaste grew. I was not at all sure that I wanted to be part of an enormous 120-square-mile commune, eventually holding a million people. We were already tearing the land apart in our haste to build, build, build, and Bhagwan did not seem to care about the ecological onslaught. Instead of wanting to harmonise with nature, as all spiritually minded people should, he had simply said: "Nature does not care for us, why should we care for nature?" He reminded people of what had happened to the culvert dams: he could not easily forget the bridge that had been washed away three times.

After the session, the photographer confided to me that he had no intention of coming to this place. "I don't want to lose myself in the commune and leave the world behind," he said. "It's *my* goddam house there. I don't want to give it to Sheela. I've worked all my life to get that place. I'm fifty now, and who knows what may happen in the future? If Bhagwan went somewhere else then where would I be? This place is for you young cowboys and pioneers. I like my metalled roads and concert halls." He wrote Bhagwan a note expressing his feelings, and went back to Boston.

A week later as I came home from work, tired, dirty and exhausted, the chief chambermaid asked me to carry the heavy video screen into Bhagwan's room. She assured me that he was not in the room, so I could go in unwashed. In Poona he had read ten or fifteen books a day, and now he watched videos just as avidly. It was the fulltime job of three sannyasis to make sure he had a constant supply of videos. His favourite films were George C. Scott's *Patton*, and *The Ten Commandments*. He had watched *Patton* five or six times already.

As I pushed my way into the room with the screen, I was suddenly aware of somebody there, over by the far wall. The samurai in me was instantly alert, and in the split second before I realised that it was Bhagwan himself, my sixth sense, long trained to make instant evaluations, sensed an empty shell of a man, a defeated relic with only sadness and ruined pride in his eyes.

I had caught myself unawares. I had finally seen my Master without my disciple's conditioned vision. When he saw it was me his eyes widened and his forehead tightened. "Good, Shiva, good," he said quietly, almost sadly. My 'good disciple' mask responded, slamming down like the visor of a medieval knight about to ride into battle.

In that moment I knew that he had seen my penetrating look — after all, it was he that had taught it to me and complimented me upon it.

Later that day one of Bhagwan's favourite anecdotes came back to me. In a Zen monastery in old Japan, a novice was assigned to the kitchen to clean rice. Unlike his fellow novices, he was not permitted to join the communal meditations. After more than a year of this ignominy he begged for an audience with his Master, and asked him why his teaching had not yet begun. "Ha!" exclaimed the Master, "So you want teaching. So you are ready! Tomorrow your teaching begins."

The next afternoon, when the novice was beginning to wonder when his teaching would start, he was carrying a tray of freshly-cleaned rice into the kitchen. The Master jumped out from a hiding place and struck him with a short staff, nearly knocking him and the rice flying. The Master laughed softly and walked away.

Nothing more happened for two months, and the novice had almost forgotten the incident when once again a surprise attack caught him daydreaming.

After a year of this the novice could sense when his Master was about, and could avoid being hit, but while he was asleep one night, the Master dealt him a blow across the shoulders and scuttled off, chortling. After two more years the Master found it impossible to attack the novice undetected, even at night.

One fine spring day the novice was out collecting mushrooms, and saw his Master hiding behind a tree waiting for him, his back turned towards the novice. Very quietly the novice crept up behind the Master and sprang on him, seizing his collar and crying "Aha!"

The Master turned, smiled radiantly, and said: "Come, you wouldn't hit an old man, would you, graduate monk?"

So it seemed that I had caught my Master hiding behind his tree. More than that: I had glimpsed an inner reality that was shocking in its barren intensity. If this was to be my graduation, it had come too suddenly. It was shocking to see him like that, to really see him. I remembered what Teertha had said when I asked him how he found Bhagwan after Teertha's year away. Teertha, ever the cautious diplomat, paused for a long time. Then, carefully measuring each word, he said: "He's very far away now, isn't he?" Somendra, another Poona protégé, had a similar encounter. "The guy simply was not there," he confided to me, "not in the here and now, anyway."

On the ranch things became steadily more fascist and degenerate. In mid-April, soon after the Antelope elections, the resident medical staff met with Sheela. She briefed us on how to deal with the large numbers of people who were becoming seriously ill. "I have a message for you all from Bhagwan," she announced triumphantly. "When people come to see you and complain of exhaustion, you give them an injection and send them straight back to work." No specific injection or dosage was mentioned. "Remember that it is negativity," (this pronounced with palpable distaste) "that makes them ill. You should let them feel they are being taken care of. Reassure them, and send them straight back to work. OK? Any questions?"

My friend the doctor and I looked at each other and sighed. Those who became sick were utterly exhausted. Their nervous systems could not cope any longer, and their simple wounds were no longer healing as they should. They were coming down with injuries and secondary infections, and could not seem to recover. The house allocated to be the ward for sick and injured people was zoned to hold six people, but was regularly filled with as many as twenty-eight at a time. The medical staff requested a second house, but were told no, there was not a spare house available. I was working at the medical centre daily now, and seeing at least one new acute back case every day. I felt I could not stand by and watch these people getting more ill by the minute. The doctor and I decided to keep sending people to the ward, and soon Sheela would have no choice but to allocate another house. We were not prepared to let a non-medically-qualified person tell us how to treat patients, even if that person was supposed to have total power over us. Like watching an overinflated balloon, the doctor and I stood back to await developments.

Sheela went on to make a public address to the rest of the sannyasis — now numbering about two and a half thousand — and reminded them of the need for discretion and secrecy. She said there was every possibility that government raids would start before long, and that there were very probably government spies among us sannyasis. "Be careful what you say everywhere, especially at meal times," she said. "County and Federal inspectors may be coming disguised as visitors. Also," she went on, "quite a few people are getting sick. I asked Bhagwan what provision to make for them, and he said that the majority of sick people were negative, and that everyone who really loved him would find the energy to go on working for him, even when they are having to put in a twenty-hour day at the hardest of tasks. Negative people, on the other hand, get sick on the slightest pretext."

Sheela had her own plans about what to do about overcrowding on the ward. She came to visit it one day, and told my patients who were lying in bed sick that if they did not get up and work immediately, they would not be allowed to leave the ward at all until after the festival, which was still three months away. All but one of my twelve patients left the same day. I felt the crack in my heart begin to widen. I resolved never to work in the medical centre again.

Then the first real tragedy occurred at the ranch. It happened to a friend of mine, Ambara, one of the original fifty samurai, as the result of a canoeing accident. His canoe overturned and he was washed down river. The two friends who were with him were able to scramble out on to the bank, but Ambara was not able to make it. The others ran, wringing wet, to the nearest farmhouse to try and get help.

The farmer was not pleased to see them. "You people ain't gettin' no help from this family," he said irately, seeing their malas, "not after what you bin doin' round here. Get off my property, *now!*" The sannyasis were shocked at his anger, especially in an emergency like this. We had not realised how deep the alienation had already gone. In a close-knit farming community like this, a response of this sort would usually be unthinkable. A mile or two down the road, another farmer allowed them to ring Sheela. A group of mechanics were sent out on motorcycles to look for Ambara, but they had no success. Up to this point I had kept out of the search and maintained a low profile, but now I had to do something for my friend. The most obvious way to look for Ambara was by helicopter. I went on the CB radio to suggest to Sheela that she hire a helicopter immediately. I knew this was a very provocative thing to do, but a man's life was far more important than my staying out of trouble. "That has been considered" was my answer. I later learnt that Sheela had said no because of the adverse publicity it might arouse.

By midnight, six of us had checked a mile or so up the river from a bridge about twelve miles below the accident site, while another group checked downriver from where the accident had happened. Neither of us had found anything. Now we were ordered to abandon the search, but I asked for more time to check out other parts of the river. My radioed request met with a negative response: "Everyone has to come back now. No more search."

"Well," I persisted, "can I have the OK to stay here by myself in case Ambara comes in off the fields between now and dawn? That's another four hours." The co-ordinator came back on the air with: "Am having radio trouble. Cannot distinguish last request. proceed as you think appropriate. Out." I blessed her.

I had a partner with me, an Italian plumber, and by daybreak we had walked twelve or fifteen miles, calling out Ambara's name. We found his cowboy hat about ten miles downstream from the accident. By morning a County Police Department aircraft was conducting a pattern search, and our own twin-engined aircraft had joined it.

At about eight in the morning I met Richard, Vivek's new boyfriend. "I've covered for you," he said.

"Whatever do you mean?" I asked.

"I mean that when you said you were staying, all the other teams decided to stay on and search too," he said. "Sheela is furious, and she's blaming you for everything."

I felt a great pit at the bottom of my stomach. It was true, the 'work' was more important than anything, even a man's life. I asked Richard where the other search parties were now, and he told me they had been cancelled. "Sheela said the work must not suffer any more, and that given the water temperature Ambara must have died by nine last night at the latest"

But what if he hadn't died? I knew Ambara — he was one tough and determined son of a Canadian farmer, and certainly no quitter. What if he had broken a leg and was lying on a bank somewhere waiting for help? I suppressed as best I could the tide of anger and indignation that was rising up in me. If I gave vent to it, Sheela would certainly have me off the ranch in an instant.

That evening, my heavy equipment supervisor and his girlfriend joined me in a secret attempt to hire a helicopter for a further search. I managed to sneak a Portland Yellow Pages out of Sheela's office and got to the only unsupervised phone on the ranch. Although it was

Sunday evening, I managed to locate a helicopter hire company who could have a search helicopter ready for us at first light the next morning. The three of us then went to solicit money for the hire, which would cost $400 an hour.

But Sheela got to hear of it, and the helicopter hire idea was immediately squashed. I felt sicker than ever. What was this place coming to? 'Work' had taken precedence over life, and everything had gone mad. Erecting instant plastic housing and building culvert dams that got washed away, keeping a team of mechanics patching up ageing dump trucks, crushing rock into gravel because this was the cheapest way of doing it, planting fields far too late to yield any harvest — was this the great 'work'? What was the use of it if we did not even take care of our own people?

The County Police were continuing their search, but our own plane was called off by mid-morning. I heard that the police could not believe our lack of interest in the search. Our own search had stopped after only eight hours, with less than two per cent of the population of the ranch participating.

What upset me most was that the person who was lost was somebody who Sheela considered to be unimportant. If it had been one of her chosen few, we would all have been out there, two thousand of us, combing every metre of river bank. There would have been a fleet of helicopters searching, and we would not have given up until either the person or the body was found. Expense was certainly no problem. Bhagwan by now had over forty Rolls Royces, and the material wealth of the ranch was enormous.

Isabel told me that Sheela had been furious about our attempt to hire a helicopter on our own initiative. I should have requested official permission to hire the helicopter, Isabel said, then it could all have been arranged properly. She told me that for 'public relations reasons' it had been decided to resume the search the next day, which would be the third day after the accident. I was getting more heavy-hearted with every day that passed.

Now was the time to take the three-week holiday for which I had been granted permission. I had not yet decided to leave Bhagwan and the ranch for good, but I certainly needed time to cool off and consider my future.

I managed to raise the money for a new motorcycle, and decided to travel round the western states. It was the first holiday I had had for nine years. The first day I travelled nearly a thousand miles, and it felt wonderful to be out of the ranch and on my own.

Isabel and I had discussed what we would do in the event of my not being allowed back on the ranch, since although she was married to Niren, an American lawyer, and thus had no visa problems, it was clear that she was seriously thinking about leaving. We were still good friends. We had worked out a telephone code to circumvent the ranch phone censors — 'negatives' was our word for airline tickets, and if Isabel wanted to join me she would ask me to send her some of my holiday negatives.

A week after I left the ranch, I called her. "A lot has been happening here," she said, "and things have changed. Sheela held a public meeting and denounced you for what you did. She said that it was clear that Ambara must have been dead for hours when you insisted on continuing the search. She also said that you had started ordering people around as though you were the big chief samurai again. Then she said that your supervisor and his girlfriend had already apologised to Sheela for the helicopter affair."

Apologised? What was everybody doing? I could not believe my ears, and it felt like the final betrayal from those who I thought were my friends. Isabel went on to say that since Sheela did not believe that people had the maturity to use their days off properly, they had now been cancelled altogether, and since festival time was approaching and fifteen thousand sannyasis were expected to attend, the work load was being increased to a minimum of fifteen hours a day, seven days a week. She made no mention at all of the negatives. It seemed as though she was aligning herself with Sheela again, and I was the villain.

A week later I spoke to Isabel again. She told me that the police had found Ambara's body on an island forty miles downstream. I wanted to know whether he had died from drowning or exposure, but didn't ask. I was saddened by his death, and it put yet another nail in the coffin of my relationship with what had once been a united and compassionate family. Although I had known he must be dead, I had not yet let the reality sink in.

During the three weeks of my holiday I travelled six thousand miles, and it was sheer exhilaration. I relied on intution to let me know when radar checks were in operation, and never once got a ticket for speeding.

When the three weeks were up I returned to the ranch with trepidation. I found Sheela in her trailer and we had a superficial conversation. None of my past actions were mentioned, and it seemed that she was willing to let bygones be bygones. I discovered that while I had been away Vivek had had a bad motor accident, and Gayan and another German sannyasin had been injured. More rules and restrictions were being posted. I read the latest rules and the new list of sexual quarantines in the canteen, and realised that it was going to be impossible to continue to live like this. As I went into the ward to visit the German girl with the neck injuries, which had received no proper treatment, I heard my inner voice saying, stronger than ever: you're finished with this place.

That night I went to bed early, to get some rest before starting work with the bulldozer the next day. I could not sleep for that voice saying over and over: you're finished with this place. After ten years of being with Bhagwan it had come to this. At eleven o'clock I got dressed and went outside, determined to ask Bhagwan about it psychically. I remembered the time in New Jersey, when in my extreme exhaustion I had asked him for his mercy. This was another such moment. He could not be blind to what was going on, and he alone could change things here if he wanted to.

Because he was in silence I could not contact Bhagwan directly, but I could communicate with him telepathically. I went and sat on the lawn outside his room and meditated for ten minutes, focusing my energy towards him, with the question in my heart: "Bhagwan, am I finished with this place — and you — or not?" I opened my eyes. All the lights in his room suddenly went out. It seemed symbolic, as though my period of illumination was over. Now it was time to make my way on my own.

I had an image of Bhagwan sitting in front of his video screen for hours on end, saw his driving accidents, his speeding tickets, the bitterness he had expressed to the Boston photographer, and the day I had walked into his room and seen him clearly as a hollow shell. It was all so different from his public persona. He was supposed to be the Enlightened One, the Master, the Omniscient One, the man of perfect awareness. What was he doing now? Watching movies, driving incompetently and dangerously, issuing commands about making money to Sheela, and buying new Rolls Royces every week. The videos had now become so important to him that the sannyasis whose job it was to keep him satisfied were flying to Portland or San Francisco almost every day to provide new movies — an enormously costly indulgence. How different from the man who read ten or

fifteen erudite books every day, and who amazed five thousand
people at Poona with his oratory, his love, and his perception, and
kept them spellbound for hours at a time.

When I realised that this was indeed the end of the road for me, I
was overjoyed. I rolled over and over in the dewy grass with delight
and relief. There was no more need for shilly-shallying — I knew
what I had to do.

The next morning I saw Isabel before she went off to work, and
told her that I was definitely going. She said she understood, and
even started talking about 'negatives' again. Then I went to see
Sheela, and explained that I was not happy here, and that it was time
for me to go. She agreed, adding that I should be 'very careful'. I
knew by now exactly what she meant. After collecting my few
belongings in the ranch yard, I bumped into the woman who had
helped me try to hire the helicopter. "Why ever did you apologise to
Sheela?" I asked. She looked at me in amazement. "We didn't," she
said. "We never apologised. Sheela made that up to try and alienate
you, to prove that you were the only one who was still
unsurrendered.".

I was off the ranch that same day, but not before I had seen Vivek.
She was in the kitchen, looking soft and gentle. "Hi, Vivek," I said.
"Listen. I'm going to leave." She looked me straight in the eye,
silently asking me to elaborate on my reasons. It was the eyes you had
to watch with Vivek.

I told her about Sheela putting everybody out of the hospital ward,
making them work when they were too ill. Then I explained how I
felt about Ambara, that I thought it had been callous and discom-
passionate, and I said that I wasn't happy with the way we had treated
the old people in Antelope. I didn't tell her my feelings about
Bhagwan, but I did say that my heart wasn't in the place any more.
"Could you tell Bhagwan why I'm leaving," I said, "and give him my
love?" Vivek said that she would, but added no comment of her own.
I felt glad that I had told her, and had therefore squared my accounts
with Bhagwan.

My first stop after leaving the ranch was at Carmel, California,
where I was to stay with a former sannyasi who had offered me a job
ten days earlier. When I arrived on his doorstep, I found that the job
offer had evaporated. I felt like a modern version of Rip Van Winkle,
awakening after a ten year hibernation to find myself in a foreign
country with very little money, a broken heart, and little idea of how

to conduct myself in the world at large. I soon began to miss my extended family on the ranch. It seemed as though I had no identity other than as a sannyasi living in Bhagwan's commune. However was I going to make my way in the world once more?

I discovered that I had become so institutionalised that I was afraid to do even simple things like opening a bank account. After so many years of being told what to do at every turn, I had lost confidence in being able to make decisions for myself. I felt particularly torn whenever I remembered that the first World Festival was to begin at Rajneeshpuram in six weeks time. It seemed that everybody I loved was either going or was there already. Part of me knew for certain that it was all over, but another part clung to the old and familiar, and to that wonderful extended orange family.

I found the outside world very inhospitable. I didn't know anybody, and nobody knew or cared about me. I didn't know how to go about getting a job, and I had an acute bout of homesickness for the ranch. I went to see the newly-released movie, *ET*, and when I heard the message "ET phone home" it brought tears to my eyes. I wanted to go home too, whatever the cost. I decided to write to Bhagwan first, to let him know exactly what had caused me to leave. I wanted to put it all on record, to make sure Bhagwan knew exactly how I felt and why I could no longer stay. I wrote the letter and sent it off, but received no reply.

In desperation I phoned Sheela, who told me that Bhagwan had said my letter was 'nonsense'. But, she said, I could come back if I was ready to drop my friendships with all those people who had left Bhagwan, including Laxmi, Deeksha, and everyone who had left in the last few months. It was too much. I replied that it was not up to me to decide whether or not they were negative, but they were my friends, and I couldn't just cut them off like that. Sheela told me that Bhagwan had said the reason that I was miserable was that I had insisted on communicating with 'negative' people. I told Sheela that the conditions she was imposing for my return were unacceptable, and that she could pass on my apologies to Bhagwan for wasting his time. In a surprisingly soft voice she said she would do that, and asked me again to take good care of myself.

Two weeks after this I wrote Bhagwan another letter. I didn't know whether Sheela had told Bhagwan what I had said, or even if she showed him my letters, but by this time I was getting desperate. The friends who visited me in Carmel thought I was going mad. My continuing indecision was tearing me apart. The rational part of me knew the truth about what was happening on the ranch, but the emotional part yearned for contact with the people who had become my only friends. The second letter I wrote to Bhagwan was conciliatory and fawning. At the time I wrote it I wanted to be back at all costs. The Festival had already started, and I did not see how I could stay away from it.

When Sheela got the letter, her reply was not at all what I had expected. She phoned me as soon as she received it, and said that Bhagwan, like me, could change his mind. He had been ready to have me back, but now he had changed his mind. He wanted me to know that I had missed a great opportunity, and that I could have become enlightened in this lifetime if I had stayed with him. Now, though, it was too late. I was not welcome at Rancho Rajneesh.

At first I felt shattered and dejected as I let the words sink in, but then I felt angry. Who the hell was he to play God and predict whether or not I could become enlightened? Why should he imagine that he knows everything? So, I could not go back. There was nothing for it but to try and find work in Carmel. Luckily I was able to do my Chinese massage, and work seemed to appear just as my money was running out. When I was down to my last eighty dollars I decided to sell my motorcycle, and was offered $2,500 for it. I told the dealer I would go away and think about it, then the next day the bike broke down seriously. As I was wondering what to do I had another phone call from the ranch, this time from the chief accountant, Savita, or Sally Anne Croft. She informed me that I could come back if I was prepared to drop all my negativity, but if I did come back, I was to understand that I would be on bulldozer work fulltime. She added that I would not be living in Bhagwan's house any more.

To return now would probably mean living in a tent, but I was desperate, and agreed to her terms. Perhaps Bhagwan's messages had been tests to help me see the light. The important thing was that I could now go back if I wanted to. "Come on home, lovely one," said Savita, "come on home! There are lots of people waiting to welcome you back." My heart swelled up and tears of joy came to my eyes. I wondered if Isabel would still be there for me.

It meant that I had missed the Festival, but at that point I was ready to go back regardless of anything. I knew it would be hard, but I would give it everything I had just one more time, and if it didn't work out I could always leave a final time.

When I reached Portland airport I saw the ranch's aircraft with the twin bird symbol that I had designed, and nausea shot through me. Suddenly I wanted to run, run for my life and my freedom. But now I was hooked. The pull was too strong. I had to give it one more try.

When I got back I was immediately allocated to my old bulldozer and assigned work. Everybody treated me as though I had just returned from the dead. My old co-ordinator nicknamed me Lazarus: "Ain't nobody ever came back like you just did," he said.

I was very sad that I had missed the Festival, which from all accounts had been a resounding success. Fifteen thousand people had come from all over the world. In her press releases, Sheela claimed six hundred thousand disciples worldwide. Nine months earlier the old Poona records, which showed only twenty thousand at most, had been shredded and buried under a newly-made road to the lake. Now we had no legal connection at all with that bunch of criminals who had left India secretly one Sunday afternoon over a year ago without paying their taxes.

During the Festival money had apparently poured in, though it was officially considered a financial failure. The commercial department had produced souvenirs and trinkets, such as the stickers saying 'I've been to the Ranch' and the favourite 'Moses Invests, Jesus Saves, Bhagwan Spends!'. T-shirts with the slogan 'Warning — Delicate Ego' had sold well, but plasticky key-rings showing Bhagwan driving were less popular, as was the genuine cowboy gear as worn by the Rancho Rajneesh ranch hands. Most of the visitors had spent all their money simply getting there and paying the large registration fee.

Nothing was free at Rajneeshpuram. Snacks, books, tapes, souvenirs, courses and boutique items all sold for top prices. One US State Department official, in a report about Rajneeshpuram, said that Bhagwan's followers seemed to have applied the same money-making techniques as those used in Disneyland and Disneyworld, where everything you could possibly need was for sale on the site. This meant that no cash would 'escape' into the local community. You could buy anything within the ashram, from rosewood beads to houseplants, even a slightly used but 'blessed' Rolls Royce.

After the Festival there was a protracted fuss about Bhagwan's new clothes. As he watched video replays of himself he noticed that his socks did not perfectly match his robes. First he castigated his three seamstresses and his tailor, then the video team was broadsided. A full week before the next celebration a few months later, the tailoring team and the video crew assembled at exactly the right time of day to take footage of Bhagwan's new robes, together with his socks and hat, hanging over a chair. The results were scrutinised carefully, and a copy of the film then sent to Lao Tzu House for Bhagwan's seal of approval.

In October, Bhagwan visited the lake about eight miles away, and the video crew filmed the events. Bhagwan, Vivek and Sheela were seen paddling about in a shallow-bottomed boat, Bhagwan looking very glum. Suddenly the photographer's boat collided with the video team's boat, and the next part of the film, amidst the confused footage showing where the camera had been upset, also showed very clearly the beam of delight on Bhagwan's face resulting from this minor contretemps. It had made his day.

The film continued with an interview on the banks of the lake. Sheela asked Bhagwan if he would like a house built here for him, right on the lake, air-conditioned, private, with a lawn and surrounded by lots of trees. "You would like that, wouldn't you, Bhagwan?"

"Yes, Sheela, I'm tired of all this *brown*!" he said with something approaching venom.

"And then you can come out here every day, sit in your own *special* air-conditioned house, and *enjoy*! My workers will have it ready for you within a month, and the new road too. It will be a beautiful drive, you will see."

"Yes Sheela, but what will I *do* here?"

This question left Sheela at a loss. The man who once boasted that he could stay in his room for weeks on end, doing little or nothing except reading, now desperately seemed to need entertainment. It was painful to see Sheela fawning over Bhagwan while constantly manipulating him, like the rich owner of an expensive poodle.

All this time the US Immigration and Naturalisation Service was continuing its investigation. This had been stepped up when Edwin M. Meese, then Counsellor to President Reagan and now US Attorney General, had received a letter proposing a thorough overhaul of all Rajneeshee applications for residency. The letter found its way to the Portland office, which upgraded their investigation immediately.

The man deputed to handle the Rajneesh immigration investigations, Tom Casey, had started working for the immigration service in 1972. He had had less than twelve weeks' formal training for the job, and now he found himself up against a multinational organization with almost limitless funds, six full-time attorneys devoted solely to immigration matters, and no interest in or time for conventional Christian morality or fair play. On top of this, President Reagan had just slashed the INS budget by a massive 40% at a time when there were an estimated five million illegal immigrants already in the USA, so the immigration service was overwhelmed and understaffed.

For the first year of the investigation, Casey worked alone from a shared open-plan office in the Federal Building in downtown Portland. There is every indication that, from the earliest days, Sheela had an informant planted right in his office, and another higher up in the Federal bureaucracy. This second informer later leaked word to the ranch the day before Bhagwan was due to be arrested. At the time of writing, a Federal Grand Jury is desperately trying to discover the identity of this high-ranking official. Sheela certainly knew all the time what was going on, and the possibility of setting up and financing an informant was discussed at length at one of the 'secret' co-ordinators' meetings. There was Casey, battling all alone against a formidable group of female sannyasins, who were working with six full time highly qualified and experienced sannyasi lawyers. We also had a limitless expense account, and many people with nothing to do but bamboozle, confuse and confound poor old Tom Casey. No wonder he didn't know what had hit him. Even if he had been the most brilliant immigration investigator in the history of the INS, he would have been no match for our lot. He was on his own, working a forty-hour week in a shared office, and had to ask permission every time he wanted to make a long-distance call. How could he ever hope to pin anything on us?

At first he tried valiantly to handle it by himself. He made a total of eight trips to the ranch, earning himself a reputation as a bully. During the summer of 1982, Casey at last realised what he was up against, but it was not until the following year that Washington took notice and he was assigned one deputy.

By the autumn of 1982 we were under siege both inside and out. The neighbouring farmers and the local people were determined to fight our aggrandisement in the courts, in the press, and on television. Federal and State investigators were constantly prowling around. Key Rajneeshee people started to leave. During the Festival Sheela had publicly denounced Somendra, once Bhagwan's favourite disciple. He was no longer a sannyasi. Power and greed had corrupted him, Sheela said, and he had been ordered to hand back his mala. He was denounced in the most damaging terms, and not a soul in the audience of several thousand had attempted to speak up for him. The following day three more sannyasis were excommunicated, including the Brazilian musician that Sheela had sent away penniless from the New Jersey castle.

Sheela had made some more announcements on Bhagwan's behalf: within a few years the world would be destroyed by atomic war; California would be hit by a major earthquake in 1984; and a new phase of work would begin after the Festival, that of building an elaborate system of tunnels in the surrounding hillside. These would be equipped with atom bomb and radiation proof doors, so everyone in the commune could take shelter for several years, until the air was breathable again. We were to take with us into the tunnels one example of every piece of high technology available to start the new world with. Only sannyasis would survive the holocaust, and to prepare ourselves for the day we would have to gradually adapt our diets, so that eventually we would be able to live on vitamin and mineral capsules. After the announcement, some work crews went up to Sheela to offer help with the tunnels. It all sounded so familiar. In Bombay we had heard Bhagwan predict that the world would end in 1978. When it didn't, he altered the date to 1980, and so it went on. Destruction was always about five years in the future — like his 'soon', the future was very elastic. Sheela said that Bhagwan wanted total surrender from everybody *now* because there was so little time left. I later heard that Bhagwan had been watching the film *Nostradamus* the day before he made his latest apocalyptic announcements.

My visa renewal application was not going well. Within a month of returning to the ranch I was summoned to Portland for an interview with the infamous Tom Casey. For a week before the interview I was briefed daily by two sannyasin women who were legal experts on what questions to expect, and how I should answer them. It was nerve-racking, as just about every aspect of the ranch either contravened American law or was not what the official PR handouts about the ranch stated. When I arrived I was amused to see a newspaper clipping pinned to the wall with the headline 'Let Bhagwans Be Bhagwans'. Tom Casey's approach had been accurately assessed by the ranch experts, and in an hour of solid questioning he only asked me one unexpected question: did I know what he was trying to do?

Three months after I returned to the ranch I suffered a severely-sprained elbow, and took myself off bulldozers. I took a new job manning the CB radio in the heavy equipment office. Haridas was jealous of my move, as he was thoroughly exhausted from working on bulldozers. "I am far more sick zan you. Vot for you get so lucky, huh?" he demanded to know. Jeannie was transferred to my office too, and we began to have fun together. The decision to return began to seem like the right one.

Jeannie and I started to talk about our feelings of dissilusionment. I still wanted to try and stick it out in the hope that it would get better. Jeannie was sure that she and her boyfriend, the doctor, would be leaving soon. She was quite distressed about Bhagwan's recent behaviour. "It's the old angry guru trip all over again," she said. "He's just lashing out at all comers. Now the people he and Sheela have been walking all over are hitting back and it's beginning to get very messy. You can't fool with the Federal Government for long without getting your fingers rapped. All this non-payment of bills, the lying, the PR deceit — why do we have to do it this way? We could have had our paradise legally and above board, and build our commune in complete peace. This way of doing things just makes me sick!"

Bhagwan, still in 'silence', now started to make short guided tours of the main work departments. According to Sheela, this was in response to sannyasis saying that they never saw him, and felt isolated from him. All that most of us ever saw of him now was his bearded face as he drove by. Wherever he went, a team of photographers and video operators would record the event, and in the evening we had the pleasure of watching Bhagwan on television, touring the plumbers' department or going round the cleaning works. The canteen, which was zoned to accommodate 250 people, was now serving 2,500 sannasis with meals every day.

In October, Bhagwan himself was called for an interview in Portland with the Immigration Service. He flew to Portland in the ranch's new twin-engined Mitsubishi turbo-prop aircraft. His personal physician had to approve the plane for noise level and comfort, since Bhagwan had never flown in anything less distinguished than a Lear Jet before. He wore his $150,000 Cartier watch, the first time he had put it on since it had been given to him in 1975. Perhaps he aimed to impress the INS investigators, or maybe it just made him feel good.

On the morning that Bhagwan was due to leave for Portland, the entire ranch community was asked to come and bid him *bon voyage*. In her pep talk to us, Sheela instructed us to be one hundred per cent positive, as then Bhagwan was sure to have his visa application granted. He had applied for a change of status from that of a tourist on a temporary visa to a religious teacher with permanent residency. He now had to prove that he was a genuine religious teacher.

When they arrived at the INS office, Bhagwan was ushered into a specially-cleaned room. Sheela was specifically excluded. Bhagwan was questioned for two hours, and the interview was tape recorded. The first machine, however, broke down after only two or three minutes — until then it had worked flawlessly for five years — and a second recorder was brought in. Bhagwan was still able to jinx machinery!

He had been thoroughly briefed about how he should answer. "I am a super, super, super teacher," he expounded, having been advised by his Washington attorneys not to call himself a Master or a Guru.

"Well, Mr Mohan, if you are such a super, super, super teacher, then surely some of your disciples must be enlightened, as you are. After all, you have been teaching for twenty years, have you not?"

"Yes. Thirty of my disciples are indeed enlightened."

"Ah. Who are they? What are their names?"

"Well, you have to understand that I cannot give you their names. This would upset the others in the commune."

"Is Sheela enlightened?"

"No, but it can happen any moment!"

"Is Teertha enlightened? Is Vivek? Is Laxmi?"

"No, they are not enlightened, but a few of them are very close."

"Why did you send Laxmi away?"

"Because I had no further use for her."

After he had left, the official who had been interviewing him swivelled his chair around and sat pondering the view for ten minutes. Back at the ranch the next day, Sheela cited this as evidence of the tremendous impact that Bhagwan had, even on lowly officials. I thought it was far more likely that he was considering just how he could get Bhagwan out of the country as fast as possible.

Their verdict did not take long to prepare. His application was turned down, and he was given until February 1983 to leave the country.

Back at the ranch, the rules and regulations were still being tightened up. A complicated system of sexual quarantine, instigated during the Festival, remained in force. Everybody had to wear a coloured wrist band denoting their sexual quarantine category. Orange was for ranch workers who were 'clean', blue was for short-stay visitors who were 'suspect', and green for longer-stay visitors who had not been vetted one way or the other. A coloured bead also had to be worn on the mala, signifying 'clean', 'dubious' or 'un-vetted'. The system might have been effective if it had been rigidly adhered to, but sexual passion is a hard thing to legislate or control, and the system was doomed to failure. It seemed to me that we were simply going through another re-run of the Kailash 'increase the rules' scenario. Couldn't Bhagwan do something original, something really inspired and beautiful, instead? I had heard it all before. If free sex had been as important to me now as it had once been, then perhaps the system would have been worth it. But it wasn't.

By September 1982 more and more of the original sannyasis had left or had been denounced, and their places were being taken by very young brash Americans, who now formed the bulk of the commune. Few were educated, or had travelled, or had the same ideals as those embraced by the original members. Their average age was about twenty-two, and at thirty-four I felt distinctly old among them. They were also very noisy and arrogant. When the ranch had started it had been peopled by quiet and serene meditators.

In September four sannyasi mechanics left in one week, and it became even more difficult to keep our battered fleet together. Sheela announced that our monthly fuel bill now exceeded $200,000. In the lawyer's office the stress of lying and deceit had become so great that two lawyers asked to be transferred to the farming department. Back in February, five lawyers had left the ranch in as many weeks. They could not handle the unethical way in which Sheela asked them to behave. There is only so much that a lawyer will agree to do. These people were all legally qualified and trained to keep within the law, and Sheela and Bhagwan were constantly asking them to find ways of breaking that law.

Although I felt at home again for a while, the feeling did not last. It was freezing cold again, and it was a mile's walk every morning to the heavy equipment office. As I set out at seven in the morning, wave after wave of rolling juniper-spotted hills spread out and disappeared into the distance. Gently falling snow subdued the early light of dawn. I kept wondering what I was still doing here. As I trudged through the mud and slush I asked myself: is there something wrong with me, or is there something wrong with him? The dream had become such a sordid nightmare.

One October day a sannyasi carpenter who lived in my trailer disappeared. I decided I had had enough of keeping a low profile. I threw caution to the winds, and asked the journalist in charge of our fortnightly news-sheet, a former reporter with the *Birmingham Post*, how he could write such blatant propaganda. Surely after his career as a parliamentary correspondent for a respectable paper he had some regard for the truth? He stared at me, amazed at my outspokenness, and made sure he never sat with me again.

On another occasion I spoke out against the unhygienic practices of the canteen supervisors. I had just gone down with amoebic dysentery again, something I had had no trace of in my last two years in India. At the ranch medical centre, which had grown and was now staffed by six doctors and three nurses, all fully-qualified, I was told to take Indian drugs for the infection. I was told that these were cheaper. But I wanted real Flagyl, by far the most effective remedy. A surrendered disciple was expected to help the ranch to save money. I knew I would get reported for having caused another confrontation, and I was. Although I was so exhausted because of the dysentery, I could not just lie back and accept it. My body was beginning to crack up after years of malnutrition and tropical disease, followed by this punishing physical labour. This body which was once so strong was just not up to it any longer. I thought of Teertha, who had recently arrived back from a world money-raising tour. He had become so exhausted that he had been advised to have a pacemaker fitted for his heart.

A week or so later, Bhagwan's personal physician asked me to take a barium meal and be X-rayed. He explained that this was to test the X-ray machine in the newly-built operating theatre in Bhagwan's house. Bhagwan had always feared that he would die of cancer, and his hypochondria was well known. For many years it had been one of my jobs to act as Bhagwan's living mannequin, but I was not going to take medical risks on his account. I suggested he should try it out on one of Bhagwan's brothers, several of whom had now found their way to the ranch.

Saying no to the ranch was, I knew, tantamount to treason, but I had had enough. I remembered a quote from Carlos Castaneda that I had once read: "The basic difference between an ordinary man and a warrior is that a warrior takes everything as a challenge while an ordinary man takes everything either as a blessing or a curse." It was up to me to face this challenge like a warrior.

Those who had already left Bhagwan were gradually being wiped out of existence. Yatri, the English graphic artist who had produced all the books in Poona, met me for coffee one day, and told me that Bhagwan had said that nobody who had left the commune could appear in new books. I remembered Bhagwan's fierce assertion in Poona that the truth was the truth, and could never be altered, and now here we were, altering our records to further his personal vendettas.

One morning in November, I was summoned out of the blue to see Sheela in her trailer. I decided that this must be the final showdown. She came straight to the point. "Shiva, I have been receiving disturbing reports about you. You have become negative again. Now last time when you left, it was only through Bhagwan's grace that you were allowed to return at all. I myself would not have let you come back. But now Bhagwan has told me that your negativity is disturbing one of our best workers, Jeannie. So you have a choice. Either you drop this negativity of you leave the ranch. You can keep the mala or not. Now what do you want to do?"

I looked at her shifty gangster eyes as she added: "We asked Jeannie if she had been influenced by your negativity, and she said no, not at all. I went back to Bhagwan, but he said that regardless of anything Jeannie might say Shiva has still made her nagative. So do you have anything to say?"

I told her my heart was not in it any more, and that I would leave. I asked her for a ticket back to London, but she refused to help. She told me to go and beg for money in the commune. She did agree to help me with the paperwork I would need to leave the country, then in carefully measured tones she told me again to be very careful when I left. I had heard and seen enough of Sheela's more dubious activities to know exactly what Sheela would be prepared to do to me if I was not 'careful'. Outside the trailer I met Isabel and told her what had happened. She looked sad, and asked me if I still loved Bhagwan. "Yes," I said, "that has not changed." We gave each other a last lingering hug, and I went off in search of Jeannie.

It turned out that she had been visited twice the previous night by

Sheela, who had become almost hysterical. Jeannie had been planning to go to Colorado to pick up some second-hand trucks that Sheela had bought cheaply, but Sheela had misunderstood, and thought that Jeannie was leaving for good. Jeannie had said that she was planning to leave sooner or later if things didn't improve. "There are a lot of things wrong with this place," she told Sheela, "and I certainly don't need Shiva or anyone else to point that out. I'm not afraid to tell you or Bhagwan what I feel about it!"

Sheela had then gone on to tell Jeannie that I was going round upsetting people, and showed her a report which had been compiled about my activities. It detailed all the people I had been in contact with, and everything they had said about me. Nothing in it was really true, but it was very damaging.

As I had no money, I asked Jeannie if she could help me buy my ticket back to Britain. Jeannie's family were well-off landowners, which was part of the reason why Sheela was so worried about her leaving. Sheela liked having monied people around her, and didn't want any good source of cash to dry up.

Before I could leave I had to train somebody to take over my new job with the sewage disposal truck. Sewage had become a major problem, as the tanks were only designed to cope with the ranch's official population, and our actual population was about ten times that. The canteen sewage system was now having to be attended to daily instead of monthly, and the waste was being illegally dumped into a lagoon which had only been registered for sewage dumping as a temporary measure during the Festival. Bhagwan had named this lagoon after one of his contemporaries for whom he had no respect, but who had a large following in America — it was called the Muktananda Sewage Lagoon.

The chief co-ordinator sought me out to tell me I had to be off the ranch by sunset. I said I would not leave until I had enough money to fly home. Towards the end of the day Karuna, who was in charge of the ranch visa department, told me that Casey wanted to see me for another interview in Portland. He had apparently said: "That fella' ain't leaving the country until he sees me!" I was asked to go back to the office and go over all the briefings again. Now that I could do them damage if I said the wrong things, they were all over me again. After a four-hour briefing, Karuna said that she would drive me over to Portland herself the next day with Gayan and Gayan's daughter, who had just arrived on the ranch from her father's house in

Germany. We were still technically married, though we had obtained our *decree nisi* and were only six weeks away from being fully divorced. Karuna decided that Casey should not be told this, as Gayan's visa application would be affected by my decision to leave.

Casey was now quite aware of who he was dealing with. The ranch and its present organisation, Rajneesh Foundation International, had already become quite notorious in Portland. He knew that I had fallen out with Sheela the day before, and he also knew about my involvement in the search for Ambara. Perhaps he had a spy in the ranch just as the ranch had a spy in his office. "You know, Hugh," he said in a friendly way, "I've been making a few enquiries about you, and everybody agrees that you are a very loyal disciple of Bhagwan's, perhaps *the* most loyal. That's why he made you a bodyguard. Now, what I can't understand is why somebody decent like you should be associating with somebody like Sheela, who surrounds herself with a bunch of yes-women and sycophants. I can understand why you were so upset about Ambara — anyone would have been. I feel if I were run over by a motor grader on the ranch tomorrow, Sheela would actually be glad. How can you associate with her?"

I saw the trap and did my best to cover for Sheela. "I know she has a hard exterior," I said, "but underneath she has a good heart." Casey continued to look me straight in the eye. Both he and I knew that I was lying. His skilled cross-examination went on for four hours. Gayan and her little daughter, Hasya, were given a separate interview. Casey was very gentle with Hasya. I wrote some farewell notes for Gayan to distribute for me.

I did not go back to the ranch after my interview, but flew to southern Oregon and stayed with some ex-sannyasi friends there. Three days later, Jeannie phoned me to say there had been a co-ordinators' meeting at the ranch, at which Sheela had mentioned that Swami Shiva had left, with all his negativity. She went on to say that I had betrayed Bhagwan to Casey, that I had told him everything about Bhagwan and the commune, and that as a result Bhagwan would now have to leave the States. All the positivity of the commune had been betrayed by one person's negativity. After the meeting Jeannie's boyfriend told her that he was leaving whether Jeannie came with him or not. He had had all that he could take.

Jeannie and the doctor realised that if Sheela knew about their plans she would try and prevent them leaving, so they decided to leave that night. The English nurse, Jaya, and her boyfriend decided to leave with them, driven by Bob Harvey. They hid under the seats of a long-distance truck, and passed through both ranch check points unnoticed. But one of them had accidentally left a suitcase on the seat. Bob told the sannyasi perimeter guards that it was his overnight bag, and the escapees breathed a sigh of relief when he was allowed through. They left Oregon from a south Oregon airport, using assumed names and buying new clothes in case Sheela had tipped off the police using a trumped-up theft charge.

It was eight o'clock the next morning before Sheela learned that anybody had left. There were now three thousand people on the ranch, far too many for Sheela to keep an eye on, so it was a while before she could tell whether just a few people had left, or whether there had been a general exodus. A round-up was ordered, and Sheela called another emergency meeting. At the meeting both she and Vivek were on the stage in tears. With her arm round Vivek's shoulder to comfort her, Sheela announced: "Bhagwan says that if one more person leaves the commune like that, he is going to leave his body immediately. The commune will be disbanded, and his work will come to an end.

"You know that Vivek and I have had a few differences of opinion in the past two years," she went on, "but here we are standing together in front of you, united. We are one. This is a vitally important time. We have to stick together, drop our differences, and devote all our energy to making *his* dream a reality. Nobody must leave without permission."

When faced with this ultimate blackmail three more people who had been on the point of leaving unpacked their bags. Nobody wanted to be held responsible for Bhagwan's death. On the fourth day after I left I sent back my mala, as I did not want to incur another bout of homesickness which vould have me crawling back yet again. This time it had to be final, absolute. I vowed that I would never go back, however difficult things got in the outside world.

I met Jeannie and a few others in New Mexico, and Jeannie told me that the cheques that she and three other people on the ranch had given me to buy my ticket to England had been cancelled by Sheela. In itself that did not matter too much, as I had now sold my motorcycle and had enough money to return home, but it was a foretaste of the persecution yet to come.

Back in London, I went straight to the main Rajneesh meditation centre in Oak Village. I wore a new black track suit. My welcome could not have been cooler. The sannyasin in charge motioned me into her office. "You are not to come here any more," she said. "You are not to go to any Rajneesh centre anywhere in the world. That is the ruling from the ranch. You are not to contact any sannyasis anywhere in the world."

"I guessed as much," I said as breezily as I could. "I just called in to collect my divorce papers. The authorities were going to send them here." She informed me that they had been sent to Oregon, where they would do nothing but delay the divorce. Now I must leave; she could not help me any more. After ten years away from my native land it was a bitter homecoming.

Chapter Sixteen
LIFE AFTER BHAGWAN

I knew that I was going to find it difficult to re-establish myself in the outside world. Who was I? What was left of 'me'? Where was I going to live and what was I going to do?

In the lobby of the London meditation centre, an attractive woman — the very first sannyasin *Penthouse* centrefold girl, who wore her mala but nothing else for the pictures — was waiting for me with a message. It was to say that the door back to Rajneeshpuram was still open, and that I could still return to the ranch. The message came from Sushila, Sheela's deputy, with whom she had just had breakfast at the London Hilton. It was clear that I was going to have to be very careful. The ranch tried all sorts of methods to find out where I was going to live, how much money I had, and what my plans were for the future. I soon realised that I knew very few peole who were not or had never been sannyasis. I went to stay with a sannyasi friend in Paris. We met in the Gare du Nord. After we had embraced, she said: "Eh, cheri, you are all over ze international newsletter. You 'ave got ze 'ole page, you are famous. Whatever 'ave you done to Sheela to upset 'er so much?"

Sheela's American husband, Jayananda, flew from Cologne to Paris with the leader of the main German centre to try and locate me. I had mistakenly told a sannyasi friend in London that I was going to Paris, and Jayananda and his assistant phoned every sannyasi residence in the city to try and find out where I was. The friend I was staying with received his call, and I listened as she took it. I did sound like a dangerous fellow! The letter excommunicating me was read out to her on the phone.

When I got to see the *Newsletter*, I discovered that it included a cleverly-worded and damning denunciation of me. Even reading it now, three years after the event, puts a chill in my heart. It is typical of the distortions and half-truths that characterised Rajneeshpuram at this time. "Beloved Friends," the letter started, "Love." — Bhagwan's habitual salutation.

"Hugh Milne, formerly Swami Shivamurti, is no longer a disciple of Bhagwan. By his own choice he has left Rajneeshpuram and declared that he has nothing to do with Bhagwan and His work. This is an event from which we can all learn.

"The first thing to understand is that a true disciple of an Enlightened Master does not demand power or privileged status. If the disciple is given great responsibility or simple tasks like cleaning, it is all the same. A true disciple understands that Bhagwan's love is given unconditionally to all.

"So when situations change and a disciple who has been in a position of authority is suddenly without power, this is both a test and an opportunity. If the disciple can drop the attachment to power, then he, or she, can easily transcend. If not, a great opportunity is missed.

"For ten years, Hugh Milne was in a position of responsibility. But his whole concern was with power, not with his connection to Bhagwan. He exploited his position in Poona as head of 300 guards and as a constant attendant at Bhagwan's meetings with His disciples.

"At Rajneeshpuram, Hugh Milne did not have the opportunity for power, and immediately his discontent began to surface. He did not like being an ordinary member of the commune, helping in its construction.

"He left once, then wrote a letter apologizing and asking to return. Out of Bhagwan's compassion and love, he was welcomed back, but again he consciously hankered for special status in the commune. When he left a second time, he displayed a crude cunningness in the manner of his departure which again revealed that he was not a true disciple.

"In a letter to his Master, he said 'If ever there is a real need, I am always there for you.' This is a total distortion of the Master-disciple relationship. A Master does not need anyone, or anything. A Master is utterly fulfilled. His only desire is to share His love with His disciples. Again, this shows Hugh Milne's desire to be recognized as special.

"In his letter to Bhagwan, he said that he was enclosing the locket from his mala, but did not do so. A small slit had been made in the envelope, as if to imply that it could have

fallen out by accident." (I assume this was done either by
the Federal investigators or a clumsy censor on the ranch)
"The truth is that Hugh Milne kept the locket while at the
same time declaring that he has stopped being a sannyasin.

"In an interview with the US Immigration service, he said
that he was traveling to London to earn money and take
care of his wife and child, who live at Rajneeshpuram. Yet
he did not show that love and care to them. He left the
ranch without telling his wife what he was doing.

"Hugh Milne will not be allowed to return to the ranch
again and, even though he has kept his locket, he is no
longer a disciple of Bhagwan. No Rajneesh centers,
communes or ashrams should support him in any way, or
have anything to do with him.

"Innocent people, especially new sannyasins, may think
that because Hugh Milne has been seen in so many photographs sitting by Bhagwan's side that he is someone special.
In reality he is just a cunning and clever individual who will
not hesitate to exploit Bhagwan's disciples.

"We do not wish to have any individuals involved with
Bhagwan's work who are interested in power and exploit-
ation. It is better that people with such negative, exploit-
ative minds leave now, rather than hinder His work and
prevent His love from reaching those who are thirsty.

"His blessings,

Ma Anand Sheela
Personal Secretary to Bhagwan"

I learnt a month later, when one of the newsletter editors left the
ranch, that although Sheela had signed the letter, Bhagwan had
written it himself. It did sound very like his handiwork. I was worried
and nervous, and began to fear physical attack. I wondered just how
desperate and just how violent Bhagwan could be. While still on the
ranch, I had learned that a lot of things at Poona had not been what
they appeared to be at the time. The sannyasi — Sukhavi — who had
been beaten up for supposedly making a pass at an Indian woman had
in fact, on Laxmi's orders, been raiding the flat of a government tax
inspector. He was a professional housebreaker with a British criminal
record. The landlord who had been accused of rape at Saswat had
been set up by the Rajneeshees — an attractive Rajneeshee woman
had been sent, scantily-dressed, to his apartment late one evening,

while a bunch of male sannyasis waited within earshot for her pre-arranged scream. One of Sheela's boyfriends at Saswat had blown up the generator and set off the firebomb outside the medical centre. Now it seemed I was fair game, too, and the stakes were much higher.

I went to Berlin to visit another old friend, from where I phoned Jeannie. She was still in hiding in America. She asked me to be discreet, as she was sure her phone was being tapped. She told me that the government investigation into Bhagwan's activities had been stepped up, and it seemed certain that he would soon have to leave the country. Then I travelled to Zürich, to find that spies from the ranch had already been alerted to my plans. It all became quite a strange and distressing nightmare.

I learnt that the 'quit USA' notice that Bhagwan had been served after his interview in Portland was taken back to the ranch, where the six ranch attorneys had pored over it all night. They found a technical flaw in it, and the deportation order was thrown out. Tom Casey's team had erred disastrously. It was to take them another three years to get their man out of the country.

While I was in Switzerland the German magazine *Stern*, which had always shown an interest in our activities, published a long article on the ranch. Two paragraphs were devoted to my own departure, which was ascribed to my fury over Ambara's death. The magazine asked: "How much aviation fuel is a human life worth?" I wrote a strongly-worded letter to *Stern*, saying how pervasive the fascist regime at the ranch had become, how good they were at persecuting people who had left, and how the ranch had become "a prison run by a ruthless despot". They published the letter prominently, together with a picture of me and a naked Gayan posing Hollywood-style under a waterfall, a picture their own photographer had taken outside Poona five years previously.

During the month I spent working in Zürich I met Deeksha. In her distress she had sought out Krishnamurti, the only person Bhagwan had ever acknowledged as an equal. Krishnamurti had no time for Bhagwan, and particularly objected to the use of the word 'Bhagwan'; nobody other than God himself should use that title, he said. Krishnamurti had told Deeksha: "I have received thousands of letters from all over the world asking why I do not speak out in public against this man. But I will not, as it is not my way. The man is a criminal. You have to understand this very clearly. What he is doing to people in the name of spirituality is criminal. One must never give to another human being — and he is simply a human being — your ultimate manifestation of consciousness, which is your ability to make decisions for yourself. You have made a great mistake in giving him that power for twelve years, but understand this: no man has power except the power his followers give him. That is why he needs people around him all the time, and the more the better."

Deeksha found comfort in his observations. She told me that the names of certain people were recorded under a special access code on the ranch computer. These names were of housebreakers, forgers, confidence tricksters, drug runners and contract killers, people who might be very useful in the future. Deeksha added conversationally that both the contract killers were German. I wondered if I knew them.

As the ranch grew in notoriety, more people in the world of alternative lifestyles started questioning Bhagwan's methods. It was at about this time that Becky James, the daughter of Jenny James, the woman who founded the Atlantis community in Ireland, gave a psychic reading on Bhagwan. Relaxed and holding the paper with his name on it between her hands without knowing what was written on it, she concentrated her mind and came up with the following monologue. When I read the passage in *Atlantis Magic* I was amazed at how accurately she had 'become' the man she had never met, and did not even 'know' she was being. It was extraordinarily accurate. Only a very few people in the world actually knew Rajneesh as intimately as was being described here.

"The first thing that comes to me," she said, "is that I don't mind if I wear a long dress. I'm the sort of person who has felt what it's like to be tied up and conventional and now I feel like wearing 'cosmic' clothes. I wear particular clothes to make me a particular person. I'm very conscious of everything I do. I'm a very toned down, quite boring person really. Here I am, flat out, bored out of my mind, wearing my particular clothes, listening to particular music and to the tick tock of the clock. I don't feel any joy or laughter. I'm waiting for something to happen. I'm impatient and annoyed when everything doesn't go right.

"I'm a serious person trying to have fun. It's a Good Idea to have fun, yet it feels terrible, really empty, tight and strained. I feel glum. I've got masses of time and space to myself: I've organised it that way. Everything is white and clean and plastic and smooth. I couldn't cope with things being in a mess. But now I'm left with nothingness. I've put myself on the outside of it all and I'm not involved. I don't relate personally to anybody. I've got other people to organise the others and I'm left bored with headaches, backaches, leg ache and arm ache."

Becky said that the feeling she had was of stagnation, of something decrepit, hard, fraught, dried up.

The publishers sent a copy of the book to Sheela at the ranch, and received the following reply:

"Beloved, Love.

"Thank you for your letter. Our first impression of the is that, in this time of economic recession and soaring publishing costs, it is a miracle that a publishing corporation has wasted so much time and money producing such a collection of garbage as *Atlantis Magic*.

"We read the passages which are supposed to refer to Bhagwan Shree Rajneesh and had a good laugh at their absurdity. Bhagwan's own comment was that he had met idiots in his time, but that Jenny James and her friends top them all.

"Becky does not even come close to describing the qualities of Bhagwan. It's pure drivel and nothing else — a spewing out of Becky's own psychological neurosis. In fact, James would probably have come closer to an accurate description if she had recorded Becky's verbal diarrhoea as a continuous stream, and had then drawn names of public figures out of a hat and stuck them on at random.

"We strongly suggest that James begins a new career as a library assistant. Then she will at least be handling the books of good writers. That is about as close as she will come to being one herself.

"His blessings,

Ma Anand Sheela, President."

After Zürich I decided to go into hiding. A wise and charming lady, an exponent of Jungian thought, invited me to stay with her in the country. In the next two months I wrote the original manuscript of this book. Dissatisfied with it, and aware of Bhagwan's wrath should I publish it, I resolved to wait until distance gave me more objectivity before I rewrote it.

When I arrived back in London in May 1983, I set up practice with a group of therapists. It wasn't long before they became aware that my presence was damaging their own practices. All their patients who were sannyasis had stopped coming for treatment, on orders from the London centre. I learned that a secret general meeting had been held at the London Sannyas Centre where I had been called 'evil', 'negative', and 'The Judas'. It was impossible for me to go on working in the group practice, and I dropped out in August. Some sannyasis continued to see me, but I never knew whether they were genuine friends or whether they had been sent on official spying missions. One ex-Rajneeshee later told me that she had been instructed to visit me, ask me certain questions, write down all the answers and send them on to the ranch. A psychologist, she said that she had never witnessed a more systematic witch-hunt in all her life. I fell in love with a sannyasin woman, and found out only after our relationship had ended that she had been working as a prostitute in London to earn enough money to go to Rajneeshpuram. If there was anything left in my heart to break, that finally broke it.

In the meantime the investigation into illegal immigrations continued in Oregon. Tom Casey learned of my whereabouts and contacted me, hoping that as I was now an 'ex' I would be able to help him in his enquiries. After some initial interest, I heard what had happened to my friend the doctor, who had moved to New Mexico. In order to work there he sat the state medical examination, and since he was not able to practise until he heard the results, he took a temporary job as a taxi driver. Casey's new assistant, a fresh-faced young man called Feher, had interviewed the doctor about the ranch. Suspecting the doctor of holding back information, Feher had written to the New Mexico Examination Board — quite illegally — asking them to hold back his licence. It was nearly six months before the doctor learned what had happened, and he then successfully fought the ban. This single action put back the INS investigations for at least a year, as sannyasis all over the world stopped whatever co-operation they had been giving Casey's crew until then. When I heard this, I wanted nothing more to do with Casey and told him so.

Two detective inspectors from Scotland Yard rang me to ask if they could send a car and bring me to the Yard for questioning. I learned that I did not have to co-operate with them, so I decided not to. It later turned out that Casey had asked them to make the call. He had come to London to pursue me and his investigations, but did not have the authority or the grounds to arrest me. Since I was already being

pursued by Rajneesh Foundation International, the last thing I
wanted was to be harassed by American immigration officials and
Scotland Yard as well. Casey's methods left a lot to be desired, and
his approaches tended to be inept. I also learned later that at least
one sannyasi photographer had been instructed to watch New
Scotland Yard carefully, and photograph me or any other ex-sannyasi
if we ever went there. It was a very nerve-racking period.

While I was trying to re-integrate myself and lessen my dependence
on the Rajneesh community, I consulted a Jungian analyst from Los
Angeles, Hal Stone. He was the first medically-trained person who
understood my predicament, and he went some way towards
explaining it in Jungian terms. He was an unusually perceptive man,
and said: "Hugh, there is a group of people somewhere out there
trying to kill you. They want you out of their way. They know they
can reach you telepathically on a kind of shared wavelength, and they
are doing that every day. It's just like ju-ju or voodoo. They have put
a curse on you, and you will have to shield yourself from them,
otherwise they will be able to get you. These people wish you harm
because you have left them — which they can't tolerate — and they
now find you very threatening. You are their betrayer, their main
public enemy. You have to find ways of protecting yourself."

His advice made sense, but I seemed to lack the will to get well.
Some friends in London suggested that I should see a famous psychic
healer. I had never done anything like this before, and was very
hesitant, but since ordinary medical treatments had done nothing for
my nervous and depressed state, I decided in my desperation to give
it a try. When I phoned her up to make an appointment, she told me
that she had a two-month waiting list, but she must have picked up
the distress in my voice, because she called me back half an hour later
to say that she had a cancellation, and could I come the following
day?

I went full of trepidation. Her flat was extraordinary, with models
of frogs all over the place. She had a tiny crystal ball, half covered in
velvet. She sat opposite me and asked a few simple questions. I gave
my name simply as 'Hugh', and told her my age and a little about my
home background. Then her eyes went blank, as I had seen
Bhagwan's do ten years earlier, while she asked a few more
questions. "You had a God's name," she said to my amazement. "A
man gave you this name, an Indian man. He should not have done
that. You did not do anything to deserve this name. It should only be

given to those who have earned it. You have *not* earned it. You must not use it again. This Indian man, he has gone a little crazy. He has left his native village. While he was there he spoke the truth, but once he left he became greedy and got corrupted.Now he's been taken over. A group of women, a circle, they have taken him over and they are more powerful than he is. His name is Bhavna, no, Bharka, wait, I can't quite get it. It's close to Bhavna, so that's what I'll call him. He is wearing something funny on his head, a cap of some kind. It looks silly on him and he knows that. He is wearing it because he knows there is nothing left inside, so he is trying to hide that from others.

"The people where he has gone, in the United States I see, do not like him. He has upset them. He is going to come to a violent end. His group of people, who were originally in it because his teachings were genuine, are now in it for the money. Some of them are going to have nervous breakdowns." Though I did not know it at that time, soon after she left the ranch Laxmi did indeed have a nervous breakdown, as did Isabel's husband Niren, who was now part of Sheela's inner circle.

"These people are trying to kill you. They are trying to give you a heart attack. You are an embarrassment to them, and they want you out of the way. They are sending energy patterns to you in an effort to destroy you." At that I started — it was exactly what the Jungian analyst had said. "This man, this Bhavna, he made you something, a shield. He should not have done that. He should not even have needed a shield. He needed a shield because he was upsetting people, and that shows he does not really know what he does. A real seer will not need a shield. He used you to collect all the negativity that was aimed at him, to fence it off so that he remained safe. You stopped the bad energies from reaching him." I suddenly realised that that was what all the security arrangements, including the pre-darshan sniffing, were about. We had been the filters which prevented anything hostile ever reaching Bhagwan.

The psychic went on to say that 'Bhavna' had given me many things. She said that when the gifts were given he meant well, but now he was trying to control me through those things. She told me I had to get rid of them, as these people were not good people any more.

"Do you know how to clean your aura?" she asked. "Do you know how to deflect harmful energy patterns?" I said that I didn't.

She asked me how long I had been with these people, and when I told her ten years, she was incredulous. "What did they teach you?" she asked. I suddenly felt very small and stupid.

Bhagwan had indeed been operating on a psychic wavelength. A large part of the original attraction for me had been his psychic gifts, his ability to know what people were feeling and thinking. I now knew why I had been so shocked when Bhagwan had refused to have a guard outside his room in Oregon, saying that if he did the guard would soon be there 'to keep him in'. Though at the time everybody had treated it as one of his jokes, I should have realised that this was his cry for help, his acknowledgement of his loss of freedom, personal power and authority.

I felt certain that Sheela was trying to drum me out of practice completely, and make it impossible for me to earn my living. I lost confidence in myself both as an osteopath and as a human being. They were experts in the art of harassment, intimidation and disorientation, carefully ensuring that nothing could later be proved against them. It had worked. Like skilled Chinese torture, it had destroyed my sense of identity.

I didn't know who to turn to for help. My brother, though sympathetic, simply could not understand what was happening to me, and my father could not fathom it either. In despair, I eventually admitted myself to a psychiatric ward, since I knew I could not cope on my own. I had some idea that if I hid in the cuckoo's nest, Sheela would claim victory and stop trying to silence me. And I would be safe from the contract killers and the other 'special skills' sannyasis.

After a week in hospital I was discharged, but kept on Valium. I was still hopelessly depressed. All the joy and laughter had gone out of my life, and I felt that I was now doomed to perpetual failure. I remembered the early days with Bhagwan as a golden age that would never be repeated. While I was in this dangerous state of mind I tried to kill myself. But that still small inner voice came to me and said: "Oh no, we're not finished with you yet. You can't die now. We still have something for you to do."

I sought the advice of a London psychiatrist, who thought the best thing would be for me to go back to the ranch. I was appalled by his assessment. I spent three more weeks in psychiatric hospital, convinced at first that I would never be able to leave. Then an old Poona friend who I trusted completely came to visit me in hospital. We went out and had a pub lunch together; he encouraged me to think about living rather than dying, and said that on no account should I go back to the ranch. He kept on visiting me until I was ready to stand on my own feet again. I tried a tentative massage on a friend, and to my relief found that I had not lost my gift. I started working again in London.

A month later I returned to Zürich, where a friend helped me to set up a practice, and by June I had a thriving business once more. Then I had a bad motorcycle accident, which put me back in hospital. While I was there I had a call from the States; it was the sannyasin woman who had appeared in *Penthouse.*

She had a special message for me from Bhagwan. He had announced that twenty-one of his disciples were now enlightened, and I was one of the chosen. She felt it would be a good idea if I wrote to him to tell him what a wonderful teacher he had been. My God, I thought, when will they leave me alone? Would I never be free? At the same time there was a thrill at having a positive mention after being denounced as the most evil thing ever to have come into contact with the Rajneesh movement.

Two weeks after this I received a letter from Sheela, enclosing one of Bhagwan's new gold-embossed letterheads. I discovered I now had a new title: 'Bhodhisatva Swami Shivamurti' — 'Bhodhisatva' means 'one who will achieve enlightenment in this lifetime'. There were even initials after my name: MM, D.Phil.M. No mention of the ex-Swami, the cunning and manipulative wife and child deserter. Sheela's letter was addressed to 'Beloved Shiva' rather than to 'Hugh'. How things had changed! I wrote a short reply, thanking Bhagwan for his good wishes for my recovery. I was also tempted to ask whether this latest gift came with the same elastic band that was attached to all Bhagwan's presents. To make my new position absolutely clear I signed the letter 'Hugh'.

Three months later I heard that Bhagwan had proclaimed that the whole 'enlightened ones' announcement was a joke, and the honorary degrees from the Rajneesh International Meditation University, which was non-accredited, were cancelled.

What was left of me now? For ten years Bhagwan had conditioned and instilled, directed and ordered every aspect of my life. The instructions not to read or write had put me out of touch wiith any outside source of stimulation or dissent. My relationships with women had been coloured by the influence of the commune, and none of them had really lasted, the longest being my four-year relationship with Isabel. From 1976 onwards the 'work' had

increasingly taken precedence over relationships, and we had been
encouraged — indeed forced — to look upon our relationship with
Bhagwan as the only one that mattered. New relationships had
become rather like new cars, looking for the model that was the most
attractive and gave the best performance. When it gave any trouble,
you merely exchanged it for a new one. This attitude was
encouraged, so that normal human relationships became unimportant. In the atmosphere of the commune it was impossible to make
any commitment to another person, and since there was a deliberate
shortage of women at the New Jersey castle, men had been officially
directed to share lovers. Parents had usually had a traumatic time,
especially at Poona, and couples would typically break up, with one
partner returning to the West with the child or children. Gayan had
chosen to leave her daughter to be close to Bhagwan and to me.
Hundreds of other parents had done the same. Bhagwan encouraged
separation of children from their mothers, saying that "if you look at
history and psychology, all the damage that is done to a child is done
by the mother."

At the Festival in 1984, Sheela annunced that three sannyasis had
died of AIDS, though they were never named. Sheela proposed to
Bhagwan that condoms and rubber gloves should be introduced to
counteract the threat of spreading the virus. This he approved, along
with some directives designed to inhibit sexual freedom between his
disciples. What a change from the heady days of Bombay when he
had proclaimed that sex was divine! Oral and anal sex were
prohibited, and all kissing was summarily banned. A section of the
Newsletter was devoted to interviews with sannyasis, saying how
exciting this new directive was, and how tired everyone was of the
slovenly and unhygienic habit of kissing. Isabel denounced such
behaviour, saying she had had enough kissing to last a lifetime.

Gay couples were ordered to leave all Rajneesh communes, and in
London the sannyasi community was treated to a demonstration of
the correct use of the three pairs of rubber gloves which should be
used when making love — the third pair was to take off the other two
after intercourse without risk of contaminating yourself. In the new
hotel that had just been built on the ranch, each bedroom was now
equipped with a neatly-wrapped package of condoms and gloves,
carefully laid on the bed, together with detailed instructions. All
ranch residents were similarly supplied, and notices went up in all the
trailer bathrooms. "AIDS will kill two-thirds of humanity," predicted

Bhagwan. In August 1984 the sannyasi grapevine reported that eight people had been thrown off the ranch for not making love in the approved manner. A new directive instructed that only couples who had been monogamous and entirely faithful to each other for at least seven years could make love without using rubberware. No such Rajneeshee couple existed.

Journalists from Europe and America continued to pay visits to the ranch. Two British journalists, Simon Winchester and Sue Arnold, came and wrote up their impressions. Though rather tongue-in-cheek, neither of their accounts indicated that they saw what was really going on. Sue Arnold sent up the organisation, but did not perceive the evil that lay just beneath the smooth PR exterior. Both journalists saw an essentially happy community, which was flourishing and growing fast.

In 1985 I enrolled in a class to learn about hypnosis, and as I listened, many of Bhagwan's methods became abundantly clear. I learned, for instance, about the 'yes response' as a method of persuasion. When a large crowd was gathered to hear him speak, Bhagwan would start by saying: "You are all here searching for truth, for happiness, for enlightenment, and you are all with me today in this hall because you are following this path, because you all want to be fulfilled." Nobody could possibly reply 'no' to such an obvious series of truisms, and so a whole audience could thus be lulled into receptivity. Then Bhagwan, like a skilled hypnotist, would slide in his hypnotic suggestion. "A Master is required, an Enlightened Master, to show you the way. I am the one." Once this basic requirement for hypnotic trance was fulfilled, it was important not to allow it to be broken in any way, hence the cough-free zones, the dulcet voice. Oh yes, Bhagwan, I thought. Now I begin to understand.

The professional hypnotist knows how important it is never to make a statement that might be rejected by the trance subject, so builds up through statements that will elicit the yes response ("You all need guidance, you want to be happy") to what appears to be a perfectly logical conclusion ("There is only one enlightened Master"). Once the initial programming which produces a trance has been established, a skilled hypnotist can return a subject to the trance state with a single word, gesture or touch. Bhagwan often used a particular hand signal in lectures, and I remembered the time he had touched my third eye during the energy darshan. A hypnotist breaks a trance by asking the subject to perform a habitual task, or answer a mundane question. What had Bhagwan ordered me to do at the end of my energy darshan? Take some photographs, of course.

In contrast to the yes response, what the hypnotist must avoid at all costs is the 'no' response. I remembered a time in Bombay when I had just returned from England. Bhagwan had asked me how things had been in the West, and I had said "Not very good." He had quickly jumped in and said: "Yes, there is nothing of beauty out there." I had been quite startled, and had disagreed with him. The classical architecture of The British Museum had flashed into my mind, and broken the spell.

Bhagwan's way of imitating cadence, mood, even accent, was something I had remarked upon even in those early darshans. I now learned that these can all be used to 'get inside' a subject and lower their defences. What can be more assuring and acceptable than someone who talks just like your brother?

I could now see that his distinction between 'positive' and 'negative' disciples could easily be explained as a distinction between those who were responsive and suggestible, and those who were not good trance subjects. These people were termed 'closed', 'resistant' and 'hard'. 'Surrender' took on a whole new meaning to me.

Bhagwan clearly operated on both a hypnotic and a psychic level at once. That is how he was able to 'call me back' from the hill station in 1973. His reading and erudition, together with his long periods of concentration in a curtained room, gave him a chance to focus the energy he needed to 'call' people over long distances, as he had 'called' me several times. He always gave himself enough time to keep his energy as high as possible, and in order to replenish this energy he organised his lectures and darshans at opposite ends of the day.

His disciples, on the other hand, were encouraged not to read, and worked long hours, usually with large groups of other people. Only the very wealthy had a separate room, so the love and devotion that he instilled were always being reinforced by the people around you. The love, devotion and uncritical admiration that Bhagwan evoked and instilled in his followers meant that they were ready to go through any kind of hardship in order to stay near him.

Though the power that Bhagwan amplified through hypnosis and psychic awareness captivated thousands of people, others saw through it immediately. While his 'power of oratory' was able to deceive Bernard Levin, Werner Erhart had not been impressed.

While Levin is rational, scientific and educated, Erhart operates partly on an intuitive level himself, and so could be far more perceptive about what was going on. This distinction goes a long way towards explaining why Bhagwan was so attractive to professional people — lawyers, doctors and engineers. He addressed their intelligence rather than their feelings, and they were flattered.

When Krishnamurti called Bhagwan a criminal, I suspect he was not referring to the breaking of civil laws. He was referring to his misuse of hypnosis and psychic powers. Perhaps the most obvious of the psychic links that sannyasis have with Bhagwan is their mala, and it comes as no surprise to learn that when sannyasis were given their mala at darshan, they were told that if ever they stopped wearing it they should return it personally to Bhagwan.

After three years of silence, Bhagwan started speaking again in November 1984, and in one of the first lectures he gave he referred to me. "Shiva has been my bodyguard for years," he said, "but then he dropped sannyas. He wrote articles in German magazines against me. But if he comes again and wants to be my bodyguard, he will again be by my side. I know perfectly well what he has done, and if Shiva wants to be my bodyguard again, I will be immensely happy to have him."

The day the lecture was delivered I was told by phone what Bhagwan had said, and no less than two cassettes of the lecture were subsequently posted to me. Bhagwan had told one sannyasi that I was sure to come back when I heard what he had said, but I was not flattered. The number of machine guns on the ranch was multiplying, and I had no desire to be a murderer. Machine guns seemed like the very antithesis of love and meditation.

By now I was running very successful practices in London and Zürich, and felt I was free of the long tentacles of the ranch. A little while after this I went to visit a girlfriend in Portland. While I was there she received a desperate call from a friend on the ranch, demanding to know whether I had gone off on my own while I had been staying with her. She refused to comment. It was clear to me that the reason for the panic was the ranch's concern that I had been visiting the INS investigators.

For more than two years the commune had been permeated by rumours that a grand jury was considering the evidence against Bhagwan and the Foundation. Grand juries were discontinued in Britain in the 1930s, but are still part of the American judicial system, and are used to ascertain whether a State or the Federal government has sufficient evidence to prosecute a case successfully. Evidence is heard by a jury of eleven to thirteen ordinary citizens sitting with up to three judges, and anybody called to witness to the jury must do so, or can be sent to jail.

The power of a grand jury lies in its secrecy; witnesses are heard individually, and cannot be accompanied by their legal advisers. Individual witnesses thus have no idea what other witnesses have said, or even who those witnesses are. All testimony, including the names of witnesses, is kept secret, and even the timing and location of jury sittings are disclosed only to those who are taking part. It is easy to see why Sheela was so concerned; if the State had taken the case to grand jury then the ranch was about to meet its match.

Sheela grew so nervous about a possible grand jury in 1985 that she filed a massive counter-suit, claiming unfair and unlawful persecution by the government. In fact the grand jury was not convened for another ten months, but when it was set up, the government did not go in for half measures. In the event two Federal Grand Juries and one State Grand Jury were set up consecutively, the power of which was guaranteed to swamp even Rajneeshpuram's legal and espionage capabilities. One of the Federal juries was convened to investigate immigration fraud charges, including sham marriages and other deliberate illegal practices, the other to assess the charge of racketeering, or organised crime, a charge normally applied to the mafia.

It was well known in Poona that if you wanted to stay in the commune you didn't complain, let alone criticise. If you wanted to get ahead all you had to do was worship and adulate, and never say a harsh word. Since nobody who wanted to stay dared to complain, years of collective pain went unacknowledged, and the weight of unexpressed bad feelings grew and grew. When people refuse, or are not allowed, to express their feelings of anger, mistrust, fear and frustration, these feelings can become projected on others or on to the world at large. This was already happening in Poona, and grew to frightening proportions in Rajneeshpuram. The collective sum of disowned anger found a scapegoat in the world beyond the gates, and the commune started to cast itself in the victim role. Soon after the takeover of Antelope, the commune's spokespeople began predicting bloody confrontation, violence, and the use of weapons.

In September 1984 Sheela was quoted as saying: "I don't believe in

Jesus' way of turning the other cheek. I go for both cheeks. We are very well-equipped, and have arms for our protection." An investigator from *The Oregonian* newspaper wrote in detail about the arsenal amassed by the commune. "They have more .223 machine gun ammunition than all the other police departments in Oregon combined," he wrote, "together with six SGW CAR-15 assault rifles, fifteen Galil assault rifles, seven Springfield M1A1 assault rifles, three Ruger Mini-14 rifles, and sixteen Uzi semi-automatic carbines." It is worth remembering that the state of Oregon is about the size of West Germany. About 150 sannyasis were formed into a 'Peace Force' and trained in the use of these weapons. Beginning in late 1984, Bhagwan and Sheela began installing bugging and wiretapping equipment throughout Rajneeshpuram, spending $100,000 a month on it.

The anger and frustration that any normal person would feel in such a patrolled and regimented environment was turned around by the sannyasis and focused on the outside world. As the Rajneeshees started to lose court cases and the zoning plan for the new city started to look hopeless, hatred and paranoia were increasingly turned outwards.

In public, Sheela sank to new depths of hatred. At a televised school hearing in Antelope she accused a recently-widowed young woman of having caused her husband's death—he had died in a hunting accident. Without any evidence whatsoever, Sheela accused her of having been unfaithful to her husband, and asserted that he had killed himself when he had found out.

The City Mayor of Rajneeshpuram told the commune that Rajneeshpuram was receiving constant threats. "They say they're going to kill us, burn us out, kidnap our children," he said at a press conference. "But we're ready to take care of it!" The press were invited to the firing range, where twenty sannyasis were firing machine guns at human-silhouette targets. The Rajneeshpuram City Attorney, Ma Prem Sangeet, sent a message to the Federal Mediator saying: "If outsiders touch one person in this valley, I will take fifteen of their heads in self-defense. Anything the Rajneeshees do, they do properly."

When Wasco County threatened to demolish illegally used houses on the ranch, Sheela held yet another press conference. "We are willing to die for human freedom," she said. "I will paint the bulldozers with my blood. I have one hundred per cent support from my people." At the Third World Festival in 1984 she said: "We are being simultaneously attacked by all kinds of fascist forces. As far as our community is concerned we are determined to protest, and to protect our truth and our freedom with the very last drop of our blood."

Bhagwan himself added his pint to the bitter brew. In a videotaped deposition to the Multnomah County Court in 1984 he turned on the prosecuting lawyer, saying: "I have never come across such a stupid person in my entire life. I was hoping some intelligent person was going to be here. How much IQ have you got? The way you are behaving here, you are insane!" When asked if he had made statements linking Oregonians to bigotry, Rajneesh replied "I have rarely come across a person who is not a bigot."

Calling Oregonians bigots was certainly one of Sheela's specialities. In 1984 a local country and western group came out with a song sung to an old Beatles tune. It was titled *Shut Up Sheela*, and it immediately became a bestseller:

"Sweet little Sheela, Ma Anand Sheela,
You're the Bhagwan's right hand gal.
Big mouth Sheela, Ma Anand Sheela,
You should take the silence vow.
Shut up Sheela, on the news we see ya
Sayin' words you should not say.
She's a red disaster, and that is why we ask her
To move right up and blow away."

In June 1984, in a combined talk and press conference, Bhagwan said that if the newly-created city of Rajneeshpuram violated land use laws, then those laws "were bogus and should be burned." In October of the same year Sheela invited state officials to inspect facilities at the ranch, and told them that the only hope that existed in Oregon was the Rajneeshees. "And the Rajneeshees are not going," she added. "If you want us gone, then you'll have to bomb us here."

In 1982 there had been a minor bomb incident at the Portland Rajneesh Hotel in circumstances very reminiscent of the fires and bombings in Poona just before we had left, but apart from this there was nothing to suggest violence towards the Rajneesh community, and certainly nothing to justify the ranch's militant stance. So far only civil action had been taken, and that had been instigated by the ranch. A former Antelope resident, Donna Smith Quick, said on television that "Violence was a word I never heard used except from Rajneeshees." For this and similar public statements she was served with a $990,000 defamation suit by the Rajneeshpuram Mayor, Krishna Deva, while the two of them were appearing live on a Portland TV show.

Dissenters in what had once been called Antelope fared badly. A colourful character called Jim Opray erected a sign near the main road saying 'The Wages of Sin is Death'. One day he discovered the dismantled sign on the town dump, along with a rather guilty-looking sannyasi. A local reporter described the ensuing conversation as "a discussion about manure." Opray repositioned his sign. Soon afterwards he picketed the Rajneesh Café with a placard reading 'Unfair to Antelope Residents — Patrol Car Harassment'. Later the same day four sannyasi police officers arrested Opray in his own home under a charge of 'menacing', and drove him the seventy-five miles to the District Attorney's office in The Dalles. Bernie Smith, the Attorney, said the sannyasis had no authority whatsoever to enter Opray's house, and dismissed the charge as ridiculous.

By this time most of the original Antelope residents who remained in the town were quite open about their feelings. Rosemary McGreer, the neighbouring farmer, observed that "Pretty much everybody in Antelope that did any serious thinking had a lawsuit against them, and most of us still do." The only course open to many sannyasi dissenters was to leave, usually in secret. It was not so easy for the retirees.

Before the Third World Festival in 1984, an 'official' rumour was put about that Bhagwan was going to die at the Festival. A great announcement was going to be made, and since this was going to be the last and most important World Festival, all loyal sannyasis should come, whatever their personal difficulties. There were perhaps fourteen thousand sannyasis at the Festival, and many of them had a very good time, but Bhagwan's rumour turned out to be a cheap trick. He announced that he was going to die at a Festival, but not this one.

Dissatisfaction and dissent on the ranch, though silent, was now rife. To prevent people leaving, mind-altering drugs began to be prescribed to treat people who made it known that they wanted to leave. The euphoric mood-altering drug 'Ecstasy' was discreetly slipped into rich sannyasi's drinks just before fund-raising interviews. It was infinitely more productive than Sushila's brandy. One old friend of mine, a construction supervisor, made the mistake of telling Sheela that he was thinking of leaving. She told him to take drugs until he felt his normal self again. He was given Haldol, a powerful drug which produces a comatose state for up to forty-eight hours. His girlfriend was so shocked when she saw him drugged out that they both left secretly a week later.

The ranch now had eleven armed watchtowers, and a whole series of checkpoints to ensure that no unwanted visitors could get in and no sannyasis could get out. The armed police worked out a detailed code to identify unwelcome vehicles and people — Tom Casey was honoured with his own special code, 9-20, which meant he was very dangerous indeed. I am sure Tom was flattered. During the 1984 Festival, one of the best of the Poona group leaders, Amida, visited Rajneeshpuram, where her daughter was still living. When she saw the guns she didn't know at first what they were. On being told they were machine guns, she was thunderstruck.

After my departure, people who left Rajneeshpuram were known as 'dead' sannyasis, and this was more than a play on words. I was not the only one to find that the whole weight of Rajneesh International Foundation could be used to track down and silence fleeing dissidents. When Shanti, Vivek's assistant for eleven years since joining the movement at the age of sixteen, left, she was forced to go into hiding for two years. A woman from Portland who left in 1982 received abusive midnight telephone calls from the ranch for six months. Sannyasi children shouted obscenities down the phone. An ex-sannyasi who sent a package of silk robes to a friend on the ranch had them returned, together with a note that said: "For us you no longer exist. You are a dead person. We will have nothing more to do with you or your dead clothes. Take them back." Other gifts were simply incinerated.

Rajneeshees infiltrated the local election system and thus become part of the voting community. In November 1984 pro-sannyasi votes were desperately needed for a Wasco County judicial election, so three and a half thousand homeless people were bused to the ranch before polling day, all of whom were nominally eligible to vote. The idea behind the project was to put sannyasi judges on the Wasco County judiciary, and thus remove the threat of having Wasco County disincorporate the city of Rajneeshpuram. For more than a month everybody on the ranch denied that these people were being bused in simply for their voting power. No, this was Bhagwan's way of sharing his beautiful commune with the world, and of showing America that his way could succeed where theirs had failed. Nobody would be forced to vote, the ranch PR department added.

As the homeless people were bused into the commune, the Rajneesh medical unit ordered huge supplies of tranquillisers and mood-altering drugs, especially Haldol. Any connection between the two events was strenuously denied, but when one transient died, potentially lethal quantities of Haldol were found in his bloodstream. His body was driven nearly a hundred miles from the ranch and dumped in the snow outside a tavern to make it look like a case of alcoholic disorientation. The police also suspect that another person died as a result of the drug abuse, and was secretly buried on the ranch. The senior medical officer at the ranch, Puja, told the police that the drug in question — Haldol — had been sent back to the manufacturer, but the next day she told the press that this was not in fact true; she had been joking. No one laughed.

The ranch medical people had laced the homeless people's beer with Haldol. It was also stirred into their mashed potatoes to ensure their continued docility, as many of them were hardened criminals and rejects from mental institutions. Adding such a potent drug in such uncontrolled doses to people's food is totally unnethical, illegal, and highly dangerous. Anyone who organises such activities deserves no quarter from the law. In 1985 the medical officer in charge of the drugging, Ma Anand Puja, earned herself the sobriquet 'Nurse Mengele'.

Suspecting electoral fraud, Wasco County officials announced that they would interview every new voting applicant, to ascertain their intention to remain in the county once voting was over. Rajneesh and Sheela realised they had been outmanoeuvred, and hundreds of homeless people were immediately offloaded in Madras or Portland. Those who had been promised a return ticket home were given one, but many others were dumped in sleepy local towns without a cent. By December 1984 some 2,500 homeless people had been bused off the ranch.

They had come because they had been promised a heaven on earth, and as they were homeless anyway they had nothing to lose. In the end the Salvation Army had to pay for many of them to travel back to their home counties, and considered suing the ranch for the costs thus incurred. Groups of homeless people started picketing the Rajneesh Hotel in Portland. Violent scenes erupted and sannyasis were beaten up in the streets.

When it became clear that the busing of the homeless people was not going to work, Plan B was swiftly put into operation. If new voters could not be used to shift the balance, the only other way to ensure a seat for Rajneeshees on the judiciary was to make sure the turn-out for the election was well below normal. If enough of the electorate became ill on polling day, the Rajneeshees could still outvote the rest of the population without the aid of additional voters, and ensure that the city status of Rajneeshpuram, and the survival of Bhagwan's commune, were guaranteed.

Some time before polling day undercover sannyasis sprinkled salmonella bacteria over the salad bars at several large restaurants in The Dalles, the county's capital and largest town. Around seven hundred people subsequently became ill; nobody died. This was merely a sample poisoning, to see if the technique would work. In the event, the technique was not used just before the election itself. This macabre ploy must be quite unique in the electoral history of America.

Chapter Seventeen
SHOWDOWN

1985 was not a good year for Rajneesh or his predictions. While there was a minor tremor near Monterey, California did not suffer the catastrophic earthquake he had predicted. Although in October 1985 Rajneesh claimed to have more than a million disciples, only twelve thousand turned up for the Fourth World Festival, several thousand less than the First, three years earlier. Thousands of European sannyasis left the movement following the rubber gloves edict, and the number of Rajneesh centres around the world started to decline drastically. Sheela said it was a sign of strength; she was merging companies, "and people do that when their businesses are booming."

By the end of the year only the Ranch and California's Laguna Beach remained open in the USA. In Britain, the London Meditation Centre closed in the summer, and Medina Rajneesh at Herringswell in Suffolk was sold in November for £500,000. Only in Switzerland and Germany were there still active Rajneesh organisations, and even here it was often only because Rajneesh discotheques remained popular — the one in Berlin was considered the best in town.

The Rajneesh movement now had more than twenty-eight bank accounts in five countries other than the USA, including at least twelve in Switzerland. Twenty-four corporations, foundations, institutions and universities had been set up by Rajneeshees worldwide. But the movement still owed more than $4 million in unpaid taxes in India, and its federal taxes were under scrutiny in the USA. A sannyasi graduate from New Mexico won a $1.7 million settlement against Sheela for non-repayment of a loan arranged in Poona. During the trial in Portland, the judge had to order Rajneeshees to halt their pernicious harassment of witnesses in lifts and hallways. During this trial Rajneesh Foundation assets in 1983 were estimated at $30.8 million. Bob Harvey, kicked out of the ranch in 1983 on a trumped-up charge, won $140,000 in damages, and Rosemary McGreer, an independent and fearless critic of the ranch's duplicity, and the woman whose farm I had photographed from the air in 1981, won $75,000. The woman that Sheela had insulted over the death of her husband in a hunting accident was awarded $620,000 in damages. The State of Oregon fined the ranch $4.2 million for breaking zoning laws.

As the year progressed, the ranch succumbed to its own unacknowledged hatred, and gradually fell apart. Puja, the chief medical officer, kept eleven people in total isolation for months, telling them that the AIDS virus had been found in their bloodstreams. In fact there was no AIDS virus—the truth was that these eleven people knew about the wiretapping and bugging, and were being kept out of the way. One of these, a gay garage mechanic called Lazarus, eventually died in the isolation ward. Many suspect that Puja may have slowly poisoned him.

In the summer of 1985, *The Oregonian* ran a thorough and damning twenty-part investigation of Rajneeshee activities, beginning at the early days before Bombay. The series was entitled 'For Love or Money', and was very well researched. Shortly after the series started, two sannyasin women posing as cleaners tried to gain access to *The Oregonian* offices to destroy the researchers' material. Though they obtained the correct uniform they were refused admittance, since they did not have proper identity badges.

In November 1985 a plot to kill Portland Attorney General Charles Turner was uncovered. Sheela and five others had obtained false identity papers in New York, then flown to Texas to purchase hand guns, thus ensuring that the murder weapons would be virtually impossible to trace.

In September, probably acting on a tip-off about the imminent Federal Grand Jury, Sheela left the ranch suddenly and flew to Germany. Almost immediately Rajneesh blew the whistle on her secret activities. He denounced Sheela with something approaching apoplectic rage. "She turned the ranch into a concentration camp," he said, outraged. "She was a dictator." It reminded me of what I had written in *Stern* three years earlier, "The ranch is a prison run by a ruthless despot," but I was referring to Rajneesh, not to Sheela. In a poignant revelation, Rajneesh said that Sheela had, in effect, ended the life of her first husband, Chinmaya, by removing his oxygen mask. What he did not admit was that he had told her to do it.

The Immigration Service, the FBI, the Customs Department and State investigators were all called in to be his guests, and to conduct investigations into her excesses. Rajneesh started to give frequent press and TV interviews. When asked by one of the interviewers why he always wore a hat, he answered: "Because there are stupid people out there trying to get inside my head, and the hats stop them". I remembered what the psychic healer had said in London two years earlier. He was wearing his hats because of what other people thought, after all.

Rajneesh went on to detail the twenty-odd outrages that he maintained Sheela had perpetrated and of which, because of his total isolation, he claimed he knew nothing. He expressed a horror bordering on sheer disbelief when he explained that he had discovered how Sheela had been poisoning his very own cow, in an attempt to kill him through its milk. How comically appropriate that, even if it were true, Sheela should have been plotting to bring down one sacred cow by poisoning another.

After Sheela's rapid departure she was replaced by Ma Prem Hasya, a forty-eight-year-old French-born Los Angeles socialite, formerly the wife of Al Ruddy, producer of the film of *The Godfather*.

Meanwhile the grand juries, the immigration authorities and the State investigators were closing in on Rajneesh. They had enough evidence to prove without doubt that he was in the country under false pretences, that he had lied to the INS, that he had arranged bogus marriages, and that contrary to the American statute which demands a separation of church and state, he had used his 'religious' standing to influence county and state elections. The INS investigation team handling Rajneeshee affairs had now grown to seven full-time staff.

The Portland INS authorities were well aware that if Rajneesh had any indication that charges were about to be brought, he would in all probability try to leave the country, just as he had left India in 1981. They worked in what they thought was complete secrecy, but the ranch had ways of knowing how rapidly the tide was turning. On the morning of Sunday October 23rd, Rajneesh learned from an informer high up in the grand jury bureaucracy that if he did not leave the country immediately, he would be arrested without bail within forty-eight hours, and indicted on some thirty-five counts. If convicted on all the charges he would be liable to 175 years in jail. The informer was able to say exactly who was mentioned in the supposedly sealed and secret indictment.

Once they knew that arrest was imminent, Rajneesh and his

cohorts acted quickly. At 2pm a Lear Jet operator in Portland was called by the ranch and asked if he could have an aircraft at Rajneeshpuram within the hour. The pilot arrived mid-afternoon, and the $10,000 rental was paid by credit card. Another Lear Jet, which had just flown in from California, was already on the ranch. As darkness fell, the two white Lear Jets took off with Rajneesh and eight sannyasis on board, including Vivek, Hasya, and a Swami called Dhyan John, who had risen to prominence in the six weeks since Sheela had left.

Alerted by a disenchanted sannyasi informer who had watched the aircraft take off, the federal Aeronautics Aviation Administration in Seattle began monitoring the flight. The informer had seen a Rolls Royce driving up to one of the jets, but at this stage nobody was certain that Rajneesh was in fact on board either of the planes. The two jets sped off in different directions, one stopping to refuel at Pueblo in Colorado, the other at Salt Lake City in Utah. Then they both headed east, on flight paths which would converge near Charlotte, North Carolina. By now, radio contact seemed to confirm that Rajneesh was indeed aboard one of them.

Frantic efforts were being made by the Rajneeshees both on the ground and in the Lear jets to charter a jet from Charlotte to take the passengers to Bermuda or Nassau straightaway, since these were the only places accessible from the USA where Rajneesh could stay without a visa, and the Lears were not capable of making the ocean crossing. The best hotels had already been vetted in advance. When it proved impossible to hire a charter, they attempted at short notice to buy an aircraft outright, offering several million dollars cash to anybody who would sell.

The Charlotte police were notified that the passengers on the jets were fleeing subpoenas and indictments in Oregon, and were warned that they were probably armed with hand guns or Uzis, automatic weapons. Armed agents hid in the underbrush near the jet fuel pumps at the Charlotte airport in the early hours of Monday morning as the two Lear Jets taxied up, and surrounded them at gunpoint. Everybody on board was searched and taken into custody. After the occupants of the aircraft had been taken away for identification and questioning, a plastic bag containing the passports of everybody on board and a .38 hand gun was found on the runway a short distance away. The gun was loaded with Teflon bullets, designed to penetrate bullet-proof vests.

At Charlotte courthouse later the same day, Rajneesh was accused
of unlawful inter-state flight, but due to a legal slip-up by the government, he was wrongly indicted, and the charge had to be dropped. He
was also charged with arranging sham marriages and of lying to immigration officials. Vivek, Devaraj (Rajneesh's personal physician) and
Chetena (Vivek's new deputy) were charged with aiding and abetting
the flight of a fugitive, but were released on a bail of $25,000 each
after spending four nights in jail. A total of $58,000 in cash and some
thirty-five platinum, gold, diamond and emerald watches and brace-
lets were found on the aircraft, with a total value of more than a
million dollars. Rajneesh was held alone in a cell in the hospital wing,
and since there were fears that he might commit suicide while in
custody, a nurse was stationed to watch him twenty-four hours a day.

Despite her protestations about wanting to leave the ranch three
years earlier, Isabel was still on hand to hastily arrange an entire day
of television interviews for Rajneesh. Ted Koppel interviewed him
for the popular *Nightline* show. Rajneesh appeared wearing his grey
flannel prison suit and no hat. He looked awful. His verbatim re-
sponses illuminate the destructive dualities muddling his mind.

Q:"Bhagwan, some of your followers are concerned about your welfare. How are you being treated?"

B:"I am being treated perfectly well. Particularly the sheriff and his
department, the nurses are being very respectful and loving. But I
had been treated very badly by the US Marshal's department. Without any arrest warrant I have been arrested, on the point of the guns.
Unnecessarily they had put me in a place where I suffered. My back
pain has returned. My coughing is coming back. My asthma may start
any moment. And this is for no reason at all. I have not committed
any crime."

Q:"Well, there is some question about whether or not you have
committed a crime, and that obviously will be up to the courts to
decide. But maybe you can explain to me—why were you heading to
Bermuda?"

B:"I was receiving many threats to my life. Few of my friends thought
that they should take me to a safe place till the indictment comes, then
they can fly me back immediately to Oregon. That was the reason. I
was not flying from the indictment. I had no knowledge of it, when
it was happening, because it was continuously happening for one
year. So I would have waited here. And the planes were ready

to take me back any moment, so this was just a safety measure. I was not flying anywhere. I am a fighter, and when there is fight, I am the last to fly from it."

Q:"Now, Bhagwan, let me suggest to you that you have a rather flexible way of approaching things. Only a month ago you were on this broadcast with my friend Charlie Gibson, and you told him at that time that under no circumstances would you leave Oregon."

B:"Yes, under no circumstances."

Q:"But you did."

B:"No, I have not done."

Q:"Oh, I mean you left Oregon, you were on your way to Bermuda, and if you were fearful for your life . . .?"

B:"But I have not left America . . ."

Q:"Well, you were trying to."

B:"No."

Q:"Well Bermuda's not part of the United States the last time I looked."

B:"No. I was going to be somewhere in the United States. I don't know where my friends were taking me."

Q:"Well, your pilot had chartered a course for Bermuda. Does that surprise you?"

B:"I don't know. I had no idea where they were taking me."

Q:"Well it must . . . uh, uh, I suspect that even you can understand that it must seem somewhat strange to those of us who are not part of your group, who are not among your followers, that whenever, that whenever you get into . . ."

B:"I don't care about anybody. I'm simply stating the truth."

Q:"And the truth is what?"

B:"Truth is this: that I had no idea where they were taking me. And I had not even asked them. I was simply sleeping in the plane."

Q:"Well you do have a will of your own, so let me ask you, now that things to a certain degree are, have been taken out of your hands — if you had the opportunity now to go wherever you wanted, where would you like to go?"

B:"Nothing has been taken out of my hands."

Q:"Well you're in jail."

B:"That does not matter."

Q:"Well it matters in so far as your freedom is concerned . . . It matters in so far as your ability to move around is concerned."

B:"Nothing to be worried — it is a question only of few days — and a little bit my health will suffer, but it does not matter at all. My fight will continue."

Q:"Where?"

B:"It is continuing here, and I will soon be back in Oregon, and fighting. I have no intention to leave America till I am victorious in my fight."

Q:"Bhagwan, I don't mean to be offensive, but I must tell you it stretches credulity that a man would get on an aircraft and not know where he's going."

B:"I . . . depend on my people for almost everything."

Q:"What do you mean your people? — your followers?"

B:"Yes."

Q:"Yes. Your followers?"

B:"Yes."

Q:"Now I come back once again to a conversation you had with my friend Charlie Gibson less than a month ago. You swore up and down you had no followers."

B:"You are calling them followers."

Q:"I asked you, I asked you twice. That's why I repeated it."

B:"You asked me, and I said yes, because those people think them followers. I think myself they are my friends. There's one thing you are forgetting: that I was in that whole period in isolation and in silence. So whatever happened in that period, I am not responsible."

Q:"I know, you are also the same man who was asleep when you got on the plane and you didn't know . . ."

B:"Yes."

Q:" . . . where you were going but it, I mean, it always seems . . ."

B:"Yes."

Q:" . . . as though you are conveniently unconscious or out of the way when things are going on about which you don't want to know. All right, so you, you have no religion, you are not a leader of any group . . ."

B:"No, I am not a leader; I am a friend and a guide."

Q:"A friend and guide who has received a great deal of money from people who are not his followers?"

B:"Yes, but they are my friends, and I can receive . . ."

Q:"You can indeed, but I must tell you ninety Rolls Royces seem a little bit . . . excessive even for a very close friendship."

B:"Nothing is excessive to me."

Q:"Why not?"

B:"Even nine hundred will not be excessive. And I am absolutely certain about being victorious in the courts of America, because I trust in the American constitution, and I love the people of America, and I feel that America is the only hope for the whole human race. So I am not going to leave this country. I am going to fight for American constitution against American politicians. They are prostituting the democracy and the constitution both. Yes, they are my friends. Just the idea is new to you, that's why they feel confused."

Q:"No, I must confess I certainly don't have friends who are thrusting diamond-encrusted watches on me or Rolls Royces on me. That kind of friendship I am not familiar with."

On the same day as Rajneesh and his co-conspirators were being charged in Charlotte, Sheela and her two assistants, Shanti Bhadra and Nurse Mengele, Puja, were arrested in Germany during a raid on their hotel rooms. FBI and Oregon State agents were present as observers and assisted with the arrests. They were charged with attempted murder, conspiracy to commit murder, and first degree assault, and sent to a women's prison.

Rajneesh's new secretary, Hasya, followed in Sheela's footsteps in lashing out at the American authorities. In court in Charlotte she launched into her own assessment of the presiding judge. "I am furious," she told the court. "I think the judge is looking for a political situation for herself and is playing footsie with the government. I think it's outrageous. I would have thought that in a born-again Christian country judgement would not come down against Bhagwan, but now I see prejudice is going on. Bhagwan has expressed his love for this country, for the people of this country, for the constitution of this country, and for four years he has fought to live here." She did, however, concede that there had been a tentative plan to take him on to Bermuda. In court Rajneesh rubbed his back meaningfully and complained so much about backache that the judge was moved to point out that he could always have stayed at home. Hasya told television reporters that she was worried that Bhagwan was going to die in jail. Despite his ailments, however, Rajneesh insisted that he was going to fight on. "I am a fighter," he said. "We are going to fight."

An 'official' story to explain the circumstances of Rajneesh's flight was aired by Hasya on several occasions to the unbelieving media. The guru had merely been flying to North Carolina "for a rest". He loved America so much that he had no intention of leaving, and would shortly be back in Oregon to resume his duties.

This last prediction was fulfilled amost immediately. After more than two weeks spent in various state jails across the country, Rajneesh appeared before a court in Portland on November 13th, and softly pleaded 'guilty' to several counts of arranging sham marriages and two counts of lying to officials. He was fined $400,000, ordered to leave the country and given a ten year suspended sentence. Rajneesh also signed a twelve-page summary of evidence and agreed that it was sufficient to convict him on all thirty-five counts. His attorneys concurred. The main concern of the authorities was to get him out of the country as quickly as possible, as they knew this would lead to the break-up of Rancho Rajneesh. He was also given a ten-year suspended sentence and put on probation for five years.

While all this drama was being enacted I was in the States. As I watched Rajneesh on television being led from the courthouse shackled and wearing handcuffs, I saw a worn, lost, disillusioned look on his face. Then as soon as he walked into the camera lights his old showman's grin crossed his face as he bowed to the press and TV. He regarded himself as a superstar, and played the part to the very end.

Thousands of sannyasis all round the world must have been clinging to every development. One of my old sannyasi friends, now working as a psychiatrist in New York, wrote to me about his impressions of watching Rajneesh on television. "It was frightening and pathetic to see what had happened to him," he wrote. "What he could get away with in India where there was no one to challenge him was vapid and ridiculous in the face of the interviewer's simple persistence. Rajneesh's rage and frustration and greed and duplicity were totally evident."

As soon as Rajneesh had left the ranch, things there fell apart completely. Two weeks after his departure it was 'officially' announced that the ranch was closing, and more than a thousand sannyasis who still remained found themselves in a situation similar to the demise of Poona, but with no hope of a communal resurrection and with winter temperatures often twenty below freezing. Many had only the clothes they stood up in, and no money at all. They were certainly given no financial assistance by the ranch. A few years earlier a system of credit cards—known as 'Debit Cards'— had been instigated on the ranch, whereby each sannyasi's 'account' was debited each time a purchase was made in a ranch store. On

November 22nd the use of these cards was suspended, and the sannyasi's 'credit' frozen. Money stopped being paid to ranch creditors under the pretext that the ranch was 'going bankrupt', and a repeat performance of the Poona exodus was set in motion. People started to call friends and relatives, usually collect, to ask for money and tickets home. After the first three hundred people left, the ranch ran out of suitcases, so cardboard boxes lined up by the bus stop.

While all this was happening it is my reasoned estimate that Rajneesh Foundation International and its associated companies and institutions was collectively worth around fifty million dollars, though the true figure will not emerge even after the Federal investigations are complete, since so much is kept in Swiss banks. All but nine of the Rolls Royces — which it had been planned to ship in great secrecy to India — were sold to a Texas dealer for about $5 million. $4 million was still owed to the finance companies who had provided the money for the cars. Rolls Royce USA discovered that the sannyasi mechanics had rolled some of the odometers back.

After all the efforts by the authorities to expose and discredit Rajneesh, he had escaped an immeasurably wealthy man, living in plush hotels reserved for his exclusive use and with many of his luxury playthings intact. There were ugly scenes back at the ranch as sannyasis realised the implications of the material discrepancies between their guru's fate and their own. The much-vaunted love and peace evaporated rapidly as the survivors tried to get out of the slushy, icy wilderness and back home, if they had a home any more. They had been abandoned, penniless, by a guru who had promised them his unconditional love if they surrendered totally to him.

Some time before Rajneesh's departure, Laxmi had been taken back into the fold by her guru, and given the task of finding a place for Rajneesh to stay on his return to India. In the three years since she had been denounced as cunning and deceitful she had been very ill with cancer and had undergone a hysterectomy operation, but she had been summoned to the Fourth World Festival, and was apparently forgiven. Several people who had seen her at the Festival remarked that she had looked very ill, and close to death. Given important work to do for Rajneesh, however, she sprang back into action, and a few days later flew back to India to arrange his next port of call.

Once back in India, Rajneesh lost no time in lambasting America as the most repugnant and evil of places. "If you want to experience hell," he said, "visit America." He claimed that his commune had held a shining light up to the rest of the world. During its four years of existence, he said, there had been no crime, no rape, and to counter the population explosion, no children had been born. While extolling the virtues of the commune, Rajneesh forebore to mention the 150-strong police force with its forty-seven automatic weapons, the rigidly-enforced wearing of condoms and rubber gloves for lovemaking, or the widespread use of mind-altering drugs to maintain law and order. Nor did he mention the false AIDS readings, the isolation ward for the rebellious, the extensive wiretapping, the opening of all mail, the bugging of telephone calls, the spate of vicious lawsuits issued against honest and innocent local people, or the eventual internal backlash which finally killed the community.

He did not talk about his own deliberate and cavalier flouting of American law — "We are the law," Sheela had once said. While castigating America, Rajneesh did not mention the busing and drugging of homeless people, the mass poisoning at The Dalles, the arson at the Wasco County courthouse, the Portland bombing or the murders that had been committed. To those who did not already know the alternative version he made himself out to be a lily-white spiritual recluse who practised only what he preached — peace, love and gentle co-existence. If there had been any excesses, he said, Sheela had committed them while he was 'in silence and seclusion' for three years.

According to Rajneesh, he had only been forced to leave because the commune had been so successful, because it held up such an embarrassing mirror to the rest of American society. Rajneesh-puram, he claimed, had been threatening the very cultural basis of America itself, showing it up for the sham it really was. The authorities had harassed this poor, harmless, enlightened sage and thrown him unfairly into jail. It pleased Rajneesh to play the martyr's role, but he elicited no sympathy except from his dwindling band of 'friends'.

As soon as he arrived back in India, the Indian authorities seized the Poona ashram, as part of a concerted international effort to recoup losses from the outstanding debts from the ranch, said to be at least $35 million. Both the Indian and American governments wanted to ensure that no illegal transfer of funds took place. At last Rajneesh was being outmanoeuvred at his own international game.

For his first month in India, Rajneesh lived with Laxmi in a luxury hotel. They left this hotel in the middle of the night, leaving behind an unpaid $20,000 bill. His financial habits never change! He is now in Ireland, apparently on another short-stay tourist visa, looking for a site for a new commune, but will any country welcome him now? Canada and Fiji—the site of his dream island—have already turned him down.

More than twenty other people from the ranch were indicted as a result of the grand jury sittings. Rajneeshpuram Mayor, Swami Krishna Deva, was indicted on racketeering charges, pleaded guilty, and was given a ten year sentence. He then agreed to turn state's evidence, and officials undertook to change his identity, both legally and by plastic surgery, in recognition of the serious nature of threats and reprisals against him from his organised crime affiliations.

Five ranch women who had helped to organise sham marriages also pleaded guilty. In February 1986 Sheela was successfully extradited from West Germany, along with Shanti Bhadra and 'Nurse Mengele' Puja. The largest manhunt and investigation of crime and fraud the Oregon state authorities had ever undertaken had now moved into its final stage, in the public courts. In her defence Sheela apparently had an enormous collection of cassette tapes, which she recorded secretly in her daily work sessions with Rajneesh, when he instructed her how to run the commune and deal with both internal and external threats. While these tapes were nominally inadmissible as court evidence, they will undoubtedly affect the hearing of the case if they are admitted as circumstantial testimony. Should these recordings ever be proved genuine and made public they will show once and for all who was the real mastermind behind what went on at Rajneeshpuram. Whatever the outcome of Sheela's case, the tapes are unlikely to present a glowing picture of the man who describes himself as the only Enlightened Master in the world. He is not very enlightened in private.

When I left the movement for good, several of my friends told me that it would probably take at least a year 'to find myself'. It was more like three before I really felt like myself again, and only now am I beginning to re-establish myself as a normal, free, happy person again. It is very noticeable that almost everybody who has been with Rajneesh for an extended period of time goes through a period of intense disorientation combined with anger, bitterness, and an inability to settle down to any self-disciplined lifestyle. Most people spend a period of time wandering from place to place, unemployed and hopelessly inarticulate, often verging on mental breakdown and catatonia. Many people who left found it was just too difficult in the outside world, and returned to the fold within a year. Now that the Rajneeshee fold is in disarray, many sannyasis and ex-sannyasis have turned to other charismatic figures. The guru-disciple relationship, as I know from my own experience, is not an easy addiction to kick.

When I cut myself off from Bhagwan's energy source I found it very difficult to become part of the ordinary world again. I had lost the support of an enormous world-wide family, and there was precious little to replace it with. There are many thousands of people all over the world who must be going through exactly the same experiences following the disappearance of their guru, and my heart goes out to them. At least I have had three years in which to recover, and it has taken all that time to regain the self-confidence I had before I met Rajneesh. I am fortunate—I have a busy practice and run teaching seminars in Cranial Osteopathy all over the U.S.A. What of the others?

My friend Haridas flew to India just after Rajneesh, but was only given a three-week non-extendable visa—the Indian authorities are very wary of a repeat performance of Poona. He then flew to Nepal where Rajneesh joined him a week later. Vivek, together with Rajneesh's physician, the Englishman Devaraj, were also only granted three-week visas. They then flew to Greece to stay with Mukta, before flying back to Nepal to be with their 'friend'. The guru habit dies hard.

Isabel flew to Chile, and she is talking about making it again on her own in the real world. Her husband, Niren, went on to visit Rajneesh while he was in Uruguay, and was apparently thrilled by the experience. Somendra, now Mike Barnett again, set himself up as a Teacher and therapy leader in Zürich after 'graduating' from the movement in 1982, and has just bought himself a new Ferrari—not, I hope, the first of many! Teertha, the former Quaesitor leader Paul Lowe, is in Las Vegas, the gambling capital of the USA, living with a rich acquaintance and probably still wondering what has happened to him, falling from grace as rapidly as he did. I hope that Teertha, one of the most insightful of human beings, is not finding the transition to the ordinary world too difficult.

John du Cane—Rishi—was freed from prison with a Royal Pardon. Jeannie is practising acupuncture in the USA. Deeksha is living in hiding in Australia, as is Shanti, once Vivek's assistant, in America. And the photographer from Boston who told me that on no account was Sheela going to get her hands on the house he'd saved up for all his life is still happily living in it, long after Rajneeshpuram has ceased to exist.

A false master has to have as many unquestioning people around him as possible, and Rajneesh was a brilliant manipulator of the unquestioning disciple. He needed to have more disciples all the time so that he could feel secure in his gurudom, which had become his sole identity. The phenomenon, when one has the freedom to explore historical precedents, is well known. Rasputin, Hitler and Mussolini were all powerful, charismatic leaders who could draw people to themselves, seducing and manipulating them into giving up their own principles and finally their own integrity. The obvious example in recent times is that of the Jonestown massacre, where Jim Jones' disciples had lost their separate identities and virtually become one with their master. Several sannyasis told me that if Rajneesh asked them to die for him they would. I remember Sharon Ryan, a sannyasin whose father — American Senator Leo Ryan — was killed as he went to investigate Jonestown and thus precipitated the mass suicide, saying that people had told her they would die for Bhagwan. "I don't know if my trust in him is that total," she said, "but I would like it to be." In subtle ways the unquestioning disciple adds to the guru's power, and secrecy and wealth multiply it further.

The *Rajneesh Times* often made a point of remarking that when Sheela told Rajneesh about some particularly volatile issue, such as the impending rescindment of Rajneeshpuram's city status, "it was the first that Bhagwan knew about this matter." This was simply not true. He knew as much as the head of any large multi-national corporation knows what is going on in his organisation. He chose all his top executives, manipulated and controlled their public and private lives, and used a peculiar form of economic blackmail to keep them in harness. He allowed them to amass enormous personal fortunes, then used greed as a lever to obtain precisely what he wanted, including ninety-three Rolls Royces, a private turboprop aircraft, a palatial mansion with its own operating theatre, and an endless supply of adoring 'friends'. Then after they left him — like Sheela, Laxmi and Deeksha — he accused them of embezzling enormous sums of money, in order to alienate his disciples from them.

Rajneesh's non-attachment both to human relationships and to the material world was never what it appeared to be. It was, on close and dispassionate inspection, closer to outright manipulation. I remember once in Poona when Rajneesh was asked by an English disciple if he might borrow a book. The 'Enlightened Master' stiffly refused. His pattern of collecting things, whether it was books, pens, watches or cars, verged on the pathological. As soon as he tired of collecting something, he gave the entire collection away in one cathartic handout. Even his meticulously-kept library was given away in this fashion to the newly-founded Rajneesh University. It was the same with human relationships. While he preached total non-possessiveness and rearranged thousands of people's relationships, his relationship with Vivek was inviolable. Then one day he dropped her, completely severing the relationship.

Rajneesh always held that his truth was the only real truth, and he castigated and ridiculed anybody who disagreed in a forthright, decisive, and often devastating fashion. Yet he always carefully prevented anybody from telling their version of the truth about their relationship with him and his organisation. From the very earliest days the hallmarks of his empire were secrecy, duplicity, propaganda and shameless exaggeration.

It remains a moot point whether Rajneesh planned the whole Rajneeshpuram scenario from the very beginning, or whether it was some uncontrollable urge for power which, once in motion, took him over. The question is probably as unanswerable as discovering whether Sheela was Rajneesh's puppet, or he hers. Deeksha said it was a 'mutual manipulation', which probably best describes what was going on during the American years. Whichever it was, it left a great deal of human detritus clinging by the wayside clutching cardboard boxes as the last Rolls Royce purred out of the ranch.

The total ban on dissent within the movement, so effectively managed in Oregon, is what finally led to its downfall. In a rare moment of largesse in 1984, Rajneesh allowed that I, one of his most vocal and intimate dissenters, could say what I liked. "If Shiva feels happy to write about me," he said, "perfectly good." We shall see.

The yogic guru is obliged by his teaching to be celibate and ascetic. The tantric guru is free to teach by example a far more zesty discipline. But there are human, legal and compassionate limits to what any leader can ask of his disciples. Rajneesh exceeded them all. If it was a spiritual lesson of any kind, it was one by bad example. No amount of historical revisionism ("There were no sterilisations";

"There is no organisation") or creative interpretation ("Bhagwan knew all along, and planned it like this to show how corrupt the American constitution really is") can hide the simple fact that what for many people was promised as an oasis in the desert rapidly became a murderous quicksand which devoured, mostly through spiritual emasculation, those it pretended to be helping.

It is not a simple phenomenon to understand. I hope this account will help to put it in perspective, shedding light on how and why sane and intelligent people are attracted to gifted, charismatic and manipulative leaders like Rajneesh. As Krishnamurti said, it is vitally important never to give another person the power to make your decisions for you.

APPENDIX

During their eventful years in America, the activities of Rajneesh Foundation International—later renamed Rajneesh Friends International—became increasingly complex. For the guidance of the reader, here is a simplified and updated summary of events from June 1981, when Sheela bought the Big Muddy Ranch in Oregon, to January 1987, when Rajneesh was back in Bombay, and Sheela was in jail in California.

On July 10th, 1981, the New Jersey Meditation Centre bought the former Big Muddy ranch for $5.75 million. Bhagwan Shree Rajneesh himself arrived on the ranch on August 29th, and it was publicly announced that he would not be staying there permanently. He was only 'paying a visit'. By October 1981 the Portland district office of the US Immigration and Naturalisation Service had started to investigate the Rajneeshees for immigration frauds. To begin with the investigation was handled singlehandedly by Tom Casey at the Portland office.

The Rajneeshees quickly built fifty houses inside the ranch, which they named Rancho Rajneesh. In May 1982 they voted 154-0 to incorporate a separate city, which would be called Rajneeshpuram, on 2,013 acres of the 64,229 acres of the ranch. The American authorities considered the incorporation of Rajneeshpuram as a city a violation of laws governing the separation of church and state, and accordingly Oregon Attorney General Dave Frohnmayer challenged the incorporation in November 1983.

Sheela, who was Rajneesh's right hand woman and chief executive, held the supreme position on the ranch, until she suddenly left the organisation in September 1985, taking with her several of her colleagues and a large number of secret recordings of her conversations with Rajneesh, and fled to Germany. Two days later ten more Rajneeshee officials, including the Mayor of Rajneeshpuram, also left the commune.

After Sheela and her friends had left, Rajneesh lost no time in denouncing both his former secretary and 'her fascist gang' of all kinds of serious crimes. He invited the police and the FBI to come in and investigate her activities. Law enforcement agencies, both local and federal, created a task force together with the Rajneeshees to investigate Sheela's many alleged illegal activities.

In October, the following month, a federal grand jury in Portland secretly indicted Rajneesh and seven others, charging them with immigration fraud. Two days later a Wasco County grand jury indicted Sheela and two of her friends, Shanti Bhadra and Anand Puja, on charges that they tried to kill Rajneesh's personal physician, Devaraj.

Having been forewarned that he was about to be arrested on a federal charge, Rajneesh arranged to leave the ranch by Lear jet. He was arrested in Charlotte, North Carolina, on October 28th, 1985. The same day, Sheela, Shanti Bhadra and Puja were arrested in Hausern, West Germany.

On November 8th, 1985, Rajneesh was released on $500,000 bail after being returned to Portland from Charlotte. He pleaded guilty to two federal felonies, was fined $400,000, given a suspended prison sentence of ten years, and placed on probation for five years. He immediately left Oregon for India.

On November 22nd, David Knapp, the former Mayor of Rajneeshpuram and once Sheela's most trusted lieutenant, appeared in Wasco County Circuit Court, where he pleaded guilty to a state racketeering charge and an immigration conspiracy charge. Knapp—Krishna Deva—then signed a plea bargain agreement with local and federal authorities, agreeing to become a prosecution witness, and was then given five years probation. The new Mayor of Rajneeshpuram, Isabel's husband Niren, told commune members that the ranch would now be shut down and sold. Within four weeks the ranch was reduced from 1,500 people to 120 caretakers.

The Rolls Royces were put up for sale, and eighty-five were bought by a Texan car dealer, Robert Toethlisberger. On December 5th, Dave Frohnmayer filed a racketeering case in Wasco County Circuit Court against twenty-six different Rajneeshee organisations.

US District Court Judge Helen Frye declared Rajneeshpuram illegal on December 5th, saying that it violated constitutional provisions separating church and state. On the same day, US bankruptcy judge Elizabeth Perris appointed two trustees to oversee the liquidation of the commune.

On December 13, five Rajneeshee co-ordinators pleaded guilty to immigration charges in Portland District Court. The town of

Rajneesh, formerly Antelope and taken over by the Rajneeshees in 1982, had officially changed its name back to Antelope, and non-Rajneeshees were sworn in as mayor and council members. This act formally ended the Rajneeshee rule of the tiny town. On December 19th, two more Rajneeshees pleaded guilty to conspiracy to commit electronic eavesdropping, and on December 20th, a US District Court grand jury in Portland indicted Sheela and twenty more Rajneeshees on electronic eavesdropping charges.

Altogether, thirty-four Rajneeshees, including Rajneesh himself, have been charged with twelve different kinds of State and Federal charges. They include attempted murder, first-degree assault, second-degree assault, first-degree arson, burglary, racketeering, harbouring a fugitive, electronic eavesdropping, immigration conspiracies, lying to the US authorities, and criminal conspiracy.

Before the commune was disbanded, Sheela was replaced as Rajneesh's personal secretary by Prem Hasya, aged forty-eight, a Los Angeles socialite formerly married to film producer Al Ruddy, and subsequently married to Rajneesh's doctor, Devaraj. Hasya followed the Rajneesh tradition of conspicuous wealth by driving a gold-flecked Rolls Royce over the ranch.

During the winter of 1984-85, Sheela, while still in command, travelled all over the world, mainly to raise funds, and on one trip secretly married her third husband, Dhyan Dipo, a Swiss also known as Urs Birnstiel, in New Mexico. Only then, according to Rajneesh, did she get divorced from her existing husband. Dipo was instrumental in managing Rajneesh International finances.

Also in 1984, the Rajneesh Humanity Trust's 'Share a Home' programme bused in 3,500 street people from across the country to swell the voting numbers so that the Rajneeshees could win seats at the Wasco County Court. When local officials got wise to this, the homeless people were dumped out of the ranch without funds, after having their beer and mashed potatoes laced with Haldol, a powerful tranquilliser, to make them more docile. As a result at least one homeless person died. This attempt to win the election reportedly cost the Rajneeshees over $1 million.

After this, things started to go against the ranch. A Portland District Court awarded $1.7 million to a former disciple, Helen Byron, aged sixty-six. In 1980 Helen Byron had lent Rajneesh Foundation International nearly $310,000, which Sheela claimed was a contribution. The US Internal Revenue Service then informed

Sheela that they were investigating her own personal income tax.

Throughout 1984 and 1985 the US Immigration and Naturalisation Service accelerated its investigation of sham marriages. In response to this, Sheela organised a series of counter-attacks, which included:

— Plotting to kill Charles H. Turner, a US attorney in Portland, and several other people alleged to be enemies of the Rajneeshees. A group of Rajneeshees watched Turner's house and observed him for several days. They planned to stop him on his way to work and shoot him, but the plan was never carried out. Others on the 'hit list' included Helen Byron, Laxmi, my friend Jeannie, an *Oregonian* reporter, and Oregon Attorney General Dave Frohnmayer.

— Attempting to sabotage the computer system used by *The Oregonian* reporting team, to prevent publication of their twenty-part exposé of the Rajneesh organisation.

— Setting fire to the Wasco County Planning Department Office, which held the files on disputes involving Rajneeshees. The fire, on January 14th, 1985, damaged the office and destroyed about one third of the county's files. The Rajneesh Neo-Sannyas International Commune then tendered for renovation and repairs to the damaged office, but their quotation was not accepted.

At the same time, the commune undertook extensive electronic bugging of its own ranch. Bugs were installed in several trailers, and by October 1984 the commune was spending $100,000 a month to complete the purchase of the equipment. After Sheela left, police discovered listening devices in thirty hotel and guest rooms, public meeting places, and inside Rajneesh's own chair. Sheela used this last microphone to record their daily private work sessions.

When Sheela left the ranch, disciples danced in the streets to celebrate. Rajneesh said she had taken $45 million with her, which was in a Swiss bank account, and left the commune $55 million in debt. From exile in Germany, Sheela retaliated by giving interviews to German magazines, saying that Rajneesh had vastly exaggerated the numbers of his disciples. He only had 30,000, she said, not a million. She said on Swiss television that he had ordered her to organise drug smuggling to raise money, and she had had to leave him. She also claimed that the new leadership had spiked refreshments with the drug 'Ecstasy' to encourage donations. Rajneesh, she told interviewers, took sixty milligrams of Valium a day, and was addicted to twice-daily doses of nitrous oxide or laughing gas. On October 28, 1985, Sheela and her assistants Shanti Bhadra and Puja were arrested in West Germany, and subsequently extradited to the U.S.A. on the attempted murder charge.

By the time the various investigations were completed in December 1986, a complex pattern of criminal conspiracies, attempted murders, racketeering, and immigration fraud had been investigated, established, and finally proven. Before his deportation in November 1985, Rajneesh had personally signed a twelve-page summary of the evidence prepared against him, in addition to his more public admission of guilt for defrauding the government and concealing his intention to stay in the States. The summary included the admission of complicity in the Poona book warehouse arson, shortly before he left India. His lawyers signed a similar but longer summary, and also agreed that the evidence was sufficient to convict their client on all counts.

Rajneeshees meanwhile defended their guru's guilty plea as a 'technical one', which had been made under a specific clause allowing someone to plead guilty, whilst maintaining their innocence, if this was done for health reasons, or to protect the welfare of others. Very few, if any, Rajneeshees seemed aware of the twelve-page summary of evidence that their guru had signed.

Dave Frohnmayer described the investigation as 'among the most serious in Oregon history'. It was unquestionably the most sensational.

When Krishna Deva agreed to co-operate with the state and federal authorities in November 1985, he did so on the understanding that further charges would not be brought against him. He specifically instanced the salmonella poisoning in The Dalles in this respect. Deva had been recognised by a worker at one of the restaurants concerned, and his role in this event had apparently been confirmed by other exRajneeshee informers. Addressing Judge Jelderks at his trial, Deva referred to his activities while on the ranch, and said: 'If I had had any backbone at all, I would have left many times'. Jelderks gave Deva five years' probation and fined him $5,000.

On November 24, 1986, Deva was again in court for sentencing, this time on federal immigration conspiracy charges. U.S. Attorney Charles Turner had recommended to the federal judge, Edward Levy, that Deva be given probation in view of the continuous co-operation that he had given to the authorities. Levy chose not to follow Turner's recommendations, and sentenced Deva to two years

After his deportation from the U.S.A., Rajneesh flew by private aircraft to Delhi, where he stayed at the Delhi Hyatt Hotel. From there he went to Manali, a beautiful resort in the foothills of the Himalayas. Giving interviews to the press, he declared that he 'would never leave India again', in addition to repudiating America, at great length, as an evil and repugnant place. After two weeks he left the Manali hotel that had been rented exclusively for him, without paying his $20,000 bill. Laxmi, he said later, was supposed to have paid it for him.

From India Rajneesh flew to Nepal, where, beset with visa problems for his dwindling entourage, he was unable to stay for more than a month. During early 1986 he visited the Bahamas and Crete. In Crete the old chauvinistic foolishness re-emerged, and a printed form was sent out to all sannyasis inviting them to come and be with Bhagwan Shree, who was only there on a tourist visa. It included advice on what to say when applying for visas, and where to stay once you arrived. Money was prominently mentioned. An Australian TV crew flew out to film this phenomenon of the much travelled guru and his now rapidly expanding flock. Curious but relatively disinterested, in prison. The authorities were secretive about where he would be sent to jail. Whilst the agencies with whom Deva had co-operated were shocked at Levy's sentencing, and his dismissal of the plea for clemency, the two-year sentence was in fact a light one, if you considered that the Dalles poisoning was a Class A felony, for which the maximum sentence is twenty years.

However, it did seem a draconian punishment in terms of the 1985 plea bargain arrangement and its specific exclusion of the poisoning incident. Those others charged with similar immigration fraud charges—notably Sheela and Rajneesh—seemed to be treated far more lightly. And neither of them co-operated in any meaningful way with the authorities, whereas Deva had done so for a year. Perhaps his being an American citizen worked against him. Certainly there is no obvious reason, given his previous low ranking in the Ranch hierarchy as regards immigration conspiracy, for his being singled out in this way. . . .

The Dalles poisoning was designed to make so many voters ill that the numerically deficient Rajneeshees could still win the judicial election. This would secure the future of their city's precious zoning status, with or without the voting clout of the 3,500 homeless people bussed in specially for the occasion.

they waited in a courtyard for Rajneesh to appear. Their cameraman, a gruff and hearty bloke of thirty-five, told me what it was like: 'Well, you know it was just another job, flying out to Crete to take some footage of this geezer. We had hardly heard anything about him. I thought to myself, looking around, at all these coots in their orange clothes, funny lot these are, but if that's what they want to do good luck to them. Didn't have much of an opinion about the main bloke. Then this door opens and this geezer wafts out and I think to myself—Jesus, he looks like God incarnate! He just had such an incredible presence, a magnetism, to him. I thought as long as I live I will never see such an awesome man. Then I could understand what all these people were doing sitting on the ground like that. Then this geezer sits down and'—the cameraman strikes his forehead in shock—'starts to talk and I think to myself "Oh why did you start to talk?" It was awful! If only he would shut up he would do O.K.'

His description seemed to sum up so perfectly the destructive divisiveness within Rajneesh's mind. The magnetic presence was still there, the enlightened consciousness was nowhere to be found. Two days later, alarmed by Rajneesh's acerbic lecture comments on the Greek Orthodox religion, and seeing the influx of sannyasis—about three hundred had arrived within a week—the authorities arrested Rajneesh and summarily deported him.

From there he flew to England's Heathrow airport, where he was denied permission to enter the country. A short stay in Ireland was followed by a visit to Jamaica, followed by a further unsuccessful attempt to enter England. From there he flew to Uruguay, where, the Rajneesh rumour mill put it out, he had a one-year visa. Possibly chastised by the Cretan debacle, no immediate invitations to join him were issued. However, excitement grew amongst the faithful over the possibility that Rajneesh would set up a new commune in Uruguay. An international Newsletter was distributed in the summer of 1986, outlining Rajneesh's newly projected 'mystery school'. This would be held in Uruguay in the near future, and was to be one of the pinnacles of His Work on Earth. Loyal disciples should stand by for further news.

Meanwhile the Newsletter was taken up by a series of vitriolic denouncements, signed by his new secretary but obviously penned by Rajneesh himself. The tone and content was exactly similar to all those previous letters of excommunication. This time it was his group leaders who caught the weight of the guru's icy anger. Teertha and two of the other foremost group leaders, Rajen and Amitabh, were summed up as power-hungry manipulators or mentally retarded imbeciles (Teertha) and sannyasis were instructed to disassociate from them in particular, and all group leaders in general. The same issue of the Newsletter was full of advertisements from the very same group leaders, offering 'feel like Poona all over again' groups. Something had to give. Two issues later, Rajneesh declared that it had all been a joke, and his people could see group leaders again. But everyone should remember that no one ever got Enlightened by doing a group. They would have to come to him for that. He was still the boss.

Teertha set up a commune near Lake Maggiore in northern Italy. He started calling himself Paul Lowe again. His first wife, Poonam, the erstwhile dragon-in-charge of the London Centre, also dropped sannyas and wrote a heated open letter to Bhagwan in the European Newsletter. She remarked pointedly about all the things she had lost by being a sannyasi. Mike Barnet (Somendra) replied in the following Newsletter that she should 'come off it'—that everyone had lost something, and most people who had played this particular game had lost everything. So she should stop crying. Poonam set about opening a new London Encounter Group Centre. It would be called Quaesitor 2, after the Centre she and Teertha gave up to stay with Rajneesh in 1973. Privately she sent me a message regretting that she had followed orders and had treated me so badly from 1982 to 1984 in London.

Meanwhile I went to London for the launch of the British edition of this book. I did a live radio phone-in show, which was supposed to feature myself sitting opposite Rajneesh's dentist, Devageet. Thirty minutes into the programme, Davageet turned up and immediately accused our host of engineering his late arrival as part of a systematic plot to deny his Bhagwan proper representation. The 'master's' paranoia seemed to be catching. The subsequently phoned-in questions were, with one exception, entirely from sannyasis desperately seeking to destroy my credibility. Devageet's sole purpose was to follow the instructions he had received from India, which was to blame everything on Sheela. This he did with blind devotion. One of the more distinguished radio reviewers commented in the English press that it sounded like a family quarrel with everyone picking on the person who had left home.

Back on the still unsold Ranch in May, the young English woman who had once stopped my farewell cheque was now in charge. The judges who had been appointed as receivers for the sale of the once-bankrupt farm had insisted that some thirty Rajneeshee office holders in the Foundation must all be paid a monthly retainer of at least $1,000. A month or two after this arrangement was instituted, a phone call came from Rajneesh's secretary, Hasya, in Uruguay. When Bhagwan had heard the news about the $1,000 pay checks on his Ranch, she said dramatically, he collapsed, clutching his chest. Hasya said she rushed to get him medication, and when he recovered he said to tell the people in Oregon that in Uruguay he had hardly enough money on which to live. He said when he heard 'the news' it felt as if someone had hit him with a club. The young Englishwoman replied demurely that since she was only a co-ordinator and not a boss, she did not feel it was her role to tell the remaining sannyasis on the Ranch what to do with their money. But, she suggested, if Hasya would write her a letter giving Bhagwan's name and address in Uruguay, and stating that he was out of money, she would put it up on the noticeboard, and on the next pay day, anyone who wanted to send their money to Uruguay could do so. No letter ever arrived.

Meanwhile the huge earth dam on the Ranch suffered severe damage in a flood and emergency repairs were undertaken by the handful of construction workers still there. Everyone hoped it would not blow while so many people still lived downwater from it. The repairs worked. All of the original fifty 'trailers'—the mobile double wides— were sold and towed unceremoniously off the Ranch. The helicopter that had been the airborne gunship when Rajneesh went for his daily drives was sold to a local pilot. He brought it back a week later: it had machine gun bullet holes in one rotor. Would the Ranch kindly replace it with a new rotor? They did. It turned out that during machine gun meditation one day the gunners on board had loosed off a volley at a hillside target above the helicopter, while the chopper was banked in a turn. The gunners fired straight through the arc of the blades. Luckily they only hit one rotor. A ranch craftsman hid the holes with filler, for the new owner to discover later.

Meanwhile, in Portland, Sheela's lawyers negotiated with the federal and state authorities for a full six months to gain a favourable plea bargain arrangement. In July she was sentenced in federal court for wiretapping and causing the salmonella poisoning in The Dalles. Under the terms of the plea bargain she also pleaded guilty to immigration fraud, conspiracy to arrange sham marriages, and otherwise defraud the government. In state court Sheela pleaded guilty to the attempted murder of Rajneesh's physician, Devaraj, and to poisoning two local county officials when they visited the Ranch by giving them each a glass of poisoned drinking water. (One of the two nearly died.) She also pleaded guilty to causing the fire that nearly destroyed the Wasco County Planning Office in January 1985.

Sheela received the maximum possible prison term for each of the charges, 20 years. She is actually expected to serve only two and a half years in a medium security prison in California, before being deported back to India. She was fined $400,000—the exact fine Rajneesh had paid nine months earlier—and ordered to pay $70,000 in restitution for the damage caused by the fire. Her assistants Puja and Shanti Bhadra received similar but lesser sentences.

Oregon Attorney General Dave Frohnmayer (the same man the Ranch 'dirty tricks department' had plotted to kill a year earlier— Puja had even gone to his house in 1985 disguised as a Bible saleswoman, as part of the research for the group) said at a news conference that the plea bargain arrangement had saved the state at least one million dollars which it would otherwise have had to spend trying the three women. The sannyasi who actually set fire to the Planning Office, Anugiten, fled his native U.S.A. and has disappeared.

It turned out that Uruguay had never granted Rajneesh a one-year visa after all. After staying there for six months, he was denied a visa extension and flew to Jamaica, all hope of the promised mystery school lost for the time being. From there he landed briefly in Canada before taking off again, this time in India. Despite his earlier protestations of poverty, he still flew in a private jet. It looked like he would finally have to pay the $4 million he owed the Indian Inland Revenue in personal back taxes and penalties. And he would have to stay in India because no other country would have him. 'You will see me in many jails' he had said after being deported from Crete, 'because I speak the Truth, and the world is not ready to hear Truth. . . .'

He set up residency in Juhu Beach, a relatively up-market suburb of Bombay, and began giving audiences and lectures all over again. One of his oldest disciples, the Poona gynecologist who did so many female sannyasi's sterilisations, commented ruefully in a recent letter that he did not want to visit his ex-guru. 'Yes, it felt beautiful to be with Bhagwan at the time, but I have been receiving hundreds of letters from all over the world asking me for details of the sterilisations I did, and if they have a chance of reversal. (Some of the girls were only fourteen at the time.) Bhagwan should have stopped the sterilisations, not encouraged them. . . .And some of the friends here, the old sannyasis, they went down to Juhu to see him, full of hope and longing in their hearts. But they came back so shocked that he seemed to be such an angry old man now. They said every day he is making new enemies in Bombay, as if he did not have enough old ones already. . . .'

The irrepressible Laxmi swept into Poona to raise money for the establishment of a new Rajneesh restaurant in Delhi, another Zorba the Buddha. She got enough money from 'the friends' to make the venture work. She went back to Delhi and bought a new Mercedes with the money. *Populus vulti decepi, ergo decepiatur. . . .*

In the early afternoon of October 4th, 1986, a fire ravaged a Portland apartment where all of the records from the ranch had been transferred. The two Rajneeshee women who lived there were out shopping at the time. The fire did considerable damage to the business records stored there, and destroyed a telefax machine. The local authorities are investigating the fire as a case of arson.

An Indian journalist who interviewed Rajneesh in his new quarters in a bungalow in Juhu Beach, just north of Bombay, reported that he was 'presiding over a shrunken flock'. Referring to the fact that Rajneesh had just declared himself to be an Acharya again—that is, only a mere professor—she said that 'obviously, there is confusion in the mind of the Bhagwan'. The journalist added her impression that this new version of Rajneesh, whether he be Acharya or Bhagwan, lacked something of his earlier self. 'To me, there will always be two Rajneeshs—the vintage model, exquisite, bubbly and charismatic; and the eighties version, when the fizz somehow went out, and the bottle was refilled with hype and hypocrisy'. An accompanying photograph shows Rajneesh, still dressed in his sumptuous robes, blessing an audience of a scant twenty, mostly Indian, disciples. It made the scene look eerily desolate.

Back in the U.S.A., *Car and Driver* magazine selected Rajneesh as one of its "Ten Best Losers" in its January 1987 review of the past years events: 'What else can you call Bhagwan Shree Rajneesh, who was not only thrown out of the country after his girlfriend skipped with $40 million of his money, but had to skate without his fleet of 85 Rolls Royces? Bhagwan, you big wienie. Didn't anyone ever tell you that expensive cars and machine-gun-toting bodyguards just get in the way of True Enlightenment?'

Finally, counting the costs of their exhaustive investigative report of the Rajneeshee affair, *The Oregonian* staff noted that they had spent $40,000 fighting the Immigration Service for rights that they felt they were due under the Freedom of Information Act. The lawyers at the Ranch seemed to have fared better, since they knew much of the information given to the INS by ex-Rajneeshee informers during the course of the investigation, such as fraudulent marriage testimony. They had obtained this information through the same Act that *The Oregonian* fought so hard to access.

While the affair has been treated with great tact and secrecy, the identity of the informer in the government offices who tipped off Rajneesh's lawyers of his impending arrest did seem to emerge from the veils. A gentle retirement seems to have been arranged. . . .

A British TV researcher visited the ranch in late December 1986. She reported that there were about six Rajneeshees still living there as caretakers. The place was still unsold, although many of the mobile homes had been bought by an Alaskan concern, and had already been trucked out. 'The people left are really scared, spooked. People keep shooting out windows, sniping at them during the night. They think that it is not local people, so much as people from farther afield, who are doing it. As if they are bidding their own kind of farewell to the infamous settlement. Antelope is full of tourist families, complete with grandmother and dog, who have come to see the site of the great religious battlefield. . . .'

In a riposte to my private theory that the "attempted murder" charge of Rajneesh's physician, Devaraj, might have been a deliberate frame-up designed to get Sheela back into the U.S.A., a former member of the Ranch's 'dirty tricks department' had this to say: 'Oh no, that wasn't the case at all. We tried to kill him so many times, he was like Rasputin, he just would not die. . . .' No sane answer as to why things had reached this point has ever been explained to me. Rumours of a mutual suicide pact between Rajneesh and his physician are floated, but are hard to believe. The man's tenacity to life— in spite of his frequent threats to 'leave'—seems far too well developed. But his oft-quoted prediction of dying a martyr's death seems more likely, especially in a country as volatile as India, with Rajneesh 'making new enemies every day'.

It is as if martyrdom is the only fame he has left to claim.